PENGUIN BOOKS

WHO REALLY RUNS IRELAND?

In over twenty years as a reporter (*Business & Finance, Sunday Business Post, Irish Independent*) and editor (*Sunday Tribune*), and now as a broadcaster (he presents 'The Last Word' on Today FM) and columnist (*Sunday Times, Irish Examiner*), Matt Cooper has enjoyed proximity and access to the most significant people in Irish politics and business, hearing from them and hearing about them from a variety of sources. His depth of experience means he is in an unrivalled position to assess and interpret the actions of the powerful and their implications for us all.

D0767682

MATT COOPER

Who Really Runs Ireland?

*The story of the elite who led Ireland
from bust to boom . . . and back again*

PENGUIN BOOKS

PENGUIN BOOKS

Published by the Penguin Group
Penguin Books Ltd, 80 Strand, London WC2R ORL, England
Penguin Group (USA) Inc., 375 Hudson Street, New York, New York 10014, USA
Penguin Group (Canada), 90 Eglinton Avenue East, Suite 700, Toronto, Ontario, Canada M4P 2Y3
(a division of Pearson Penguin Canada Inc.)
Penguin Ireland, 25 St Stephen's Green, Dublin 2, Ireland (a division of Penguin Books Ltd)
Penguin Group (Australia), 250 Camberwell Road, Camberwell, Victoria 3124, Australia
(a division of Pearson Australia Group Pty Ltd)
Penguin Books India Pvt Ltd, 11 Community Centre, Panchsheel Park, New Delhi – 110 017, India
Penguin Group (NZ), 67 Apollo Drive, Rosedale, North Shore 0632, New Zealand
(a division of Pearson New Zealand Ltd)
Penguin Books (South Africa) (Pty) Ltd, 24 Sturdee Avenue, Rosebank,
Johannesburg 2196, South Africa

Penguin Books Ltd, Registered Offices: 80 Strand, London WC2R ORL, England

www.penguin.com

First published by Penguin Ireland 2009
Published with a new Conclusion and Postscript in Penguin Books 2010
005

ISBN: 978-1-844-88167-3

www.greenpenguin.co.uk

ALWAYS LEARNING   **PEARSON**

To my family, Andie, Aimee, Millie, Zach and Harry,
and, of course, Aileen

Contents

PART III

Tax is for the little people

PART IV

They haven't gone away, you know

PART V

Bringing down the house

PART VI
Playing with the big boys

PART VII
Two barons fall to earth

PART VIII
The failures of regulation

PART IX
After the boom is over . . .

CONTENTS

PART X
The comeback kings

PART XI
And in conclusion . . . Update for the 2010 edition

Introduction: The hard landing

Monday, 29 September 2008, was the evening when the most powerful people in Ireland felt almost powerless. They were grappling with a once-in-a-lifetime crisis, on a scale none of them had ever expected to experience, or had even feared. The continued existence of the Irish banks was under threat and with it much of the country's future. The standards of living that our citizens had come to enjoy hinged on the decisions that these men would take.

The Taoiseach, Brian Cowen, and his Minister for Finance, Brian Lenihan, sat in Government Buildings along with the governor of the Central Bank, John Hurley, the chief executive of the Financial Services Regulatory Authority, Patrick Neary, and the secretary generals of the departments of An Taoiseach and Finance, Dermot McCarthy and David Doyle. They were joined soon by the attorney general, Paul Gallagher. A retinue of their advisers flocked around the building, popping in and out when asked. Almost overwhelmed by what was happening, they were seeking information, offering and assessing options, and taking calls from people with advice – but they were also trying to ensure that nobody outside found out what was happening before the necessary decisions were taken, implemented and announced.

Power resided with these people, but so did extraordinary responsibility. These men had to battle to establish the government's sovereign responsibility for our future. What if they were to choose the wrong course of action? What if they were to do nothing at all? Would that be for good or bad?

'I had to inform the minister that the risks to financial stability were becoming unacceptably high, with knock-on effects for the wider economy,' Central Bank governor John Hurley explained days later. 'A major consideration was that the highly concentrated nature of the Irish banking system created a high risk of contagion. Decisive action to protect the stability of the economy and its financial system was needed.'

In plain English, that meant that some banks were running out of money. If one were to go out of business, as seemed likely, the risk became that much higher that this could happen to all of them, although – and here was the rub – that was by no means a certainty. If the main banks closed suddenly, and citizens and companies were unable to get at their cash, there could be riots in the street. External forces seemingly had taken control of Ireland's economic destiny and, by extension, its social stability.

The bankers were outside, sitting in the nearby Sycamore Room. The four men there represented the country's two biggest and most important banks: the chairmen of Allied Irish Banks and Bank of Ireland respectively, Dermot Gleeson and Richard Burrows, and their chief executives, Eugene Sheehy and Brian Goggin.

Sheehy and Goggin had come together at 6.30 p.m. to ring Cowen, requesting the meeting. They feared the imminent collapse of Anglo Irish Bank and possibly Irish Nationwide Building Society, and that such an event would create a domino effect, sweeping away their banks too. Anglo shares had fallen 46 per cent that day alone, the latest and most significant in a series of major price falls. The news got worse within minutes of the phone call. Just before 7 p.m., after the Irish markets had closed, the US House of Representatives delivered a shock rejection to the Bush administration's $700 billion plan to re-stimulate the US economy; the Dow Jones fell sharply, ending by 9 p.m. Irish time with the highest one-day fall of all time and the worst performance since Black Monday in October 1987.

The following day threatened to be dreadful for the Irish banks unless action was taken. Irish banks were massively reliant on borrowed money from overseas, and regularly had to borrow new money for old loans that were due for repayment. Suddenly this money was less readily available, and the fear was that nobody would lend to any bank in Ireland if one or two were seen to die. Liquidity – money in the system, like oil lubricating a machine – is essential to the banks and to the overall economy. If it dried up, as suddenly looked possible, it would not merely ruin the banks but also the entire economy. AIB and Bank of Ireland provided the bulk of this cash flow, which is why they were regarded as being of 'systemic importance'.

The bankers, very experienced, tough men, responsible for tens of thousands of employees, billions in shareholders' investments, and the deposits and loans of millions of customers worldwide, had arrived at Government Buildings around 9.30 p.m. They were made to know their place: it was two hours before they were granted an audience with Cowen and his entourage.

The government was not unprepared. For weeks it had been in crisis mode, although it hid this from the public for fear of undermining public confidence. The problems were multiple: the instability of international markets, made worse by the collapse in mid-September of massive US investment bank Lehman Brothers and the expensive rescue of insurance giant AIG, something that made money more expensive and harder to get; the increasing belief that Irish banks had lent too much money for property speculation and that this would never be recovered; a flight of deposits out of the Irish banks, Anglo in particular, from which big businesses were moving hundreds of millions of euro at a time.

Expert groups had been set up to prepare contingency plans. EU Commissioner and former finance minister Charlie McCreevy was consulted by Lenihan, and others were canvassed as well. On Saturday, 20 September, Lenihan made a sudden announcement that the state guarantee on all bank deposits was to be increased from €20,000 to €100,000. He accompanied this with the assertion that the Irish banking system was full of 'soundness and stability'. 'I want it to be known that the government is confident about the strength and resilience of the Irish financial system,' he said.

Frantic work went on behind the scenes to try to protect the banks, with the European Central Bank asked for help. In public Lenihan got into a row with RTÉ's *Liveline* when callers told presenter Joe Duffy the truth: people were taking their money out of banks for fear of losing it. Efforts to maintain confidence failed. Now the wolves were at the door.

The four bankers made their pitch for help and were then questioned. They were sent out by Cowen, only to be recalled later and informed of decisions taken in their absence.

Others were heard as well, via telephone, during the evening. Logs detailing who called in and who was called have not been made available, but, regardless of who had input, a consensus was reached quickly. The nationalization – or taking into state ownership – of the banks was not considered an acceptable solution; nor was letting a bank collapse. Something else had to be done.

The buck stopped with Cowen, subject to his cabinet's approval, having taken the advice of those around him. This was probably the closest a Taoiseach has ever been to deciding to go to war, a powerful yet vulnerable position to be in. The war was to be with faceless investors in international money markets who had an arsenal with which they could destroy the Irish economy.

It was an evening for cool heads, rigorous analysis and firm decision-making, when trust and confidence in one another was of primary importance.

Lenihan was struggling to convince that he had been the right man to succeed Cowen as Minister for Finance. Although clearly highly intelligent and principled, he was a barrister hampered by having had absolutely no experience of either finance or economics prior to his appointment. He was a man who needed guidance.

Neary had become a poor joke with the public in previous weeks, because of television and public appearances in which he insisted that everything was fine and dandy in Irish banking, just short of shouting, 'Don't panic!' He had work to do to convince everyone else present that he could make a valuable contribution.

Hurley was one of the highest-paid central bankers in the world, but it was not a reward for his powers of foresight; he had not beaten down the doors of government to warn of impending doom because of excessive and dangerous lending by the banks. He had reinforced, rather than challenged, the government's wishful thinking about a so-called 'soft landing' but was required now to disagree strongly with the politicians, drawing on all of his presumed expertise to do so.

McCarthy had spent the last decade as a conciliator, a man who struck deals and compromises, particularly with the social partners: trade unions, employers and non-governmental organizations that engaged in the long-standing process of negotiation with government over economic plans and national pay agreements. Reaching those deals, as well as working on the peace process in Northern Ireland, coming up with solutions that were acceptable to all, had required great patience and stamina. This, however, was a night for speed of thought and decisive action.

Doyle was a brusque man who had worked his way up through the civil service over many years. He was in charge of a department that had shed nearly all its staff of trained economists and that had a woeful record of predicting the annual likely tax take – a basic requisite for planning – and other important statistics. While it was an evening for decisiveness, it was also a time for listening to other points of view.

Nobody doubted Gallagher's legal brain or analytical brilliance. He could be relied upon to ensure that no laws were broken, but, while he would be able to tell people what they could do legally, along with what they couldn't do, that didn't necessarily mean that he would initiate any useful ideas.

What these people thought of each other, and of Cowen – in terms of character, experience and ability – was crucial to the dynamic of the evening. They also had to make judgements about the quality of the information that was about to be conveyed by the four bankers, and to be aware of the agendas that would drive the manner of its delivery.

Sheehy was a career banker who had been only four years at the helm at AIB, with a confident, almost arrogant demeanour that had also been typical of his predecessors. He had not foreseen or prepared AIB for the sharp downturn, and it had become clear that he had gambled the bank's enormous resources in the property market. Sheehy's chairman was well known to most of those in the room: Gleeson, a former attorney general appointed by the last Fine Gael Taoiseach, John Bruton, had been highly regarded for his intellect, much as Gallagher was now, but he tended to emphasize the legal principle over the practical position. Gleeson had weakened his own authority just a few months earlier by authorizing a massive and unaffordable increase in AIB's interim dividend payment to shareholders. It was a futile gesture in a bid to prove that the bank had no need for additional reserves to cope with a rise in bad debts.

Burrows was the former managing director of Irish Distillers, a whiskey manufacturer that had been purchased by the French Pernod Ricard group in a controversial takeover battle twenty years ago. He had stayed with the French, working his way up to the very top of the group, while also taking on a part-time position with Bank of Ireland a few years earlier. Under Burrows's approving eye, Goggin had only weeks before he began the long-overdue, painful process of telling shareholders things were not as good at the bank as they had believed. They cut the dividend and raised estimates of bad debts. The reward for this belated candour was a continuously falling share price.

The officials and politicians had to treat these bankers with scepticism. These highly paid men – all with seven-figure annual incomes – had created their own crises, albeit under the indulgent eye of those with the responsibility for reining them in. Their immediate problem was the lack of international liquidity available to Ireland, but this stemmed from their own excessive borrowing on international money markets and the use of that money in overly optimistic property lending. AIB, in particular, did not have a good track record as a responsible corporate citizen, with its history of defrauding the state and its own customers, and requiring state assistance to get it out of trouble. Back in 1986 it sought government help after its disastrous purchase of Insurance Corporation of Ireland; it claimed to need £100 million – an enormous sum at the time, just when the country had mass unemployment and high exchequer deficits. The scale of the rescue it received may not actually have been necessary. So the government had reason to be wary of AIB's requests.

Now, however, the government was not in a position to take a chance. It had information from a variety of other sources and had to assume that potential disaster was afoot.

There were various options. It could take its chances and allow Anglo to fall, on the assumption that the domino effect would not necessarily knock the other banks as well. However, the experience of Lehman's fall in the US only a fortnight previously did not encourage that approach – and there was also the possibility that many powerful and wealthy owners of Anglo shares and borrowers from it might suffer enormous losses. It could take Anglo into public ownership, as the British had done with Northern Rock, but that would not be good for Ireland's international image; there would be knock-on financial consequences; and Anglo's stakeholders would be as upset by this as they would be by a decision to let the bank fall.

There seemed to be a third way. Just as success has many fathers and failure is an orphan, so those who first sought credit for the chosen idea have since been quiet in repeating their stake to the claim. Economist David McWilliams and solicitor-turned-property developer Noel Smyth both wrote newspaper articles advocating many aspects of this approach in the weeks before it was actually adopted. There were rumours, never confirmed and treated by departmental insiders as bizarre, that it came from Swiss tax resident and money-market speculator J. P. McManus. Regardless of where the idea came from, the government was about to make an extraordinary gamble: it was going to wager the reputation and finances of the state on a scheme to guarantee all of the deposits and liabilities of the major Irish-owned and regulated financial institutions.

AIB, Bank of Ireland, Irish Life & Permanent, Anglo Irish Bank, Irish Nationwide Building Society and EBS Building Society were all to be included (and other smaller institutions were added subsequently). The amount of money covered by the guarantee from the state was €440 billion.

Cowen had taken an enormous chance, but, in retrospect, it may have been the easiest of the available options and therefore in keeping with the character of the man. He did not want to allow a bank to fail and he did not want to take it into public ownership.

So what did everyone in the room that night make of Cowen, the man who ultimately had all the power and responsibility?

Brian Cowen had been a somewhat passive Minister for Finance during his four years in office, offering little real change, always cautious in his actions and careful not to rock the boat. He had developed a reputation for readily understanding what was going on, but his decisions were based on likely immediate political consequences rather than on long-term economic requirements. He was not known for making tough, brave and unpopular calls. He relied extensively on his civil servants. He followed the lead set down by his Taoiseach, Bertie Ahern.

However, he was struggling to adjust to the demands of being Taoiseach, a job he had held for less than five months, as the economic downturn gathered pace and as political events went against him.

The 48-year-old from Offaly, a qualified solicitor who was elected a TD for Laois-Offaly in 1984, after his father Ber (Bernard) died aged just fifty-one, had become leader of Fianna Fáil by acclamation. No one contested the election to the vacancy caused by Ahern's sudden resignation because Cowen was regarded as unbeatable. He had been heir apparent for years, the logical successor to Ahern because of his popularity within Fianna Fáil, his reputation enhanced by his starring role in the successful 2007 general election campaign and his obvious devotion to the party.

His relative underachievement in ministerial office – at Labour, Transport, Energy and Communications, Health, and Foreign Affairs, where he had little or no track record of innovation or major accomplishments – was ignored. That he had been Minister for Finance at a time when the boom was in full flow was seen as enough. His leadership credentials were never really examined, just assumed. His appeal to the general public – rather than to just the Fianna Fáil family – was not considered a major flaw, given Ahern's electoral appeal across party lines.

Cowen indulged Ahern by letting him have a four-week political wake before the handover of power was completed. Cowen got no honeymoon period, however. He was pitched immediately into the Lisbon Treaty referendum campaign, which had to be won if Ireland was to endorse the European Union structural reform agreed by the other twenty-six member states. He had the support of all the other main political parties, with the exception of Sinn Féin. While legislation required broadcasters to be neutral, the domestically owned print media campaigned enthusiastically for ratification. Endorsement from the farming organizations and trade unions was slow in coming but did arrive eventually.

Meanwhile, an apparently wealthy businessman called Declan Ganley, London-born of Irish parents and living in Galway but active in the US, Iraq and Eastern Europe, emerged to front a 'vote no' campaign, funding for which remained undisclosed. His rhetoric appealed to the increasingly nervous middle classes – as the economic slump threatened – and suddenly it looked as if his campaign might be successful in defeating the establishment powers, as it added to the impact of the traditional 'no' vote on the left. An opinion poll in the *Irish Times* a week before polling day suggested that the vote was going to be lost. Suddenly Cowen was under pressure to deliver.

Two days before the referendum, on 9 June 2008, Cowen joined me for an interview on *The Last Word*. He had a big sales pitch to make in what would be his penultimate radio interview of the campaign. He arrived in the studio with a minimum of fuss and fanfare, as is his way. As we waited during the news headlines before going live on air, I asked him how he was finding his new job, compared to how he had expected it to be.

I'd known Cowen fifteen years at this stage. When he puts his mind to it, he is one of the best interviewees in Irish politics, answering questions directly and intelligently and convincingly; when he doesn't, his choice of words and delivery are leaden and cliché-ridden. You just hope you'll catch him on a good day.

In response to my casual question, Cowen showed himself at his most likeable. He paused to gather his thoughts and then gave a straightforward answer. He said that it was different to what he had expected and that it had required getting used to, even though he had thought he was prepared because of his previous close proximity to the job.

It struck me as a sensible answer as well as an honest one. However well a politician prepares for taking office – and because of Ahern's mounting credibility deficit, Cowen had known for some time that the job was almost certainly coming to him – the extent of the power and responsibility that comes with the job must dawn on the occupant only once it has been taken. And clearly it was becoming more difficult than he could have anticipated.

Cowen's answers in the rest of the interview seemed more rehearsed and, even if logical and delivered with personal conviction, lacked that certain something that might have convinced a sceptical audience. It was much the same in other broadcast interviews. By 12 June the referendum had been lost, a savage blow not just to the establishment's authority and possibly Ireland's position in Europe, but to Cowen himself, calling his ability to lead into question at a very early stage.

Just a little over a year before, in late May 2007, Cowen had contributed enormously to a Fianna Fáil campaign that led to a third term for the party and government under Ahern's leadership.

It had been an extraordinary and often exciting election campaign, overshadowed by revelations about Ahern's personal, and apparently unethical, financial dealings from over a decade earlier, when he had been Minister for Finance and about to take over as leader of Fianna Fáil.

Many had wanted the election campaign to concentrate on threats to continued economic prosperity. The warning signs were flashing that the property bubble was deflating quickly and that there would be serious adverse consequences for the rest of the economy as jobs were lost and tax revenues fell.

In April 2007 RTÉ broadcast a brilliant but chilling documentary called *Future Shock: Property Crash*. Journalist Richard Curran forecast the consequences – lost jobs, falling incomes and a sudden large drop in tax revenue – if the property market were to fall by 10, 20 or 30 per cent. He was backed up by a range of articulate economists, such as UCD's Professor Morgan Kelly, who were particularly worried that the concept of a 'soft landing', as often voiced by vested interests, had been shown to be a myth in other countries at various times in economic history.

The hype merchants in the property industry were appalled and rushed to condemn the documentary as alarmist and unduly pessimistic. Two days later I conducted the first of two lengthy pre-election interviews with Ahern for *The Last Word*. Ahern dismissed the RTÉ programme as 'irresponsible and inaccurate' and added that he 'disagreed with almost everything in it'.

What else could he say? If he admitted there was anything of substance to the programme's predictions, it would have been a repudiation of the policies he had espoused in the preceding years, when he had allowed his friends in the construction sector to let rip, encouraged by the availability of cheap money from the banks. No government goes into an election campaign rejecting its own economic performance.

Ahern called the election shortly after that programme was broadcast, but the campaign floundered under the weight of the unfolding allegations about his financial past. There was an extraordinary press conference at the Mansion House for the launch of the Fianna Fáil manifesto, where journalist Vincent Browne harangued Ahern into addressing those issues. A hunched Ahern visibly pulled back his shoulders and came out fighting, but it was clearly putting an enormous strain on him. This campaign was nothing like the previous two, in which an ebullient Ahern had bounded from street to street, smiling widely as he met people, never stopping for more than the briefest of chats before heading off again, allowing Fianna Fáil to feed off his enormous energy. Instead he went to ground and when he emerged he stayed silent when asked awkward questions, the silences then becoming even more awkward than the questions. The opinion polls suggested he was going to lose power. One of his ministerial colleagues subsequently told me: 'We were being led by a broken man.'

The Monday after the party's campaign launch, Ahern came into *The Last Word* studio for another lengthy interview, his only public appearance of the day and also the media's only photo opportunity. The interview was to start just after the 5 p.m. news. Ahern arrived early, and, as an item that we had recorded earlier went out, Ahern and I settled into our seats, sitting alone together in the sound-proofed room. Outside the glass wall of the studio, photographers scrambled to take shots, flashes from their cameras repeating incessantly. We had a few minutes to wait before the red studio light went on to indicate that we were live on the air.

As I knew well from many encounters over the previous fifteen years, making small talk with Ahern is not easy. Despite his image, he is not particularly sociable, with journalists at least. As this wasn't the time to ask about Manchester United or the Dubs, and he had few interests outside of politics, I asked him a bland question about how he was finding the campaign, just to get his tongue loosened. I expected the usual spin that it was all going well and how encouraged he was by the reaction he was getting from the people.

His reply was startling and disarming. He shrugged his shoulders forcibly, sighed loudly and said he was largely fed up with it, fed up with what he was going through, and wondered at times why he bothered.

He was just minutes away from a chance to defend his record in office publicly, to explain his public and private interactions with the Planning Tribunal that was investigating his financial history and to say why the people should re-elect him. Yet he was indicating that he'd reached a point where he no longer cared.

I was thrown momentarily. This was not the Ahern I had expected, although in retrospect it was in keeping with his dismal personal performance in the first week of the campaign.

I decided that it couldn't be true that he didn't want power any more. Ahern lived for holding and exercising power, both at local and national levels. Nationally Ahern had been leader of Fianna Fáil for almost thirteen years. He had been Taoiseach for ten years and had put it to excellent use in securing political settlements in the North of Ireland. He was still getting kudos for his stewardship of the economic boom, even if some of us were accusing him of not preparing sufficiently for the inevitable downturn. Bizarrely, he had spoken the previous week of wanting to step down before the next general election – giving a hostage to fortune that no politician should and repeating the mistake made by his good friend Tony Blair. But to do that, he had to win this one first.

Maybe he just wanted me to be a little bit more sympathetic during the interview. Ahern wore his power lightly, a wonderful talent for a politician. One of his greatest skills was an ability to make himself seem the same as everyone else, the common man, as if he were not really the leader at all. He had a reputation for making people feel as if they were close to him. By placing his trust in me it could have made me like him a little bit more. On the other hand Ahern had shown a personal weakness that I could have exploited during the interview. With Ahern you just never knew, which made him one of the most fascinating subjects I've ever interviewed for radio.

Once we were live, the professional Ahern kicked into gear. He performed. There was no doubt in his voice as he stood by his record. He wanted to be Taoiseach again and he wanted people to vote for him.

Ahern won the election, of course, his personal popularity essential to that success. Indeed, he received some sympathy because of the excessive pressure he was under from the media to explain his financial dealings from the distant past. Fianna Fáil's loss of seats was minimal, because, although the economy was slowing, it was believed that Fianna Fáil always did better than others in handling such situations. He formed a new coalition government quickly by adding the six Green Party TDs to the existing combination with the Progressive Democrats, who were down to two TDs. It was a shrewd move that established a comfortable majority for the difficult times he must have sensed were coming, both for him personally and for the nation.

His supporters claimed that the election outcome was a ringing endorsement of Ahern's suitability for office, as if some form of referendum had taken place. They said that nobody cared about the allegations of financial irregularities being investigated at the Planning Tribunal and that the electorate believed them to be unimportant. A feisty Ahern gave an interview to Mark Little on RTÉ the night of his victory that vacillated from justifiably satisfied to snarling, as he snapped at the journalists who had dogged him.

Further revelations from the Planning Tribunal over the coming months, which started shortly after the election, eroded his strength. Just as the country needed its Taoiseach to be focused, his attention kept getting diverted to the tribunal that stalked him. Senior figures in Fianna Fáil worried that his credibility – and, by extension, the government's – was being damaged, but they continued to support him in public, although ever more reluctantly. He suddenly quit the following April, nearly four years ahead of the schedule he had set for himself.

During the month of his political wake Ahern was celebrated more than generously, giving lie to the criticism of the Irish that we are a fair race in that we all speak ill of each other. Ahern's political sins were largely overlooked and his achievements lauded to the hilt. His long lap of honour, which included a speech to Congress in Washington, was a stunning final exercise of political theatre, which many took as the start of a bid to become President in 2011.

In retrospect, while the extended handover suited Ahern, it was an unwelcome distraction from the rapidly developing economic crisis and did nothing to further the Fianna Fáil campaign for the Lisbon Treaty referendum.

The political establishment was convinced that membership of the European Union was essential to our prosperity. Since 1973 the EU had given us much of the money we needed to develop as a modern economy but, perhaps as importantly, had changed our attitudes by requiring us to look at things differently. Whereas once Ireland looked to Rome, because of the adherence of the majority of the population to the Catholic Church, it now looked to Brussels. EU membership transformed the country economically and socially, and brought about an enormous shift in power.

It gave us trading opportunities that reached beyond our previously dominant partner, Britain. It forced us to abandon protectionism and to embrace competition. It provided us with money. It made us more attractive as a location for foreign investment and allowed for better-paid employment. Its institutions forced us to change many of our Church-dominated social laws. Our horizons broadened as our citizens travelled more widely in the countries of our fellow EU members, breaking the old obsession with the English-speaking nations of Britain and the United States of America.

The European Union had power over us but ironically that helped to liberate us and made us take more responsibility for ourselves. Yes, we were dependent, even more so after we abandoned our currency to become members of the Economic and Monetary Union – joining the new currency, the euro, in 1999, with the notes and coins arriving in 2002 – but the requirements of entry to membership imposed useful financial disciplines on our government. While the euro turned out to be a mixed blessing, overall the EU gave us more options and more opportunities, as we became an open economy and a more open society.

Indeed things went so well that we thought that we had it made, that we had become an example to the rest of Europe, even the world, in how to become prosperous in a short space of time.

And now, suddenly, unexpectedly, it had all gone wrong. It turned out that we had lost the run of ourselves, so much so that we decided we were going to stop the rest of the European Union from ratifying the Lisbon Treaty, because, really, we knew better.

As Ahern departed and Cowen took power, we faced a dizzying plunge, not just into economic recession but into depression and a return to something approaching the relative poverty of the recent decades.

In September 2008, just weeks before the introduction of the state guarantee for the banks, the famous naval training ship the *Asgard II* sank mysteriously in French waters. Its insurance was not enough to cover the cost of replacing it, and the government decided that it could not afford to raise it from its watery grave. It became something of a symbol of the new era.

Ahern had left Cowen to take the helm of a nation buffeted by the enormous waves of a near-perfect storm on the seas of international finance. The government, the banks, the property developers and the general population found themselves frantically trying to bail out losses that threatened to sink everyone. The government had blown the proceeds of the boom on ill-thought-out increases in public expenditure that did not deliver value for money. Businesses had wasted billions through bad investments, including buying their own shares at overly high prices, making excessive payments to top executives and overpaying for other companies using too much borrowed money. Some of the most prominent men in Irish business were humbled. Consumers had loaded up on debt, either to finance conspicuous consumption or to buy overvalued properties here and abroad. The banks had recklessly provided the money for all of this, undermining their own strength in the process. The property developers who, with their conspicuous consumption, had been the visible embodiment of new wealth suddenly had little or no cash left to play with; their assets were devalued and effectively taken into the ownership of the state.

The seductive power of excessively cheap money had ruined us. Membership of the euro had given us very low interest rates by historical standards and we binged on debt. While the last major recession, in the 1980s, was marked by excessive government debt, this time it is a generation of mainly younger people who find themselves massively stretched. Whereas once it was the national debt held by the state on our behalf that was a millstone (and soon will be again), loans that individuals and families hold have become an enormous problem as job losses mount and incomes fall sharply. Irish people are the most heavily borrowed in Europe. Per head of population Irish people have the highest levels of personal debt in the European Union. A decade ago we would have been nearer the bottom of such league tables.

The European Central Bank sets interest rates and the banks took advantage of this by lending large sums. This fuelled an investment surge, particularly in property. But the absolute amount of borrowing – heading for €400 billion – is extraordinary in a country of just over four million people and the pace of increase in extra borrowing has been far too fast. We thought we had wealth, but, really, all we had was leverage.

It needn't have come to this. The warning signs were clear that economic growth from 2004 onwards was based on unsustainable construction activity. Unfortunately too many people bought into some extraordinary guff that this was somehow natural as well as desirable. We were told that our youthful demographics, and our need to compensate for a lack of infrastructural investment in the past, somehow made us immune to the normal cycles of economic history. When it became clear that this wishful thinking wouldn't hold, we were peddled another myth, the comforting promise of a 'soft landing'. Instead, we sailed at full speed on to the rocks and, as the economy capsized, assumptions about the possession of power, wealth and influence in the new order of Irish life were challenged and, in places, destroyed.

Ahern jumped ship at just the right time. His claim that it all went wrong for the economy after he left and that there had been no sign of a downturn before he did so beggared belief. Ahern had taken a conscious decision in 2004 to go for mad-cap growth as he sought to shore up failing political support. Coincidence or not, he did this when he realized that the Planning Tribunal was making sensitive inquiries about him, although the public was not to know that for another two years.

Cowen, unwittingly perhaps, had implemented Ahern's policies for him. Now he was to reap the consequences. His decision to guarantee all the deposits and liabilities of the banks was taken in the early hours of 30 September 2008, and was ratified by sleepy ministers during a telephone conference-call meeting of the cabinet. They trusted that those on site that evening knew what they were doing. It wasn't until the following day's cabinet meeting that they started to ask questions. A drained Cowen muttered that 'we came very close to the brink' the previous night.

He was to discover subsequently that the government, and the country, would find it almost impossible to move away from the brink and would continue to totter there, as crisis after crisis emerged and the nation's confidence, much like everything else, sank. The problems with the banks intensified, consumer spending plummeted and jobs were lost at the fastest rate in the history of the state. The exchequer finances, pride and joy of the resurgent Republic over the past decade and held up as an example to the other member states of the European Union, went into deficit at a speed that could scarcely be believed. Taxes on income had to be increased savagely – removing at a stroke all of the improvements of a decade – but the government couldn't or wouldn't make the required cuts in public spending.

It isn't possible to kill an economy – because there will always be some trade, some activity – but it can be left in a state of near-paralysis. How the hell, why the hell, had we crashed? Why hadn't we seen this coming and prepared earlier? Who was to blame? What could be done? Who would get us out of this? Who really runs the country?

PART I

The media baron

I

Friends in high places

A single framed photograph sat on Tony O'Reilly's tidy desk in his office at Independent News and Media's City West headquarters in Dublin. It showed the newspaper group's controlling shareholder and his wife Chryss in the company of another couple: An Taoiseach Bertie Ahern and his then partner Celia Larkin.

It was September 2002, and the men in the picture were arguably the most powerful in Ireland. O'Reilly was reckoned to be not just the richest man in the country – a billionaire – but also the most influential non-elected figure because of his control of INM. Although a multinational business, it owned an array of daily, Sunday and provincial newspapers in Ireland with enormous readerships. Ahern had been re-elected as Taoiseach that summer. Such was his popularity that Fianna Fáil came close to securing an overall majority in the general election, something pundits had thought was no longer possible with the vagaries of voting patterns in multi-seat constituencies.

I was somewhat surprised by the photograph. Although I'd worked for O'Reilly for nearly a decade – as editor of the *Sunday Tribune* for six years, before that business editor at the *Irish Independent* for nearly four – I had never been aware of this apparent closeness between the two men. Why was the photo there? Was it a sign of O'Reilly's genuine respect and affection for Ahern? Was it there for others to see, both his staff and visitors, because he wanted them to know of the relationship and that he, O'Reilly, was giving his approval?

O'Reilly was not present for this particular meeting at City West. It was with his son Gavin, one of his directors, Ivan Fallon (previously his biographer), and Liam Healy, his long-standing group chief executive and one of INM's nominees to the board of the *Sunday Tribune*. The only topic for discussion was cost-cutting at the *Tribune*, a newspaper

INM insisted publicly that it did not control, despite providing all of the funding to keep it in business.

I said nothing about the story that I knew was to appear the following Sunday, which made use of official state documents. These showed how Minister for Finance Charlie McCreevy had secretly demanded cuts in public spending from his cabinet colleagues in the run-up to that year's general election and how, once these pleas had been ignored, he warned that they would have to happen immediately after the election. This story flatly contradicted denials from both Ahern and McCreevy that they had any plans for cutbacks in public spending if re-elected. The following Sunday's story created a considerable political storm – although I was never to hear any comment on it from INM's management.

O'Reilly had many photographs of international figures that he could have displayed on that desk. He had collected a series of international politicians and statesmen over the years as business contacts and personal friends and had brought many of them to Ireland. Nelson Mandela, Bill Clinton, Henry Kissinger, Chris Patten, F. W. de Klerk and Desmond Tutu, among others, had come to Dublin to deliver the grandly titled 'Independent Lecture', for about 400 invited guests each time, with each speech appearing in full in the following day's *Irish Independent*. His editors – and sometimes even those from other newspapers – all had lunch with these men too, giving us the type of access and conversation that we would most likely never otherwise have had. Everyone present benefited from O'Reilly's patronage and we became even more aware of his status as one of the world's most prominent Irishmen.

So why was Ahern, and not any of those men, in the sole photograph on O'Reilly's desk?

Ahern was now a significant international figure himself, closer in many ways to Clinton and Tony Blair, for example, than to the older O'Reilly, with his more conservative economic views. But as Taoiseach, Ahern had enjoyed considerable success in two areas of long-standing and genuine interest to O'Reilly. Ahern had overseen a boom in the Irish economy between 1997 and 2002, based on many of the market capitalism ideals O'Reilly had espoused. Ahern had signed the historic Belfast Agreement in 1998, which effectively brought an end to 'The Troubles' and created a sustained peace on the island. This appealed deeply to O'Reilly's long-held anti-terrorist convictions and his committed and sincere efforts to help bring about peace through his own charitable and business endeavours. O'Reilly was impressed by what Ahern had achieved and clearly approved.

O'Reilly had been a considerable financial beneficiary of both of Ahern's achievements. The booming economy – and the peace – was producing extraordinarily enhanced advertising revenues on both sides of the border. Independent bought the *Belfast Telegraph* in 1999, making it an all-Ireland publisher. Dramatically increased profits in Ireland – and abroad – allowed for the payment of bigger dividends and strong growth in the capital value of Independent's shares. Ahern had been good for O'Reilly's main business interest.

That Tony O'Reilly was in Ahern's debt may go some way towards explaining how Ahern's greatest support in his time of political need, between late 2006 and 2008, came from O'Reilly's flagship domestic title, the *Sunday Independent*. It almost outdid all of Ahern's Fianna Fáil colleagues in fighting his corner. But then O'Reilly had other reasons to be grateful to Ahern: over the years the politician or his governments had made many decisions that were of enormous financial benefit to the businessman.

Ahern, as Minister for Finance in 1994, had changed the rules regarding the amount of time so-called 'tax non-residents' could spend in the country, making them more favourable to non-residents. O'Reilly was the most prominent of what was then a small enough bunch of expatriates who lived most of the year elsewhere but who still liked to return 'home' to do business without surrendering a large part of their worldwide income or capital gains in tax to this country.

This was crucial to O'Reilly's enjoyment of his tax-efficient profits from an investment in Eircom, the state's main telecommunications company, in the early part of the decade, as well as his investment in Independent. Ahern's government also actively helped O'Reilly bid for Eircom by introducing special tax legislation, without which he might not have been able to take control of the company.

The government had sold Telecom Éireann out of public ownership via a stock market flotation in 1999. It raised €5.5 billion, which was used to start the National Pension Reserve Fund; this later became essential when it came to providing the money for re-capitalizing the banks. However, losing control of the company – renamed Eircom when it joined the stock market – came to be considered a major economic mistake, as a lack of investment in broadband by a series of new owners – all of whom were too busy taking cash from the company to pay back the loans incurred to buy it – left Ireland badly serviced by comparison with other developed countries.

The initial sale of Eircom had seemed to be a wonderful success, especially for those who bought shares in the flotation and sold them quickly at a profit. However, the share price slumped in late 2000 and early 2001 as the dotcom bubble burst, creating large losses for those who still held the shares. Eircom decided to sell its mobile phone business to Vodafone, leaving it with the traditional fixed-line business. With a low share price, it was vulnerable to takeover.

Entrepreneur Denis O'Brien seemed the most likely bidder. He was one of the most prominent multimillionaires operating in Ireland. He controlled Esat Digifone when it won a state competition for a second mobile phone licence in 1995, and had received a personal profit of over €200 million on the sale of Esat Telecom (which owned the shares in Esat Digifone) in 2000. He had defeated an O'Reilly-backed consortium – as well as three other bidders, including one led by a hitherto unknown young businessman from Galway, via London, called Declan Ganley – to win the licence. He formed a company called e-Island but unions at the former semi-state – who retained a sizeable shareholding in Eircom – recoiled in horror. O'Brien had made a public virtue of challenging unions during his time as principal at Esat. The unions wanted almost anybody else, even O'Reilly.

O'Reilly, still somewhat chastened by his defeat by O'Brien and deeply suspicious of the circumstances in which the Rainbow government's Minister for Communications, Michael Lowry, had awarded the licence, spotted his opportunity. He became the Irish front for a consortium that involved the legendary currency speculator and investor George Soros and a foreign venture capitalist called Providence Equity. They called their consortium Valentia and set out not only to top the offer made by O'Brien but to seduce the staff shareholders as well. O'Reilly charmed Con Scanlon, a Kerryman who had succeeded David Begg as head of the Communications Workers Union, and the Employee Share Ownership Trust (ESOT), which owned about 15 per cent of the shares, opted to support him.

To finance the purchase of Eircom, Valentia needed to give ESOT an even bigger slice of the company but it did not want ESOT to have too many votes: it wanted to ensure that business decisions could be taken that might not suit the usual trade union objectives. The solution was the creation of preference shares for ESOT, which would provide a guaranteed annual return on the investment but not voting rights. The problem was that the existing tax rules did not permit such an arrangement: cash would have had to be distributed among members of the ESOT and that would have triggered an immediate tax bill for the workers. Help was needed. Finance minister Charlie McCreevy, a regular at soirées at O'Reilly's Castlemartin mansion in McCreevy's Kildare constituency, received a request from tax advisers to both Valentia and the unions, asking for a change in the tax laws.

As McCreevy subsequently admitted, O'Reilly's consortium could not have beaten O'Brien without the necessary tax change. He excused it on the basis that it had been done to benefit the workers. 'If this change had not been made, it would have favoured the Denis O'Brien consortium and the deputy can imagine the hullabaloo that would have caused,' McCreevy told the Dáil in 2003. 'The legislative changes simply provided the membership of the Eircom ESOT with a level playing field to choose to support whichever bid they wished to support . . . Both Valentia and e-Island had the same chance to strike a deal with the Eircom workers and I understand the ESOT was more inclined to vote for the Valentia consortium.'

Valentia sold the company again in 2004 by way of another stock market flotation. Irish Congress of Trade Unions economist Paul Sweeney has quantified the total gains made by the members of the Valentia consortium in just thirty months at around €950 million. The Soros Fund made €177 million, O'Reilly €35 million and Providence Equity €443 million. This was a return of 141 per cent, facilitated in part by a re-registration of Eircom as a foreign company, again to avoid tax legally, despite the fact all of its assets were in Ireland.

O'Reilly remained as chairman and in 2006 oversaw Eircom's latest exit from the stock market, when the non-staff shareholding was bought by an Australian investor called Babcock and Brown. By this stage the workers had taken €424 million in cash tax-free from the myriad deals, an average of over €87,000 per employee tax-free. But the deal proved disastrous for the state. The Australians borrowed too much to buy

Eircom and then tried to utilize much of the company's cash to repay debts of over €4 billion. Necessary investment in broadband was not undertaken. Eircom became a 'zombie company', worth less than the amount it owed its creditors. A vital national asset had been substantially damaged and diminished, and by mid-2009 a debate about taking Eircom back into state ownership had begun, as it became clear that the Australians had made a bad situation worse and could not continue with their ownership.

Tony O'Reilly enjoys prestige almost as much as he does money. Whatever about the financial benefits that Ahern's actions conferred upon O'Reilly, his decision to allow O'Reilly to become the first citizen of the Republic of Ireland to receive a knighthood from a British monarch, and to simultaneously retain his citizenship of this state, was one that O'Reilly appreciated considerably.

O'Reilly was told of his selection for a knighthood in late 2000, as a reward for his 'long and distinguished service to Northern Ireland'. It was to be announced in Britain's New Year's Honours List. However, article 40.2.2 of the Irish Constitution states: 'No title of nobility or honour may be accepted by any citizen except with the prior approval of the government.' Without permission, O'Reilly would have been forced to relinquish his Irish citizenship, an admittedly unlikely occurrence. Quite apart from his own pride in his Irishness, the potential for a public backlash in Ireland that would have damaged his domestic business interests loomed large, so he would probably not have taken that 'nuclear' option. His aim was to have his cake and to eat it: revelling in his Irish citizenship, while holding a British title, just as he boasted of the Irish credentials of most of his businesses while remaining non-resident for tax purposes.

O'Reilly had his excuses ready: he claimed he had always maintained dual citizenship because he had been born in Ireland prior to our leaving the British Commonwealth in 1949. This was somewhat surprising, given that his father was a civil servant to the Irish Free State. The Irish government was contacted by both O'Reilly's aides and by the British government and asked for the relevant permission. Several ministers were canvassed by civil servants for their views, but a recommendation that O'Reilly be allowed to accept the honour was made at a cabinet meeting and the decision was officially recorded.

Ahern could have followed the Canadian government's example. Two years earlier its Prime Minister Jean Chrétien had rebuked his British counterpart Blair for approving honours for two British-Canadian citizens, including the since disgraced and jailed owner of the *Daily Telegraph*, Conrad Black. A major row ensued, in which Black's Canadian newspapers championed the cause of their master, but Chrétien would not back down. Black later renounced his Canadian citizenship. There would be no such controversy in Ireland.

O'Reilly – who bowed the knee to Queen Elizabeth in a summer ceremony in 2001 and received the regal tap of the ceremonial sword on both shoulders before being presented with an insignia denoting the Knights Bachelor – had done something that many regarded as deeply controversial. However, he is not the only Irish businessman to have received a knighthood: former attorney general and European Commissioner Peter Sutherland was appointed a Knight Commander of the Order of St Michael and St George, while former Unilever chairman Niall FitzGerald was made a Knight Commander of the British Empire. But, while Sutherland scoffed at the idea of using the title 'Sir', Tony (usually referred to as Dr A. J. F. O'Reilly in his own newspapers prior to that, having earned a PhD in agricultural marketing from Bradford University) wished in future to be called Sir Anthony O'Reilly and for his wife to be called Lady O'Reilly.

One can only imagine what Ahern, an avowed Republican and a Dubliner who had grown up within a couple of miles of O'Reilly's home on the Northside of the city, thought privately. But there were gains to be made from accommodating O'Reilly – and the possibility of hostile media coverage had he denied him.

Ahern may reveal his true opinion of O'Reilly – and explain their dealings – when his own autobiography is published, but, given Ahern's dispersal of information on a need-to-know basis, that is by no means certain. Their personalities, backgrounds and world-views appear to be so different that it's hard to believe their relationship was based on much more than the mutual exercise of power.

Power is clearly essential to both of them but for different reasons. O'Reilly is interested in the wealth and social standing that power provides; how others see him is essential. Ahern is not without vanity or a desire to be liked, as his selfish vote-getting in Dublin Central has proved; he has complained bitterly since leaving office that he has not been appreciated sufficiently for all he believes he did for the country. Yet he did not have O'Reilly's spending needs (although the revelations of the Planning Tribunal show that having at least some financial cushion was very important to him). While O'Reilly was obsessed with appearances, decorum and shows of wealth that were quasi-aristocratic, Ahern has traded on his apparent ordinariness, revelling in his image as an anorak wearer, even after his former partner Celia Larkin, a 'beauty and image' consultant, tidied him up and he started spending €30,000 a year, at the state's expense, on make-up.

O'Reilly is a more polished performer, both publicly and privately. He is a fluent speaker, an erudite conversationalist and a keen mimic, who can be somewhat cruel and indiscreet in his comments about those who have fallen foul of him or who are out of favour. He is capable of listening, something which not all powerful businessmen do after a certain stage, although he does not hide his displeasure if he doesn't like what he hears. It is possible to spend time in his company comfortably.

By contrast it is hard to spend more than a few moments with Ahern before awkward silences intrude that you, and occasionally he, must fill. Enda Kenny, leader of Fine Gael and his long-time political opponent, described Ahern perceptively as a 'social loner' – somebody who gives an impression of openness and affability that is not borne out by reality. Ahern rarely spends long with anybody other than his close friends or those with whom he is having political dealings. Ahern is not a top-rank public speaker. While many believe this is deliberate, especially when his meanderings appear more endearing than deliberately obfuscatory, his use of a professional acting coach suggests it is a real problem.

O'Reilly was born in 1936, grew up on the relatively prosperous Griffith Avenue and was pushed in a professional direction by his ambitious parents, who sent him to the famed Jesuit school Belvedere, where he excelled in both academic subjects and in rugby. O'Reilly was an Irish rugby international at eighteen and within the year a famous winger on the British and Irish Lions rugby team. He studied law at University College Dublin and, despite qualifying as a solicitor, quickly immersed himself in business and talked his way into senior jobs at a young age. He was head of the state dairy board, An Bord Bainne, at the age of twenty-six and, after a series of moves, became the boss of the world-famous Heinz food group before he reached the age of forty.

Although based in Pittsburgh, and resident in Lyford Quay in the Bahamas, O'Reilly decided to retain an involvement in Ireland through business. He had taken control of Independent Newspapers in 1973 (four years before Ahern was first elected to the Dáil), formed an investment vehicle called Fitzwilton that was quoted on the Irish stock market, and was the main figure in a highly controversial oil exploration company called Atlantic Resources that made, but largely lost, fortunes during the 1980s. It was his use of Independent, however, that made him such a prominent and powerful Irish figure.

Ahern was born fifteen years after O'Reilly and grew up nearby on the Northside of Dublin but in the more modest circumstances of Drumcondra. Whereas O'Reilly's father was a senior civil servant, Ahern's was a gardener. Ahern's sporting interests were in Gaelic football and Manchester United – as a supporter rather than as a player – and his schooling was with the Christian Brothers. He did not go to university and only partly qualified as an accountant; claims that he had studied at the London School of Economics were exaggerated. He spent time working in the accounts department at the Mater Hospital but from an early age was obsessed with politics and the sport it provided. He was elected to Dublin City Council and was a surprise success for Fianna Fáil in the 1977 general election. Charlie Haughey made him chief whip in 1981 and when Fianna Fáil was out of power for five years in the mid-eighties he built up his profile during a very useful term as Lord Mayor of Dublin.

It isn't known when Ahern's and O'Reilly's paths first crossed. O'Reilly had been considered so close to Jack Lynch when he led Fianna Fáil that there was much speculation about a domestic political career for the businessman. O'Reilly had enjoyed Haughey's company in the early days but became distrustful of his brand of nationalism and suspicious of his financial position. The antipathy was mutual, particularly when the Independent titles were unsparing in their criticism of Haughey during his time in power, although O'Reilly supported Haughey's conversion to tight fiscal management for the state between 1987 and 1991.

This conflict was something that Haughey's press secretary P. J. Mara was often called upon to manage. Mara, who sprang to public fame because of his characterization in the satirical radio show of that time called *Scrap Saturday*, used a combination of affability and shrewdness to diffuse dangerous situations. He later drew on his experiences of this time to great effect, becoming one of the most powerful back-room figures in Irish business and politics. He became a bridge between O'Reilly and Ahern, a paid consultant to the former and a confidant of the latter, serving as Fianna Fáil director of elections for all of Ahern's three successful general election campaigns.

Mara had come to regard the fighting between the Independent group and Haughey (and, by extension, Fianna Fáil) as a political mistake that he was determined Ahern would not repeat once he came into the leadership of the party. Ahern did not need much telling. He had seen how O'Reilly had flexed his power: not just against Fianna Fáil but also Dick Spring during the Labour leader's tenure as Minister for Energy in the mid-1980s; and then Fine Gael's John Bruton during his time as Taoiseach. Ahern needed O'Reilly as a friend, not as an enemy.

2

Payback

It was to become the most infamous editorial in the history of Irish newspapers. On 5 June 1997, the day before the 1997 general election, the *Irish Independent* broke with tradition and published its editorial across the top of its front page, just below the masthead. It was a jaw-dropping contribution that strongly advocated ditching the Rainbow Coalition of Fine Gael, Labour and Democratic Left. 'On any objective analysis, it is a vote for Fianna Fáil and the Progressive Democrats tomorrow which offers the better chance of securing our future. We have had decades of harsh tax regimes. Let us start to enjoy some payback.'

The editorial may not have influenced voting decisions – opinion polls had predicted accurately the eventual outcome of a Fianna Fáil–PD coalition, supported by independents – but it outraged those who ended up on the losing side. 'I'm calling on Dick Spring, as a friend, to do a service to the party and to the country and give his side of the story, to clear the air as regards Independent Newspapers,' pleaded ejected Cork North Central TD Toddy O'Sullivan of Labour, live on television.

Spring was calculated in his response, going no further than to describe the editorial as 'disgraceful and despicable, a new low in Irish journalism'. Later, Bruton said he thought 'the fact that the *Irish Independent* chose to put an editorial on the front page of its newspaper, urging people not to vote for a government which had succeeded in recording a 9 per cent annual growth rate in the economy during its term of office, does indicate a certain perversity of political opinion on the part of that newspaper.'

Over time it emerged that there had been plenty of contact and conflict between the government and the company, including a contentious and highly significant personal meeting between Bruton and O'Reilly. This suggested that Independent Newspapers and O'Reilly had motive for wishing to punish the outgoing government for what it perceived as animus towards their business interests. There was a corresponding desire to see Fianna Fáil return to power, with its perceived more 'progressive' approach to helping business and the willingness of certain senior individuals, such as Ray Burke, a close friend of Mara, to help.

Burke was a character of whom the media was deeply suspicious. Ironically, in light of what was to follow, it was the *Sunday Independent* that almost did for him in the 1970s. It linked him clearly to all sorts of nefarious goings-on with a notorious pair of builders called Tom Brennan and Joe McGowan, who had built Burke's house in Swords and who were also associated with a controversial auctioneer called John Finnegan.

Despite owning the newspaper that had been central to revealing Burke's dealings to the public, it was Burke to whom O'Reilly's executives became close in the late 1980s. He held cabinet responsibility for two areas close to O'Reilly's heart and wallet: oil exploration and media.

Until Burke came back into office in 1987, O'Reilly had not enjoyed as much luck in exploration as he would have liked. O'Reilly told *Forbes* magazine in the 1980s that he had 'influence' among Irish politicians by virtue of his wealth and his ownership of leading newspapers. 'Since I own 35 per cent of the newspapers in Ireland I have close contact with the politicians. I got the blocks he [the geologist] wanted,' he said. But that statement was at odds with how others would have seen it, most notably Ivan Fallon in his 1994 biography of O'Reilly, *The Player*. 'In the mid-1970s, the coalition government introduced a series of measures, including the abandonment of export tax relief and a combination of royalties, state ownership rights and corporation tax, which added up to an effective tax rate of 85 per cent on profits, killing exploration for the rest of the decade,' Fallon wrote.

Spring gave O'Reilly little when he became Minister for Energy. He refused to deliver all of the terms and conditions for oil exploration that O'Reilly wanted, especially in relation to tax on any exploration costs and a stake in any possible finds. The young leader of the Labour Party had ideals that were diametrically opposed to those of O'Reilly, although they found common ground on Northern Ireland. A shared passion for rugby didn't help to thaw a frosty relationship: the normal bond that exists between former rugby internationals, even those of a different generation, was absent.

Fallon alleged that Spring showed 'a complete lack of commercial awareness' in refusing to change the rules to any significant degree when he amended them in 1985 and 1986. O'Reilly believed that oil companies often found their terms toughened after they had made a discovery, but that it was a 'huge mistake' to put conditions in place before a discovery was even made. O'Reilly said, 'the world of oil exploration is a poker game and we simply don't know how to play it. 1983 was the year to show we understood the business and the politicians failed the test.' Fallon has written that 'a later Fianna Fáil government, recognizing Spring's folly, made the terms much more favourable, but it was too late: a unique opportunity to make Ireland self-sufficient in oil and gas had gone.'

Burke doesn't feature in Fallon's book, but he was the figure who, as Minister for Energy in 1987, significantly improved the terms for oil companies prospecting off the Irish coast. Royalties were abolished and the state relinquished any stake in an eventual oil or gas find. 'I am realistic enough to appreciate that we cannot have our cake and eat it,' Burke said on 30 September1987, when announcing new licensing terms for the offshore sector. 'Perhaps when we are a recognized oil province, we will be able to afford the luxury of more stringent terms, but for now it is clear that concessions of a radical nature are necessary to offset to the greatest possible extent the effects of low oil prices on exploration in Ireland and the recent disappointing results.'

Burke said the terms were similar to those in Britain and Spain, but it subsequently turned out that, not for the first or last time, Burke's decision was something of a solo run. It had followed a meeting with the oil companies that took place contrary to the advice of a senior adviser in his department. It didn't do O'Reilly much good. His involvement with Atlantic Resources, one of the most hyped and ultimately underperforming stock market companies of the eighties, was one of the many expensive disappointments that he has endured in investing money in Ireland.

But Burke was to continue to feature in O'Reilly's corporate life. When Haughey returned to power in 1987, he gave Burke responsibility for communications as well as for energy. Burke's job appeared to be to frighten the state-funded RTÉ editorially and to undermine it commercially. With many private radio operators operating as 'pirates' and broadcasting illegally in local areas, Burke had an opportunity to regularize and legalize the situation. He set up the Independent Radio and Television Commission, which awarded the first national commercial radio licence to Century Radio in 1989 and then a range of local licences. Nearly a decade later it emerged that Burke had received a corrupt payment of £35,000 from one of Century's backers, a Cork-born music promoter called Oliver Barry. Burke made merry during the 1989 general election campaign, taking donations that may have amounted to £80,000 from two building companies, JMSE and Bovale, as subsequently outlined in startling detail at the same Planning Tribunal that would eventually destroy Ahern.

Crucially, however, the tribunal did not investigate in public another intriguing payment of £30,000 to Burke. This one came from Fitzwilton, a public company under the control of O'Reilly.

On 7 June 1989 two directors of Fitzwilton, Robin Rennicks and Paul Power, travelled to Burke's home. Rennicks was a new Fitzwilton director, having sold it his road-sign company Rennicks Manufacturing. The two men handed over a cheque, made out to cash, on behalf of Fitzwilton but drawn on the Rennicks account.

Fitzwilton was a regular donor to political parties, but normally the company gave its money to Fianna Fáil headquarters. This payment stood out because it was the first time that the cheque was made out to cash, was not given to the party's election fund and was paid via a minister. Fianna Fáil headquarters was informed of the donation, however. Burke later passed on £10,000 of this money to the party by way of a draft, but kept the rest, telling headquarters officials who sought the full amount: 'That's as much as you're getting. Good luck.' All involved have said consistently that the money was intended to be a normal political contribution (although Burke's credibility in that regard is shot).

Other O'Reilly-controlled companies also had reason to want Fianna Fáil returned to office.

As Minister for Communications, Burke was responsible for the issuing of licences for the operation of what was known as the Multichannel Multipoint Distribution Service (MMDS). In the pre-satellite era, MMDS was a wireless cable system that enabled operators to distribute foreign television channels into rural Irish homes. However, the country was littered with many illegal deflector masts, erected on hill and mountain tops, which captured the British TV signals and re-routed them to those who had roof-top aerials, all for little or no cost to the recipients.

Burke suggested that Independent apply for licences to supply a legal service, saying that he would allow this but not a bid for radio licences. The unspoken fear was that O'Reilly would then have too much power over media content. Burke was considering the applications from Independent at the time of the sudden 1989 election – and the Fitzwilton donation. He retained responsibility for communications when the new coalition with the Progressive Democrats was formed under Haughey, even though he also received the onerous duties of the Department of Justice.

Four months later Burke issued twenty-nine MMDS licences, seven of which went to Independent directly, and another eleven to companies in which Independent was a minority shareholder. The new holders were given exclusive rights in the areas they covered. Independent invested heavily in the expensive equipment, but the illegal operators continued, and the take-up of the new service was low. Independent's American co-investors and bankers were furious.

Joe Hayes, the managing director of Independent's Irish operations, contacted Burke. He secured a 'letter of comfort'. In it, Burke stated 'Immediately MMDS service is available in any of your franchise regions, my department will apply the full rigours of the law to illegal operations affecting that franchise region. My department will use its best endeavours to ensure that there are no illegal broadcasting systems affecting that region within six months after the commencement of MMDS transmissions.' Significantly, notation on the letter included a coding rarely used by civil servants to indicate that the content came from the minister and not the department. This implied that Burke was departing from official advice.

Notwithstanding Burke's promises, nothing was done. In late 1992 Burke was booted out of cabinet by the new Taoiseach, Albert Reynolds.

After Fianna Fáil lost power in late 1994, John Bruton's new Rainbow government appointed Fine Gael's Michael Lowry to the Department of Transport, Energy and Communications. He was to prove a worthy successor to Burke, with his similar liking for tax evasion and relationships with wealthy businessmen.

In his new position, Lowry became central to O'Reilly's ambitions for zinc mining at Galmoy in County Kilkenny (through Arcon, a family-controlled company that had grown out of the Atlantic Resources), the commercial performance of the MMDS licences and Independent's plan to be part of a successful bid for the country's second mobile phone licence.

Independent was part of a consortium called Irish Cellular Telephones, which also included the American telecoms giant AT&T for ballast and credibility. Neutral observers never gave Independent much of a chance of success, believing the government would balk at giving O'Reilly another potentially very valuable licence. But that didn't stop O'Reilly hoping or believing that he could win.

In September 1995 Lowry officiated at the opening of the Galmoy mine. Lowry was embroiled in controversy because he had claimed to be 'under surveillance' by mysterious forces who, he alleged, were involved in 'cosy cartels' that aimed to win contracts from state companies. Lowry's credibility was being called into question, and by the *Irish Independent* in particular, where reporter Sam Smyth and I had worked together on a series of investigative stories about his activities.

Lowry was not in a good mood that day, probably because after weeks in which he had not featured in the headlines Smyth had catapulted Lowry back on to page one with another scoop. At the end of the lunch Lowry spotted me and gestured across the marquee for me to stay where I was, that he wanted to talk to me. He walked over and greeted me with the words 'You and Sam Smyth are trying to fuck me.' I slowly and deliberately told him: 'No, Minister, Sam Smyth and I are not trying to fuck you. That is not our job or our intention. You are a government minister making highly controversial claims that Sam and I have investigated and have found difficult to substantiate, which is what we have reported.' Lowry then insisted that the rest of the conversation was off the record and went on to explain, in colourful terms, his version of events in relation to mysterious figures allegedly following him, and others, in white hi-ace vans.

After Lowry left my company I ran into O'Reilly. He wasn't as happy as I would have expected, having just opened a major mine that would employ hundreds and presumably make major profits. Having politely congratulated him on the opening of the mine, I asked him how confident he was about winning the mobile phone licence competition, which was nearing completion. He told me that Lowry had said to him, 'Your fellas didn't do so well today.' O'Reilly was aghast. 'He made it out that AT&T, one of the biggest and most experienced companies in the world, didn't know what they were doing.' He told me this on the agreement that it was not to appear in print at that time.

There was far more significance to that remark than Lowry's apparent dismissal of the credentials of the Irish Cellular Telephones bid. The process was supposed to be 'hermetically sealed' from interference by the minister. He should not have known what was going on at the interview stages, although it is possible that he was merely winding up O'Reilly because of his displeasure at what had appeared in that day's *Irish Independent*.

Years later, when the licence award came under examination at the Moriarty Tribunal, O'Reilly would be accused, wrongly, of making up the comment and of informing the tribunal of the exchange with Lowry out of a sense of malice. Lowry denied to the tribunal that he had ever said it. Fighting for his reputation, he would also tell of a meeting with O'Reilly at the Curragh Racecourse in June 1995, again during the competition process, at which O'Reilly expressed his 'expectation' that his consortium would win. However, he later provided a supplemental statement to the tribunal clarifying that O'Reilly was only expressing a confident opinion rather than making a specific demand.

The competition was won by Denis O'Brien's Esat consortium and O'Reilly did not complain publicly. He wrote a personal letter to O'Brien, congratulating him on his good fortune. But the loss clearly rankled, and when Taoiseach John Bruton visited O'Reilly's holiday home in Glandore in West Cork in late July 1996 he was told of what he later described as O'Reilly's 'extreme displeasure' at the loss. The meeting was private, no notes were taken and some of what was said was subsequently disputed, with O'Reilly denying that he had complained to Bruton about the mobile phone licence. But both men agree that the main issue under dispute that day was the government's failure to crack down on the illegal deflector mast operators.

Three months earlier O'Reilly, in the chairman's letter included in the annual report of Independent Newspapers, had publicly attacked the Rainbow government for failing to protect its investment in the MMDS licences. Its subsidiary, Princes Holdings Limited (PHL), had lost £26 million by this stage, as the availability of pirated alternatives meant the subscriber take-up was much lower than expected. Burke's written promise was not being honoured, and Lowry, as the relevant minister, was being blamed.

Lowry had support for his inaction. Attorney general Dermot Gleeson held that Burke had acted unlawfully and *ultra vires* of his authority. And a factor of political, though not legal, importance was the possibility that Fine Gael might lose seats at the following year's general election if the pirates were closed.

But O'Reilly's complaints against the government went beyond the MMDS issue and continued in even more detail in a letter he sent to Bruton the day after the July meeting. He said that the grants made available to big American food company Heinz (where he was chairman and chief executive at the time) for a manufacturing facility in County Louth had not been made available to Arcon, despite the employment and tax revenue the mine would generate. He warned that failure to protect the indigenous sector would allow Rupert Murdoch – 'whose affection for Ireland is not among his most discerning characteristics'– to take control of the market. 'I and my colleagues are alarmed at the inattention of certain ministers and equally alarmed that we have become something of a political football in other areas of our business . . . I have to say that we have not, in any of our enterprises, received any help or encouragement from the present government or the ministers,' he wrote to Bruton. He added, portentously, that 'we are under acute pressure from our partners in the [MMDS] venture in relation to the terms under which they made their original investment.'

Bruton asked his senior adviser, Sean Donlon – a former civil servant and executive in the high-profile aircraft leasing company GPA – to see if he could do anything for O'Reilly 'in the areas in which proper discretion could be exercised'. A meeting was arranged for early September 1996 at which Independent was represented by Liam Healy, director Brendan Hopkins and external consultant Mike Burns. Donlon warned that Fine Gael could lose four seats by taking the action demanded of it with regard to MMDS licenses. Independent was unimpressed, making it clear that the US shareholders in PHL were anxious to take the state to court over its failure to 'police the exclusivity of the licences'.

Hopkins wrote a memo afterwards that recorded, 'We said they [the government] would lose Independent Newspapers as friends and [this] would mean any future administration would have to pay a large bill.'

O'Reilly, when giving evidence on this to the Moriarty Tribunal eight years later, said 'that this particular use of the word "friends" related specifically to losing us as friends in this debate internally within our consortium [PHL], to stop them [the US shareholders] from taking the state to law, and allowing us to exhaust all the various means that we could to remedy the deflector crisis'. He said the US shareholders had been 'seething with us as well as with the government, at the amount of money they were losing in Ireland'. Similarly, Healy rejected any suggestion that there had been a threat to use the group's newspapers to criticize the government.

Donlon reported back to Bruton that Michael Lowry was persona non grata with Independent and that the meeting left him 'in no doubt about Independent Newspapers' hostility to the government parties if outstanding issues were not resolved to their satisfaction'. In his 2004 evidence to the Moriarty Tribunal, Bruton said he would have taken the reference to losing Independent as friends to mean hostile coverage of the government parties in the newspapers, and not a threat of litigation. He said this could be seen as a 'threat'.

After that September meeting O'Reilly wrote to Bruton again, asking if it was his government's policy to 'encourage pirates'. He said Bruton's answer to the question 'will be of great importance to us and to our position in assessing our future plans'. He never received a reply.

Coincidence or not, Bruton's next communication from the O'Reilly stable was that famous payback editorial of June 1997.

It wasn't until a year later that the details of the Fitzwilton payment to Ray Burke in 1989 were revealed. Details of the row between Fine Gael and the government over the MMDS licences also began to emerge at that time.

The revelation put pressure on Ahern's government to widen the terms of reference of the Planning Tribunal. Whatever about dodgy builders bunging Burke cash to pay for planning decisions, the idea that a company owned by the country's richest man and most powerful media baron could also have been investigated by the tribunal was far more significant.

When it looked as if O'Reilly was going to be called to account in public, he hired the services of one of the country's toughest and best-connected barristers, Corkman Dermot Gleeson, to represent him in the initial private hearings.

Gleeson brought some good fortune as well as good advice to O'Reilly. Despite widespread political and media comment, the tribunal never publicly investigated the full circumstances of the Fitzwilton payment or who was responsible for it. For reasons that were not explained at the time of its initial decision, the Planning Tribunal decided not to proceed to public hearings, despite conducting lengthy private investigations. But then, following a demand by the government in December 2004 that the tribunal declare what it would do in public before it finished its work, an effort was made by tribunal officials to bring the Fitzwilton issue back on to its agenda.

Fitzwilton, however, was not to return to the tribunal's public hearings. Following legal action by O'Reilly's company alleging that the tribunal had misinterpreted its terms of reference and that public hearings should not go ahead, the Supreme Court in 2006 agreed that the way in which the tribunal's response to the Oireachtas had been drafted did not comply with its amended terms of reference. O'Reilly was off this particular hook.

3

His master's voices

I can imagine how relieved Tony O'Reilly must have been when the Supreme Court ruled that the Planning Tribunal could not publicly investigate the Fitzwilton payment to Ray Burke. O'Reilly is obsessive about his personal reputation. That anyone might even consider that he had corrupted the political process would be anathema to him.

Shortly after the *Magill* report on the Fitzwilton payment appeared in 1998, a front-page news report in the *Sunday Tribune* referred to the possibility of investigation into the payment to Burke by Fitzwilton, 'a company in which Tony O'Reilly is the controlling shareholder'. It may have been a plain statement of fact, but that and the offending paragraph's positioning down near the bottom of the report did not spare me the wrath of O'Reilly's proxy.

Late that Sunday afternoon I received a phone call from a senior independent executive. He was furious that the reference to O'Reilly had been included. He told me that Gleeson had advised O'Reilly that he had grounds for a libel action, even though it would be against his own newspaper. He wanted to hold the reporter who had written the story responsible, but I told him that I'd been fully aware of the text before publication and had approved it. I was forced to assure him that 'greater care' would be taken before any further references would be made in the future. I didn't much look forward to my next meeting with O'Reilly, although nothing more was said about it.

The issue of editorial control of the newspaper was a sensitive one. I had to tread a line between what I saw as my responsibility to the readers and the reality that the loss-making newspaper was dependent on Independent for finance to survive. There had been political and legal issues relating to Independent's involvement with the paper. The purchase of a 29 per cent shareholding in Tribune Publications –

publisher of the *Sunday Tribune* – was completed in 1990, despite the strenuous objections of the then Minister for Industry and Commerce, Des O'Malley. The Progressive Democrat leader – who ironically would have shared many of O'Reilly's ideas on business and the North of Ireland – believed that O'Reilly's influence in the domestic newspaper market had become too large. Using the powers given to him under company law, O'Malley blocked a full takeover of the company, although he was unable to force Independent Newspapers to divest itself of its shares. As the law referred only to ordinary shares, which gave voting control, Independent eventually got around this by the creation of preference shares, which gave complete financial control (preference shares, and subsequent loans, were due repayment and dividends before the ordinary shares). While there were non-Independent members on the board, knowledge that Independent paid all the bills tempered any decisions that might have been inimical to its interests.

When the issue of the *Sunday Tribune*'s editorial independence was under discussion, the Competition Authority was shown an O'Reilly quotation that had been modelled on the style book of the *Washington Post*, of which he was a director. 'In a world where the ownership of newspapers is increasingly concentrated amongst a smaller group of names . . . the newspaper's duty is to its readers and to the public at large and not to the private interests of the owner.'

I clung to that in my editorial management of the newspaper, even though the idea that the *Sunday Tribune* was somehow independent of the control of Independent was a sham. I was appointed to the position of editor in September 1996 without even an application or an interview, and, given that I'd celebrated my thirtieth birthday only two months earlier, I suspect it was thought that I'd be easily controlled.

I was in the job less than a week when I received two instructions. The first, which came directly from O'Reilly, was that there was never to be any support in the paper for the IRA. I had no problem with that. An instruction from a proprietor not to support an illegal organization was more than fair and reasonable.

The second came from another Independent executive and it was to sack three journalists whom O'Reilly didn't like: Eamon McCann, Frank Fitzgibbon and the since deceased Des Crowley. I refused. Unfortunately, no sooner had I made this stand than Fitzgibbon quit anyway to become a columnist at the *Sunday Times* (where he is now editor and I'm one of his columnists), making me wish he'd told me this just a few hours earlier. Fitzgibbon was a feisty business journalist who had not been known to bow the knee to O'Reilly or others.

McCann, a hard-line socialist, stayed for my six years as editor, writing about sport, religion and the Bloody Sunday Tribunal, and continued in his other role as a columnist with the *Belfast Telegraph* after Independent bought it. However, I bowed to subsequent sustained pressure two years later to make Crowley redundant from our business department. Crowley delighted in writing stories that embarrassed senior business figures and was reviled in many quarters, not because of inaccuracy but because he had become a useful conduit for the disaffected. Much of what he wrote infuriated O'Reilly particularly. I wasn't proud of my decision but felt I had no option but to make it when I relied on Independent not to slash my editorial budgets.

The biggest pressure on me was to cut costs. The *Sunday Tribune* had made large losses consistently in the years before I joined it and that didn't end under my stewardship, despite increased circulation and higher advertising revenues. All we did manage to do was reduce the weekly losses. Money had to come from Independent to keep the paper running.

The cost to INM of the investment since 1990 has amounted to over €60 million; the newspaper consistently failed to match its revenues to its costs. INM, while maintaining the fiction of non-control, wanted us to do some things and not others, and would not allow us the funds for major investment when there was no guarantee it would get the required return, or where such investment might give competitors grounds to allege unfair competition. And with the *Sunday Independent*'s senior editors complaining bitterly that their profits were being used to sustain a newspaper they disparaged – funds that they felt they could have put to better use – our room for manoeuvre was limited.

The corporate imperative was different, however, to that of the flagship newspaper title. My task was clear, if never explicitly put into writing: it was to make enough sales to block any circulation advances by the *Sunday Times* at the top end of the market. What was never said, although it was implied, was that we weren't to impinge too much on the *Sunday Independent* (or indeed on other titles within the parent group) in terms of both advertising revenue and sales of the paper itself. When the *Sunday Tribune*'s managing director, Frank Cronin, decided to launch a property section in 1997, he was instructed by Independent, as main shareholder, not to do so on the Friday before it was due to appear for the first time, even though many advertisements had already been booked by estate agents. Independent didn't want us undercutting the rates of the *Irish Independent*'s profitable Friday property section. We, however, wanted to raise advertising revenue that was previously unavailable to us. I could see why it wanted to stop us, but I knew how important to us such new revenue could be. We went ahead anyway, but other decisions as to how we spent our money received much tougher scrutiny thereafter.

I discovered that there were those who would take it upon themselves to remind me of my paper's difficult financial position, should I do anything that seemed contrary to the wishes of Independent's main man. This came to a head for me in early 2001, when I came under pressure from others within the Independent group literally to stop the presses to prevent publication of an editorial the *Sunday Tribune* was carrying that referred directly to O'Reilly's business interests. The pressure to toe the line did not come from Independent's directors but from some of its middle-management, who seemingly acted out of fear of being seen to dissent from what they perceived to be their boss's – and therefore their own – interests.

O'Reilly's emergence as a likely buyer of Eircom was to be the litmus test. For the edition of 28 April 2001 I had written an editorial under the headline: 'Don't sell your shares, no matter who buys Eircom'; in addition, I'd put a picture of O'Reilly, Denis O'Brien and Dermot Desmond (also rumoured as a likely bidder for Eircom) on the front page above the masthead, accompanied by a line saying don't sell Eircom shares to any of these men. In the editorial I suggested that the share price did not reflect Eircom's real value. 'Investors should be slow to accept whatever offers come from any of the parties,' I wrote, and said the fall in the share price had much more to do with international developments than with Eircom's own failings and that it was a far better business than many people gave it credit for. I went on to argue:

It has cash on hand rather than borrowings, a sizeable market position in Ireland, no dubious overseas investments and is profitable. The danger, however, is that Eircom, either under existing management or new owners, will decelerate investment programmes to suit the financial requirements of investors.

Why doesn't one of the multimillionaires involved satisfy himself with buying just 29.9 per cent of the company, the maximum amount permitted under stock exchange rules before triggering a full bid? A 29 per cent share in these circumstances should be enough to secure management control and would obviate the need to buy out the workers' shares. It would also mean that existing investors would share in whatever uplift O'Brien or O'Reilly or Desmond could bring to the company. That certainly makes more sense than selling to them cheaply.

The *Sunday Tribune* was printed at Terenure Printers, home to the *Sunday World*. Not long after the first copies were off the presses I received a phone call from a senior editorial figure in the group, who worked at another newspaper. He had received a phone call from someone who'd seen a first edition of the paper and who had urged him to use his influence with me to have the editorial and front-page picture removed. He said he was worried that I was going to do my career serious damage and that I was bringing trouble upon myself unnecessarily. I explained to him the content of the editorial in more detail than his original source had and why I thought it was important for the *Sunday Tribune* to have its own editorial line on this. I also told him that I didn't think it would cause a problem.

It didn't. Some days later I was told by a third party involved in the Valentia bid that the editorial had come up for discussion in O'Reilly's presence at a meeting where the next moves in the Eircom takeover were being plotted. Somebody did complain about it and I was told that it was O'Reilly who defended my independence. He said it was useful in that it confirmed he did not interfere with editorial decisions. I imagine that he knew its publication was never going to make much difference to the eventual outcome.

In 1999 the *Irish Times* political editor Geraldine Kennedy revealed considerable new detail about the payment to Burke and the coincidence of the award of the MMDS licences to Independent. Bruton – still smarting from his experience during the 1997 election – seized upon this in the Dáil, and both he and the *Irish Times* were to feel the wrath of many titles in the Independent group in return. A front-page comment in the *Irish Independent* proclaimed that a 'vicious, calculated and damaging smear campaign' had been instigated against its parent company.

The *Irish Times* replied in an editorial, noting 'a series of articles, some signed, some anonymous, that accused the *Irish Times* of a "travesty of fair reporting"'; this series of articles also stridently denied a range of offences that the *Irish Times* never alleged to have taken place at all. The *Irish Times* editorial noted that RTÉ had also drawn Independent's ire, finding itself charged with begrudgery against O'Reilly on the grounds that he was 'rich, successful and self-made':

On the contrary, the *Irish Times* has lauded his entrepreneurial skill, his leadership and his courage, which have brought the Independent group to a position of international strength and influence. The *Irish Times* has always recognized and applauded his practical patriotism, his love of country and his immense contribution both financial and cultural. But none of this means that one should be blind to the dangers of concentration of ownership in media or of corporate linkages between media organizations and other commercial companies.

It is a matter of public record that Dr O'Reilly does not intervene in the editorial content of his newspapers. It is remarkable therefore that so many on his payroll, unbidden and unprompted, will respond with one unvarying and uncritical voice at a time like this. This is employee loyalty of a kind which is all too rarely to be found in today's world and Dr O'Reilly and his fellow-shareholders must consider themselves exceptionally fortunate to be its recipients.

The *Irish Times* was clearly enjoying itself, and Bruton wasn't going to miss the opportunity to put the boot in either. 'It is an abuse of press power for a major newspaper group to use their columns and editorials over four days running to concoct replies on behalf of their owner to one speech in the Dáil,' said Bruton. He accused the newspaper group of being in a 'state of denial' about the matter, citing an editorial in which it accused him of abusing Dáil privilege to link Independent Newspapers and its chairman with payments to a politician. Bruton said: 'The statement I made on that matter is factual in that Dr O'Reilly is chairman of the company that made the payment, so there is a link between him and the payment, whether or not he consented to or was aware of the payment . . . So that is a statement that could be made anywhere without benefit of privilege.'

A spokesman for Independent Newspapers said: 'Mr Bruton was wrong to attempt to create a link between Independent Newspapers and Fitzwilton.'

Bruton's opportunity to finally ventilate the issues between Fine Gael and O'Reilly arose in the forum of the Moriarty Tribunal; there, however, he was standing on somewhat shakier ground. Bruton had been Taoiseach at the time of Michael Lowry's forced resignation as Minister for Transport, Energy and Communications in December 1996. Lowry's dodgy dealings finally caught up with him when Sam Smyth revealed that Lowry had secretly accepted Ben Dunne's largesse, a £300,000 plus gift of an extension to his mansion in Tipperary. This revelation led to a chain of events that included Haughey's unmasking as another beneficiary of Dunne's millions, the establishment of the McCracken Tribunal and, subsequently, in order to continue the investigation of Lowry and Haughey, the creation of the Moriarty Tribunal.

While the Moriarty Tribunal did not deal specifically with the matter of the payment to Burke by Fitzwilton, it came up in the course of the tribunal's investigation into Lowry's handling of the mobile phone licence award in 1995. Independent had been part of a bidding consortium, so its relationship with Lowry came into question. And Lowry, having been brought down originally by the *Irish Independent*, was more than happy to drag O'Reilly's rows with the government back into the spotlight.

This meant O'Reilly had to endure examination in the witness box at Dublin Castle and issue statements of further 'clarification' as to his knowledge of the payment to Burke. He claimed that he had learned only ten years after the event that the 1989 general election payment to Fianna Fáil had been made via Burke and that Burke had kept two thirds of it for himself.

O'Reilly defended the payback editorial by pointing out that Fine Gael actually increased its vote in the 1997 election. 'It could be that the front-page editorial helped them,' he contended. O'Reilly agreed that the editorial was 'unusual' but denied he'd had any input into it or knowledge that it would be published. He said the board of INM did not interfere in the editorial policies of its titles. 'That can be ascertained by direct contact with any of the editors in the group ... The general view, I would say, about Independent News and Media is that governments always feel they are being maligned by it, whatever government, and opposition feel that they are being ignored.'

It is hard to find anyone with sympathy for O'Reilly. There is an extraordinary antipathy towards him from people in politics and business to whom I have spoken over the years. Even if they accept that

O'Reilly has had no direct involvement in newspaper content, some blame him none the less for not reining in certain editors. That said, had he done so, he might have been subjected to accusations of undue editorial interference. The problems have been caused by the manner in which the *Sunday Independent* does its work, a manner that owes much to sensationalism and much to partisanship. And that partisanship was never more apparent than in its treatment of Bertie Ahern.

PART II

The Taoiseach

4

The great defender

It was 26 May, the Saturday morning after the 2007 general election, and Fianna Fáil had won enough seats to allow it to return to power. Fintan O'Toole of the *Irish Times* was one of the guests in studio in *The Last Word* post-election special. He wanted to know, as a matter of public interest, what had been discussed and agreed when Bertie Ahern and Brian Cowen went to Tony O'Reilly's house on Fitzwilliam Square in Dublin in the weeks running up to the election.

Eoghan Harris, one of the leading commentators employed by the *Sunday Independent*, entered the studio, clearly furious despite Fianna Fáil's victory, which he had advocated and predicted. He took a seat beside O'Toole, directly across the desk from me. And when he started talking it provided what is known as 'radio gold', one of those compelling episodes that stops listeners in their tracks.

Harris launched an extraordinary attack on O'Toole's newspaper for what he called its failed attempt to bring down Ahern by publishing a series of reports on his financial dealings. He accused it of trying to deny that this had been a deliberate strategy. He decried what he regarded as an attempt to ascribe a sinister motive – or 'murky agenda' – to the 'Cowen–O'Reilly meeting', as Harris called it, implying that Ahern had not attended.

It wasn't until a few weeks after the meeting took place that Fianna Fáil was challenged publicly about what had passed between the party's most senior officers and the country's most powerful newspaper interests. At a press conference during the election campaign Cowen confirmed the meeting – 'an opportunity had arisen'– but refused to say what had been discussed. 'Any meetings that are private are private. It wasn't about anything other than Fianna Fáil putting its position formally to a proprietor of newspapers to see what way we can get our message across.' This raised the question as to why, given his insistence that he did not interfere with the editorial policies of the newspapers, O'Reilly failed to direct the politicians to his editors when they sought a meeting for such purposes.

Six weeks before the general election the *Observer*'s Ireland correspondent, Henry McDonald, delivered a remarkable scoop, declaring baldly that 'Sir Tony O'Reilly is to swing his Independent Newspapers group behind Bertie Ahern in the Irish general election next month.' McDonald quoted Fianna Fáil sources: 'the party was "cracking open the champagne this weekend" over the news.' He wrote: 'as well as editorials supporting the current Fianna Fáil–Progressive Democrat coalition, high-profile Independent Group columnists such as Eoghan Harris in the *Sunday Independent* are also expected to call for the coalition's re-election.'

But something significant did happen on 22 April, the very day the *Observer* published its story. McDonald was shown to be entirely correct in his predictions.

The *Sunday Independent* had been shaping up to be a major thorn in Fianna Fáil's side for the election campaign. It was running its own pre-election campaign to bring about a change in the rates of stamp duty charged on residential property transactions, claiming that it was an unfair tax, that it was acting as a disincentive to purchases and that it was causing the market to slow. This was somewhat bizarre, given that at that stage the property bubble looked as if it was only beginning to deflate. Indeed the *Sunday Independent* seemed obsessed with the escalating property market and devoted phenomenal coverage to it during the boom.

The campaign intensified as the election neared. For example, on 4 March 2007 the front-page headline read 'Bertie sinks as house market goes under', and there was an article inside under the headline 'How Cowen drives young people into the arms of moneylenders'. Two weeks later the front-page headline read 'Home tax: ministers snubbed by Cowen', claiming some of the cabinet were 'privately admitting' the party had missed an electoral opportunity by failing to reform stamp duty. A week later the headline read 'FF resorts to auction politics to woo voters' but bemoaned the absence of stamp duty proposals. Two weeks later again a banner across the front page of the newspaper ran: 'Election 2007 – the issue: it's stamp duty, stupid'. On 15 April editor

Aengus Fanning wrote a piece for the front page under the headline: 'Labour and Fine Gael unite on stamp duty', stating that they, and not the government, understood what was the most important issue for voters.

The *Sunday Independent*'s campaign was helping to set the political agenda. Other political parties promised to reform or abolish the tax within months of a new government being formed. On Tuesday, 17 April, the *Irish Times* headlined a piece 'Stamp duty reform key battleground in election campaign'.

The cumulative effect of dozens of articles, week after week, about residential property stamp duty got its result. Ahern buckled. On 22 April, a week after the newspaper had given Ahern a good kicking on its front page and after the visit to O'Reilly's central Dublin home, the *Sunday Independent* switched tack.

On that day the front-page headline on the *Sunday Independent* read: 'Ahern set for quick reform of home tax', a story that had been delivered exclusively to the paper, although it did not quote any sources directly. (Ahern effectively confirmed its accuracy to me in a radio interview the following day, saying that something would be announced before the general election – which it was, again through the pages of the *Sunday Independent*.) At the bottom of the front page on 22 April there was a piece in which Fanning personally attacked Enda Kenny. One front-page banner for an inside-page story read: 'How Fine Gael lost the election' and there was another for a piece entitled: 'My pain during Bertiegate: Miriam Ahern'. Inside, Eoghan Harris said that he had been 'hammering out one hard message' on stamp duty for six months and that the campaign was now bearing fruit.

There was one curiosity in the *Sunday Independent* that day: in the same edition in which it loudly proclaimed its success in setting the electoral agenda, it also carried an opinion poll, by a reputable polling company, that ranked stamp duty in joint-last place of all the fourteen issues presented to those polled for assessment.

It's hard to imagine that O'Reilly was personally concerned about stamp duty rates and that he'd ordered his newspaper to conduct a campaign about it, although the state of the property market would impact on advertising volumes and rates. It's not hard to believe, though, that those under pressure from their ultimate bosses to keep up profits would have seen it as a good idea.

Confirmation of the *Sunday Independent*'s deliberate actions came from Harris during his on-air row with O'Toole in my studio. 'When we got what we wanted on stamp duty we turned back to Fianna Fáil,' he announced. He took issue with what he perceived to be O'Toole's belief that the *Sunday Independent* campaign against stamp duty was not acceptable because it had an 'agenda', whereas the *Irish Times* campaign of leaks was 'information' and therefore without an agenda.

There is little doubt in political circles that the *Sunday Independent* is regarded as influential – or that it is feared. It does not have the largest newspaper circulation in the country – that accolade goes to its sister paper, the *Sunday World* – but it has about one million readers every Sunday and they are of an age and disposition that makes them more likely to vote. While the *Irish Times* is the most respected newspaper in the country, and is turned to first by the most powerful in the country and opinion formers, it may not have as much influence as the *Sunday Independent* because it has fewer readers. Indeed this is something that the *Sunday Independent* liked to state regularly when it went through a lengthy period of deliberately disparaging the *Irish Times*'s content and opinions.

The editor of the *Sunday Independent*, Aengus Fanning, and his deputy, Anne Harris, a couple who became engaged a few years ago, are the driving force behind the paper. Anne Harris, as editor of *Image* magazine, was hired by Fanning not long after he took the job in 1984. Many of those who have worked with the newspaper believe that whatever editorial line is in vogue is set primarily by her. A forceful and strongly spoken individual, but capable too of great charm towards those who are in favour, she is credited with having read the market correctly by bringing a magazine-like approach to the newspaper.

The paper was something of a trail-blazer under their editorship, becoming a type of publication that had not been previously seen in the Irish media. New wealth and consumption were celebrated and promoted, even before the Celtic Tiger came into being. The emphasis was on comment and analysis, and many of its journalists were (and still are) selected for their skill in constructing forceful and persuasive arguments, rather than for their ability to deliver objective news stories. Comment verged on invective, deliberately targeting issues and, more controversially, people in an attempt to stir things up. The newspaper set agendas, especially by the use of attack dogs such as Eamon Dunphy, who, having specialized in savaging sporting figures like Irish soccer manager Jack Charlton, turned to Irish political and cultural icons such as John Hume, Seamus Heaney, Pat Kenny and Roddy Doyle. This aspect of the paper appalled people and many complained to O'Reilly as proprietor. However, he did not interfere, quite liking the promotion of capitalism, the vehement opposition to the IRA and the profits brought in by high circulation.

Indeed, some critics have charged that O'Reilly was happy because the *Sunday Independent* targeted his opponents by proxy. Chief among these has been Vincent Browne: he has alleged the journalists are used by some of these newspapers as hit-men, attacking outside journalists who are questioning and critical. 'The way in which, for instance, the *Sunday Independent* targets any critics of O'Reilly itself borders on the corrupt,' he wrote once. 'It is implausible that O'Reilly has ordered this but certainly the editors know they will win his approval and commendation if that is what they do.'

Yet the *Sunday Independent* has a great defence against any charges of bias. It has perfected the art of simultaneously running campaigns while giving the alternative within the same pages. It is full of dissident voices from within at the same time as it appears to be following an agenda. Excellent journalists such as Gene Kerrigan, Alan Ruddock and John Drennan often write contrary to the perceived editorial line of the newspaper – and that gives the *Sunday Independent* a good defence against the charge that it is deliberately manipulative and tries to exercise power by proxy.

We asked Eoghan Harris to join us on our post-election programme because he had been unapologetic and unwavering in his support for Ahern since the first allegations of financial irregularities emerged in September 2006. If Dunphy was the *Sunday Independent*'s box-office controversialist in the late 1980s and early 1990s, Anne Harris's ex-husband filled the role in this decade. For two years he used his column in the *Sunday Independent* and appearances in the broadcast media to defend the beleaguered Taoiseach.

Harris claimed Ahern was the subject of a deliberate campaign to undermine him, which was being achieved by the selective leaking of information from the Planning Tribunal. He argued that the sums of money involved were trivial – especially if compared to those involved when Charles Haughey used his office to enrich himself – and could be explained easily by the domestic circumstances in which Ahern found himself. He suspected a plot by Republican elements, presumably to help Sinn Féin in the general election at Fianna Fáil's expense. Harris insisted that any balanced assessment of Ahern's achievements, especially in relation to Northern Ireland, and indeed the economy, would convince the electorate that he remained the best-qualified politician to lead the country. He went against the media consensus in saying so and gloried in pointing this out.

Harris had travelled the full political spectrum as an activist, from radical left-wing politics in the 1960s to supporting Fianna Fáil – or, more pertinently, Ahern – in the 2000s, with opposition to militant Republicanism as the common element in his ideological evolution. He never pretended to separate his political beliefs from his media work and his desire to influence public opinion. Throughout the election campaign Harris was Ahern's strongest and most provocative champion, predicting not just that Ahern would be returned to power but that he and the *Sunday Independent* would be shown to have understood the Irish people better than anyone else in the media by insisting that the issue of Ahern's money simply didn't matter. Before the election Harris wrote that:

Ahern himself is a class act who does not come from the correct class. And the correct class, which controls the media, is basically a politically correct class. That being so, I suspect that some of them sneer at Ahern the same way they sneer at the *Sunday Independent*. Big mistake. Because Ahern and the *Sunday Independent* are in touch with the Irish people.

By and large, Irish people do not like the new Puritan priesthood of the media which calls politicians to a public life of Platonic perfection which it will not apply to its own profession. To the media, all sins are mortal and all sins are the same.

Whatever impact all of that may have had on the readers of the *Sunday Independent*, a performance by Harris on RTÉ's *The Late Late Show* on the Friday evening before the election may have been even more important. As part of a panel with Eamon Dunphy and John Waters, Harris used his formidable rhetorical skills to defend Ahern to the hilt, earning rousing applause from the audience in doing so. His task may have been made a bit easier by the widespread perception – again not reported in much of the media – that Ahern had outperformed Fine Gael leader Enda Kenny in a television debate the previous evening. But it is also possible that his eloquent and passionate dismissal of Ahern's accusers was instrumental in swaying undecided voters towards Fianna Fáil.

Not everybody at RTÉ was thrilled, despite the compelling nature of the television. Senior RTÉ executives such as director-general Cathal Goan and managing director of news Ed Mulhall later told an Oireachtas committee that they had been uncomfortable with the item. But Goan pointed out that the independent Broadcasting Complaints Commission had found no imbalance when it adjudicated on a formal complaint, so, as far as he was concerned, RTÉ had 'fulfilled its statutory duty'.

Just days before the election Ahern formalized his promise to remove stamp duty for all first-time buyers regardless of the value of the house if he were to be returned to power. He did so in an exclusive article he wrote for the *Sunday Independent*. Ahern said uncertainty had the potential to damage the housing market, and that this would in turn have knock-on effects on the wider economy because of the potential impact on the construction sector. 'We need to bring that uncertainty to an end,' he wrote.

It wasn't the only exclusive that Ahern delivered to the *Sunday Independent* in this period. The dissolution of the Dáil and the naming of the date for the general election were announced exclusively to the *Sunday Independent*, which carried the story on its front page on the same morning that Ahern went to Áras an Uachtaráin to seek the approval of President Mary McAleese. The news was carried immediately on the broadcast media from very early that morning, but it was too late for the *Sunday Independent*'s rivals, who were put at a serious commercial disadvantage.

The following August, when Ahern announced his eleven nominees for Seanad Éireann, there were surprises. Ivor Callely, who had lost his seat in the general election, and who had been forced to resign as a junior minister when it emerged in late 2005 that he had allowed businessmen to pay for the refurbishment of his private residence, was one of the appointments. But overshadowing all of this was the choice of Eoghan Harris. It was extraordinary by any standards, given his status as cheerleader-in-chief in the defence of Ahern. It wasn't just a reward for Harris but a clear rebuff to everyone else in the media. How reassured Ahern must have been subsequently to read this conclusion to one of Harris's articles in the *Sunday Independent*: 'Because as long as I am around, Bertie will never walk alone.'

5

The fund-raiser

A former ministerial colleague of Bertie Ahern's ruefully reminded me of an old Irish political maxim that his erstwhile party leader had failed to follow: 'It was the late John Healy [a legendary Irish political journalist] who said that leaders should worry not about what their enemies might do to them but what their friends might do for them.' It was a pointed reference to the role of Des Richardson in Ahern's life.

Richardson served Ahern loyally but his fingerprints are on several of the financial mistakes that Ahern made before becoming leader of Fianna Fáil. Richardson is also Ahern's connection to many of the property developers who prospered during Ahern's reign as Taoiseach and who floundered almost as soon as he departed.

The two met during the 1980s and, while Richardson never became a member of Fianna Fáil, the Dubliner became essential to Ahern's financing of his constituency organization and his personal financial affairs. Crucially, he operated in a manner that left Ahern open to all sorts of investigation and innuendo and provided a link to a very colourful cast of characters, including disgraced lobbyist Frank Dunlop, Ansbacher depositor John Finnegan and property developer Owen O'Callaghan.

Despite his key role in Irish political life for nearly two decades, especially in organizing the infamous Fianna Fáil fund-raising tent at the Galway Races, the public was never properly introduced to Richardson until the broadcast of the RTÉ documentary series *Bertie* in late 2008. (He was bullish in his defence of his actions in raising money for the former Taoiseach, but his attitude did his friend few favours.) Although he had made a number of appearances at the Planning Tribunal, the lack of televised coverage of those hearings and his relatively low profile meant that he had never registered as a significant player.

The first many had heard of him was when Ahern named him in September 2006 as one of his 'dig-out' men, the group of friends who Ahern claimed had helped him with money when he was struggling with the financial implications of the end of his marriage.

I rang Richardson the day after Ahern's tearful interview with Bryan Dobson, asking him to contribute to a *The Last Word* piece we planned to do on the 'dig-out' friends whom Ahern had named. Richardson declined but told me that he and the other donors were 'being forced to take money back that we don't want'. This was strange, as Ahern had emphasized that the money he received was only a loan; here was one of the donors effectively suggesting that it was a gift after all.

I'd had an earlier phone conversation with Richardson about the subject of money for Ahern. In early December 2001 he rang me at the *Sunday Tribune* to berate me for the headline that had appeared on the front page of the previous week's paper: 'Ahern takes cash from Ansbacher figure'. 'Vicious and most unfair,' he complained. The story, by political correspondent Shane Coleman, had given details of the guest list at the annual fund-raising dinner for the O'Donovan Rossa constituency organization at Clontarf Castle the previous weekend. Among those present were property developers Seán Dunne, Bernard McNamara and Jim Mansfield, auctioneer Ken McDonald of Hooke & McDonald, David McKenna, chief executive of recruitment company Marlborough, publican Charlie Chawke, hotelier Noel O'Callaghan and Central Bank director Jim Nugent. Also there as usual were two old friends of Ahern: Robert White, who had unsuccessfully proposed developing the old Phoenix Park Racecourse into a national conference centre, stadium and casino; and Joe Burke, part of his tightly knit 'Drumcondra Mafia'– the men who had helped Ahern win and hold his Dáil seat – and soon to be his nominee for chairman of the Dublin Port Authority. The presence of Ryanair boss Michael O'Leary was very unusual, but this was during the brief period when O'Leary was being mannerly to politicians before resuming normal service and targeting Ahern in particular for failing to give him what he wanted.

One name jumped out: that of auctioneer John Finnegan. He was known both as an associate of former Taoiseach Charles Haughey and as one of his fellow depositors in the infamous Ansbacher tax evasion scheme constructed by the accountant and adviser to Haughey, Des Traynor. Ansbacher, a bank in the Cayman Islands, had been used by certain Irish investors to deposit money and evade tax. To have use of their money, the investors 'borrowed' it back, the interest rate being their fee for the service. An affidavit lodged with the High Court in 1999 by an investigating officer into the Ansbacher scam said that Finnegan had received a £1.88 million 'loan' from the accounts of Ansbacher Cayman and that this was 'adequately secured'. While Finnegan hadn't been named formally as an Ansbacher tax evader at this stage, the dogs in the street knew him to be one, and Ahern had been aware of written confirmation of that for nearly three years.

That wasn't all. Evidence at the Planning Tribunal showed that Finnegan had given money secretly to disgraced former minister Ray Burke and was an investor in development projects with other Burke donors, including builders Tom Brennan and Joe McGowan. He had testified to the Planning Tribunal only after it secured a High Court order against him; there he had argued that he was unable to give details of his illegal offshore accounts because the trustees were refusing to give him information about his own money. That made him a suspected tax-cheat, implied he was corrupt and showed contempt for a proper investigation by the state.

As a result of the *Tribune* report Ahern was put under pressure in the Dáil to justify taking money from some of the characters with whom he socialized. 'I have not taken money from anybody or asked anybody for money, regardless of whether they are involved in a tribunal,' he claimed. 'If a constituency organizes a function and I attend as guest of honour, I neither vet nor organize who else attends, nor do I handle the money.' As to the question of who attended or did not attend such functions, Ahern said it was 'a free country'.

Our point had been whether it was appropriate for Ahern's constituency to have taken money from someone like Finnegan, hidden or not. Surely anyone with any kind of political savvy would have distanced themselves from someone as toxic as Finnegan? Instead, Finnegan had hosted his table at this annual event as he had done for most of the previous fifteen years.

But it wasn't the *Sunday Tribune*'s questioning of Finnegan's suitability to be a guest at the O'Donovan Rossa cumann fund-raiser that worried Richardson. He took exception to the implications of the word 'cash' in the headline. 'It wasn't cash,' Richardson thundered down the phone. 'It was a cheque.' He explained that the method of payment was crucial because the cheque proved that Finnegan hadn't tried to hide his contribution and that it had not been for more money than was allowed under the statutory limits. There was nothing underhand about the payment, he insisted. The wider point, that some people might not be suitable donors to a serving Taoiseach, even if the amount was within the limits and declared, either escaped or didn't concern him. The suggestion contained in the article that Ahern, or indeed Richardson as the fund-raiser, should exercise some discretion didn't seem to matter.

Richardson had been organizing Ahern's annual constituency fund-raiser for well over a decade. He had organized the purchase of Ahern's constituency office, St Luke's in Drumcondra, above which Ahern lived for many years following his marital separation, and set up the trust fund to control it. The money he raised for the constituency was vast and allowed Ahern to operate the most formidable personal vote-getting machine in the country. But it was not until Richardson stepped away from his other role as party fund-raiser that it was discovered Richardson had been both giving money to Ahern personally and organizing for others to do it for more than two years.

Richardson was given the job of party fund-raiser with Fianna Fáil because Ahern had insisted upon it. Ahern just missed out on becoming leader of Fianna Fáil, Albert Reynolds getting the job instead, when Haughey finally bowed out in early 1992. Reynolds gave Ahern the rather unenviable job of national treasurer with responsibility for clearing the party's debt of over £3 million. Ahern reluctantly took on the task but only on the condition that Richardson was employed to raise funds. Richardson was paid £5,000 per month, a sizeable fee in those days, apparently rising to £6,500 later. He operated from the same suite in the Berkeley Court Hotel that Des Traynor had used years earlier, reputedly reducing the deficit to nearly zero by the time of the 1997 general election campaign.

However, Richardson didn't restrict himself to serving Fianna Fáil. He had an office at David McKenna's Marlborough recruitment company, where he was a part-time director, and he also acted as an adviser to many of the people and companies from whom he was getting money for Fianna Fáil. What isn't known is whether Ahern personally authorized Richardson's decision to top up his income in this way. The biggest question of all is whether Richardson's activities – on behalf of the party, constituency and Ahern personally – influenced Ahern's actions as Minister for Finance between 1992 and 1994, consciously or not.

As finance minister Ahern did a lot to benefit the rich and powerful. Far from tackling tax evasion, as he subsequently boasted of doing, he introduced the highly controversial and regressive tax amnesty of 1993 (following on from the previous 'once-in-a-lifetime' amnesty of five years earlier). Those who availed themselves of the amnesty paid just 15 per cent of the money that they properly owed. The Labour members of cabinet were stunned by his proposal because Ahern had told Tánaiste Dick Spring only the night before that he was against the idea, which was being floated by Reynolds. The Taoiseach was insistent, however, and now with Ahern proposing the measure Labour felt that it had to give support or a major issue of disagreement would cause great trouble to the stability of the coalition at an early stage.

Ahern changed the rules governing tax residency. The effect of this was to make legal tax avoidance far easier for a wealthy elite who wanted to spend only a portion of the year in Ireland. He oversaw a regime of generous special tax breaks for developers of car parks and inner-city projects, and signed off on shopping centres too, claiming that it was to stimulate economic activity.

Not long into the fund-raising job Richardson came up with a wheeze that was to produce a lot of money for Fianna Fáil but that would later have far-reaching and expensive consequences. Richardson decided to organize a series of private gatherings in the homes of wealthy businessmen to which other similarly wealthy people would be invited. There they would meet both Reynolds and Ahern for a gentlemanly chat about the economy and politics. After the gourmet food with fine wines, followed by brandies and cigars, very large cheques – and sometimes wads of cash – were collected by Richardson for the party's use. One such dinner was held in 1993 at a period mansion in Enniskerry, County Wicklow, belonging to the multimillionaire commercial property developer Ken Rohan.

The favour was returned in a big way. In early 1994 Ahern introduced a late amendment to the Finance Act as it went through the Dáil. The amendment to Section 19 of the 1982 Finance Act did not attract much attention when it was introduced. It merely appeared to be an extension of the existing rules governing so-called stately homes, to which the public were allowed access at limited times so they could admire this part of the nation's heritage. But it went much deeper than that. Although the new retrospective tax relief could be claimed by any taxpayer who came within the criteria of it, it seemed specifically designed to suit the owner of the house where Ahern and Reynolds had met with up to twenty senior business figures late the previous year. It may have saved Rohan as much as £1.5 million in tax that the Revenue Commissioners had intended to claim from him because, uniquely, Ahern's new tax law applied retrospectively to the previous twelve years.

Rohan was in dispute with the Revenue Commissioners. He had filled parts of the house with expensive antique furniture and paintings using money from his company Airspace Investments. He 'borrowed' the items that the company had bought instead of leaving them at the corporate premises. These included an eighteenth-century suite of furniture made by Thomas Chippendale, which is regarded as the largest set by Chippendale still intact in a private collection; the Coolattin Barrets, a set of three paintings by George Barret dating from the 1760s; a very early Irish topographical painting of Stradbally Hall, County Laois, by an unknown artist from 1710; and a 1798 view of Dublin Bay by William Ashford.

The Revenue Commissioners decided that, as Rohan had not used his personal income to buy the furniture, a benefit-in-kind tax payment was required, just as when an employee has a company-supplied car. They therefore levied a tax bill under the benefit-in-kind rules for just two years in the mid-1980s. The amount claimed was 12.5 per cent of the value of the items per annum, which would have resulted in a bill of over £150,000 per year. Had the Revenue won these cases it might have been able to levy tax for all the other years that Airspace had been 'lending' its owner the items, which could have amounted to £1.5 million for twelve years.

Rohan appealed this assessment and won his case at the Appeal Commissioners in May 1993. However, the Revenue Commissioners indicated their displeasure at the judgment and said that they would raise another assessment for the tax year 1992/3. If the Appeal Commissioners again found in Rohan's favour, the Revenue Commissioners would appeal that judgment to the High Court, as is allowed by law. Should the Revenue Commissioners win there, they would then try to raise taxes for all the other years to which the arrangement had applied. The cost to Rohan threatened to be enormous.

Rohan organized an extensive lobbying campaign to gather support, involving the Irish Georgian Society, the Department of Arts, Culture, Heritage and the Gaeltacht, and Bord Fáilte, even before the first case had been won at the Appeal Commissioners. The first representations had been made by the Irish Georgian Society in February 1993 when it said that some of its members were very concerned by what they believed was a new proposal by the Revenue Commissioners to tax art collections in the state. The society claimed that 'if the proposal to levy tax on such collections was ratified, it would no longer be possible for many of these owners to maintain their art collections and, as a result, priceless and irreplaceable works will no longer be on view and many would undoubtedly be sold.'

But there was no 'new proposal' as claimed by the Irish Georgian Society; the relevant legislation was already in place and no private owner was under the threat of a new tax bill because of it. The problem arose only for those who did not own their homes or contents personally, but through a company instead. Rohan put on extra pressure by applying for an export licence for some of the major works of art owned by the company he controlled, effectively threatening to remove the heritage items from Ireland unless legislation was introduced to suit his financial position.

Ahern may have been influenced by a letter Rohan had sent him in October 1993, around the time he got to see the furniture and paintings for himself at Enniskerry. 'I do think you would be doing a great service to Irish heritage if this amendment could be introduced into the next Finance Act. I cannot tell you how concerned people are and are considering moving works of art out of the country for sale.' Rohan also included the draft of a proposed amendment to the law, written for him by his accountants at SKC.

Rohan's arguments did not impress state officials, according to Department of Finance documents from the time. The Revenue Commissioners are not allowed by statute to make recommendations, but they were asked by the Department of Finance to provide 'observations' on the proposed legislation submitted by Rohan and the arguments of his friends in the Irish Georgian Society. The Revenue's response was carefully written and clearly outlined all of the reasons why a change to the tax laws should not be introduced. It particularly noted that 'the provision of works of art by a body corporate for its directors or employees, where no market value rent is involved, constitutes a chargeable benefit-in-kind.'

Using this, the Department of Finance officials drafted a response to Rohan's arguments, citing in detail the four specific reasons why they had been rejected. They presented this to the minister for his endorsement. Ahern did not sign the draft response. Instead, a line was drawn through both pages of the document and a couple of handwritten notes were scribbled at the top of its front page. These stated that the minister wanted legislation introduced on the lines sought by Rohan and his accountants. The files suggest that this was a shock both to the department officials and to the Revenue.

In almost all cases, changes to the tax laws apply only to the present and the future – which meant that the proposed legislation would not solve Rohan's problem with tax bills from the past. In an extraordinary twist, Ahern's new legislation was given retrospective effect for twelve years, thereby preventing the Revenue from mounting a challenge in the courts for previously unpaid tax. The Revenue Commissioners were snookered, although it was claimed in the *Sunday Independent* months after the story broke that the Revenue Commissioners had asked for the retrospection, to make the tax treatment 'consistent'.

Few other than those directly involved noticed the change to the tax laws when they were introduced in early 1994. There was no media coverage. I was told about it in late 1998 and, after weeks of investigation, put the story into the public domain on the front page of the *Sunday Tribune* in late January 1999. The government swiftly spun its response to what was a complicated story, one for which not all the facts were available at that time.

Ahern complained that I had not given him enough time to answer the detailed questions that I submitted the day before publication. On the following Tuesday two civil servants were wheeled out to give their interpretation of events; it was a highly unusual move to get them involved in what was a political issue. They said that Ahern had not departed from normal procedures. A government spokesman said afterwards that the Department of Finance files showed that the normal process of administration and government was followed to the letter and that 'the spurious issues raised about the Taoiseach's role in them are without foundation.' The departments of the Taoiseach and Finance both said the decision to introduce the section retrospectively was to 'make it consistent' with the period to which the relief for expenditure on significant buildings already applied. 'The real beneficiaries, of course, are the public, who can visit the houses and view the furnishings and works of art.'

Several months later, in May 1999, finance minister Charlie McCreevy admitted to the Dáil that 'measures to test the issue in the courts by way of a further appeal were in train when the matter was overtaken by the proposed amending legislation.' He also said that 'I understand from the Revenue Commissioners that one taxpayer has applied for and benefited from the section since its introduction', but argued that the legislation applied generally. 'It was not confined to a sole beneficiary, as has been claimed in the media.'

There was a postscript that put it in an even more serious light. Four years later, in 2003, the *Sunday Business Post* revealed that Richardson had been in receipt of regular fees from Rohan. Richardson had been getting £1,000 per month from Rohan for an unspecified period before receiving a severance payment of £10,000 in 1997. He was being paid a retainer by Rohan for strategic consultancy advice.

During this era, there were no laws to cover this sort of thing; ethics legislation has since been introduced that requires such payments to be disclosed. Fianna Fáil and Richardson were not required to say where money for the party came from or how much was received. Nor was Richardson prohibited from working as a lobbyist or adviser in addition to his work for Fianna Fáil, even if it was on behalf of people or companies who were making payments to the party. He did not have to tell anyone in Fianna Fáil or at a body such as the Standards in Public Office (SIPO) Commission who else he represented or helped or how much they paid him. But, in retrospect, it raises enormous questions about the potential for crossover and conflict of interests.

Ahern survived the fuss over the *Sunday Tribune* story because it seemed that many people found it too complicated – and the Richardson angle was not known then. Several months later the *Sunday Independent* wrote that it was not a scandal and that it was doubtful whether it was even improper. 'More a case of having money and influencing the right people. Legitimately, of course.' Rohan was subsequently appointed to the board of the National Gallery by Ahern's government.

The episode was never explored at the Planning Tribunal because it did not fall under its terms of reference. Although Richardson's accounts were made available to the tribunal – detailing payments and sources – they could not be examined in public or form part of its eventual findings unless they applied to planning decisions. However, another in the series of dinners organized by Richardson did involve a major player in the property business, and, while Ahern wasn't even present at the event, it was to be at the root of many of the problems that eventually brought him down.

6

The money labyrinth

The Fianna Fáil fund-raising dinner that took place in Cork on 11 March 1994 was very like the one that took place in Ken Rohan's house: an opportunity for business movers and shakers to meet the most important politicians in the country and to make donations to the ruling party.

Accountant Niall Welch was the host and the guests included Taoiseach Albert Reynolds, Des Richardson and the prominent property developer Owen O'Callaghan.

The Corkman had enjoyed success in rejuvenating Cork city centre with a number of large shopping centres. Now with ambitions far beyond his native county, he had hitched up with another developer called Tom Gilmartin, who had a plan to build a massive shopping centre complex on a site in West Dublin, near the M50.

O'Callaghan's key ally in getting planning permission for the Quarryvale development was public relations consultant and lobbyist Frank Dunlop. O'Callaghan gave him a 'war chest' of £1 million to campaign on behalf of the Quarryvale plan. The Planning Tribunal established later that Dunlop took some for himself and used the rest to bribe politicians. He told the tribunal that he bribed over a dozen councillors with O'Callaghan's money, but the Corkman has denied that this money was given to Frank Dunlop for any purpose other than legitimate campaigning. Dunlop has stated that O'Callaghan was not aware that Dunlop was using the money to bribe politicians and councillors.

Even though he didn't attend Welch's dinner, Dunlop had none the less been involved – and it wasn't through his client O'Callaghan either. Dunlop had prepared a thank you speech for Richardson to deliver on the night.

What happened before and after this gathering in Cork is central to the allegations about Bertie Ahern's financial affairs that consumed so much time at the Planning Tribunal.

Two days before the dinner Ahern met with Richardson and Welch for breakfast at the Shelbourne Hotel in Dublin. Richardson later provided the Planning Tribunal with his expenses record for the day and on it is an entry for £33.15 and a note that says 'the Cork event'. But Ahern said it wasn't discussed, not even who was coming and how much might be collected. Shown Richardson's note, Ahern, national treasurer at the time of the dinner, said he wasn't changing his evidence.

O'Callaghan – who had been asked before Christmas 1993 by Fianna Fáil's Ray MacSharry for a £100,000 contribution to the party – made a political donation of £10,000 on the night. Unfortunately, while Richardson said it was his practice to write thank you notes to donors after receiving substantial donations, there was no record of this gesture being made to any of those who donated on this particular night, even though £50,000 was raised in total.

Two weeks after the Cork dinner, on 24 March, O'Callaghan met with Ahern in Dublin at the Department of Finance. O'Callaghan recalled Dunlop setting up the meeting, but Ahern can't even remember if it took place, leaving everyone to rely on O'Callaghan's version of events. He said he was looking for reassurance from Ahern that a rival shopping centre being developed at Blanchardstown by Green Property (where Ray MacSharry was a director) would not get special urban tax designation. That would have given it a competitive advantage in the area and put funding for his nearby Quarryvale centre at risk. When Ahern was asked about this by the tribunal during a hearing in September 2008, he accepted O'Callaghan's evidence that he had told the Corkman that neither Blanchardstown nor Quarryvale would be getting urban tax designation. Ahern said he would merely have been telling O'Callaghan what was well-known government policy at the time.

Whatever way he put it, O'Callaghan was so reassured by what he heard that he went off to meet with his bank, AIB, and his partner Tom Gilmartin to tell them the good news. Gilmartin told the Planning Tribunal that the Corkman told him privately after that meeting that he had paid Ahern £30,000 in return for the assurance (this is denied by O'Callaghan). Gilmartin's allegations about this and other alleged uses of O'Callaghan's money are what eventually brought Ahern to the attention of the Planning Tribunal a decade later.

Ahern's diary reveals a visit to his office from Frank Dunlop one month after his meeting with O'Callaghan, on 25 April 1994. On the same day Ahern lodged £30,000 in cash in a special savings account in AIB O'Connell Street, Dublin, that he had just opened, having apparently operated without bank accounts for the previous seven years. Ahern explained that this was the first in a series of lodgements of cash; he was depositing money that had accumulated over a number of years in his safe at his St Luke's constituency office. Asked by tribunal counsel Des O'Neill if there was any connection between this payment and the meeting with O'Callaghan a month earlier, Ahern said 'Absolutely not.'

Ahern has insisted consistently that he never received 'a penny or a cent in today's money' from O'Callaghan. Nor, he told the tribunal, had he known that O'Callaghan was one of those approached in an effort to clear the party's debts. He said he had been aware that O'Callaghan had been at the Cork fund-raising dinner, but wouldn't have known about his donation that night.

Gilmartin – who was manoeuvred out of the Quarryvale consortium, though the project had been his idea – made many more allegations about O'Callaghan. He claimed O'Callaghan had paid £150,000 to Reynolds for tax designation for a shopping centre at Golden Island in Athlone, which was partly owned by O'Callaghan, and that this deal had been struck at the Cork dinner. O'Callaghan has denied that he ever made this payment.

On 14 December 1994, one day before he left office, Ahern signed a statutory instrument giving tax designation to Golden Island. He said he had done so at the request of the Department of the Environment, which dealt with applications. Ahern said that he was unaware of the identities of the individuals or companies that owned land that benefited from the tax designations he granted in 1994, which coincidentally included Richardson and Dunlop, who owned land in Navan, County Meath.

Owen O'Callaghan's second visit to Ahern's office was in late November 1994. Dunlop attended, as did representatives from an American investment firm called Chilton & O'Connor.

Ahern had already met with Chilton & O'Connor in early March 1994 at Los Angeles Airport, some months after Taoiseach Albert

Reynolds had done so. It was backing O'Callaghan's plan for a £50 million sports stadium at Neilstown, West Dublin. It would have been home to the Dublin Dons, which is what English Premier League side Wimbledon would have been renamed had it been given permission to relocate to Dublin and stay in its league.

Ahern said the sports stadium may have been mentioned at the first meeting in Los Angeles but he remembered the conversation being mainly about the company's licence for the International Financial Services Centre. Records supplied by Niall Lawlor (son of the late Fianna Fáil TD Liam Lawlor), who happened to work for Chilton & O'Connor, suggested that the stadium was the main issue discussed

O'Callaghan said that when he met with Ahern two weeks later, for the Quarryvale tax designation discussion, he spoke briefly about his stadium plan, but Ahern never mentioned that he had met with its financiers in the US two weeks previously.

It seemed that Ahern wanted to tell the Planning Tribunal little about his dealings with this US bank. In his 2003 written response to early queries from the tribunal, Ahern didn't mention that Dunlop had sent him an outline of the stadium plan in December 1993 or that he'd met with the company at Los Angeles Airport in March 1994. He also failed to disclose that a detailed analysis of the stadium project had been sent to the Department of Finance by Chilton & O'Connor in August 1994, prior to the November 1994 meeting.

Within days of that second meeting with O'Callaghan, Ahern's partner Celia Larkin went to the AIB on O'Connell Street and made a deposit of what he said was sterling. This equated to exactly $45,000, according to the tribunal lawyers. AIB has no record of a sterling lodgement on that day but it did take in that amount in dollars. This deposit was made on 5 December 1994, the day before he was expected to become Taoiseach but didn't.

All of this became known when the tribunal sought Ahern's bank records in the course of examining the allegation that he'd received money from O'Callaghan. It was told that Ahern had no bank records for part of the period under examination and that he had chosen to deal in cash because of his separation from his wife.

Ahern told the tribunal the money that went into the AIB account in December came from Michael Wall, an Irish emigrant to Manchester. He said Wall had given him £30,000 in cash that month to pay for the refurbishment of a house in Beresford Avenue in Drumcondra that he and Larkin were renting from Wall.

Wall had come to Dublin with the cash, which, on the evening he went to Ahern's annual constituency fund-raiser, he had kept in a suitcase in the Ashling Hotel near the Phoenix Park – wedged into a wardrobe in his room. The following day he brought it to Ahern's constituency office and put most of this money – uncounted – on to Ahern's desk. Ahern didn't count it either, but he did put it into a safe in his office and a couple of days later Larkin took it to the bank.

Days later, after his expected elevation to Taoiseach had not materialized – because Fianna Fáil's erstwhile partner Labour decided to go into power with Fine Gael and Democratic Left instead – Ahern drove Larkin to the bank to get the money back.

Further probing at the Planning Tribunal revealed the claim that Wall, a man of apparently modest means, had been prepared to buy the house – which Larkin located and viewed before purchase and which he didn't even see until after the deal was done – and then rent it to Ahern. He had had it done up to Larkin's standards, including the construction of a conservatory, and agreed to sell it to Ahern at a later date at a predetermined price.

Wall made out a will in favour of his tenant, apparently without Ahern's knowledge. Des Richardson's close friend, a solicitor called Gerry Brennan, who died prematurely in 1997, handled the will, the original 1995 conveyancing when Wall bought the house and the subsequent 1997 transaction when ownership formally moved to Ahern.

Gerry Brennan has been cited as central, alongside Des Richardson, to the first alleged 'dig-out' for Ahern that took place a year earlier in December 1993. The duo, apparently wrongly believing Ahern to be skint, decided to have a whip-round among friends.

Ahern said – both to the Planning Tribunal and to Bryan Dobson in his *Six One News* interview in September 2006 – that he received an amount of £22,500 that month, nearly all of which was in cash, from a group of friends who were interested only in doing him a good turn; their intention was to help him out of the financial problems that had arisen from his separation.

Eight people – Paddy Reilly, Des Richardson, Padraic O'Connor (who denied later that he was a friend), Jim Nugent, David McKenna, Fintan

Gunne, Mick Collins and Charlie Chawke – are said to have given the £22,500 in late 1993. In a remarkable demonstration of the cash economy that seemed to operate at the time, most of the men said the money came from personal cash resources; withdrawals that would have been recorded in bank archives hadn't been necessary for them. This meant that the only money that left a trail was a bank draft for £5,000 from O'Connor and a cheque for £2,500 written on the account of a company called Willdover. It was controlled by Richardson and was the company through which he invoiced Fianna Fáil for the fund-raising he did on its behalf.

In mid-December the Willdover bank account was overdrawn but it had invoiced Fianna Fáil for £18,744. Willdover got its money just before Christmas, when it received a cheque from a Fianna Fáil account that was used by Richardson to raise funds. The Fianna Fáil cheque was signed for him by Ahern. Richardson lodged it and then wrote a cheque to cash on the Willdover account for £2,500, which he gave to Ahern. According to Richardson's evidence to the tribunal, the fact that a cheque from Fianna Fáil had allowed him to make the payment to Ahern was simply a coincidence. A false entry was made in Willdover's book saying the cheque made to cash was related to the annual Kilmainham constituency fund-raiser.

The bank draft of £5,000 from NCB Stockbrokers (Padraic O'Connor was then its managing director) was made out to a Richardson-controlled company called Euroworkforce on the basis of a bogus invoice. It was used by Richardson to purchase another bank draft made out in Ahern's favour. The manner of the payment was odd, as NCB could have made out the payment directly to Fianna Fáil or Ahern. However, it could be that the cheque was part of the 'pick-me-up' scheme that Richardson was operating at this time, in which donors to Fianna Fáil were asked to pick up bills that the party had to pay.

Padraic O'Connor said it was to defray constituency expenses, not to support Ahern personally, and that it was not a loan. He was supported in this by NCB's former finance director Chris McHugh in tribunal evidence. This meant that, if the Planning Tribunal concurred, Ahern had put a political donation to personal use.

It seems that by late 1993 Richardson had three roles: a paid job raising funds for Fianna Fáil; a voluntary one raising funds for the constituency;

and one raising money for Ahern. In November and December 1993 he lodged £50,000 and £100,000 for the party; about £35,000 for the constituency through the annual dinner at the Royal Hospital Kilmainham; and, with Gerry Brennan, raised £22,500 that was given to Ahern on 27 December. It's not known if he was doing anything for himself that month as a consultant to others.

Adding to the confusion was the fact that Richardson had never registered as a shareholder or director of Willdover, the company that invoiced Fianna Fáil for his fund-raising services. Its registered office was 50 City Quay, Dublin 2; these premises had been developed by one of Richardson's property companies. Willdover did not make returns to the Companies Office and was struck off in 1999. Such unorthodox behaviour comes as no surprise, given the revelations from the Planning Tribunal as to how Richardson did business and its discoveries about his involvement with another company called Berraway.

From 1992 until it was dissolved in 1999, Berraway traded from 25 Upper Mount Street, Dublin 2, which just happened to be the address of the public relations firm Frank Dunlop & Associates. Dunlop was a shareholder in Berraway, but the company was controlled by a property developer in Navan called Eamon Duignan. Duignan told the tribunal he left the firm in 1995, passing control to Richardson. However, Richardson's new position, either as shareholder or director, was not notified to the Companies Registration Office, nor was Duignan's resignation.

While Richardson used Willdover to bill Fianna Fáil for his work for the party, he used Berraway to invoice clients for consultancy work. Ken Rohan paid him in this way, with some payments coming after the millionaire received the tax break on his Wicklow mansion's contents.

In 1997, after Ahern came to power, Richardson formed a more formal business partnership with Dunlop. Asked by the Planning Tribunal to explain how he came to be working for Dunlop after the 1997 general election, he said that he had done so for just a year and after carrying out 'background checks'. This seemed a very odd comment, considering Dunlop's prominence as a previous government press secretary, his role in helping Richardson at the Cork fund-raiser in 1994, his work for O'Callaghan and his contribution to a large catering bill of £11,250 from the Galway Races Fianna Fáil tent in 1996.

What attracted these two men to each other? What were the financial arrangements? Why did it end? What did Richardson do for the already very well-connected Dunlop? Make further introductions? Provide the perception of easier access to the new Taoiseach?

Dunlop clearly had excellent access to Ahern. The tribunal was told how, when Ahern was leader of the opposition in 1996, Dunlop and O'Callaghan had 'dropped in' to give Ahern an update on the Neilstown stadium project (one that never came to fruition). Dunlop testified that he and Ahern were in regular phone contact when Ahern was a minister and later when he was Taoiseach. 'Bertie would go out of his way on some occasions to facilitate any requests I made of him,' Dunlop said.

Quarryvale got built eventually and was renamed the Liffey Valley Shopping Centre. When it was due to open in 1998, Dunlop and O'Callaghan wanted Ahern to perform the official ceremony. Dunlop's first written request to book a date with Ahern was addressed not to the Taoiseach's office, where his diary was, but to Richardson at his suite in the Berkeley Court Hotel.

7

What friends are for

In his interview for the 2008 television documentary *Bertie*, the former Taoiseach said that he did 'absolutely nothing wrong' in accepting money from friends and supporters. As a 'principle', he added, he was 'probably wrong to take the money from anyone'. He said that he wouldn't have taken the money had he known how much grief it was going to cause him, which suggested his regret was prompted not by any sense of morality but by getting caught.

Ahern might well have been thinking of the mauling he got over a second alleged dig-out he received in 1994. This time it was from a group of friends who were having a few pints in the Beaumont House pub in October 1994 when they decided that the Minister for Finance needed a few quid. These men – Joe Burke, Dermot Carew, Barry English and another Paddy Reilly, this one 'Paddy the Plasterer' – gave evidence to the effect that they collected £16,500 in cash for Ahern. Again, there was no paper trail.

The tribunal seemed unconvinced and pointed out that the amount Ahern lodged to his AIB account after receiving this second dig-out equated to exactly £25,000 sterling. Ahern said the balance of the money came from a whip-round after a speaking engagement in Manchester; the audience had collected and given him £8,000 sterling on the spur of the moment.

Ahern said he'd had no problem in taking either sum. The first he described as a 'debt of honour', a loan on which he had failed to make repayments or to pay interest, at least until it was 'disclosed' to the public. Then he gave back the money. He emphasized that it was not a gift; a gift would be liable for tax. The second payment, the Manchester one, was described as a 'gift', but, because the money was received outside the state, no tax was payable on it. While ministers are not supposed to accept payment from third parties for speaking engagements, Ahern explained he was in Manchester in a 'personal capacity'. His contention was that a group of British and Irish businessmen had wanted to hear the Irish Minister for Finance speak in a personal capacity and were so impressed by what they'd heard that they raised £8,000 for him on the spot.

If Ahern's friends and associates were generous to him, he, in turn, was generous to those he described as friends. At a rather inconsequential level, Paddy Reilly and his wife received tickets for attending the Winter Solstice at Newgrange, courtesy of the Office of Public Works, in late 2006, not long after his name first became known to the public. And in early 2007 he accompanied Ahern to the famous first rugby international against England at Croke Park, in what was interpreted as a defiant gesture by an increasingly beleaguered Ahern.

More significantly, however, Ahern gave some of his friends and alleged donors state positions and was open about it. In his interview with Bryan Dobson in September 2006, in which he attempted to explain and defend the operation of his finances on RTÉ's *Six One News*, Ahern didn't attempt to argue that people were appointed because they were the best people for the job: 'I might have appointed somebody but I appointed them because they were friends, not because of anything they had given me.'

Friends who received appointments included Richardson and Christy Wall, who were both appointed to the board of Aer Lingus when it was fully in state control. Neither had any experience of the aviation industry, but they were able to avail themselves of free and discounted flights when serving the airline, as well as draw modest fees.

David McKenna, the recruitment consultant who had hired Richardson to work in his business before it ran into financial trouble, joined the board of Enterprise Ireland. Economist Padraic O'Connor was appointed to the board of ACC Bank before it was sold to Rabobank. Jim Nugent was a regular at constituency fund-raisers. He was appointed to the boards of Cert – which dealt with training and standards in the hotel, catering and tourism industries – and the Central Bank, a critically important position.

Perhaps the most interesting of Ahern's donors was Joe Burke, who was given two terms as chairman of the Dublin Port Company in highly controversial circumstances. Burke was a trustee of St Luke's, chairman of St Luke's house committee, involved in election fund-raising and a signatory to one of the Fianna Fáil constituency accounts along with Ahern. He was regarded as one of Ahern's key lieutenants.

Burke came to public prominence in the summer of 1999 as a central figure in a controversy that came very close to derailing the Fianna Fáil–Progressive Democrats coalition government. In October 1997 a young architect, Philip Sheedy, was jailed for four years for killing, while driving drunk, Anne Ryan, a Tallaght mother of two young children. Sheedy spent six months in Mountjoy and was then transferred to the open prison at Shelton Abbey. Burke visited him there on 14 October 1998. Soon after, in November 1998, Sheedy's case was re-listed and he was released from prison.

When the circumstances of the re-listing and release emerged into the public domain, there was uproar. It turned out that Supreme Court Judge Hugh O'Flaherty had made inquiries about the status of the case. This was highly unusual because there was an appeals process under way. A higher court judge questioning the decision of a lower court, when there is no suggestion that anything untoward has taken place in the original conduct of the case, is frowned upon.

The circuit judge who released Sheedy, Cyril Kelly, was forced to resign when he was unable to explain the circumstances in which he sanctioned early release. The public outcry resulted in O'Flaherty going too, in April 1999, but, pointedly, Ahern and Larkin were photographed visiting his house on the evening of his resignation, offering their sympathies. Meanwhile, Sheedy returned voluntarily to jail to serve the balance of his sentence.

But there was to be an added twist. In May 1999 the *Sunday Tribune*'s Catherine Cleary discovered that Sheedy had been working as an architect for Joe Burke's pub refurbishment business at the time he had killed Anne Ryan. Then the newspaper revealed that in July 1998 the Taoiseach's private secretary, acting on Ahern's instructions, had made oral inquiries to his counterpart in the Department of Justice about the possibility of regular day release for Sheedy. The Taoiseach's inquiry was recorded in a written note by his secretary simply as 'Justice – what's the story?'

Bad enough as that was, the bigger political problem was that Ahern had revealed none of this during the row over O'Flaherty's and Kelly's resignations. When the controversy broke, and he was reminded of his actions by his private secretary, he told the cabinet what he had done and undertook to convey the information to the Dáil. But he failed to do so and the information was revealed instead by the *Sunday Tribune* days later.

Ahern then assured everyone that it was 'nonsense to suggest that the Government showed any special sympathy to Mr Sheedy . . . I applied no political pressure to get Mr Sheedy's early release.' Ahern explained that he had said nothing when he had the opportunity because of a 'legitimate concern not to feed conspiracy theories, or by juxtaposing irrelevant information to imply or signal the probability of some hidden connection'.

He also said that he had never discussed the case with Burke. There is no evidence to the contrary, but a decade later there has never been a satisfactory explanation as to why the various judges acted as they did in the case. It was an enormous crisis because it implied not just political interference in the judicial process but interference at a level unprecedented in the history of the state.

Nearly ten years later, during an interview with producer Steve Carson for the *Bertie* documentary, Ahern dismissed the Sheedy affair as 'nothing'. That is a rewriting of history. Tánaiste Mary Harney had been furious about Ahern's handling of events and it came nearer than anything else – other than his own personal finances – to bringing down the government.

In 2000 there was a final turn to the tale, which allowed cynics to ask just how far Fianna Fáil would go to try to look after its own. The Irish government was in a position to nominate a vice-president to the European Investment Bank, a lucrative position paying a six-figure salary. Minister for Finance Charlie McCreevy nominated Hugh O'Flaherty. The Sheedy controversy was reignited and few could believe the chutzpah involved. O'Flaherty, realizing that his hell of a year earlier was about to be revisited, withdrew his acceptance of the nomination and returned to his enforced retirement, comforted by things such as the friendship of Tony O'Reilly, at whose parties he was a regular guest.

Two years later Joe Burke was to receive his own elevation. In the dying days of the 1997–2002 government, as Ahern prepared to form a new administration after a successful general election, Burke was nominated to the position of chairman of the state-controlled Dublin Port Authority. Given that Burke specialized in pub refurbishments, and considering Ahern's subsequent comments, it seems that friendship was the most logical explanation for the appointment.

Burke is from Donegal originally and served a term as a Fianna Fáil councillor with Ahern from 1987 to 1991. In evidence to the Planning Tribunal in 2008 he revealed just how close he was to Ahern when he described how Ahern had stayed with his family 'on and off' after his marriage ended, on one occasion for two weeks. He explained his £3,500 cash contribution to the alleged 1994 dig-out on the basis of his friendship with Ahern. 'I didn't give it to the Minister of Finance, I didn't give it to a politician, I gave it to a personal friend of long standing,' he said. He said that he made the payment at this time because Ahern's living arrangements had been an impediment to his becoming leader of Fianna Fáil two and a half years earlier, although he couldn't explain why he had waited so long to do something about it if he was so worried.

Burke had been involved in the purchase of a house for Ahern many years earlier: his constituency headquarters and occasional residence, St Luke's in Drumcondra. The story goes that a group of Fianna Fáil supporters (most of whom have never been named) came together for a meeting at the Gresham Hotel on 3 December 1987 and decided upon a plan whereby twenty-five people would give £5,000 each over five years in £1,000 instalments to buy the house for Ahern's use; the house would then be held in trust for Fianna Fáil.

Untangling the various operations centred on St Luke's may help to illustrate the workings of Bertie Ahern's finances up to the mid-1990s. What baffled was that at a time when Ahern said he didn't have the money to buy a new house, it turned out that he had in his possession substantial savings, loans and gifts from supporters. And, despite dealing with substantial amounts of foreign currency, he denied ever having had a bank or building society account outside Ireland. That the man running the country's finances – and Fianna Fáil's too – kept huge amounts of cash, both Irish pounds and sterling, in a safe in his office, when he could have earned significant interest by keeping the money in a bank account, seemed very strange and was not easily explained by reference to the breakdown of his marriage.

Burke hit hard times from 2004, ironically because of a major change to the law brought in by Fianna Fáil. The 2004 ban on smoking in the workplace meant that many pubs went out of business. Those that remained spent less on refurbishments and extensions. Burke's business – J. H. Burke & Sons Ltd – went into liquidation in December 2006 with debts of some €2.3 million. Mr Justice Kevin Feeney ruled that a Section 150 order against Burke – restricting him from acting as a director of a company for five years – was merited because Burke had not acted responsibly in some aspects of the conduct of his company's affairs. The only saving grace for Burke was the finding that he had acted honestly. The judge also put a 'stay' on the Section 150 order, pending an appeal, which was important, given his role at the Dublin Port Authority.

Ahern acted quickly to support his old friend. On 13 June 2007, the government's last day in office before the formation of the next coalition, the outgoing Minister for Transport, Martin Cullen, wrote to Joe Burke and to five other members of the Dublin Port Authority, informing them of their reappointment. Cullen acted at Ahern's behest. The opposition was furious that Ahern's mate was being rewarded again, notwithstanding the findings that had been made about his conduct in his main business.

Ahern was brazen about it. He justified Burke's reappointment 'on the basis of the knowledge, expertise and experience he brings to the job'. Ahern said Burke 'as a member and chairman of the board for many years, has carried out a hugely successful reform of the port company and is recognized as having done so across all political persuasions'. He said the improvements in industrial relations, the increased productivity of the company and the other changes Burke had made over many years 'stand up to scrutiny by anyone'. Soon afterwards Ahern conferred another indirect favour upon Burke: he appointed to the Senate an up-and-coming councillor in the Dublin South constituency called Maria Corrigan, who was then Burke's girlfriend.

Cynics noted that Ahern may have had another good reason for standing by Joe Burke. His friend was about to provide evidence to the Planning Tribunal, in relation to the allegations being made by Tom Gilmartin.

The property developer claimed to have had dealings with Ahern back in May 1989, a month before that year's general election. Gilmartin said that he had complained to Ahern about being blocked from purchasing Dublin Corporation land in West Dublin; he needed this land to complete the Quarryvale development site. He told Ahern that local TD Liam Lawlor was shaking him down for money.

Gilmartin said that Ahern put him in touch with Joe Burke and that the sale later went through, although only after Burke had asked him for £500,000. Burke described the allegation as 'outrageous' and said he had never solicited money on behalf of Ahern and had never been asked to do so. Burke said the discussion with Gilmartin was about his plans for a major development at Bachelors Walk in the city centre, a scheme on which Lawlor was employed as a consultant. He refuted colourful suggestions of driving Gilmartin around in a pick-up truck – which he denied even having – looking for Ahern in various Dublin 3 and 9 pubs before taking Gilmartin to the airport to catch a flight.

A later appearance at the tribunal, in early 2008, would find Burke answering questions about his stewardship of St Luke's and his role as a trustee of what was called the B/T account – which some said was related to the St Luke's building trust but others believed was a fund controlled by Ahern and a friend called Tim Collins (hence, B/T for Bertie/Tim). These questions led to the knotty matter of where Bertie Ahern's political and personal affairs began and ended because of the account's use as the source of a loan to Celia Larkin in 1994. It was another loan for which no legal documents existed; nor was there a repayment schedule or terms of interest. The £30,000 loan remained unpaid until after it was uncovered by the tribunal.

8

Bertie's closest confidante

Few could understand it when Bertie Ahern's government nominated Celia Larkin to the board of the new National Consumer Agency (NCA) – and nobody believed Fianna Fáil's suggestion that she was the minister Micheál Martin's choice rather than Ahern's. It wouldn't have been done without Ahern's approval and the idea that somebody would have suggested it to Ahern in the first place is unlikely.

It was the summer of 2005, and the Ahern–Larkin personal relationship had ended at least two years earlier. So what the heck was happening now? Why this very public display of patronage? Why did she want an appointment and why did he want to give it? Such a decision would only have invited speculation and scorn from the opposition and intrusion by the media, most of whom had treated the couple's break-up with respect by largely ignoring it.

Larkin had been important to Ahern in lots of ways. Apart from their personal connection, she had helped to sharpen up his image. Ahern was not a social animal or adept at small talk, while Larkin was gregarious and charming in social situations: he didn't have to introduce her; she was the one who stepped forward to say hello and have a chat. She might have been outgoing, but she was also discreet and never conducted a tell-all, no-holds-barred interview about her time with Ahern. Nor did she cause him any embarrassment or trouble at her Planning Tribunal appearances. Despite considerable speculation that she might get into difficulties under questioning at the tribunal, she was feisty, defensive and consistent. This may have much to do with the fact that her finances were inextricably bound up with Ahern's, which she knew would subject her to intense scrutiny.

Ahern explained his bizarre financial affairs in the early 1990s by referring to the difficulties of his marital separation. But Ahern had been separated since 1987. In what he described as the 'dark and difficult' period of 1993–5, when he claims to have been the recipient of 'dig-outs' from friends and without payments from any other source, he was setting up a new home with Larkin. It is this that might better explain his need for cash and the strange circumstances in which he rented his new house for over two years before completing its purchase.

As for Larkin, her financial arrangements during her time as Ahern's partner became of considerable public interest because of the extent to which they were entwined with Ahern's. Larkin never held elected office. She got her first paid gig from the public purse in 1997, when the new Taoiseach appointed her to run his constituency office. However, for over five years her name appeared on many official state invitations as Ahern's partner. She also became his official partner for foreign visits. He described her as his 'life partner'.

The revelation in early 2008 that Larkin was the beneficiary of a £30,000 loan from what Ahern has described as a Fianna Fáil constituency account was of enormous significance. Ultimately it was the humiliation of Ahern's secretary Gráinne Carruth at the tribunal (she broke down in tears when finally confessing to lodging sterling, rather than punts, to Ahern's bank accounts and was clearly distraught that she could not sustain a story that was central to his defence) that accelerated Ahern's decision to resign as Taoiseach. Carruth's ordeal shamed Ahern more than some of the more dramatic information about his finances. But the Larkin revelation weeks earlier had been seminal. His political money – if that's what it was – had been put to her personal use. The argument that there was a line between personal and political – one that Ahern used regularly in the face of the tribunal's sustained and forensic inquiries and in his now infamous Bryan Dobson TV interview in September 2006 – collapsed when the Larkin payment was uncovered. There was no way of explaining it away. Here was something that the public could understand clearly amid all of the confusion about currencies and myriad bank accounts and apparently no bank accounts and it had nothing to do with Ahern's proclaimed marital issues.

Ahern claimed that he knew nothing about the transfer of £30,000 from the B/T account to Larkin, which was used to purchase the house in which her elderly relatives lived. The house was valued at £40,100 and had been put up for sale by the family of the former landlord, who had died. Ahern said the first he knew of it was after the house had been bought.

We were expected to believe that Larkin did not tell him about this interest-free loan, which had no security in place for the lender (Fianna Fáil), such as a charge over the title on the property. Solicitor Gerry Brennan – who had acted for Ahern in his separation proceedings and as a witness for Larkin when she executed the purchase of her aunt's house in April 1993 – didn't tell Ahern either, at least not until it was all done.

Larkin got her loan at a time when Ahern, as Fianna Fáil national treasurer, was responsible for raising money to clear the party's massive debts and was engaged in an attempted centralization of Fianna Fáil finances to eliminate constituency discretion over funds. The idea that a Fianna Fáil constituency organization would advance a loan of that size at a time when the party was trying to clear its debts seems extraordinary.

Larkin left the state payroll in 2000 to follow her own career path as a fashion consultant and media celebrity. The relationship with Ahern, after considerable speculation about marriage and children, ended in late 2002.

Her qualifications for the board of the NCA went little further than her relevant experience in offering cosmetic and beauty services to customers of her shop. 'For the first time, the consumer in Ireland really has a say,' Larkin said when asked about her appointment. 'There's nothing like a bit of controversy to raise the profile of a board like this . . . It's a voluntary board, so I'm giving my time voluntarily. That's an important point, and the public aren't aware of it.' (Since joining in 2006 she has received fees and expenses of €55,000.)

Micheál Martin gallantly came to her defence at the time of her appointment. 'Are people now saying because of who she is she is to be debarred from ever serving on any state board or from ever making a contribution to public affairs? If that is what people are suggesting, then I would equally argue that that's a very unfair proposition to put,' he said.

What wasn't known at the time of Larkin's appointment was that the tribunal was already engaged in a detailed investigation of Ahern's finances and in correspondence with him. Larkin probably knew more about Ahern's political and personal life than anyone else. She had been alongside him at crucial times for over a decade.

Her eventual appearance at the tribunal did him no harm. For example, she said that when Michael Wall bought the Beresford Avenue house that Ahern rented and later bought, it never crossed her mind he might have done so on behalf of Ahern or with the use of Ahern's money.

The added twist to the whole saga came when Ahern helped Larkin to clear her loan once it came to the tribunal's attention. Ahern gave his former partner €40,000 as a short-term loan early in 2008 so she could repay the money to Fianna Fáil's Dublin Central organization. She quickly took out a second mortgage on her own home and repaid Ahern. She borrowed this money from the Irish Nationwide Building Society; the loan was approved by its boss, Michael Fingleton, and, again, no security was offered. She claimed that she decided to repay the original £30,000 after a journalist called to the house where an elderly aunt still lived and started asking questions. 'It was to protect her because she was agitated by people calling to the house,' she said. She denied that her decision to repay the money, which amounted to €45,510 when interest was added, was motivated by the tribunal's discovery of the B/T building society account from which the money had come.

9

Circle of friends

It was early in 1994 and the party was in full swing but there was work to be done. P. J. Mara wanted me to meet a couple of his new clients. 'Builders, two lads from the west,' he said. 'Great characters, dying to get known by the business media, would really like to meet the *Irish Independent*.' And so I met Mick and Tom Bailey, the owners of Bovale Developments.

I'd never heard of the Roscommon natives before that. They were amiable, Tom in particular, rough and ready, despite the good suits, not like many of the other businessmen at the party, with their more polished accents. We chatted for a while but I didn't hear anything that made me think they merited an interview or a profile for the newspaper: they were too coy in answering questions – like many business people, they wanted a profile but they didn't want to give away any information about themselves other than that they were very successful. I didn't realize just how wealthy or busy as house builders they were – or just how well connected they were politically. Three years later I wrote about Mick Bailey, but not in the circumstances he would have wished.

In July 1997 I disclosed in the *Sunday Tribune* that Bailey had made a large cash payment (which I believed to be about £40,000 but the size of which has never been established) to Fianna Fáil TD Ray Burke prior to the 1989 general election. It was one of the stories that led to the establishment of the Planning Tribunal. Bailey was compelled to give evidence to it but he, his brother and his sister-in-law, Caroline, went to enormous lengths to hide their actions from the tribunal, including lying when he said Bovale paid Gogarty £150,000, falsifying financial records of the company and claiming that others were destroyed in a fire, which led to a raft of findings against them by Justice Fergus Flood for hindering and obstructing the tribunal's work. The tribunal's eventual finding was that Bailey had been present when Burke had received a corrupt payment; that Bailey knew that it was corrupt and that the payment had been made in connection with lands that Bailey had planned to co-develop. The tribunal found that Bailey had passed an envelope to Burke that others in the room believed was a payment of £40,000.

The Revenue Commissioners investigated his business, with the result that Bovale had to make a settlement for more than €22 million in unpaid tax, interest and penalties. The brothers would become the subject of a lengthy and costly investigation by the Office of the Director of Corporate Enforcement, which is seeking to have them disqualified as directors.

Ray Burke was at the party in Mara's Dublin 4 house too, as he was on other occasions. Fianna Fáil was going through its spell in opposition, with Ahern settling in as leader. Although Burke had been a victim of Reynolds's purge, he remained close to Ahern and Mara, and was back on the party front-bench. Another politician there that evening, and a regular at Mara's soirées, was G. V. Wright. Wright admitted to the tribunal in February 2008 that he had received several sums of money from Dunlop and Owen O'Callaghan totalling £15,000 but said these were political donations. One of the payments – of £2,000 in cash – was made by Dunlop in the Dáil bar in June 1991, wrapped inside a copy of the *Irish Times*. The Fianna Fáil politicians in the house had mostly been marginalized within the party since the accession of Reynolds to power and were united by their disregard for the despised 'country and western alliance' with which he had replaced them, even though Ahern was his finance minister and considered too senior even for Reynolds to drop. Just one member of that 'country and western alliance' was a guest in Mara's house on the couple of occasions that I was there: the exception who proved the rule was Brian Cowen.

Mara had gone into corporate work in 1992 after Haughey left power, serving large clients such as Tony Ryan's Guinness Peat Aviation, once the world's largest aviation finance company, based in Shannon. Elan, the pharmaceutical company based in Athlone, and Mark Kavanagh's Hardwicke Properties, one of the original developers of the International Financial Services Centre, were other major clients. He disdained writing press releases, or offering conventional PR services. Mara brought together his contacts and his clients, introduced people to each other and then left them to get on with doing business: that is what his parties were about. He held these occasions quite regularly, inviting a mix of businessmen, lawyers and the media to meet the politicians. I recall being at about half a dozen of such events over three years.

Among those in attendance were men such as Colm Barrington – who, almost fifteen years later, would be made chairman of Aer Lingus when Dermot Desmond, another friend and client of Mara, decided not to take the job – as well as various executives, past and present, from GPA. Desmond was there on at least one occasion. I can also recall meeting Denis O'Brien, himself an ex-GPA man who later brought Mara into his Digicel business as an adviser.

Journalists and broadcasters who attended on various occasions, often with partners, included Vincent Browne (then editor of the *Sunday Tribune*), Eamon Dunphy (then a writer with the *Sunday Independent*), Cliff Taylor (now editor of the *Sunday Business Post*, but then business editor of the *Irish Times*), Sam Smyth (at the time a colleague of mine at the *Irish Independent*), Vinnie Doyle (then editor of the *Irish Independent*) and Conor Brady (editor of the *Irish Times*). Barristers such as Michael McDowell (later to be Ahern's attorney general and Minister for Justice and leader of the Progressive Democrats) was a guest, as was his good friend Adrian Hardiman, a PD who was appointed to the Supreme Court by Ahern's government, and his wife, Judge Yvonne Murphy, who was appointed later to chair a state tribunal of inquiry. Other barristers such as Paul O'Higgins and Gerry Danaher were also regulars.

Mara's company was highly enjoyable. He was full of stories, extraordinarily indiscreet and bitchy in his comments about those who did not impress him. Indeed, he and his wife, Breda, were guests at my wedding in 1995.

In the early 1990s Mara had represented a consortium that wanted to build a giant conference centre, hotel, national stadium and casino at the Phoenix Park in Dublin, on the site of the old racecourse. The main Irish mover of the scheme, to be called Sonas, was Robert White. His partner in the venture was a rotund Manchester property developer called Norman Turner, an engaging character who made no secret of his Irish roots or of his ambitions to make loads more money.

Soon afterwards, the Sonas consortium received outline planning permission for the venture, but it needed approval from the government to operate a casino. Apparently, the projected profits from this were deemed essential to covering the costs of building and operating the national stadium in particular. The Rainbow coalition government set itself against granting such a licence. Asked about this at a 1996 party to celebrate receiving the planning permission – at which Cowen was the most prominent politician – White reportedly said, 'But what about the next government?'

Ahern remained non-committal because this was a very sensitive issue politically – and would become so again later when various allegations were made at the Planning Tribunal, first under Justice Fergus Flood and then under Justice Alan Mahon, threatening both times to envelop Ahern in controversy. In 1996 there was a by-election in Dublin West, in which the planned development was a major local issue. It was won by Brian Lenihan junior, who declared himself against the plan.

What few people knew at the time was that Des Richardson may have had a role in the whole enterprise. In April/May 1994 Turner gave Richardson a $10,000 payment that was not receipted or acknowledged or lodged to the party's fund-raising account. Richardson said he later used the cash, once it had been converted to pounds, to offset a bill for a party fund-raiser at the Galway Races.

At the tribunal Richardson was dragged into a row over an alleged offer of money to Liam Lawlor. Richardson denied that at a meeting in the Berkeley Court Hotel he had offered Lawlor £100,000 to act as a consultant to the proposed project. Richardson conceded that he had intervened on behalf of a friend, believed to be White, and discussed the possibility of Lawlor taking an advisory role on the project, dealing specifically with advice on community issues. 'At no time during our conversation, or at any time in my long-standing friendship and relationship with Liam Lawlor, did I offer him money on behalf of myself or anybody else for this or any other project,' Richardson said, adding that Lawlor had a moral objection to casinos.

Ahern came out against the proposed casino in advance of the 1997 general election – fearing that support for it would cost Fianna Fáil seats – and then ditched both the national stadium at the Phoenix Park and the one Owen O'Callaghan had proposed for Neilstown, opting instead for a third plan: a state-built stadium, part funded by Limerick business tycoon J. P. McManus.

*

Many people had been surprised when Ahern appointed Ray Burke to his front-bench while in opposition; they were, however, shocked when he put Burke not just into government but into the senior and important position of Minister for Foreign Affairs, at a delicate time in the peace process.

In 1996 the *Sunday Business Post* began a series of stories claiming that a prominent Fianna Fáil politician had been in receipt of payments from a property developer prior to the 1989 general election. For legal reasons Burke was not named; nor was the company, Joseph Murphy Structural Engineering (JMSE). The names of both were well known in political and media circles.

In July 1997 I was contacted by an informed source who told me that Burke, at the same meeting, had also received a payment from Mick Bailey of Bovale Developments. At the time I had forgotten my previous meeting with Bailey and could remember little enough about the extent of his business interests. I made a number of calls and, satisfied by the quality of the information I had received, named Burke on the front page of the *Sunday Tribune* as the government minister who was the subject of the speculation. The following week the *Sunday Business Post* put the name of JMSE into the public domain.

Burke had form, going back as far as 1974, when the *Sunday Independent* produced an extract from the accounts of a house-building company controlled by Joe Brennan and Tom McGowan: this showed a payment of £15,000 under the heading 'planning'. Burke was the subject of a Garda investigation (and twenty interviews by the Fraud Squad) into land rezoning in Swords that focused on his relationship with this duo. They had a remarkable knack for acquiring options to buy agricultural land around Swords that was never intended for development. However, it would then be rezoned, more often than not against the advice of Dublin County Council's planners, allowing for vast profits. No prosecutions ever ensued.

In the early 1980s Burke was given control of the Department of the Environment by Haughey, which gave him responsibility for nominations to the ultimate planning authority, An Bord Pleanála. With blatant disregard for what might be said, Burke appointed his constituency adviser, Tony Lambert, and Brennan and McGowan's architect, John P. Keenan, who just happened to have designed Burke's own house.

Ahern claimed to have conducted an investigation into the rumours clouding Burke prior to forming his first government. 'I've been just about up every tree in north County Dublin chasing all kinds of things,' he said. Soon to be minister Dermot Ahern was sent to talk to JMSE's Joseph Murphy junior, and Dublin Central constituency activist Cyprian Brady went to have a chat with Bailey, but nobody bothered talking to the man making the allegations, James Gogarty, a retired JMSE employee.

Ray Burke lasted in the cabinet for only a few months, resigning as Minister for Foreign Affairs in October 1997 after defiantly drawing a 'line in the sand' over the allegations of corruption – which then swept over the line and washed him out of office. Burke not only resigned his ministry but quit politics altogether, and Ahern chose to lash out at those whom he blamed for Burke's downfall, rather than at the bent politician himself. He condemned 'the persistent hounding of an honourable man to resign his important position, on the basis of innuendo and unproven allegations' and applied the word 'sinister' to the actions of the journalists and politicians who had pursued Burke.

Richardson was asked by Ahern – presumably in his role as paid fund-raiser – to become involved in the special investigation set up after Burke's resignation to find out from whom Burke had taken money. Burke told the Planning Tribunal that he had met Ahern and Richardson in a pub in Swords, where he mentioned to them that he had a 'political fund' – but not that it contained more than £118,000. This meeting took place on the night of the by-election to fill his seat in Dublin North in 1998. There were reports at the time that the meeting was confrontational, that Burke felt he was being treated as a scapegoat, when others who had similar arrangements were going unpunished.

Following the deluge of stories about Burke's activities, Ahern was forced to establish a tribunal to 'investigate certain matters in the planning process', but, as Dunlop has said subsequently, nobody in political and business circles really thought it would get anywhere. Eventually it was to bring about Ahern's own downfall, but before doing so it told us an enormous amount about Ahern's circle of friends and close associates.

It confirmed the widely held suspicion that Burke had acted corruptly while Minister for Communications. The tribunal uncovered a £35,000 'corrupt payment' to Burke by concert promoter Oliver Barry; this had been made in response to a demand for £30,000 cash by Burke when Barry was part of the Century Radio consortium, bidding for the first national independent radio licence in opposition to RTÉ. Other Century promoters included Wexford businessman James Stafford and Charles Haughey's son-in-law John Mulhern, who was later named as an Ansbacher tax evader.

Century Radio won the licence, and in March 1989 Burke issued a directive under which Century acquired the access it needed to RTÉ's transmission network for an annual amount that was less than half of the £614,000 RTÉ had suggested was fair. Prior to winning its licence, Century had not even entered into negotiations with RTÉ for the use of the network, apparently confident the minister would deliver in its favour. The Independent Radio and Television Commission – which had awarded the licence – complained that Burke was in 'almost daily consultation in matters that need not concern him'. Burke met with Century's bankers and assured them that he would take steps in their favour, including, if necessary, the introduction of legislation that would be to Century's financial benefit.

Burke told the tribunal that the Barry payment was an unsolicited political donation, but Justice Fergus Flood decided the money was received 'not as a political contribution, but as a bribe'. Flood also concluded that Barry's partners in Century, Stafford and Mulhern, must have known that the £35,000 was a 'corrupt' payment to the politician.

Century launched in September 1989 without Ireland's most popular broadcaster, Gay Byrne, whom it had hoped to poach from RTÉ. It was a financial disaster – a high cost base swamping small revenues, as the audience stayed with RTÉ – and within months it needed help. Burke reacted by placing caps on the amount of advertising revenue RTÉ could raise, in the hope that advertisers would turn to Century.

Had this measure and the transmission instruction not followed the payment from Barry, they may have had some legitimacy, but the corruption undermined such arguments. The tribunal found eventually that Burke had sought 'to advance the private interests of the promoters of Century and not to serve the public interest'.

The Century investigation also dragged in Mara. The tribunal investigated an allegation by Stafford that Burke and Mara had sought payments to deliver radio licences, even though awards were supposed to be the remit of the Independent Radio and Television Commission. Stafford claimed Barry told him a 'price list' was operated by Burke and Mara. The going rate for a national television licence was £90,000;

£75,000 for a Dublin radio licence; and £25,000 for a local radio licence.

Both men denied it, Mara telling the tribunal that 'the idea that Mr Ray Burke and I were wandering around Dublin like two head waiters offering licences for sale is madness.' Later, Stafford withdrew his 'cash for licences' allegation, saying it was merely 'a rumour' and he was 'unable to say' what substance there was to it. No finding was made against Mara.

While trying to get to the bottom of one thing, the tribunal often uncovered the truth about several other things, which were sources of considerable interest to the public and of considerable embarrassment to those involved.

During his time as government press secretary Mara's financial affairs were managed in a fashion that was not dissimilar to the way Ahern organized his. Mara was short of cash, so friends gave him soft loans without written repayment schedules or terms of interest. Some of the Irish pound lodgements he made to bank accounts were equivalent to round sums in foreign currencies. The money came from Oliver Barry and Dermot Desmond, one of Charlie Haughey's most significant donors.

Mara was found to have set up two offshore bank accounts on the Isle of Man and to have failed initially, in two separate sworn affidavits and in other correspondence, to reveal the existence of these accounts, although he did so later.

The only adverse finding the tribunal made against Mara was that he failed to cooperate with the tribunal by not providing it with details of one of the offshore accounts. It found Mara's explanation that he had simply forgotten about the account to be 'unlikely', given both the extensive steps that were taken to form a company there and the level of turnover in the account.

Mara's role in the 2002 general election campaign was unaffected. He reprised the successful stint he had had as director of elections five years earlier. As far as Ahern's Fianna Fáil was concerned, it could wait for a finding from the tribunal based on the evidence. The long-awaited report into the Burke module of the tribunal arrived in September 2002, just weeks before the Nice Treaty referendum campaign vote. Mara's role as director of elections became an immediate issue for the opposition and Mara resigned, saying he was 'determined to ensure nothing relating to me could be used in an attempt to damage the chances of successful outcome to the campaign'.

Ahern leaped to Mara's defence. 'The fact is that P. J. Mara, who is a very hard-working individual for Fianna Fáil, has been found innocent of the offences that were put before him,' he said. 'That is the fact. But he has been reprimanded in the lowest scale because his affidavit was not complete.' It didn't seem to matter to Ahern that Mara had given evidence relating to a secret offshore account. Instead, he said he hoped Mara would 'work again with us in the future'. He did too, as director of elections during the 2007 election campaign, and he could be found on stage in the Mansion House at the launch of the Fianna Fáil manifesto, when Ahern had to take a series of questions from Vincent Browne about his financial affairs.

The authorities had no option but to prosecute Burke, which resulted in a six-month prison sentence for tax evasion. Burke was found to have had his house – subsequently sold for over €3 million – built for him for nothing by the builders Brennan and McGowan; to have taken a series of corrupt payments from them via offshore bank accounts and to have taken actions, as a public representative, to their benefit. In the spring of 1989 alone he received money from Bovale, JMSE and Oliver Barry. All, he tried to argue, were legitimate political donations.

Mara has publicly defended his relationship with Burke, one of the few to have done so. Shortly after the 2002 general election campaign – but before the Flood Tribunal report – he told Vincent Browne in an *Irish Times* interview that 'I certainly would regard him as a friend of mine. We had fun times together and again, as I said, I am not in the habit of abandoning my friends.'

Mara also defended the honour of Charles Haughey, still alive at the time. 'When time elapses and when the balance sheet is totted up, the pluses and minuses, when his legislative achievements are placed in the balance against other matters, I think that his record will stand the test of time,' he said.

This attitude and the circles of friendships – as well as Ahern's own long-hidden compromised position – go a long way towards explaining why Ahern failed to tackle the lax financial and ethical standards adversely affecting Irish politics and business during his time as Taoiseach. Ahern has shown time and again that he will not abandon his friends – and that people within his circle will defend each other, almost no matter what.

Ahern came to power as Taoiseach about six months after the revelation about Fine Gael's Michael Lowry and the unmasking of Haughey as Ben Dunne's other major political client, forming a coalition government with the PDs, supported by independents. He was in power as Haughey's reputation was destroyed, as Burke came tumbling down and as EU Commissioner Pádraig Flynn was revealed as having pocketed £50,000 of Tom Gilmartin's money that was intended for Fianna Fáil. Ahern did nothing to get the party's money back, instead playing footsie with Flynn's daughter Beverley, who was shown by an RTÉ television programme in 1998 to have been involved in encouraging tax evasion when working for National Irish Bank. He was left with no option but to kick her out of the party but got her back in again in time to contest the 2002 general election for Fianna Fáil. When her Supreme Court appeal against losing her libel action against RTÉ also failed, he had to get rid of her again, but managed to slip her back into the party just before he stepped down as leader. He appeared unconcerned that she let the state-funded RTÉ pay for a sizeable chunk of the legal costs of her failed action against it, pleading inability to pay.

Each time financial scandal hit Fianna Fáil Ahern's condemnation was partial and measured, as if he could not bring himself to condemn such behaviour unequivocally. Any action against miscreants was taken only when to remain loyal would have been too damaging to himself and Fianna Fáil. Worse, wherever possible he allowed for swift rehabilitation, as if the public would forget his deeds or regard them as inconsequential. Minor Fianna Fáil TDs Denis Foley – holder of an illegal Ansbacher account alongside Charlie Haughey, to facilitate tax evasion – and Michael Collins – a straightforward tax evader – were engulfed by financial scandals that were totally at odds with the elected positions they held, but Fianna Fáil often avoided facing the facts and acted only when public opinion could no longer be ignored. Ahern made Liam Lawlor – another TD whose greed and shamelessness were legendary – the chair of the Dáil ethics committee, which suggests Ahern has either the most wicked sense of humour or the utmost disdain for political niceties. This occurred before Dunlop pronounced Lawlor the 'Mister Big' of political corruption, and before Lawlor was jailed for refusing to incriminate himself at the tribunal. However, suspicion about Lawlor's activities, particularly in the interaction between business and politics and property rezoning, had been widespread within political and media circles for many years.

Michael Lowry's financial misconduct has been laid out in detail at two tribunals, but in 2007 Ahern cut a secret deal with Lowry, just re-elected as an independent TD for Tipperary North, to secure his vote, promising that an unspecified amount of money would be spent on undisclosed projects in his constituency. The arrangement was made with Lowry notwithstanding the pending publication of the Moriarty Tribunal report into Lowry's handling of the second mobile phone licence competition that went to the Denis O'Brien-led consortium.

One section of the Moriarty Tribunal report has been published, however: the one that deals with Charles Haughey. Ahern's actions in signing blank cheques on the Fianna Fáil party leader's account, an account that Haughey put to his own personal use – to, among other things, buy Charvet shirts in Paris, where he was such a good customer that they had taken a mould of his bust, and to wine and dine his mistress Terry Keane in Le Coq Hardi – came in for limited censure. Tribunal Chairman Michael Moriarty used the words 'inappropriate and imprudent'.

All of the evidence about Haughey's wrong-doing and corruption had been available before the tribunal issued its final report and before Haughey's death. Yet Ahern delivered this tribute to Haughey during the graveside oration: 'Charles Haughey was a legend and a man. A political leader of peerless acumen and commanding talent. He was a patriot to his fingertips. I have no doubt but that the ultimate judgement of history will be positive. He was one of the most consequential of Irishmen and when the shadows have faded the light of his achievements will remain.'

Ahern's position on Haughey's guilt was in a process of flux from 1997 onwards, and depended on how he read the political sensitivities of the day. Having condemned Haughey when necessary, he moved to rehabilitate him before his death. Perhaps it was the knowledge of his own actions – and the realization that they were likely to emerge into the public domain because of the tribunal's investigations – that prompted him to emphasize that Haughey's achievements outweighed his corruption. He must hope that others within Fianna Fáil will be as kind in assessing his legacy.

10

A day at the races

It's as much a social as a sporting event, the quality of horse racing on show not being the highest. But if the Galway Races have become famous for one thing it has to be for the now defunct Fianna Fáil fund-raising tent.

It was Des Richardson's idea, as part of his fund-raising activities for the party. He spotted a trend and arguably accentuated it: at the end of July each year the newly rich decided to have an old-fashioned Irish party. Everyone who went to Ballybrit got to dress up and to drink champagne as well as stout and to eat sit-down meals instead of sandwiches. It was the Irish version of Ascot, except it was traditional national hunt racing with its jumps instead of the posh flat stuff. Instead of top hats and tails there were sharp suits, and the atmosphere was easy-going and jolly.

Fianna Fáil believed its stewardship of the economy had created much of this opportunity, so why shouldn't it profit from it when it was so extravagantly on show here? The Fianna Fáil tent was Richardson's way of putting 500 of these people in a room each day, the majority of whom would pay for the privilege – as much as €4,000 for a table of ten. For that, the donors would get reasonably good food and fine wines, easy access to the tote and possibly a little token gift too. The profit for the week was put at as much as €170,000.

It provided access to the elite, and even a sense of being part of their set. Government ministers would always be present – though some later said they regarded it more as a chore than as enjoyment – with party leader and Taoiseach Bertie Ahern moving from table to table, having a word for everyone.

Paradoxically, the party got hammered in the Dáil and in the media for doing something seemingly transparent – while meetings in hotels during the winter months got no media coverage but raised even greater sums of money.

The seeming transparency of the tent was somewhat illusory, however. Access was tightly controlled, so no media outlet was able to publish or broadcast a list of who was there. Journalists had to wait outside and hope to recognize somebody on the way in or depend on people who had been inside to tell them who else was there and what was going on.

Legislation enacted in the wake of scandals about payments to Charles Haughey, Ray Burke, Liam Lawlor and Pádraig Flynn had restricted the amounts that could be donated, publicly and privately, and donations, either individual or corporate, could not exceed €6,350 in a single year. But that didn't mean that long-standing donors, or new ones trying to get access to the system, didn't continue to make contact with politicians personally to air their views, or didn't use well-placed and well-paid lobbyists to convey requests.

Among the names reported to have been in attendance in the Ballybrit Suite – as the tent was called – over the years, at least once if not more often, were significant property developers and businessmen such as Seán Dunne, Sean Mulryan, Bernard McNamara, Ged Pierse, Johnny Ronan, Bill Cullen, Padráig Rhatigan and Paschal Taggart. Also spotted there was banker to the big builders, Michael Fingleton of the Irish Nationwide Building Society, and auctioneer Arthur French, who had been very involved with businessman Michael Smurfit over the years.

Possibly the most controversial of recent appearances was that of Ray Burke's old donor, Bovale's Michael Bailey, in 2006: this was just months after his record tax settlement, which arose from the Revenue investigations that followed disclosures made at the Planning Tribunal. Nobody in Fianna Fáil seemed to care.

Bailey's appearances in particular were grist to the mill for the likes of Socialist Party TD Joe Higgins when it came to winding up Ahern in the Dáil. One of Higgins's more entertaining attacks was his description of 'those multimillionaires who jet and helicopter their way from tax exile to tug the Taoiseach's sleeve, when, like an Arabian prince, he sets up his tent at the Galway Races each year.'

Ahern's response was to scoff. 'We run it [the tent] to make a few quid – but the old stuff that people are going on about is begrudgery and comes from people that wouldn't be able to get enough guests to fit inside a phone-box.'

But there was criticism from within the party too, especially from the local constituency organization in Galway West, which complained about 'a sense of elitism' that isolated many people and the damage it did to the image of the party, which was supposed to be all-inclusive.

Ahern was concerned about the 'elitist' claims. 'The kind of spin is that everyone who goes into the tent is a massively rich person, but the people in my constituency who come are ordinary Joe Soaps who put their hands in their pocket and have a great week in Galway,' he said in its defence. There was some bemusement when he said of the tent contributors that 'some of them are tradesmen, some of them business people, some of them builders and some of them farmers.' He also mentioned 'clerical and administrative workers – all walks of life'. At between €250 and €400 per individual ticket, depending on the day of the week, that seemed unlikely. The so-called 'ordinary Joe Soaps' to whom Ahern referred might have been there as guests of the wealthy who bought the table, or else the money being made through property speculation was more widely spread than had been thought.

Ahern said that it wasn't possible to run Fianna Fáil without this substantial source of funding. And on another occasion, during an *Irish Times* interview in 2004 to mark his ten years as leader of the party, in which he famously declared himself to be a socialist, Ahern declared that 'if there are not the guys at the Galway Races in the tent who are earning wealth, who are creating wealth, then I can't redistribute that.'

Towards the end of Ahern's time, the pressure to disband the Galway operation became more intense, even if subtly applied. 'There's nothing wrong with it,' said Seámus Brennan, Minister for Arts, Sport and Tourism. 'It's an open, transparent fund-raiser and people pay a few bob to have your meal and a bit of fun, but, given that it's been such an issue, I do think we should review it at some stage.'

Former minister Jim McDaid defended the fund-raiser and said critics were 'begrudgers and jealous'. 'The tent was a very amenable way of getting quite a large amount of funds into the coffers. It was absolutely nothing to do with corruption,' he insisted.

It's likely that had Ahern survived as Fianna Fáil party leader, the Galway tent would have survived with him. Ahern was cussed in his final years as Taoiseach, often seeming to go out of his way to do things as an affront to his critics. Keeping the tent open in the face of criticism would have given him a certain satisfaction, especially as it was Richardson's baby. But the problem for the rest of Fianna Fáil was that both the tent and the party seemed to be getting used for much the same purpose: for example, someone like Bailey was able to give two-fingers to his critics by openly flaunting his continued links to the elite.

Cowen decided to do away with the tent. Early on in his tenure as leader of Fianna Fáil, he announced that the 2008 tent was being 'suspended' as part of a 'review' of fund-raising, organization and recruitment. His supporters claimed that it was a sign of the new broom sweeping away what was wrong. The cynics suggested the decision was taken because of a realization that most of the usual donors did not have the cash to attend and that a half-empty suite would play badly politically, suggesting a loss of confidence in Fianna Fáil.

Typically, Cowen did not get the full benefit out of his decision because he couldn't bring himself to be seen admitting to a mistake or condemning those who had supported the event in the past. In a radio interview months later with Marian Finucane on RTÉ Radio One, Cowen said he 'got rid of that fund-raising thing because it wasn't worth the hassle. There was all this mythology that you were talking about . . . the signal was that there was no intention on our part at any time for anyone to think that there's an inside curve for anybody' – the implication being that there was never anything wrong in giving special access to an elite, just hassle from having to deal with the publicity shone upon it by the pesky media. It seemed that Cowen really wasn't that much different to what had gone on before after all.

He had one prominent Fianna Fáil supporter for his decision, though: the former European Commissioner Charlie McCreevy. 'I was not a great attendee at the tent,' the horse racing fanatic declared. 'I felt obliged to go for half-a-day or so when I was minister. I was expected to do so. I found it to be a pain in the arse. I won't particularly miss it at all.'

PART III

Tax is for the little people

II

Horse sense

The Galway Races was a playground where the newly rich could flaunt their wealth during the late summer, just as they did at the races at Punchestown in spring and Leopardstown at Christmas and indeed at Cheltenham in England, usually close to St Patrick's Day.

What separated the truly rich from the merely well-off was to be a player in the expensive hobby of owning and breeding racehorses, to race here in Ireland, and sometimes in France, Australia and the United States.

It was a symbol of financial virility. The ordinary Irish, particularly those of rural stock, as many of the new property multimillionaires were, had always loved horses and horse racing but had been required to tip the forelock to the landed gentry and their 'betters' who had the financial means to participate in the so-called sport of kings. That changed in modern Ireland, with no small thanks due to government policy, with support from the main opposition parties.

This hobby was subsidized massively by the state. While tax exemption for stallions – the main beneficiary of which was John Magnier at Coolmore – attracted the bulk of controversy, the straightforward subvention of horse racing was arguably far more significant. Between 2001 and 2008 inclusive €545 million was given by the taxpayer to the Horse and Greyhound Racing Fund, with an 80–20 split between the sports. The annual state subsidy per spectator at a horse-racing event worked out at more than €40 every time someone attended. No other sport came near to receiving such generous state support.

The annual subvention for horse racing for 2009 fell by 9 per cent – as the government sought to cut costs wherever possible – but there was still €56.5 million available for prize money. Irish horse-racing prize money is the richest in the world, with the exception of Japan, and its average of €24,600 per race compares to just €15,600 in Britain. It's claimed that prize money of this size is needed to attract the best horses to race in Ireland.

Over one third of prize money in Irish flat racing during 2008 went to the top ten owners. Top of the list was Swiss resident Magnier's wife, Sue, followed by the Aga Khan, the Maktoums of the United Arab Emirates, a Monaco-based former bookie called Michael Tabor, who is a close friend of Magnier, J. P. McManus, Dermot Desmond, and Lady O'Reilly, wife of Tony O'Reilly. McManus got the most prize money in the National Hunt category.

Commercial sponsors contributed negligible amounts, even though their names got plenty of media publicity for being attached to races. The few companies involved tended to be those where the owners or directors had personal interests in horse ownership or attending the attached social events. Michael Smurfit, Michael O'Leary and O'Reilly are among those who had their companies sponsor races in Ireland or at the big British National Hunt Festival of Cheltenham. Entry fees to races were not expensive, so effectively the taxpayer stumped up most of the cash competed for by the wealthy who owned horses.

This was done at the expense of other sports that were not as popular with the elite. For 2009 the overall Horse and Greyhound Racing Fund grant of €68 million accounted for one third of all spending on sport. The government stopped all funding for the Sports Capital Programme, which had supported 6,700 projects at local and national levels in the previous ten years, supplying every sport and creating many jobs. It had been given €85 million in 2007 and €56 million in 2008 before its axing. The horses outranked the humans during and even after the Celtic Tiger era when it came to getting government funding, or rather their owners did.

Finance minister Charlie McCreevy may not have been a fan of the Galway Races, but he was a regular at other meetings and was known to be a punter. His Kildare constituency depended heavily on the horse industry. His colleagues, the former Minister for Arts, Sports and Tourism John O'Donoghue and the former Minister for Agriculture Joe Walsh, were other big horse-racing enthusiasts. Ahern claimed to be a successful gambler on horses, and Cowen was another who not only enjoyed the social aspect of the races but also found time to buy part of a horse in a syndicate with other politicians. The hobbies of some of the most prominent politicians of the Celtic Tiger era coincided with the financial interests of key players in the horse industry. Hundreds of millions of euro were poured into a sector where the ultimate beneficiaries were the big stud-farm owners, large owners and the gambling industry. The explanation was that it protected 16,500 jobs.

McCreevy explained his generosity with state money in an interview with the *Racing Post* in 2000: 'The next logical step is to put racing's finances on a permanent footing. If that is not done racing will be at the whim of the government of the day and when the pressure comes for expenditure on things like health and education, racing will go down the political priority list. Now is the opportunity, while myself and Joe Walsh are ministers, to finalize the matter once and for all.' The initial scheme for the fund was for four years and he extended it by another four years just before he was exiled to Brussels. It is now being run on a year-to-year basis.

It was one of the rare funds that benefited from 'ring-fenced' tax revenues, whereby money raised from a particular source is reallocated to the same sector, rather than being funnelled into the general pot.

The money came from taxes on all betting, both off-course and on-course, in Ireland. At the time a rate of 5 per cent was levied on all bookmakers' income. However, this tax was reduced first to 2 per cent and then 1 per cent after lobbying against 'the threat posed to bookmakers' shops by online betting'. This kept the bookies happy but it meant that insufficient revenue was being raised from the designated source to meet the promised spending commitments. The deficit had to be financed from the general exchequer revenues, which attracted criticism in a special investigation in 2006 by the Economic and Social Research Institute's (ESRI's) Professor Tony Fahey and Dr Liam Delaney. It said the Horse and Greyhound Racing Fund no longer served its original function.

Another distorting factor was that the money raised was not a percentage of what was wagered on Irish horse racing but on all activities in Irish bookies, including foreign horse racing and other sports, such as soccer, rugby and golf. Less than 15 per cent of all gambling in Ireland is believed to be on Irish horse racing – but the rewards for the sport were disproportionately and unfairly huge.

McCreevy also ensured that horse-racing facilities in his constituency were looked after, the deal he did for Punchestown racecourse being one of the most controversial.

The racecourse owners – the privately owned Kildare Hunt Club – applied to the Department of Agriculture in November 1999 for €6.9 million to spend on developing Punchestown as the 'Irish Cheltenham'. A structure to be known as the Punchestown Agricultural and Equestrian Event Centre was to be included.

With rare speed, in just under two months, Department of Agriculture officials recommended to a delighted Minister Walsh that Punchestown should get what it wanted. The following day Walsh was on to McCreevy looking for the money and it took less than a week for McCreevy to decide he would use state funds to help.

Three months later the Punchestown management returned to the Department of Agriculture with a more ambitious idea that would cost not much short of twice as much: €12.8 million. As well as building the centre, the owners wanted to demolish and rebuild the racecourse's stables – to bring them up to the standards for major international events – and build a new entrance and pavilion at the course.

Without even a departmental audit or an independent assessment, Walsh wrote to McCreevy looking for another €6.4 million for their equestrian centre, which would of course benefit their mutual friends. It took McCreevy less than a fortnight to agree. He failed to have the project assessed by way of a cost-benefit analysis, as the Comptroller and Auditor General – the state's official auditor of public spending – tartly noted in a subsequent report.

There was more to come. On 17 September 2001 McCreevy received the chairman of the course, James Osborne – once Larry Goodman's solicitor and a director of Ryanair – and its chief executive, Charlie Murless, at his constituency office in Naas, County Kildare. Construction of the approved project had started, but now Kildare County Council said a new sewerage system and more parking on the site was needed. McCreevy agreed to give Punchestown an extra €1.5 million, breaching the cap set by Walsh's department.

This brought the total government spend on the centre to €14.8 million and, extraordinarily, the Kildare Hunt Club put up no money itself. Later, when McCreevy decided that the completed Punchestown should be the location for a two-day meeting of European finance ministers, the state was charged €60,000 for the hire of the facilities.

However, by this stage Punchestown badly needed the money, having debts of €8 million, despite receiving almost €25 million in state loans and grants. The cancellation of the Punchestown National Hunt Festival in April 2001 because of the foot-and-mouth crisis left the racecourse in severe financial difficulties, as the annual April event accounts for about 90 per cent of Punchestown's business. It meant that Horse Racing Ireland had to provide an emergency long-term loan of €2.5 million to keep the course in business.

The opposition made hay with McCreevy's actions. Joan Burton told the Dáil that 'if the minister of the day is seen to take a soft option in the interests of local pet projects or personal cronies while vital areas of public capital expenditure, such as health and education, are postponed or cut back, this brings the profession of politics into disrepute ... Anyone who has sought money for a new school, a falling-down school, a hospital ward to be opened or an extension to a community hall must wonder how the "tally-ho brigade" in Kildare were able to winkle such enormous amounts of money out of the minister almost like magic.'

The Public Accounts Committee (PAC) had found that the centre 'was hardly used' in its first year, and that only a third of events held there were of an equestrian or agricultural nature. 'This is 100 per cent funding with almost no conditionality,' Burton charged. 'We do not even know if the state holds some kind of security for these assets in the event of the whole project failing. All we know is that Santa's kingdom will base itself in the centre for the next few months. Not only was the minister playing Santa Claus to the Kildare hunt, but he appears determined to keep on doing so.'

McCreevy claimed that the controversy arose only because the centre was located in his constituency. 'I have no apologies to make about my involvement and I am certain the state's contribution has now resulted in a world-class event centre in which we can all take pride,' he said. He also cited proper investigation of the application by the Department of Agriculture but it later admitted that a proper appraisal had not been conducted. However, it defended the decision to fund the project, claiming a positive financial benefit to the economy from it.

It was not until 2008 that the attitude towards government funding of horse racing changed ... and arguably just at the time the industry needed financial support the most.

The economic downturn was a disaster for the sport, as many of the new owners started to bail out. Builder Sean Mulryan halved the number of horses he kept to thirty, and there were many rumours that O'Reilly was trying to sell his prized Castlemartin Stud, although these were denied. Trainers took a big hit as owners withdrew or abandoned horses. The country's main equine abattoir was booked out for months in advance as some owners destroyed expensive livestock. Bloodstock sales almost halved in 2008, with sales at public auction dropping by €77 million on the previous year to just €99.5 million, as people realized that owning horses was a luxury; the trend continued into 2009. A fall in attendances that had started a year earlier continued, and on-course betting slumped.

McCreevy went to Cheltenham in March 2009, as he did every year, where he partied in a VIP private box with Mulryan and other builders such as Mick Bailey.

Irish Times journalist Kathy Sheridan approached him for a comment about the state of the economy. The EU Commissioner for Internal Markets and Services, a job that paid €230,000 per annum, on top of a €70,000 annual pension he was already drawing from his time as a minister, was reluctant initially to comment but then told her, 'Look it. You ate three meals yesterday, didn't you? You'll be eating three meals tomorrow, won't you? And a year from now you'll still be eating three meals a day.'

12

Probably the best Minister for Finance in the world

Charlie McCreevy was named as the 'greatest' Minister for Finance in the history of the state in a survey of business people conducted by *Finance* magazine in 2004, but it didn't save him from being exiled to Brussels that year.

Bertie Ahern panicked after dreadful European and local election results, blaming McCreevy's attempts to rein in public spending for public unhappiness with Fianna Fáil. Ahern appointed Brian Cowen with a brief to continue spending, using tax revenues from the revived construction and property boom. The disastrous consequences of this were felt during 2008 and 2009.

McCreevy was considered successful because he achieved budget surpluses in most years, with tax revenues outstripping government spending. He did not curtail spending, however. In 2001 total government expenditure increased by 23 per cent, while taxes grew by a mere 3.2 per cent. Then in the December 2001 budget for 2002 McCreevy allowed for further spending increases of 14.4 per cent and gambled on tax revenues rising by 8.6 per cent. The government knew it was facing a June 2002 general election, so it spent public money to buy the favour of the electorate.

The surge in spending was explained partly by public service pay rises that arose from the 'benchmarking' episode of 2000. McCreevy had set up a special review group that recommended a range of pay increases, ostensibly to bring public sector workers into line with allegedly better-paid people in the private sector. McCreevy refused to publish details of how the review group calculated its recommendations, even though implementation permanently added €1 billion a year to the public sector wage bill. It also provided a higher base off which future increases were calculated. The suspicion that the whole exercise was devised to buy off the public sector trade unions grew when economist Jim O'Leary of Davy Stockbrokers quit the process in protest. Most of the additional pay was awarded without significant productivity increases attached and without taking the pension benefits and job security of the public sector into account. McCreevy added tens of thousands of extra workers to the public sector without properly assessing what they would do or what value they would provide. This contributed to higher pay rates in the private sector, as it competed to attract labour.

McCreevy was annoyed by accusations that he had inflated the boom and ignored the likelihood of future revenue shortfalls to cover perma- nent increases in spending. His boast was 'when you have it, you spend it and the mistake is trying to spend it when you haven't got it.'

It was a populist explanation of policy, but it ran serious risks because he was concentrating on what happened in a year rather than over a longer period. He attempted to balance the government budget between spending and revenue every year between 1997 and 2004, and when he achieved surpluses he used the money for more tax cuts, increased public spending and paying off the national debt. However, he did not save enough because he overdid the increase in public spending. This meant that when deficits re-emerged, as they always do in a longer economic cycle, he or a successor would either have to raise taxes or reduce spending on state services and capital investment.

McCreevy's instinct was actually to curb the growth in public spend- ing but every attempt he made ran into dissent at cabinet and from Ahern. Free-spending ministers knew that they would either have Ahern's support or that he would quail at helping McCreevy to tighten the screw.

To McCreevy's fury, in September 2002 the *Sunday Tribune* published secret government memoranda outlining how he had implored his col- leagues to reduce spending since the start of that year, even in advance of the election. He warned that massive financial problems loomed, but they ignored him and kept spending. During the election campaign McCreevy insisted that no spending cuts were planned for after the return to government.

Having won the election helped by these false promises, McCreevy told the reconstituted cabinet at its first meeting that hard cuts would have to be made to bring that year's expenditure in on budget. This wasn't achieved and the government continued with double-digit spending increases. He got away with it, helped by a swift international recovery from the post 9/11 economic downturn, cheaply priced money because of our entry to the euro and booming tax revenues from the resurgent construction and property sectors.

But the warning signs were there, especially from internal Department of Finance documents that told him our interest rates probably needed to be about 4 per cent higher than they were to temper asset price inflation.

Instead of dealing with things in his budget for 2003 McCreevy seemed somewhat lacking when it came to real initiatives and diverted attention with what proved to be another highly expensive wheeze: the 'decentralization' of public servants away from Dublin to a variety of rural locations. In foisting his ill-thought-out plan upon public servants without any prior consultation, he ignored the national spatial strategy that aimed to introduce sustainable regional development. Many questioned whether politics, and not economics, was the motivating factor when designating locations. To make matters worse, persuading people to move, when that was possible, cost much more than intended, and the amounts involved in buying land or new buildings to house government departments or agencies were also exorbitant.

But poor estimates of how much measures would cost were typical of McCreevy. The cost of providing free medical cards to the over-seventies was completely underestimated, for example, and led to the debacle in late 2008 when 'grey power' overturned a government attempt to remove the automatic entitlement. Many of his apparently radical reforms of the income tax system were not properly costed either, and it was noticeable that his department's spending and income projections were almost always massively wrong. But nobody seemed to care when exchequer surpluses were being achieved none the less.

While it's true that McCreevy brought the corporation tax down to 12.5 per cent, that process had already been started and crucially agreed with the European Union by his predecessor, Ruairi Quinn. This didn't stop Fianna Fáil from claiming the credit for low business taxes.

Not even his creation of the National Pension Reserve Fund was an unqualified success, even though the 2009 government was thankful to have it as a means of finding money for the recapitalization of AIB and Bank of Ireland. McCreevy used the proceeds of the sale of Eircom, together with an annual contribution of 1 per cent of national output (to be paid out of the surplus), to start the fund, the idea being that the proceeds of investments made with the money would be used to pay state pensions from 2025.

Most of the money was invested on the stock market, which was all fine and well as long as markets went up – but from late 2007 they went down steadily, wiping out much of the earlier profit. This was ironic, as McCreevy had once chided Eircom shareholders for whingeing about their losses by telling them the stock market was like 'a casino'. McCreevy was correct to highlight the pension crisis that looms as the population grows older, but the Economic and Social Research Institute (ESRI) argued strongly that the money would have been better spent on developing the infrastructure of this country to provide revenues in the future that would pay the pensions. Instead, it was invested in other countries, although the record of value-for-money spending in Ireland suggests much of it might have been wasted here too. So perhaps simply paying off the national debt in full and building up savings for the inevitable downturn might have been the best option, if politically difficult to implement.

There was considerable productivity growth up until 2002, but foreign investment and massive capital transfers from the EU were largely responsible, and the government's drive to reduce overall borrowing was dictated by the requirements of the Maastricht Treaty to ensure our entry to the euro. Tax cuts did contribute to a consumer boom, when people had more money to spend, but lower interest rates, and a greater willingness to borrow, did too.

McCreevy consistently brought income tax rates down in his first term of office. The top rate went from 48 per cent to 42 per cent – before Cowen cut it by 1 per cent more – and the standard rate from 26 per cent to 20 per cent. His failure to inflation-proof tax credits in his last two budgets meant that in real terms people ended up paying more income tax by stealth. The percentage of workers paying the top rate of income tax reached 52 per cent under McCreevy, which was the highest in the state's history, and employees on average industrial earnings were paying tax at the top rate. Yet, at the same time, he failed to tackle all of the tax breaks for the rich, as he had promised, and indeed introduced quite a few more. This meant that 117 of the top 400 highest earners paid less than 30 per cent in tax in the 1999/2000 tax year and just over half of that number paid less than 5 per cent.

What people could not escape were the high taxes on consumption. McCreevy contributed to what became known as the 'Rip-off Republic' because he maintained the very high VAT rate of 21 per cent (apart from one year, when he brought it down to 20 per cent before returning to the old level) and this helped to keep consumer prices high. Spending taxes generally hit the poor the hardest, and McCreevy's policy was to rely heavily on high indirect taxes as his major source of revenue, with almost half of all revenue being raised from spending taxes at one stage during his tenure. High taxes on spending contributed to higher inflation.

McCreevy became the darling of the middle classes, though, with his politically inspired Special Savings Investment Accounts, which were introduced in 2001/2 and which matured five years later, just in time for the 2007 general election. For every four euro that a citizen saved, the state added a euro, up to a maximum of €63 per month from the state, as long as people saved every month for each of those five years. It was, in effect, a tax-free bonus courtesy of the state. He had to admit that the take-up was way higher than he had expected – costing the state about €500 million per annum more than anticipated – and he was left to defend it on the basis that it was serving a social use in persuading people to save rather than spend. But the scheme discriminated against those who had no spare cash, and favoured those who could afford to save. In reality, it was an unfair and inequitable idea because it rewarded only those who had money to save with extra state handouts.

McCreevy did all of these things for populist reasons but they also distracted attention from his actions that helped the rich.

McCreevy changed the culture of the relationship between the state and entrepreneurs, speculators and investors. Most crucially, he halved the capital gains tax rate from 40 per cent to 20 per cent in one of the most dramatic moves ever undertaken by a politician. A number of informed sources, speaking on condition of anonymity, have insisted that McCreevy was not the instigator of this initiative, but was encouraged strongly to undertake it by Ahern, who believed it would encourage a higher level of business activity and provide extra tax revenues to spend. While the increase in revenues suggests that it worked as intended, there is also an argument that the rise would have come anyway, even at the old rates, because of the surge in economic activity; or, that if a reduction was required, it did not need to be as dramatic as the one McCreevy introduced.

In addition, McCreevy provided a raft of tax breaks to people with assets and large incomes that fuelled the unsustainable construction-led boom. He allowed special tax breaks on pensions for the super-rich that enabled them to take millions out of their companies tax-free, sometimes tens of millions. His reduction in income tax rates was enough to keep the general public happy, but it was of far less significance than his reductions in capital gains tax. It shifted the balance in favour of those with capital and away from those supplying labour. In McCreevy's Ireland everyone got richer, but the gap between rich and poor grew significantly.

13

Tax is for the young and the poor

Charlie McCreevy passed on the opportunity to visit one of the most controversial examples of what one of his tax breaks could buy. He and his wife, Noleen, were invited in 2004 to be among the select forty-four guests on board a luxury yacht called the *Christina O* that was playing host to the wedding party of property developer Seán Dunne and his new wife Gayle Killilea. McCreevy phoned the reception and was put on speaker-phone for all to hear as he offered his congratulations to the happy couple. Had he gone, he could have seen what had been bought with the tens of millions of euro the Irish taxman should have received.

As the one-time plaything of the famous Greek shipping billionaire Aristotle Socrates Onassis, the *Christina O* was one of the most famous luxury private yachts in the world. But by 2004 it had became a floating tax break for an elite circle of wealthy Irish millionaires. They bought the yacht and reduced their Irish tax by legally claiming the cost of its refurbishment as a deduction against their taxable income, before renting it to other millionaires, including Irish ones, for play.

They did this for five years, leading Labour Party leader Pat Rabbitte to complain to the Dáil about a yacht 'parked in the middle of the Mediterranean, staffed with non-Irish people, disporting itself for the rich and powerful, earning an income of €9 million a year and paying virtually no tax to this exchequer'.

The *Christina O* started its life as a 325-foot-long Canadian naval frigate built in 1943, but it was purchased by Onassis five years later. He spent six years and $4 million turning it into the most luxurious private yacht known. He named it after his daughter and spent much of his time there. The rich and famous were regular guests. Sir Winston Churchill was introduced to President Kennedy on the *Christina O*. Grace Kelly and Prince Rainier of Monaco held their wedding reception on board.

Onassis squired the widowed Jackie Kennedy on it (and of course later married her). Frank Sinatra, Marilyn Monroe, John Wayne, Greta Garbo and other movie and singing stars of the era were regular guests.

After her father's death in 1975, Christina Onassis gave the yacht to the Greek state, but it fell into disrepair. In 1998 it was bought by an American tour operator who in turn sold it to a Greek national called John Paul Papanicolaou. He partnered with an Irish syndicate to buy and refit the boat. At a Croatian shipyard, and under the watchful eye of Greek experts, 560 tonnes of steel and 140 tonnes of pipe work were replaced and fifty-six miles of new electrical wiring installed. New diesel engines and gensets gave the yacht a cruising speed of 18 knots and a top speed of 22 knots. New accommodation was added: a banquet-sized, split-level, formal dining room that seated the forty-four guests was incorporated into the middle-deck; on the main deck a new gym, massage room and beauty salon were installed; a 'sports lounge' with various gaming tables, effectively a casino, was put in, as were new lifts and a cinema. The open pool deck on the stern was retained, its centrepiece being a bronze-bordered pool inlaid with mosaic frescos of ancient Crete. Apparently, at the push of a button the bottom raises to deck level to become a dance floor – once the water has been drained.

The stools in 'Ari's Bar', which were covered, famously, in the foreskins of whales (leading to Onassis's favourite joke of asking women if they knew they were sitting on the 'biggest dick in the world'), were reupholstered in fine leather. The circular bar was adorned with footrests and handrails of ornately carved and polished whales' teeth. Paintings by Renoir were hung and the chandeliers and lamps were by Baccarat. The guest accommodation resembled a modern five-star hotel. Guests arrived by helicopter, following the installation of a helipad.

When the group of Irish businessmen bought the famous private yacht, they had it reclassified as a passenger ship for hire. The price of buying the yacht was relatively low but the cost of the refit was €65 million. That suited the Irish partnership. A solicitor at the firm of Ivor Fitzpatrick had spotted a loophole in the tax laws that allowed the cost of the capital investment to be offset against income tax falling due from all sources, and not just against the income from renting the yacht at a price of about €70,000 per day.

Fitzpatrick ran a large practice under his own name while simultaneously operating as a property developer. He was well connected politically and had represented Charles Haughey at the Moriarty Tribunal. He was appointed to the board of Aer Lingus, alongside Des Richardson, by Bertie Ahern's government.

Fitzpatrick sold the scheme to investors who borrowed much of the money from the Irish Nationwide Building Society, which held a mortgage over the vessel. The identities of most of those he introduced to the *Christina O* scheme are unknown (although property developer Paddy McKillen's name did surface); complete information on who participated has been hard to find because the partnership is registered in the Cook Islands. But it is certain that one investor was businessman Robert Harris.

Despite a very limited formal education, Harris had made a fortune by acquiring the franchise for the Japanese Hino range of trucks. He moved in property and profited massively from the quick sale of the Carysfort Educational College in Blackrock that he had bought from nuns, a deal that led to controversy involving Taoiseach Charles Haughey.

In his tax return filed in January 2002, for the tax year that finished on 5 April 2001, Harris claimed relief for trading losses, capital allowances and bank interest arising from the purchase and refurbishment of the *Christina O* by what was called the Cook Islands (CI) Partnership, of which he was a member. Harris had invested €144,000 and provided €14.3 million as a loan.

The Revenue Commissioners wanted to deny him this tax benefit and hit Harris with a bill of €9.12 million, which he paid but then appealed. In October 2004 the Appeal Commissioners decided Harris was legally entitled to avoid the taxes demanded of him. The Revenue Commissioners decided they would appeal to the High Court but in the meantime Harris demanded a refund of his money and won a separate High Court judgment. Indeed, Mr Justice Hugh Geoghegan said that the retention of the excessive tax was unlawful.

In February 2008 the Revenue Commissioners went back to the High Court and argued that, while Harris, as an Irish resident and taxpayer, could offset losses on the *Christina O* against his investment in the Cook Islands partnership, he could not offset the investment against his entire income. Harris's lawyers said the law entitled him to do so and he won his case because of a technical provision in the tax laws relating to the definition and structure of the partnership. His victory implied that the other investors in the consortium were able to reduce their tax in a similar fashion.

Back in 2003 Labour finance spokeswoman Joan Burton highlighted the unfair use of tax incentives. 'President McAleese stated recently that alcohol abuse is the dark side of our social life, but tax avoidance by the wealthy is the dark side of the economy,' she said. Having outlined a list of tax breaks that enabled wealthy persons to achieve a virtual tax-free status, she alleged that 'all of these devices, sponsored and fostered by Fianna Fáil and the Progressive Democrats, allow wealthy individuals to essentially decide how much tax to pay.'

The use of tax incentives was defended by Tom Parlon, then the PD junior minister in the Office of Public Works. On losing his seat in the 2007 general election, Parlon landed on his feet by getting the job of director-general of the Construction Industry Federation. 'Tax incentives are there to be used and to encourage investment which would not otherwise be made,' he said, although he condemned the highly artificial and 'packaged' ways the incentives (or the tax code in general) were used to greatly reduce effective tax rates on high incomes – a purpose for which they had not been intended.

The number of tax breaks provided by Charlie McCreevy that benefited the rich who stayed in Ireland is so great that it's surprising that some still opted to move their tax residency out of Ireland during the Celtic Tiger era.

One of the most extraordinary incentives that he introduced was a tax-driven pension scheme for the owners / directors of Irish companies, brought in by the Finance Act of 2000, called Approved Retirement Funds (ARF). These allowed owner-investors to pay unlimited amounts out of company profits tax-free into their personal pension funds – and conferred further tax benefits on the lucky beneficiaries once they started to draw on the money upon retirement. This was possible because ARFs gave their owners the freedom to continue investing on retirement age, rather than having to purchase an annuity – a product that provides a fixed income each year.

It was an extraordinarily tax-efficient way for a major company shareholder to get their hands on the cash in a profitable, privately owned and controlled company without having to pay income tax of 42 per cent on dividends.

A Department of Finance investigation, details of which were published in 2006, revealed that two companies had each made a payment of over €100 million to the ARF of a lucky individual. The identities of those Irish resident individuals and of the companies that made the payments were protected by confidentiality rules. But it is understood that there were many other shareholder/directors who received payments of over €10 million plus from their companies, before the rules were changed by Brian Cowen as Minister for Finance in the budget of December 2006. By that stage, however, some 6,200 people had taken advantage of ARFs.

Officials in the Department of Finance and the Revenue Commissioners agreed that some people had been treating ARFs as a tax-exempt haven for funds, rather than as the flexible revenue retirement income stream they were designed to be. The figures they produced showed that the size of these funds jumped from €19 million to €1.1 billion after the law concerning ARFs was changed in 2000 – and nothing could be done, retrospectively, to recover the tax lost.

Various investment managers had set up special units within their organizations to cater for clients who had the money to avail themselves of this super deal. Sean FitzPatrick established a special insurance division at Anglo Irish Bank for those who wanted to use ARFs. It then set up various syndicates that invested the ARF money at home and abroad and that borrowed multiples of the money to assist in the investment, usually from Anglo itself.

That the syndicate managers and investors were able to borrow was again due to McCreevy and another change to the pension rules he had introduced: he allowed owners of ARFs to borrow additional money that could then be invested in anything, including property speculation at home and abroad.

Section 16 of the Finance Act 2004 reversed a Revenue rule that had been in existence for over twenty-five years prohibiting occupational pension schemes from borrowing to increase the money available for investments. This relaxation of the rules allowed holders of both self-administered pension schemes and ARFs to borrow in order to invest in property and greatly increased the amount of money available for further inflation of the property bubble.

The idea was that the potential for borrowing within pension funds gave beneficiaries the opportunity for more choice, reducing their dependence on the stock market. It allowed investors to increase the amount of investment in residential, commercial and office property markets that they could rent to others, and in different countries, theoretically reducing risk. Previously, the size of the pension fund might not have been enough to allow for property investment, whereas access to borrowed money provided this.

For example, if there was €500,000 in a fund, the investment manager would not necessarily have been able to purchase a commercial property that was sufficiently attractive. Now three times as much could be borrowed to buy something for €2 million. Alternatively, the €500,000 could be put in a syndicate organized by the likes of Anglo, which would raise €5 million from a group of ten, borrow another €15 million from the bank and have €20 million to invest in a property deal.

In theory, this would improve returns. In practice, it helped to push property prices up further because of the 'weight of money' chasing deals. In addition, the risk of serious losses for the pension fund was increased should the value of the property fall, or rent payments fail to cover interest costs on the loans, given the amount of borrowed money now involved.

It wasn't just commercial properties that were attractive to investors. In 2004 the Revenue said it would not object to pension schemes investing in residential units that would be let. The funds began buying apartment blocks or estates, again pushing up prices for ordinary homeowners who were struggling to raise the money for a mortgage for a place to live. The only things disallowed for inclusion were holiday homes and the ownership of commercial premises that directors were using for the business.

By 2006 use of ARFs was costing the state so much in tax revenue that couldn't be collected – and was enriching the already wealthy even further so generously – that Cowen had to act.

He introduced a limit of €5 million in total on tax-free contributions to such funds; and he limited the maximum tax-free lump sum a person could draw from their pension fund to €1.25 million. This would give a male retiring at age sixty an annual pension of approximately €110,000 and a male retiring at sixty-five an annual pension of approximately €135,000 on top of the lump sum. These figures closely approximated the pensions paid to former government departmental secretaries and ministers. If those pensions were being self-funded, rather than coming out of the public cash flow, it would have required the prior construction of a pension pot of €5 million to fund the benefits.

While investment returns achieved in ARFs were exempt from tax, withdrawals of the funds from an ARF were and are liable to income tax. As holders didn't need the capital or any income from the fund because of the size of the lump sum they had received tax-free, and because they wanted to leave the residual amount to heirs in a tax-efficient way, many people just allowed profits to accumulate within the fund tax-free. If people needed extra money they borrowed from banks, secured on the money in the fund, as it was cheaper to pay interest on the loans than tax on the capital withdrawal.

Cowen introduced new rules from the start of 2008: even if no funds were withdrawn during the year, the ARF holder would be assumed to have drawn down 3 per cent of the value of the fund, with income tax payable on that calculated amount. 'I closed off excessive funding for pensions, limited the amount which can be drawn from pension products by way of tax-free lump sums and restricted the capacity of individuals to use approved retirement funds as purely long-term tax-exempt vehicles,' he said. By that stage, however, much of the damage had been done.

Rich people were able to reduce not only their pension tax but also their income tax and other tax bills. An extraordinary system appears to have been at work during the late 1990s and into this century. Many people with large incomes managed to reduce their annual tax bills to near nothing by clever use of so-called incentives.

They didn't even have to use spare after-tax income; instead, they just borrowed large sums of money to finance investments in tax-driven property projects (often new-build apartments in tax designated areas). They used the rent they received to cover the interest payments on the loans, and were also able to claim the cost of the loan against their tax bill (e.g., if an investor borrowed €200,000 over ten years and had taxable income of €100,000 annually in each of those ten years, he could subtract €20,000 – the notional annual amount he had invested in the relevant scheme – from that income before tax was calculated on it). Then, ten years later, investors sold these investments (they had to wait ten years because, according to tax legislation, if investors sold sooner they would lose some or all of the tax relief), often at huge profits, and repaid the original loan. On top of that, if an investor could somehow make a convincing case that he had resided in a tax-designated property, and hence it was his principal private residence, capital gains tax of 20 per cent did not apply. This was the cherry on the cake for these canny investors, an added bonus to the reduced income tax bills they had enjoyed during the life of the investment.

After the airing of a *Primetime Investigates* programme for RTÉ in May 2005, Cowen came under political pressure and announced that he was scrapping many of the reliefs, pledging to 'eliminate the phenomenon of tax-free millionaires'. Cowen's clamp-down on the various reliefs available was more limited than it could have been, especially as the extent to which the rich had previously availed themselves of the benefits was far greater than had been assumed. In total, the rich saved about €3 billion in tax that would have been paid to the state if the 'incentives', or tax breaks, had not been available to them. Even after Cowen's announcement the elite still had another €850 million or so that they were entitled to keep on the basis of investments already made.

Property tax breaks alone amounted to about €2 billion in lost tax. But the loss of revenue was not the only problem: while the 'incentives' facilitated necessary development in certain areas, they also contributed to unnecessary construction in unsuitable locations, solely so interested parties could claim tax relief.

This is one of the major reasons why there were 'ghost' housing estates in so many parts of the country from as early as 2005, two years before the surge in construction stopped. It led to a bidding war between investors and those looking for somewhere to live, with the investors paying inflated prices just to get the tax benefits of a particular development and the home buyers unable to compete with them, particularly in perceived 'good areas'. It allowed developers to charge excessive prices for properties or persuaded them that it was worth while spending much more in the first place to get the land upon which to build. It pushed rents up too.

Quite simply it went on far too long. Not only were the incentives unnecessary – because the capital would have been available for the investments – but they gave tax benefits on super-profits to the wealthy in society. The biggest beneficiaries were the builders and developers, who then populated Fianna Fáil's Galway Races tent. The government acquiesced, as it collected VAT and other taxes from house sales, and PAYE and PRSI receipts from construction jobs.

Those who took advantage of the system can hardly be blamed too much for doing so. It was the fault of the legislators who introduced these tax breaks. The incentives came to be regarded as a central plank of the economic policies of successive Irish governments for nearly forty years, and it was felt that tax incentives for residents encouraged Irish wealth creators to keep their money here instead of sending it abroad. 'The point that people forget is that the Celtic Tiger was not booming when those incentives were introduced,' one tax adviser told me. 'This country was on its knees.'

It is possible that the authorities did not anticipate the loss of tax revenue that would result when the economy boomed. What doesn't bear thinking about is that the politicians' actions in introducing the incentives just helped the rich get richer.

Economists have noted that high tax rates give people an incentive to take advantage of tax breaks. They make investments because they can avoid tax by doing so rather than because those investments make commercial sense in their own right.

The government's own Tax Strategy Group – made up of leading public servants – warned back in 1999 that: 'Such reliefs add to the increase in property prices generally and provide a bonus to land and property owners and investors who are usually the better off.' This partly explained the rush of developers to enter the hotel business, often with associated golf courses and relaxation spas, and the rise in capital prices – and rates to customers – that accompanied it.

The support for development of the hotel industry made sense at one point. There was a shortage of suitable stock of hotel bedrooms and associated facilities, which put Ireland at a disadvantage as a hotel destination. Unfortunately, the availability of massive capital grants to offset against income from other investments persuaded many land-owners and builders – with no experience in how to run hotels or real interest in the provision of the necessary service – to enter the hotel construction game.

Tax breaks of 15 per cent of the capital costs for the first six years and then 10 per cent in year seven were allowed. Owners invested limited equity and borrowed the rest, then wrote off the capital allowances against rental income from other investments and watched as values for hotels began to increase. Any investigation as to whether chosen locations actually needed hotels was rarely done. Many investors also had a deal in place to sell the hotel for at least the original construction price, the profit being all the tax breaks received over seven years.

The scheme helped to add 16,000 new hotel bedrooms to the national stock between 1996 and 2004, but when McCreevy moved to close it off from the end of December 2002 he received plenty of lobbying from cash-rich developers who were planning their own hotels. He extended it to the end of 2004 and there was a rush of applications from developers who wanted to qualify. A total of 217 hotel applications countrywide were lodged in the run-up to Christmas 2004, with the proposed addition of almost 15,000 bedrooms, almost as many again as had been built in the previous decade. The potential annual cost to the exchequer would be up to €100 million for the following seven years, but the government argued that it could recoup the lost tax in VAT payments, tourist revenue and new jobs. This created a dreadful over-supply of hotel rooms and not enough business to go around.

Hotel construction wasn't the only sector buoyed by tax breaks. A surplus of tax incentive-funded student apartments were built, many subsequently left vacant because of a lack of demand. Developers ploughed into these on the basis that they would sell for higher prices than non-tax-driven schemes. Many of these, bought by investors wanting to shelter existing rental income or wanting capital allowances, are now empty and not producing any income to cover mortgage repayments.

Residential properties in the designated Border-Midlands-West (BMW) region were frequently bought by city slickers as a structure to minimize tax, with higher prices paid than those any locals could afford. Many of the units were never rented, or were let at very low rates, which didn't worry investors too much as long as capital prices were still going up. The prices have since collapsed and many such investors are now sitting on negative equity, as well as struggling to meet mortgage repayments.

There were also tax breaks for the construction of multi-storey car parks at a time of soaring car ownership and enormous demand from motorists for places to park because of limited on-street spaces. The car parks would have been built anyway because of the ability of the business to yield immediate cash. Investors were able to offset all of the costs against all of their income, meaning that for many years they may have paid no tax.

The cost of tax relief for schemes such as multi-storey car parks, hotels and student accommodation in 2006 – the last year for which figures are available – was €421 million.

It suited a coterie, many of whom were well connected with Fianna Fáil, to keep it all going for as long as possible: the land-owners, the developers, the auctioneers, the solicitors, the accountants and the bankers. It created jobs and associated tax revenues, but the process destroyed fairness in the tax system . . . and resulted in massively higher property prices and rents and increases in other taxes. The impact of these incentives on the exchequer may explain why McCreevy failed to index-link movements in tax credits and tax bands for ordinary tax-payers. After re-election in 2002, he also hiked indirect taxes, such as VAT, which tend to act disproportionately against those on lower incomes.

The incentives were allowed to continue even when it became clear that they no longer served their original purpose of promoting growth that otherwise would not have happened. The availability of cheap money lit the fuse but the incentives had the effect of pouring petrol on to the blazing fire.

Cowen said in his budget speech of December 2005 that 'I was in a position to ensure that ordinary people get the benefit of the economic growth which has been driving tax revenues, while avenues for exploitation of the system by a small number of higher earners have been restricted. And the most extensive review of special tax reliefs in over a decade has directly guided my hand in deciding which of these reliefs should be phased out, and which should be continued.'

His success in rooting out such tax incentive schemes was somewhat more limited than he claimed, but it was better than nothing. And by implication it was a damning indictment of what McCreevy had put in place.

The tax laws apply to everybody in the same way. However, if you are wealthy and powerful, and have access to the best legal and accounting brains, and can afford to pay for their services, it is possible to reduce taxes in a way that, in reality, is only available in theory to others. Politicians – often in awe of business or anticipating spin-off benefits for their parties – can sometimes be slow to change the laws, or close loopholes, in a way that ensures fairness prevails, even if the potential for increased revenues is available, sometimes claiming that other wider economic benefits arise from the chosen arrangements.

Nobody likes paying more tax than they have to, which is why most individuals ensure that they claim whatever credits are available to them each year so as to reduce their income taxes. The opportunities for most people are few and far between. However, the more money that is involved, and the bigger the income of the tax payer, the more opportunities become available – and it can be done legally.

Companies – or their bosses – can be obsessive about finding ways to reduce their tax liabilities, and it provides something of a metaphorical badge of honour when completed successfully, even if the tax demands in Ireland on companies are low, with corporation tax rates set at just 12.5 per cent and capital gains tax at 20 per cent. Even those low rates have not been good enough for some corporate bosses, who have gone to extreme, and mostly legal, lengths to minimize their contribution to the Irish exchequer, sometimes by using offshore companies.

There is a necessary distinction to be drawn between tax avoidance – the lawful mitigation of a tax bill – and tax evasion, which, for example, could involve incorrectly declaring income or expenses and credits to reduce the amount of money that should be paid. The Revenue Commissioners have special anti-avoidance powers available; the Revenue can say that while a measure or scheme appears to be within the letter of the law, it is so outrageously outside of the spirit of the tax law that it cannot be allowed. However, those powers are used only very rarely.

When Frank Daly, now retired as chairman of the Revenue Commissioners but also appointed by the government to the board of Anglo Irish Bank to represent the public interest, appeared in front of the Public Accounts Committee in 2003, he said that 'in extreme cases exploiting legal loopholes is not very different from a guilty man walking free because of a legal technicality . . . Where do you cross the line when tax avoidance becomes unacceptable and drifts into tax evasion? For the people who say "You can interpret tax law any way you want and fair dues to you if you get away with an acceptable interpretation", if those people's houses were burgled or they were knocked off their bicycles and the perpetrator got away on a creative technical interpretation of the law, they would probably be the first to shout that it was wrong and would question the kind of system we have here. This is a philosophical debate.'

Another tax adviser, who preferred not to be named from this book, said 'there is no natural or inherent right on the part of the state to take part of any individual's income or wealth.' He said the obligation to pay is limited to the obligation posed by the law and all tax planning does is organize affairs so as to minimize the exposure to pay tax. 'It is not only legitimate, it is natural and sensible,' he said. His definition of tax avoidance – 'carrying out a commercial transaction in a way that does not attract tax, whereas doing it in a different way would' – would appeal to many powerful and wealthy business figures.

PART IV

They haven't gone away,
you know

14

Home and away

The economy wasn't booming when Bertie Ahern, as Minister for Finance, introduced new rules for residency back in 1994 that would have serious implications for the state's ability to raise tax and for the level of payments that those able to take advantage of the new rules would have to make.

Ahern did away with existing tax rules about 'place of abode'– where someone lived – and 'centre of vital interest' – which defined where the substantial business investments of such individuals were held. Ahern brought in a simple time rule: a non-resident – even with homes here or substantial commercial interests – could spend a maximum of 183 days in one year in Ireland, followed by just eighty in the next, and not be liable for Irish tax on his non-Irish income. The beneficiaries were much happier about this, as previously it had been near impossible to keep a major house or estate in the country and still claim not to be living here. Some prominent businessmen are understood to have opted for departure soon afterwards; it was no great hardship, as they travelled extensively anyway and were often absent from the country for lengthy periods.

Ahern's supporters said that he had good reasons for making his decision. There was a perception that newly wealthy Irish people would stop investing in this country and take their capital elsewhere if, for example, they did not get incentives that somehow matched those available to the multinational corporations coming to Ireland. The return for continuing to invest in Ireland was the ability to legitimately and legally keep some profits made offshore free of Irish tax.

It is hardly an onerous regime, either. A 1999 Revenue Commissioners document casts serious doubts on the workability of the residency rules. The document warned of 'the risk that some of the richest 100 may be officially non-resident for tax purposes and yet in reality live here', giving rise to criticism from those who felt too great a compromise had been indulged and that more tax should be taken from our non-resident rich if they continued to have major and profitable investments in Ireland. It has been estimated, in official documents, that there may be as many as 3,000 people who benefit from these tax rules.

Few, however, are likely to make too much use of the so-called 'Cinderella Rule'. This allows a non-resident to enter the country at any time after midnight and do as he likes; as long as he's gone before midnight the day spent in the country does not count for tax purposes. In the era of private jets, anecdotal evidence suggests that some seriously rich businessmen do indeed go to the ball – and leave before midnight so they do not fall foul of the Cinderella Rule. Some are said to be regular fixtures at sporting and social events and attend many business meetings in the country. Some have families who live here on a long-term basis, even when the husband is travelling.

The Revenue Commissioners have tests and what they call 'an intelligence dimension' that they won't reveal. They admit to reading the newspapers in order to see who's in town. They have legal powers too: they can uncover breaches of the residence rules. The Irish Aviation Authority keeps details, for eighteen months, of flight plans of privately owned aircraft that fly in and out of the country. But, crucially, it has no details on the passenger lists of private planes. This raises the question of how it would be possible to prove who flew where and when in the event of a dispute, considering that a private jet could come and go but the manifest might not be checked. It appears, though, that in recent years the Revenue has been far more proactive, carrying out spot checks on the Irish homes of non-residents, monitoring flights of private jets more actively, seeking phone logs, diaries and even details of cash withdrawals made from ATMs. Credit card transactions, bank statements and passport records are also sought, and in 2005 the Revenue Commissioners started a series of audits.

Ahern, during his time as Taoiseach, was put under enormous pressure in the Dáil on a number of occasions to defend and justify the tax arrangements that were available to wealthy citizens. 'There is nothing illegal about people emigrating from the state for tax reasons,' he told Socialist TD Joe Higgins in April 2000. 'There are many such people, entertainers, musicians, footballers and others. The deputy wishes to castigate them as not being good Irish people because they leave the state for tax reasons. I am sure they do so for that reason and I am sure they gain as a result.'

Ahern went further. 'I take the view that Mr J. P. McManus, like the people who have given the state an art collection recently and the people who gave the state heritage properties and so forth, does his bit . . . They are luckier in that they are wealthier than me or the deputy. It is sad that when somebody does something for the state everybody starts looking under every stone to find something they did wrong in the past. I do not know J. P. McManus – sometimes I wish I did so that I could get a few good tips on the horses – but I know of him.'

In November 2002 he told the Dáil: 'There is a reality that some people are wealthier than others and neither I nor the deputy [again Higgins] are going to change that . . . All that we can do is make the tax system as fair as possible and ensure people pay taxes. I am long enough in the world to realize that people pay taxes in different ways. One can cite the old argument but the fact remains that, when what the rich pay in tax is added up, much more tax is probably gained from them in different ways.'

Replying to Labour leader Pat Rabbitte in May 2004, Ahern said: 'The argument which has been used for a long time is that there are many people, some termed non-resident, who come here and pay tax, who spend quite a lot of money and have many businesses in this country. They generate a good deal of wealth. They could go elsewhere or stay elsewhere and it is better to have them in the country over a longer period . . . The reason for the operation of the clause is that it was agreed it was better to have these people spending as many days as possible in the state. That means they have directorships, investments and property here. They spend money while they are here, probably more than the rest of us would in the entire year.'

In late 2008 finance minister Brian Lenihan announced his intention to introduce a crackdown on the Cinderella Rule as part of his budget for 2009. The timing of this headline-grabbing move surprised some people. Not only was it going to be difficult to implement but it was going to be limited in its impact because it was coming so late in the economic cycle. Even if the Revenue Commissioners succeeded in proving that some multimillionaires and billionaires had outstayed their welcome – and were liable therefore for tax in Ireland on their worldwide income – they were likely to find that there wasn't all that much income and profit upon which taxes could be levied. Many of the Irish super-rich suffered financially during the massive economic downturn. Vast profits from the sale of Irish-based assets that these individuals held from abroad, or from assets that they assembled overseas, often from money first made in Ireland, may have become a thing of the past.

As it happened Lenihan did not introduce the anticipated changes in the 2009 Finance Act or in the supplementary budget he issued in April 2009. When I asked him why he had changed his mind, he fell back on some of the old arguments that Ahern had made before about the contribution that these people made to Irish society. He also cited the tax that they paid on their Irish assets and investments.

Lenihan launched his defence despite a very recent controversy involving a prominent businessman who had exploited the type of loophole that angers the critics so much. In early 2009 businessman Gerry McCaughey – a former PD election candidate – was appointed as the new chairman of the Dublin Docklands Development Authority. He resigned a month later when it emerged that he had avoided payment of about €4 million in capital gains tax on the sale of his shares in Century Homes to Kingspan in 2005. Although he had done nothing illegal, there was uproar on the discovery that he had taken advantage of the double taxation agreement between Ireland and Italy by selling his shares in Century to his wife, who then sold them to Kingspan as part of an overall transaction. His new wife, Sophie, had moved to Italy for one year to become tax resident in anticipation of this deal and on its completion paid only a tiny fraction of the tax that would have fallen due here. The McCaugheys were following an example set by Shane Ryan, son of the late Tony Ryan. Lorraine Kinsella, Tony's wife, moved to Italy prior to buying some of his shares in Ryanair. He gave her a loan to buy the shares; she sold them for €19 million, repaid the loan to her husband and paid tax of under €40,000 in Italy.

When he was Minister for Finance, Charlie McCreevy tightened the rules in 2002 to make it harder to avoid capital gains tax on the sale of an asset. Previously a seller had to be out of the country for three years before he could avoid tax; this was increased to five years. There is also a three-year cooling off period before an individual can start to avoid income tax by going offshore.

We are not entitled, because of provisions in the constitution, to know the exact tax status of any citizen. There is no list detailing the tax status of Irish citizens available for public consumption. Some of those who are commonly referred to as having a tax non-residence status take grave offence when this is discussed in the media. One such person once sent me a solicitor's letter warning me not to discuss his tax status and said that it had no basis in law. I had no intention of doing so.

In an interview in 2004 to mark receiving the 'man of the year' award from *Business and Finance* magazine, Dermot Desmond declared: 'I am not a tax exile. Through my various investments in Ireland, I create millions in tax revenue in Ireland. I could have all of these jobs in India. The reason I left is to have the freedom to do what I want to do. I'm avoiding politicians, I'm avoiding the press and I'm avoiding small-minded people.'

In a 1994 interview for the *Irish Independent* I asked Tony O'Reilly about his tax status. He bridled visibly and launched into a lengthy list of the taxes his companies paid in Ireland and the benefits to the state that he believed his introduction of capital created. When I made a *Primetime Investigates* documentary about legal tax avoidance in 2005, O'Reilly's public relations helper Jim Milton told that me that O'Reilly did not fall into the same category as others who had left to protect their profits or income from Irish tax; he left to go to the United States for work reasons initially and then never came back on a full-time basis, although he reinvested a sizeable portion of his fortune from food group Heinz, where he had become the boss, in Irish assets.

The Edge and Bono of U2 made similar claims when pushed on their tax status in 2009, the singer excusing the arrangements into which their company had entered on the basis that 'we are just part of a system that has benefited the nation greatly.'

Proponents of the existing system argue that to curb the amount of time these people spend in the country, or to increase the amount of tax they must pay, could be counter-productive. The fear is that there would be a flight of capital and that jobs would be lost. Other tax revenue that is dependent on their investments might suddenly disappear.

In addition to Desmond, O'Reilly and U2, some of Ireland's richest men, such as John Magnier, Michael Smurfit, J. P. McManus and Denis O'Brien, are known to spend enormous amounts of time abroad, and also to own many Irish assets; it is likely that they have structured their tax affairs to their own advantage, as is their right under the constitution as long as they follow the tax laws of the state as they apply. There is no suggestion that any of them have ever done anything other than follow the tax laws to the letter.

Judging by some media commentary, the amassing of wealth by these individuals is regarded as a great achievement and a cause of celebration, irrespective of whether worthwhile or innovative products or services have been delivered to customers, or whether they prospered by speculation. These men act as an inspiration to many up-and-coming businessmen, judging by newspaper interviews in which they're asked to name their heroes. How much tax they pay in Ireland doesn't seem to be an issue, as long as they introduce capital and create wealth and give to what is perceived to be the common good in other ways; when it comes to tax they are arranging their affairs legally, just as anybody else of rational mind would.

Many have remained very active in Irish life and have contributed greatly in their own ways, often as philanthropists. O'Reilly and O'Brien have given substantial time and money to charitable, cultural and educational projects, with O'Reilly's Ireland Fund in particular having great success globally for over thirty years and O'Brien establishing an international foundation for human rights defenders, as well as performing an acclaimed role in chairing the Special Olympics World Games in 2003. McManus is a hero in Limerick for his educational, sporting and charitable donations. As well as being a charitable donor, Desmond has been highly active in legally testing the legitimacy of planning applications in parts of Dublin, although that could also be regarded as including an element of self-interest. All have been major donors to third-level educational institutions.

These men often kept their activities out of the public eye. Such altruism does not meet with universal approval, and has prompted allegations that donations like these are 'voluntary taxes'; others have to pay into a general fund and don't have the luxury of being able to dictate which causes or locations should benefit.

The beneficiaries of favourable tax residency rules are resident in a wide variety of countries, even though regulars at many events in Ireland. Some became non-residents many years ago. Michael Smurfit said that he became non-resident after his first marriage ended and because he spent much of his time travelling on business anyway. The late Tony Ryan, founder of Ryanair, was a resident of Monaco but owned a massive estate in Mexico, where he served as Ireland's Honorary Consul, as well as the Lyons Estate near Dublin, where he died in 2007.

Smurfit was the best-known Irish tax non-resident with an address in Monaco, where he also gloried in the title of Irish Honorary Consul. The principality is practically tax-free, although it is a very expensive place to live or own property. Smurfit, however, spends much of his time on the high seas on his €50 million yacht, the *Lady Ann Magee*, for which he has commissioned a more expensive replacement, or in a house in Marbella in Spain that is reputed to have cost about €25 million to build. He also has a palatial pad overlooking the fifteenth tee at the K Club at Straffan in County Kildare, where he fulfilled his ambition of hosting golf's 2006 Ryder Cup. Bertie Ahern performed the official opening of the house.

Gibraltar is the main corporate base for Desmond. He owns a substantial property on Dublin's most expensive suburban street, Ailesbury Road in Dublin 4, and a five-storey Georgian townhouse on Merrion Square near Government Buildings. Gibraltar is also very popular because companies registered there pay no VAT or capital gains tax, and most companies pay corporation tax at a rate of less than 10 per cent. Malta is popular because it does not charge tax on assets or income not brought into the jurisdiction and requires the resident to be there for only a day or two each year. Therefore, profits made elsewhere in the world can be declared in Malta and taxed subject to its regime. O'Brien spent time there as well as in Ireland, although his actual tax residence status is not known. He owns a collection of some of the most expensive houses in Ireland, including s specially built mansion on the grounds of Mount Juliet golf course in Kilkenny.

O'Reilly was long a resident of the Bahamas – where he has a house in the gated enclosure for millionaires called Lyford Cay – but when in Ireland he has the choice of the use of an estate in Kildare called Castlemartin, a Georgian townhouse in Dublin on Fitzwilliam Square and a luxury holiday home in Glandore, County Cork, although he spends a large amount of his time in a beautiful chateau in Normandy, where legend has it William the Conqueror once lived.

Some of the super-wealthy tend to choose Switzerland as a base, possibly because both capital gains tax and inheritance taxes can be avoided in certain Swiss cantons (regions). The most famous Irish Swiss residents are the horse-racing friends J. P. McManus and John Magnier.

One deal that they completed in 2005 highlighted the advantages of foreign tax residency. The duo, through their Bahamas-based company Cubic Investments, made a highly visible purchase of nearly a quarter of the shares in Manchester United. When they sold to the American Malcolm Glazer, who remains owner, their profit was estimated at about €125 million. If, at the time of the transaction, they had established residence in one of the Swiss cantons, the profit would have been taxed in Switzerland instead of in Ireland, making it exempt from capital gains tax.

Such examples are few and far between, because usually the details of profits are kept confidential. It is estimated, however, that Desmond may have made a profit of as much as £1 billion when he sold London City Airport in an extraordinary deal in 2006. It is to be expected that the sale of shares in Esat Telecom is likely to have given rise to a very substantial tax liability in the region of €55 million. However, it is not known if any actual liability to CGT arose for O'Brien, given the fact that he lived in Portugal at the time and probably only visited Ireland under the Cinderella Rule.

These people pay some tax in Ireland and the amounts can be sizeable. The rent from any properties is taxable – although they would be able to shelter some of this income from tax by owning other particular types of property that produce designated tax benefits under the incentive schemes discussed earlier. Profits from the sale of land would be taxable, irrespective of where the owner is resident. Income from directorships of Irish companies or salaries for performing duties as an employee would also be taxable.

What they don't pay may be significant. As the profits made by many of the tax non-residents remain unknown, the Revenue struggles to know how much potential tax revenue is lost to it. The loss to the Exchequer has not been quantified publicly, because it cannot be calculated under the current system. Conceivably it may run into tens, and possibly as much as hundreds, of millions of euro each year. The beneficial rules for these people remained even when it became clear that attracting foreign capital was no longer a problem and after a more sympathetic tax regime for those living here had been put in place. Lower income and substantially lower capital gains tax rates since the late 1990s didn't encourage most tax non-residents to return to full-time living in Ireland.

15

Stay (Faraway, So Close)

The Irish launch of U2's album *No Line on the Horizon* in March 2009 certainly tested the old adage about there being no such thing as bad publicity. A brilliantly plotted international marketing campaign for the album – which resulted in masses of publicity in Britain and the United States as well as in Ireland – was accompanied by protests in Dublin and then London over U2's tax status that got a considerable amount of coverage.

The band was somewhat unlucky, as the album was launched as recession turned to depression; people prepared for massive tax increases in an emergency budget in April and a much lower standard of living as job losses soared. Many people were looking for scapegoats, as U2 drummer Larry Mullen noted in a *Sunday Independent* interview some months later in which he complained about a negative attitude towards the rich. A nation that hadn't taken too much notice of tax avoidance during the boom years had become somewhat intolerant of some of those who could afford to minimize their tax liabilities by strategic tax planning.

U2's tax status is somewhat complicated. The personal tax arrangements of its five business members – Paul Hewson (Bono), Dave Evans (The Edge), Adam Clayton, Larry Mullen and the manager, Paul McGuinness – are not known. However, some of the business assets of U2 were transferred in 2006, when U2's corporate residency was moved to the Netherlands, to allow the income they produced to be distributed to the owners in a 'tax efficient manner' because of more favourable tax rates on artistic royalties in that country. That decision has led to claims that U2 is avoiding the payment of tax in Ireland by paying a smaller amount elsewhere. It is legal, but Bono's previous exhortations to the Irish government as to how to spend its tax revenues on overseas aid were cited quickly when the perception developed that he was limiting his own contribution to the pot. Bono has said he was 'hurt' and 'stung' by the criticism he endured for this decision, but there had been criticism even before that because he, and the band, had been among the beneficiaries of another controversial, and legal, tax arrangement previously.

Up until 2006 U2 enjoyed extraordinarily favourable tax treatment in Ireland, along with many others. A special tax exemption scheme for artists had been introduced in 1969 by Minister for Finance Charles Haughey. Income derived from artistic publishing was exempt from tax. The idea of the tax break was to help struggling artists with low and uncertain income. The artists' exemption provision allowed U2's members to earn tax-free royalty income while remaining resident in Ireland.

However, the exemption for artistic income was costing the state tens of millions of euro in forgone tax, and a perception developed that this tax rule was not just helping the struggling artists but also others who had no need of such assistance. U2 was not the only target: so too was Bertie Ahern's daughter Cecelia, who had become an internationally successful writer of commercial fiction, some of which had been developed for American movies and television.

A cap of €250,000 on tax-free incomes for artists was introduced in 2006 by Minister for Finance Brian Cowen. It was only once that generous amount was surpassed that tax was levied on the rest. The new limit would be more than enough tax-free income for most people, but not necessarily when the balance on which tax of 41 per cent plus levies could be applied ran into millions of euro annually. U2 became aware of a tax loophole that the Rolling Stones had exploited, whereby the Netherlands charged a very low rate of taxation on the royalties enjoyed in music publishing.

Critics of U2 pointed out that the band and its members had been able to increase their wealth dramatically over the previous two decades by reinvesting the tax-free profits they had accrued in such a favourable environment. Having made such a fortune already, how much more did they need?

That is essentially a private matter, of course. Fans argued it was enlightened and rational self-interest to pay the minimum tax possible. It is what most people do: when they claim the cost of pension contributions against tax, for example, or the cost of having the bins collected. Why would anyone with the right accounting advice give more money to the state than legally required? Wouldn't anybody else do the same if given the opportunity? And wouldn't Bono be able to put it to better use than the government, who would only waste it?

Bono is probably the world's most influential Irishman, with ready access to the White House, the Kremlin, 10 Downing Street and Brussels, where he lobbies for Third World aid and debt relief. The occupants of the White House may change but Barack Obama is as welcoming to Bono as George Bush was; and Gordon Brown meets him just as often as Tony Blair did. He has received an honorary knighthood from Britain and various official global recognitions for his voluntary work throughout the world. He is a citizen of the world as much as Ireland but when he comes home he might be best advised to just shut up and sing.

Bono has been a tireless and outspoken advocate of improving foreign aid to Africa. Only a year before U2's company changed its corporate tax residence, Bono lectured Taoiseach Bertie Ahern from the stage of a concert at Croke Park about the government's reneging on a commitment to pay to the Third World each year a sum equivalent to 0.7 per cent of the national income by 2007. Having made the promise initially during a speech to the United Nations in Washington in 2000, as Ireland sought votes to win a UN Security Council seat, Ahern shifted the target to 2012 and said he would spend the money domestically instead. Bono engaged the crowd with his argument and it hollered its support. Earlier, in a private audience with Ahern, An Taoiseach promised that he would try to speed up efforts to realize the 0.7 per cent target sooner than 2012. He failed.

Bono has strongly advocated the unprofitable and often unpopular cause of adequate healthcare provision for those with HIV and AIDS; he has spoken forcefully for a reduction in Third World debt and for the promotion of equitable global commercial trade. He has been conscience-driven, while many others in his position would merely have enjoyed their wealth while doing little social good. The rock star shtick may repulse as many people as it attracts, with some saying that this ready access to world leaders only feeds his ego, but that is to unfairly denigrate his obvious sincerity and belief in the causes he espouses. Some of that criticism is politically motivated because he hasn't engaged in the tactics of some anti-globalization protestors, who believe bringing down Western capitalism is essential to helping the Third World poor.

When I spoke to the campaigning economist Jeffrey Sachs in Dublin in 2005, he eulogized Bono's role in the Drop the Debt campaign and subsequent events. 'He was our greatest spokesman and leader in that,' said Sachs. 'He is simply one of the most remarkable leaders in global understanding, of all the wonderful things we could do on our planet, to make life better for the poorest of the poor, to help people stay alive, to help make life safer for all of us. He has brought more people into this discussion than anyone else in the world, perhaps. I've seen it because he has his fans but he also opens doors of political leaders and gets in the villages of Africa. It's a privilege and great fun to work with him.'

But it doesn't make him immune to criticism of his own conduct at home in Ireland. Groups such as the Tax Justice Network have conducted extensive research into the international use of offshore tax havens by wealthy people and their companies, and have outlined the adverse economic effects for both rich and poor societies. The Tax Justice Network has estimated that about $250 billion per year is lost to world governments because of the use of tax shelters. The Organization for Economic Cooperation and Development has supported this, and said that use of offshore accounts is best suited to individuals who live in unstable countries where regimes may seek to seize their wealth. The OECD's centre for tax policy and administration has said that when high net worth individuals enjoy the use of offshore locations, the tax base for the countries of which these people are citizens is then reduced.

Bono's use of the Netherlands as a tax shelter for U2's royalty company has led to confrontation at embarrassing times and in unexpected places. At University College Cork in 2007, where he went to receive an honorary degree, he was asked by reporters outside afterwards to explain his tax position. 'Our tax has always been not just to the letter of the law but to the spirit of the law,' he claimed. 'This country's prosperity came out of tax innovation so it would be sort of churlish to criticize U2 for what we were encouraged to do and what brought all of these companies in the first place.'

By the spring of 2009 the pressure was really on, and Bono told the *Irish Times* that 'we pay millions and millions of dollars in tax', which was an unfortunate choice of currency given that this country trades in euro.

The Edge said, 'We do business all over the world, we pay taxes all over the world and we are totally tax compliant.' Nobody has ever accused U2 or its members of tax evasion, which is the illegal non-payment of tax. What U2 have been accused of, and which they have admitted to, is tax avoidance, legally reducing the tax payable to this state by deliberately paying it elsewhere.

Bono has attempted to elaborate upon his previous comments in Cork. 'I can understand how people outside the country wouldn't understand how Ireland got to its prosperity but everybody in Ireland knows that there are some very clever people in the government and in the Revenue who created a financial architecture that prospered the entire nation – it was a way of attracting people to this country who wouldn't normally do business here. And the financial services brought billions of dollars every year directly to the Exchequer. What's actually hypocritical is the idea that then you couldn't use a financial services centre in Holland. The real question people need to ask about Ireland's tax policy is: "Was the nation a net gain benefactor?" And of course it was – hugely so.'

Unfortunately, it was clear already that much of this 'financial architecture' had been built on very flimsy foundations and created many of the problems we are currently experiencing today.

'Anyone who knows me knows I wouldn't ask anyone to do something that I am not prepared to do myself,' Bono said in a separate interview, and his reputation suggests that is right. It's possible his own cash contribution to Africa, not to mention the time he has devoted to championing its cause, outweighs whatever taxes he has saved in Ireland. Many people in this country, however, judging by the reaction of early 2009, might have preferred him to pay the taxes in Ireland first before doing as he liked with the rest, with the result that rock music's – indeed, Ireland's – most formidable preacher has lost much of his authority to deliver further sermons in this country as to how others should behave with their money.

16

Kilmallock's answer to Santa Claus

Bertie Ahern told the Dáil in 2001 that he didn't know J. P. McManus but knew of him. He had good reason to know lots about him and to ask more. McManus had offered him £50 million towards the construction of a new national sports stadium. He had the idea before Ahern came to power in 1997, but it was Ahern who showed the interest in using it as seed capital or a deposit towards a project that got dubbed 'the Bertie Bowl'.

McManus did not offer the money as a no-strings-attached gift. It was on the condition that the sports stadium was built to McManus's standards, with no corporate name attached (in the way the name 'Hibernian Aviva' is going on to the newly redeveloped Lansdowne Road).

When Ahern set up Campus Stadium Ireland Development (CSID) in 1998 to oversee the potential project, the non-sports body representatives on the board were people well known to McManus. One was a former university lecturer called Michael Walsh, who worked for Dermot Desmond's private company International Investments and Underwriting (IIU) and represented his interests on a number of corporate boards. Another Desmond ally on CSID was Derek Keogh, formerly chief executive of the state airports authority Aer Rianta when Desmond was chairman. McManus had given Keogh the task of visiting stadia throughout the world, looking for examples of what should be emulated if McManus invested. Lucy Gaffney, one of Denis O'Brien's most trusted executives, who has regularly represented his interests on corporate boards, was also included.

The nominee with the lowest profile was a Limerick-based solicitor called John Power, who does much of his work for McManus, spending a lot of time in Geneva on his behalf.

I met Power once, at the request of public relations consultant Jim

Milton of Murray Consultants. Milton had rung to berate me for an article I'd written in the *Sunday Tribune* in which I'd criticized the apparent vulgarity of some of McManus's fund-raising exploits: for example, millionaires bidding £1 million plus to play a round of golf with Tiger Woods, or the same to buy a specially commissioned painting of McManus and friends, or spending over €600,000 on a car.

Power was very worried by what he regarded as my negative attitude towards McManus and what he perceived as his friend's generosity towards the state. He wanted to convince me of all the good McManus had done for Limerick and wanted to do for Ireland.

The donations McManus has made in Limerick are legendary. His charitable foundation has raised at least €60 million for local causes since he became non-resident for tax purposes in 1994. Cancer clinics, youth services, mental health help providers and religious organizations have benefited. He provided €5 million for a business school at the University of Limerick, named, apparently with no sense of irony, after the city's most famous and committed socialist, Jim Kemmy. He sponsored Limerick GAA with €5 million per year and gave another €4 million to wipe out most of the debts incurred in revamping the local Gaelic Grounds. It was revealed early in 2009 that he was the mystery donor who had contributed €4 million towards the cost of rebuilding the iconic Thomond Park rugby stadium, where Munster beat the New Zealand All Blacks rugby team in 1978 and came so close to doing so again in the thirtieth anniversary rematch in November 2008.

The day after that match he and his friend Padraig Harrington – winner of three golf majors by then – announced details of the 2010 golf classic that Tiger Woods would attend. The previous three, in 1995, 2000 and 2005, raised about €30 million. Woods, together with some of the world's best golfers, played alongside businessmen who had paid heavily for the privilege and local amateurs who had won their places through a special competition that cost as little as €20 to enter.

At the 2005 event Ahern got the chance to meet a man who only years earlier he had said he didn't know. Ahern and four other ministers attended the gala charity dinner, where tickets cost €2,500 per seat, alongside many other captains of industry and finance. They dug deep into their (or their company's) pockets to buy these seats or places in the pro-am (which cost €100,000 per team) or to buy prizes at the auction.

Ministers Mary Hanafin, then at education, and Willie O'Dea were in attendance with 170 guests in 2008 when McManus presented another €200,000 worth of third-level scholarships to eight students from his old school, Coláiste Mhichíl (formerly the CBS Secondary School in Limerick) – the eleventh year of the J. P. McManus Scholarship Awards. In March 2008 he announced the establishment of a €30 million national fund, devoted to the All-Ireland Scholarships, which every year gave 118 students €6,750 each to help defray the costs of attending a third-level educational establishment. In a radio interview Hanafin praised this 'good example of philanthropy' and said it was a way of having 'more social inclusion'.

One of the few voices to criticize this publicly was trade union boss Jack O'Connor of the Services, Industrial, Professional and Technical Union (SIPTU). He argued that 'philanthropy is fine as far as it goes but there should be no circumstance, whatsoever, in which people from disadvantaged backgrounds, in particular, should have to rely upon it for what is surely an entitlement.' He pointed out that Hanafin's own words of tribute to the late Donogh O'Malley – who introduced free second-level education in the 1960s – stood in sharp contrast to her praise for philanthropy. 'His [O'Malley's] legacy to all students ensured that lack of means would no longer prevent anyone from reaching their educational potential.' Accepting gifts from McManus was an implicit acknowledgement that the existing system was failing to do what was required, even before the large cutbacks of recent years.

Finding anyone to offer criticism of McManus in Limerick is difficult. He is a folk hero, his reputation being that of a Robin Hood figure who takes money off the bookmakers through his fearless gambling on horse races (and other events) and who then redistributes it to the poor.

But nobody knows just how rich he is or, most pertinently, how his largesse to the state compares with the amount of tax he has legally avoided by basing his place of residence in Switzerland. The tax lost to the state since he became non-resident after 1994 may be a multiple of the funds raised for Limerick through charitable events and donations.

It is true McManus gives money to causes that might otherwise be under-funded, particularly if the state does not provide. But the state's ability to provide is reduced by tax non-residents who don't contribute the share that we might expect from all citizens who can afford to pay.

He does not appear to have donated as much as he had intended either, as Ahern abandoned the national stadium offer after intense pressure from his coalition partners the Progressive Democrats. Indeed, it has never been confirmed officially that McManus was the one making the £50 million offer, the only legal document to support this being a letter of guarantee from Swiss bankers Pictet et Cie of Geneva, on behalf of an unknown client, saying it had the money on deposit for release in the right circumstances. The bank refused to name its client, citing confidentiality. When asked about it in the Dáil, Jim McDaid, Minister for Tourism, Sport and Recreation, replied: 'Who else do you think it is? Santa Claus?'

Mystery and secrecy have always surrounded J. P. McManus and added to the myth about his successes. His career is said to have started at the age of nine, when he put an unrecorded number of shillings on Merryman II, who went on to win the 1960 Grand National. He was just twenty when he received his first bookmaker's licence, but soon decided it could be more profitable on the other side of the track. He became a feared yet fearless punter and was given the title of the Sundance Kid as he raided events such as the annual National Hunt Festival at Cheltenham.

He had his problems in the early days. There is one tale of his putting a satchel full of cash on a 'sure thing' with a Cheltenham bookmaker and losing it all. But in 1994, after losing £30,000 on one of his own stable, Gimme Five, he bet £80,000 the following day on hot favourite Danoli, which won him £155,000 at the festival. 'That put the wheels back on the bike,' he said afterwards. He was cheered for that, rather than being seen as flash or smart-arse.

Bookies have attributed his gambling success to a tremendous mathematical brain with a remarkable facility for assessing the right odds at which to lay a wager. To work out those odds requires a rigorous application to studying form. He especially pays as much attention to the ground on which horses have run previously, as to their record of finishing positions and the opposition they have encountered. But he never chases his losses or backs for fun, as mug gamblers do. He treats it so much as a business that, at times, he has not bet on his own horses in big races because he hasn't liked the price offered by bookies.

He has long since diversified his interests, using his analytical abilities and skills of daring honed in sports gambling in playing the money markets. Dealing in currencies, bonds and derivatives also requires tremendous mathematical ability, often at high speed, and bravery to back one's own judgement, especially if one's own capital is at risk. It also requires a thorough understanding of market dynamics, the trading motivations of other dealers (which are often herd-like), human sentiment and anticipation of trends. McManus learned all of this through gambling, especially through some big bets that failed in his early years and left him with no cash. It can be presumed that the discipline he applied to his sports betting has been transferred.

It has long been rumoured that he and his great friends Dermot Desmond and John Magnier made a fortune in correctly anticipating the Mexican peso devaluation of December 1994. The profits may have run into tens of millions of pounds and provided the capital for even more speculation. The trio pool their wagers when betting on many sports events and compete together in many golf pro-am events, where they tend to be highly successful, although not always popular, because they succeed in spite of their relatively high handicaps.

McManus rode the property boom like most other wealthy Irishmen, investing heavily in expensive British properties that would be considered 'trophy assets', often alongside Magnier and young Limerickman Aidan Brooks. He has been an investor in numerous private and public companies, trading in their shares. Nobody knows how much he is worth, although it has been reported that he had an excess of assets over liabilities of over €1 billion at the height of the boom.

One of his biggest windfalls came from his investment in Manchester United alongside Magnier. Their original purchase of shares in the famous English soccer club was regarded as a gesture of friendship towards the manager Alex Ferguson, who was experiencing some difficulties in negotiating a new contract on favourable terms. However, things changed when Magnier and Ferguson fell out. Ferguson – like many figures in football, a horse-racing enthusiast who liked a bet – started his friendship with McManus and Magnier around the turn of the century. He became involved with a two-year-old horse called Rock of Gibraltar, which turned into a highly successful Group 1 winner as a three-year-old. Ferguson was described as co-owner, along with Susan Magnier, and accompanied the horse into the winners' enclosure on some of the seven occasions that it won Group 1 races. Rock of Gibraltar's success on the racetrack was lucrative in itself, but it also held out the potential for massive returns at stud. Rock's ownership was critical because in 2004, his first year at stud, his income was estimated at nearly €10 million.

Magnier informed Ferguson that he was a racing owner, but not a stud owner, of Rock of Gibraltar. The Scot was furious and threatened legal action, but he was to suffer the rare experience of being out of his league. Magnier was well experienced at this type of brinkmanship. The Irish duo bought more shares to put pressure on Ferguson and started asking questions about the Scot at shareholder meetings that caused some embarrassment. It became known that they had hired the Kroll detective agency to help them formulate the questions that they had put at an annual general meeting. Ferguson folded and was made to look like little more than a mascot for the canny Irishman, the famous front-man who had increased the publicity for the horse by guiding it into the winners' enclosure. McManus and Magnier sold to the American Malcolm Glazer and Ferguson has gone on to enjoy even greater successes as manager. But the assembly of a shareholding large enough to produce a subsequent £125 million profit – and which was free from tax in Ireland – made people realize how rich the two Irishmen were.

Vast profits such as this explain why, like Magnier, McManus moved to Switzerland in the mid-nineties, returning to his 400-acre farm, Martinstown Stud at Kilmallock in County Limerick, only at weekends. He lives officially in Geneva, in the suburb of Cologny, overlooking the lake, and each day travels to his office in the Rue du Rhone, where the view from his sixth-floor office captures the snow-capped Mont Blanc beyond the River Rhone. A mid-1990s newspaper profile of McManus's new life pointed out that he paid more attention to the computer screens showing movements on the money markets and bookmakers' ante-post prices than the beautiful view. He usually travels on his privately owned Gulfstream V jet, a €45 million plane that – like his pal Desmond's aircraft and the government jet – has a range of several thousand miles. He also has access to a Bell 403 twin-engine helicopter at the airport to bring him onwards to home, which is the biggest private residence built in the state's history.

McManus spent up to €100 million on building a new mansion at his old Martinstown Stud. The 40,000 square-foot property, which is about twenty-seven times the size of the average modern house and is 5,000 square feet larger than the official state residence at Farmleigh in the

Phoenix Park, has nine bedrooms and features a 200-seat cinema, gym with eighteen-metre pool, sauna, steam room, hot tubs, a garage with car wash, a vast wine cellar and a 'panic room'. One report has said it has a room of 2,500 square feet for the dogs. Built in a faux-Palladian style, and designed by the Swiss architect Andre Durr, the bill for the interior marble and granite may have come to €25 million, with the sandstone cladding adding a further €10 million. The staircase is among the largest ever built in Europe.

Outside is a lake of nearly 60,000 square feet (just under 1.25 acres). The original idea – which the planners rejected – was for a lake to cover an area of over five times that size, which would have been almost two and a half times the size of Croke Park. Its border was to resemble that of the Limerick county boundary but the local authority requested that the applicant, Noreen McManus, supply a revised version of the plan in which artificial embankments were minimized and gently sloping grades were used instead. When planning for the smaller lake was granted, the eleven conditions included one that no motorized vehicles be used on the lake and that the proposed boathouse, which is to be constructed near by, must not be used for any activity apart from those relating to the lake. No fish are to be stocked in the lake without prior written approval of the planning authority.

While the planning authorities may not have given him a free pass, the local county council has shown itself more obliging. In 2007, when his only daughter Sue Ann was marrying Kerryman Cian Foley, McManus paid Limerick County Council a substantial undisclosed fee to have all roads leading to the local Catholic church and his house resurfaced and drained. The work was speeded up to meet the wedding deadline, and hedges and ditches along the roads around Martinstown were cut back and trimmed in time too.

McManus also paid for a total refurbishment of the local church. According to the *Irish Independent*, 'the church ceiling received three coats of white paint, the walls are cream and the back of the altar has been painted a dark red. All the pews were removed during refurbishments and varnished.' The church grounds were completely dug up, reseeded and rolled, and landscaped. A spectacular flower bed was put at the entrance of the grounds.

A giant marquee for up to 1,000 guests was erected at the front entrance to the McManus estate because the house was not ready to host the event. The happy couple received the present of a 145-acre estate in nearby Grange, which is reputed to have cost the proud father €4.5 million.

Martinstown was 160 acres in size when McManus originally bought it, but he also purchased about 450 acres of surrounding farmland to stop the public from viewing its exterior and to provide for security. The last piece of the jigsaw was the local Staker Wallace GAA grounds. He bought its land and built a replacement venue for it near by with a pavilion and playing pitches.

Few in the area begrudge him any enjoyment of his wealth, as he remains enormously popular because of his down-to-earth manner and continuing love for the things and people with whom he grew up, despite living in an entirely different fashion now.

And few remember the controversy in which McManus was caught up in the early 1990s, when he was one of the key figures in a property deal that contributed greatly to the fall of Charles Haughey as Taoiseach.

17

Charlie's loyal friend

Businessman Ben Dunne – once in control of supermarket retail giant Dunnes Stores until his family removed him because of his erratic behaviour and bought out his shares in the company – unintentionally destroyed what remained of Charlie Haughey's reputation years after the Fianna Fáil leader stepped down both from the party helm and as Taoiseach.

Details of Dunne's multimillion-pound donations to Haughey did not come until late 1996 and early 1997, nearly five years after Haughey had left office, following the disclosure that Dunne had funded serving minister Michael Lowry's £300,000 house extension. The former boss of the Dunnes Stores retail and supermarket chain was excoriated by the Moriarty Tribunal for corrupting Haughey. Dunne was furious at the tribunal's findings. While he had no choice but to concede the making of the payments, he felt the tribunal should have recognized that when he made them his judgement was impaired because of the serious trauma he had suffered after his kidnapping by the IRA in the early 1990s.

Dunne did not face legal retribution or public opprobrium as a result of the tribunal's findings, even though it stated that Haughey had interfered with a tax assessment on Dunnes Stores. Instead, Dunne was indulged as some sort of national character to be enjoyed, especially by RTÉ, which has used him in recent years as a panellist on a television consumer show and occasionally gives him a platform for so-called 'straight talking' on political and business issues on Joe Duffy's *Liveline*. It seems that because he has been so forthright about his drink and drug addictions some have forgiven or forgotten his past.

But Dunne was not the only prominent businessman to have his financial links to Haughey outlined in detail at the Moriarty Tribunal.

Dermot Desmond – reputed at the height of the Celtic Tiger era to be a billionaire – was forced to reveal many details about his own relationship with Haughey and to debate the benefits that may have arisen in public forums, much to his displeasure.

Desmond didn't give Haughey as much money as Dunne but he gave large amounts and at significant times. Unlike Dunne, Desmond has never made any apology or excuse for it, saying about his relationship with Haughey: 'He did me the biggest favour: he believed in me.'

Desmond had returned to Ireland in the 1980s after a short spell working for the World Bank in Kabul, where he grew the distinctive moustache that has led to his being nicknamed 'The Kaiser'. He left Afghanistan after the Russian invasion. He began a money-broking business, NCB, in 1981, when he was thirty-one and expanded into stockbroking in 1984, buying a firm called Dillon and Waldron and later sacking its most high-profile employee, Shane Ross. NCB thrived and Desmond abandoned money-broking in 1988.

He timed his entry to the sector brilliantly, seeing the industry as old-fashioned and slow to react to international developments, especially in the use of technology. He was envied by his traditional rivals for the way in which he picked up new business, mocked by the private school Southside set for his Dublin Northside accent and disdained for his naked ambition. His comment in an interview that 'greed is a great motivator of people' made him seem like an Irish version of Gordon Gekko, a fictional character in the 1987 hit movie *Wall Street*.

What really irked rivals was how NCB gained state contracts, as he assiduously courted Haughey on his return to power. Between 1987 and 1991 NCB won key roles in the stock market debuts of the state-owned companies Irish Life and Irish Sugar (renamed Greencore). NCB worked for the state-owned Aer Lingus (there was controversy when a file on its helicopter division was sent, apparently mistakenly, to the Haughey family-owned Celtic Helicopters, because the courier got mixed up about the address), Telecom Éireann and the ESB.

Desmond advised Pernod Ricard, the French drinks company, in its takeover of the whiskey and spirits company Irish Distillers. Desmond's tactics were regarded as inspired, especially when he managed to secure a deal at 450p per share, although a rival bidder offered 525p. Fruit-distribution company Fyffes was a major shareholder in Irish Distillers and much was later made of a suggestion by its representative Jim Flavin that Desmond should go to Haughey's home at Kinsealy to secure the tax-clearance certificate in relation to the proposed deal. Flavin waved away the suggestion as a 'joke'.

Desmond later claimed a £2 million fee from Pernod Ricard for NCB's role in the successful takeover and wrote 'we orchestrated entirely the successful campaign to get a positive tax opinion from the Revenue Commissioners, which involved using personal contacts at the highest level, including the Minister for Finance and the secretaries of the departments of the Taoiseach and Industry and Commerce.' He also said: 'We used up a large proportion of the favours we can call upon from our political contacts – and no doubt we will pay a price on the other side.'

When this emerged during Haughey's last months as Taoiseach, there was uproar in the Dáil, and Haughey described Desmond's claims as 'absurd'. He insisted he never extended any special favours to NCB.

Desmond also developed relationships with the likes of high-profile businessman Michael Smurfit, who made NCB his company's European broker. Desmond was central to Smurfit's involvement in a major public controversy in 1991 that led to Smurfit's resignation as chairman of the state-owned Telecom Éireann. The episode further undermined an already weakened Haughey, during a period in which business scandals dominated politics and media attention.

In 1990 the *Irish Independent* reported that Smurfit had been a shareholder in the company that sold a piece of land to Telecom that year for £9.4 million. The land was the former Johnson Mooney & O'Brien bakery in Ballsbridge, which Telecom had purchased as a site on which to develop a new corporate headquarters. The story implied an enormous conflict of interest on Smurfit's part, given the use of state money. Desmond immediately contacted the newspaper to say that this was incorrect, and he forced it to publish a front-page retraction and apology to Smurfit.

That would have been that, only the *Irish Times* published its own story in September 1991 saying that Smurfit actually had a recent involvement in the history of the ownership of the land. An incredibly complicated tale emerged. A company called United Property Holdings (UPH) had originally agreed in August 1989 to buy the land from the bakery's liquidator for just £4 million. UPH was an investment company run by Desmond in which he had managed to persuade many wealthy businessmen to invest: these included Martin Naughton and Lochlann Quinn of the electrical manufacturers Glen Dimplex, and his friends J. P. McManus, John Magnier and Smurfit.

UPH, in turn, quickly sold the land to another company called Chestvale, for £6.3 million, giving UPH's shareholders an immediate and handsome profit, although, as it turned out, not as much as might have been available. It was Chestvale that was to sell the land to Telecom less than a year later for a profit of £3.1 million.

The identity of the owner of Chestvale was unknown at the time, although later a Donegal businessman called Pat Doherty emerged to claim that the company was his. Chestvale was represented legally by a solicitor called Noel Smyth, who came to prominence many years later for his role in advising Ben Dunne over his payments to Charles Haughey (Dunne had nothing to do with this particular property deal, however).

Around this time Smurfit was shown the site by auctioneer John Finnegan and was 'excited' by the possibility it offered to Telecom as a location. Smurfit apparently didn't know that the site had been briefly owned by UPH, a company in which he was a shareholder. Telecom was told that Desmond could help in securing ownership of the site and engaged him to act as an intermediary with Chestvale in buying it, not knowing, as was to emerge subsequently, that Desmond was involved with Chestvale too, although not as a shareholder.

It was the High Court-appointed inspector, solicitor John Glackin, who, in 1993, got as close to the bottom of Desmond's involvement in the convoluted transaction as was possible. Glackin discovered that Desmond told Telecom that the 'best price' he could get for the site would be £9.4 million, the price at which the deal was completed in June 1990. That would have been merely a bad business deal for the state company if Doherty, as owner of Chestvale, pocketed the profit. However, Glackin also concluded – bitterly disputed by Desmond to this day – that Chestvale's profit went to Desmond and J. P. McManus.

Glackin discovered that when Smyth had made the offer on behalf of Chestvale to buy the property from UPH, he had acted on the specific instructions of Desmond, not Doherty, Chestvale's owner. Executives in UPH agreed the sale, apparently not knowing that Desmond, the founding shareholder of UPH, was involved in buying the land from it. Glackin also concluded, based on documents he uncovered, that Desmond already believed that Telecom would be interested in buying the site when he told Smyth to make Chestvale's offer to UPH. Fellow UPH investors Naughton and Quinn were very angry when this was disclosed publicly as they appeared to have been stiffed in the deal.

Furthermore, Glackin decided that Desmond was involved in a corporate vehicle that provided Chestvale with the loans to complete the purchase from UPH and that the bulk of the profit on the eventual sale of Chestvale to Telecom went to the lenders rather than to the owner. Of the £3.1 million profit made by Chestvale, £1.3 million was paid to an Isle of Man-registered company called Freezone Investments, which Glackin said was Desmond's.

Desmond denied this and said Freezone was owned by an old friend, Colin Probets, who had supported him in the establishment of NCB. But Glackin discovered a legal agreement from June 1988 that gave Desmond the right to take control of Freezone for just £1. Glackin regarded Desmond as the beneficial owner of Freezone and therefore in control of its profits.

He was also able to show that Desmond had control over the Freezone bank account and had taken money from it to make a number of payments. Glackin found that Desmond went to the Trustee Savings Bank in Grafton Street, Dublin, in late July 1990, where he withdrew £500,000 in cash from the Freezone account. Desmond told Glackin that he kept this money in a 'tennis holdall' and then gave it to its 'owner', Probets. Glackin found this story 'very difficult to believe'. He suggested that it probably went to J. P. McManus, who, in turn, denied getting it. The inspector believed that McManus got it because he too had been involved in making loans to Chestvale to enable it to buy the land from UPH.

Glackin came across a payment of $1.5 million to Chestvale in December 1989 from an account in the names of J. and N. (John and Noreen) McMahon held by Allied Irish Banks (Channel Islands) Ltd in Jersey. The inspector was told that these were not real people but their actual identities were not disclosed to him by AIB (Channel Islands) because its client refused to allow it. However, Glackin discovered that AIB in London held three accounts in the exact same names 'and in a written document stated that the sole signatory authorized to operate these accounts was John P. McManus'. Further documents showed the holder of these accounts to be the holder of the Jersey account.

McManus told the inspector he never made 'any loan that was directly or even indirectly related to the JMOB site', but, despite opportunities, he did not deny his interest in the London accounts. No findings were made by Glackin against McManus.

Glackin found in his report that there was no evidence to show that Smurfit was aware of the affairs of UPH at the time Telecom was purchasing the Ballsbridge site but that Desmond had a financial interest in Chestvale's successful involvement in the deal. Desmond said that the findings of Glackin represented the latter's opinions and did not constitute 'facts as found by a court of competent jurisdiction'. But he admitted to the Moriarty Tribunal many years later that he had 'unfettered discretion' in the use of the assets and accounts of Freezone. He also had 'full freedom of manoeuvre' over the affairs of Freezone and various powers of attorney over the affairs of Probets. Desmond was furious when the Moriarty Tribunal, as part of its investigation into the awarding of the second mobile phone licence, decided in 2003 to read the contents of Glackin's report into the public record and took legal action to try to prevent it. His application was rejected by both the High Court and Supreme Court.

In the same period as the Ballsbridge property deal Freezone gave money to Haughey and his family. In 1998 the Moriarty Tribunal discovered that the money for the refurbishment of Charles Haughey's yacht, the *Celtic Mist*, came from Freezone and from Dedeir, Desmond's personal investment company. The sum involved, £75,000, was more than the highest gross salary Haughey had earned in any of his years as Taoiseach. This money was described subsequently by Desmond as a 'loan', but it was unsecured and had not been repaid at the time of the tribunal hearing, which made it, to all intents and purposes, a gift. The tribunal found that 'Mr Haughey's eventual settlement with the Revenue Commissioners in respect of capital gains tax included provision for these sums' and went on to state: 'the tribunal rejects the evidence that these payments were in substance loans.'

In January 1998 Desmond issued a statement that the loan to Haughey had been 'settled'. In evidence, Desmond denied that this had been an attempt to mislead the media, because he said the matter had been settled in the sense that he had made an agreement with Haughey's son Conor that the loan would be repaid if and when the yacht was sold. As the final tribunal report noted, 'there was no writing in relation to his loan agreement with Mr Haughey and no details were discussed at the time as to the terms of the agreement. He [Desmond] agreed that the loans could not be enforced, either as regards principle or interest . . . He said it was not a matter of concern to him at all as to whether or not he was going to be repaid.'

Desmond consistently denied making any payments to Haughey while he was in power but the tribunal found he made payments of about £500,000 to members of Haughey's family and to companies associated with the Haugheys in the period 1987 to 1995. These were by way of loans, commercial advances, investments and gifts. Profits on shares purchased in Feltrim Mining, an exploration company set up by Conor Haughey in 1988, were made more by accident than by design.

After Haughey left power, Desmond made straight cash donations, although again these were called loans. Desmond gave Haughey £100,000 (stg) in 1994 after the former Taoiseach said he was considering becoming a director of a German bank. Desmond did not think it appropriate that his friend should demean himself by accepting directorships just to make money. He said the money 'was made payable as a loan, with no repayment dates, no interest rate, nothing written, same Dermot Desmond style with no security'. He also paid £25,000 (stg) to Haughey in October 1996.

The Moriarty Tribunal's final report of December 2006 said 'the tribunal cannot accept Mr Desmond's evidence that these payments were ever intended by him to be repayable by Mr Haughey.' It accused him of misleading the Revenue Commissioners and pointed out that the €5 million settlement that Haughey finally made with the Revenue Commissioners included an admission that the sums of money he had received from Desmond were gifts.

The tribunal's final report noted that 'in particular, Mr Desmond testified that he made no direct payments to Mr Haughey prior to 1994, after which Mr Haughey left office.' The tribunal found that 'while it must be said that the tribunal has heard no evidence to the contrary, the tribunal cannot make a finding to that effect as neither Mr Haughey's offshore accounts nor Mr Desmond's offshore accounts were accessible to the tribunal for the purpose of verifying this matter.'

The tribunal also detailed a special NCB account operated by Haughey's bagman Des Traynor while Haughey was still in power. A shares account operated by NCB between 1988 and 1995 contained more than £300,000 and was Haughey's, although official ownership resided in the Cayman Islands.

Desmond was the 'contact man' in NCB for the account until 1991 and money from it was used to pay some of Haughey's bills. Traynor gave the instructions, along with two other key players in the Ansbacher scam, Padraig Collery and John Furze. Desmond said he did not know who the beneficial owner was. The tribunal's final report said 'Desmond must have considered these accounts to be of sufficient importance to warrant his personal involvement.'

The tribunal noted that 'Mr Desmond maintained throughout his evidence that these payments were prompted by no more than friendship for Mr Haughey, a friendship which it is clear arose in the context of Mr Haughey's office as Taoiseach. Taking all of these circumstances into account, it is the tribunal's view that they do give rise to a reasonable inference that Mr Desmond's motive for making these payments was connected with the public office of Taoiseach, which had been held formerly by Mr Haughey.'

No official action was taken against Desmond by the state after the Glackin report was published in the summer of 1993. Desmond never published an alternative report to set out the truth, as he promised. He said he couldn't because he didn't trust any journalist enough to publish it in full. Although the option of publishing his own version in full on the internet was not available to him in 1993, he could have done this at the time the Moriarty Tribunal read the Glackin findings into its public record, much to his fury.

Despite the findings of the Glackin report, Desmond did not suffer any practical difficulties in his business as a result.

There was considerable surprise in the summer of 1996 when it emerged that Dermot Desmond was a 20 per cent shareholder in Esat Digifone, the company that had won a public competition a year earlier for the licence to operate the country's second mobile phone service. Most surprised of all were those members of the government who had approved the award of the licence in October 1995, not knowing that Desmond was secretly a beneficiary.

Esat Digifone was regarded as Denis O'Brien's company, even though his operation Communicorp owned just 40 per cent of it. The Norwegian state operator Telenor had 40 per cent as well. The balance was to be held by pension funds or other such passive investors. Instead, Desmond's International Investments and Underwriting (IIU) had the balance of 20 per cent (and, as it turned out, another 5 per cent for a period, which it had taken equally from the bigger two partners before selling it back to them), and this was not disclosed publicly until May 1996, just when the licence agreement was about to be signed. Indeed, the realization that losing competitors might object to the emergence of this secret shareholder caused department of communications officials to wonder if the licence could in fact be issued. Legal opinion from the barrister Richard Nesbitt was that the licence award was safe, the government should proceed, and that any arising legal action should be dealt with afterwards.

Fine Gael minister Michael Lowry had been responsible for overseeing the competition. Before his resignation in disgrace in December 1996, following the revelation of how Ben Dunne had funded his house extension, he played a major role in defending the granting of the licence to Esat Digifone. It was awarded for an apparently bargain price of £15 million.

One of the rules of the mobile phone licence competition had been that the bidders had to declare their full ownership structure. In October 1995 Lowry told a government subcommittee comprising himself, Taoiseach John Bruton, Dick Spring, Ruairi Quinn and Pronsias de Rossa (which was meeting on a separate issue) that Esat Digifone had won the independently assessed competition for the licence. The subcommittee was told the balance of 20 per cent of shares not held by Esat Telecom and Telenor would be taken up by 'passive' institutional investors. Four institutional investors were said to be interested in buying these shares but their names were never provided – for reasons of commercial confidentiality, according to Lowry.

In the Dáil on 22 November 1995, when asked about the beneficial ownership of Esat Digifone, Lowry said, 'the intentions of the winning applicant in this regard were fully disclosed.' Indeed, in April 1996, as the department struggled to get sufficient financial and other assurances from Esat to allow for the signing of the formal contract a month later, Lowry hid behind non-existent confidentiality clauses to avoid telling the Dáil that Desmond was a shareholder in Esat Digifone. Importantly, when challenged on rumours to that effect he said Esat could give the 20 per cent to be held by institutions to anyone the main shareholders so liked, although this seemed to go against the disclosure requirements of the original competition.

It was finally disclosed in May 1996 – on the actual formal granting of the licence – that Desmond's IIU had taken up the 20 per cent 'balance'. But it was not until nearly five years later, after Esat Digifone had been sold for a vast profit, that the manner in which Desmond took possession of the shares began to be disclosed.

In early 2001 the *Sunday Tribune* revealed the existence of a letter written by Desmond's IIU to Lowry's department in September 1995, less than a month before the licence competition result was announced and two months after the closing deadline for supplying information as part of the application. The letter pledged not just to buy a 20 per cent shareholding if the unnamed institutional investors did not do so, but to pay for O'Brien's involvement as well, had O'Brien failed to come up with the cash required. This was not an implausible outcome, given O'Brien's subsequently admitted financial predicament at the time.

The letter was apparently sent because of doubts about Esat Digifone's financing raised in oral hearings with the independent assessors hired to run the competition. The department said that this letter was never forwarded to the independent team, but returned to IIU, so it could not have influenced its decision. The question then arose as to how the concerns about Esat's financing had been dispelled if the letter had not been forwarded.

It raised serious questions as to whether there was ever any intention for independent institutions to hold shares and whether Desmond's potential involvement was being underplayed. The government subcommittee, in endorsing the competition result, thought it was giving the licence to a company with a specific shareholding. Unknown to it, Dermot Desmond's IIU had an agreement with O'Brien to become a shareholder in place of the investors the government thought were getting the shares. He also underwrote O'Brien's investment in the company making the licence application. This became clear to the government only in the weeks before the formal signing of the licence, the following year.

Desmond profited immediately as a result, by an amount of about £2.6 million in June 1996 when he transferred some of his shareholding back to his partners. He received his first return on his investment nearly nine months before a single phone call had been made on the new Esat Digifone network. He was to make a profit of over £100 million eventually.

*

Weeks after Shane Coleman and I had published our investigation into Desmond's shareholding in Esat Digifone, I was given information about a payment that had been made to Fine Gael, via a businessman called David Austin, an executive with the Smurfit Group, six weeks after the licence competition had concluded. In early March 2001 the *Sunday Tribune* revealed the payment of $50,000 by Telenor (which said it had been asked to do so by Denis O'Brien) to Fine Gael. A major political controversy erupted.

This meant that the tribunal had to investigate publicly the award of the mobile phone licence in case it was linked to the financial transactions involving Lowry. Desmond's shareholding became part of that investigation.

One person called to account was Pádraig Ó hUiginn, secretary in the Department of An Taoiseach during Haughey's time and formerly the most important civil servant in the country. After retirement he went to work with O'Brien, advising on how to pitch for state contracts or licences; he particularly advised on lobbying the state about the licensing fee that should be charged to whoever won the licence.

According to Ó hUiginn's evidence, when O'Brien floated the idea of introducing Desmond as a shareholder to Esat Digifone, after the closing date for information and after the consortium's final presentation to the committee judging the licensing applications, O'hUiginn was not worried about the timing. Nor was he concerned about the likely reaction, if any, to Desmond's involvement.

He gave evidence that he thought Desmond would be a much better partner than the original four institutions selected and would be much more actively concerned about the project being a success. The institutions would only be after the money, he told the tribunal, although this begs the question: what did he think Desmond, O'Brien and all the others bidding for the mobile phone wanted?

Ó hUiginn seems to have read the civil service's lack of interest in Desmond correctly. In evidence, Martin Brennan, the civil servant who was central to organizing the contest, admitted to the tribunal that he had been unaware of the content or significance of the Glackin report when he was told of Desmond's previously secret involvement in the Esat Digifone consortium. He said he had been working in Brussels at the time the report was issued in 1993 and hadn't paid it much attention. The inaction of the state's politicians or other authorities in response to

Glackin's report may have created an impression among civil servants that it didn't really matter.

Desmond went to the courts in an attempt to have the Glackin report struck from the record of the tribunal, just as many years earlier he had fought in the courts to stifle Glackin's investigation. But the Supreme Court pointed out that Glackin had been a High Court-appointed inspector and that his report was an official document upon which the tribunal was entitled to rely.

Desmond decided then on a different tack, publishing an open letter to Moriarty that he sent with 'regret, frustration and exasperation' in October 2005. 'I am not doing this to protect my reputation but to highlight how much time and money has been utterly wasted by your tribunal,' he claimed. 'When I gave evidence before you I stated that the tribunal had lost the plot. My real concerns are that the Moriarty Tribunal has been responsible for a massive waste of costs and man hours; failed to adopt basic fair procedures; damaged reputations including those of civil servants; relied too much on hearsay and rumours; put itself in positions of conflict; veered way off course without any justification; not issued any report after eight years.'

Desmond made reference to a 37-page ruling of the previous month by the tribunal: it 'does not seem to have come up with one sustainable allegation, and merely regurgitates previous baseless allegations'. In fact, it was a very carefully written document that laid out the areas of legitimate concern and the questions that would have to be addressed. It also gave undertakings to those who might be the subject of adverse findings: they would be given sight of those findings and offered an opportunity to rebut them, as subsequently happened in late 2008.

Desmond lashed out not just at the legal costs of the tribunal itself but at those incurred by witnesses. However, he failed to acknowledge that his was one of three major legal challenges – the others were launched by Haughey and O'Brien – that had delayed the public hearings and the writing of a report.

Desmond correctly argued that 'your Terms of Reference are very simple – to see whether there was any wrongdoing by Charles Haughey or Michael Lowry when minister.' 'It does not matter whether the competition process was good or bad, what matters is whether political pressure was applied,' he wrote. 'No evidence has emerged which even remotely suggests that the licence award was compromised by Michael

Lowry or indeed anyone else – in fact the opposite is the case.' But, while Desmond was correct to write that 'the Dáil did not authorize you to conduct an audit of the competition process', it transpired that it became an essential part of the investigation into Lowry's behaviour.

As far as Desmond was concerned, the tribunal had 'lost respect, not just among the general public but also among the business community.'

A year later Justice Michael Moriarty produced his first report into the corruption of Desmond's friend, former Taoiseach Charles Haughey. Balanced, understated and scrupulous in its use of the facts, it was a devastating critique of Haughey and of those who financed him in unorthodox circumstances, Desmond included. At the time of writing, the report into Lowry's actions has not yet been produced.

The tribunal's preliminary findings were sent by Moriarty to affected parties in November 2008 for them to offer observations and rebuttals.

Denis O'Brien gave four major newspaper interviews in late July 2009 – and followed this up in a first-person *Irish Times* article at the end of the month – in which he said the preliminary findings had included seventy-nine that were relevant to him, sixty of which involved him adversely. These included the sensational claim that there was a finding that the state's award of the mobile phone licence to his consortium was 'illegally issued' and that he had a 'corrupt' relationship with Lowry. 'They are all wrong and I know how they are wrong,' he told the *Sunday Times*. He insisted that he rejected the preliminary findings in their entirety and that he would fight the tribunal 'street by street' if it attempted to formalize them in its final report. He said the tribunal itself was 'out of control' and looking 'for a scalp' to justify its multimillion euro costs. He said the procedures it used were more akin to those found in a military dictatorship. 'It's unheard of. I mean it's Burma,' he told the *Sunday Tribune*. He told the *Sunday Independent* that 'there is no sense of proper justice here and if anything this is rough justice akin to what happened in the UK in the 1970s and 1980s. This is a very dark period for justice.'

O'Brien also warned of very serious consequences for the Irish economy if the tribunal published its preliminary findings as its final assessment of the evidence it had heard. The tribunal had heard already at a public sitting in June 2009 that an adverse finding had been made against the state over its handling of the licence competition. 'The reputation of Ireland will be severely damaged,' he told the *Sunday Business Post*.

18

'Still I rise'

Taoiseach Brian Cowen passed the buck when asked in the summer of 2008 if Dermot Desmond was a suitable candidate to become the chairman of Aer Lingus, in which the government retained a 25 per cent shareholding after selling it from public ownership. 'That's a matter for the board of Aer Lingus themselves to decide, but obviously Mr Desmond has had a very fine business track record,' Cowen said. The first part of his comment was politically careful, pushing responsibility to the board (although the votes of the state's nominees would never become known publicly). But the second part could have been interpreted as an endorsement. Cowen offered no evidence to support his view that Desmond had a 'very fine business track record'.

Getting the idea past Irish Congress of Trade Unions boss David Begg – an employee representative on the board – might have been a problem, given Desmond's involvement in previous controversies. But to others, mostly in business but often in Fianna Fáil too, Desmond remains a significant and positive figure in Irish life whose contribution has not been fully appreciated or acknowledged.

P. J. Mara has said that a statue commemorating Desmond should be built at the International Financial Services Centre. Desmond didn't just have the idea; he sold it forcefully to Haughey in 1987 after the previous government failed to see its potential. The IFSC had created tens of thousands of highly paid jobs, produced billions in tax revenues for the state over two decades and inspired the regeneration of an eyesore at the gateway to Dublin on the River Liffey. Pádraig Ó hUiginn has described Desmond as an 'economic patriot', highlighting Desmond's role as the 'one and only begetter' of the IFSC. Their mutual friend Denis O'Brien said of Desmond in a speech in 2004 that he had an 'innate instinct' for business and was 'virtually always spot on'. He attributed to Desmond not just the idea for the IFSC but also the National Treasury Management Agency. O'Brien said that if Desmond was a British citizen, 'I would be introducing him as Sir Desmond', but he added that, thankfully, Desmond had not changed his colours.

When *Business & Finance* magazine nominated him as its 'Man of the Year' in 2004, Cowen, as Minister for Finance, eulogized Desmond at the awards dinner for showing how to 'transform conceptual ideas into measurable achievements'.

Despite this praise, Desmond appears to feel unappreciated. In a rare public appearance in 2004, in front of students and invited guests at a function at the National College of Industrial Relations, Desmond was asked how Ireland could learn to live with its successful entrepreneurs. 'Better than it has,' he replied, to laughter. This has been a common refrain in the few interviews and speeches he has given. He told this audience that he was Irish, his family was Irish, and he intended to die Irish. 'I have to learn to live with the strengths and weaknesses of the Irish personality, including my own.'

Desmond's company International Investments and Underwriting has its headquarters on the top floor of one of the most prominent buildings in the IFSC, one of the four original office blocks built there. Desmond had purchased the building for £30 million in the late 1980s but ran into problems while financing this that almost ruined him. He sold floors and took a mortgage from Michael Fingleton at the Irish Nationwide Building Society to bide him through before eventually buying the building back.

Desmond is the sole shareholder in IIU, and in 2004 he made it an unlimited company, which means it does not have to publish accounts. He said that he did this to 'operate away from the glare of the media'. He told *Business & Finance*: 'My business is private. I don't have any outside shareholders, I don't have any bonds. I'm not accountable to anyone and that's the way I like to keep it.'

Desmond has never been comfortable with media scrutiny. My first dealings with him were as a young business journalist in the early 1990s. At the time of the Ballsbridge property controversy, we had an uncomfortable meeting in NCB offices, during which he declared that I was his 'enemy' because of my line of questioning and stories I had written. I explained that I was merely trying to do my job. We maintained an uneasy peace over subsequent years and occasionally, after some persuasion, he spoke whenever he felt he needed to put forward his side of a story. Like Fintan O'Toole, another journalist who wrote about him over the years, I have received communications from him in the form of poetry, a welcome change from the more usual solicitor's letter. On one occasion Desmond wrote to O'Toole: 'When you write or talk about me, now or in the future, my reaction is reflected in this poem.' Enclosed was the full text of a poem called 'Still I Rise'. O'Toole recognized the piece. It was by Maya Angelou, the African-American poet, teacher and civil rights activist. The poem is an outcry in celebration of the survival of the enslaved and oppressed.

A decade after I had first met him, I went to visit Desmond in his new offices in the IFSC. He didn't like some of the things that had been written about him in the *Sunday Tribune* and his solicitors had sent us a number of letters threatening litigation. I may have been the one who requested the meeting, but there was no doubt as to what was on the agenda: what he perceived as unfair coverage of his business and personal interests.

His offices overlooked the Liffey and were the height of business opulence, with his own personal gym included. He was particularly proud of glass that, at the touch of a button, could prevent visibility into the room and provide security. Lunch was served by his personal butler. I left with Desmond accepting my assurances that no malice was intended towards him in anything my newspaper or I wrote and that we were merely trying to report fairly and accurately in the public interest. His attitude, as he explained it to me, was that he didn't want anyone writing about him but that if they did and they got anything wrong, he would sue them. He probably didn't believe my explanations but he offered to tear up the legal proceedings he had prepared against my newspaper.

Since then there have been a few telephone conversations, in the last of which he again berated me strongly for my stance when writing certain pieces, especially in relation to his evidence to the Moriarty Tribunal. That conversation, about eight years ago, ended with his announcing that he would never speak to me again and slamming down the phone. He has been as good as his word, although I did receive my own poem from him, author unknown, entitled 'Never Trust a Journalist'. If you don't agree with Desmond's view of the world, it is not just a difference of opinion: you are wrong and that may make you someone he regards as an enemy.

*

Given all the praise Desmond has received, and given his own declaration of patriotism, it is easy to understand why Anglo Irish Bank chairman Sean FitzPatrick – who was the Aer Lingus director heading the special subcommittee to find a replacement for the retiring John Sharman – wanted Desmond to take over as chair. FitzPatrick introduced his friend – who was a large borrower from Anglo – to the Aer Lingus chief executive Dermot Mannion in an attempt to smooth a path for the appointment.

Desmond has long had a profitable interest in aviation and related activities. One of his lesser-known financial successes was a profit of about €22 million on the sale of 50 per cent of Pembroke Capital, a Dublin aircraft leasing company run by P. J. Mara's brother-in-law Mike Dolan.

His best-ever deal, though, was the purchase and sale of London City Airport. Desmond bought it from the British building group Mowlem in 1995 for £23.5 million (stg). The small airport is in the heart of the London Docklands but just minutes from the financial centre of the City, and, with its notoriously short runway, handled fewer than 500,000 passengers per annum, mainly on small aircraft such as private jets and commuter services. Desmond saw great potential to compete with the much larger Heathrow, Gatwick, Stansted and Luton airports. He increased traffic and enhanced the development use of the site, increasing passenger throughput to 2.3 million passengers in a decade and securing a connection to the London Underground via its own Docklands Light Railway (DLR) station.

In 2006 Desmond sold it to a consortium involving American International Group (AIG), Credit Suisse and GE Infrastructure for a price believed to be about £1.2 billion (stg). The timing, at the top of the market, was perfect. It is not known what borrowings Desmond was carrying, but the profit gave him enormous financial clout.

Desmond has a remarkable eye for a good investment, buying assets that others would ignore and selling assets before others have realized they are overpriced. He made his first fortune by selling his stake in NCB Stockbrokers for over €17.5 million in 1994. He bought one fifth of Celtic Football Club in Glasgow in 1994, becoming its biggest individual shareholder. It is an emotional rather than financial investment, but under his direction Celtic has been run along more sensible lines than most clubs. He and McManus bought the exotic Sandy Lane

Hotel in Barbados for £38 million, the day after Desmond had enjoyed a night there. They then spent about €400 million on a four-year rebuilding programme that was said to have run massively over-budget. Tiger Woods held his wedding there as a gift from the two.

Desmond calls himself an 'eclectic investor' and says there are no rules to his investment decisions. 'If you were to go by what the majority say, you'd never do anything. We've all got to realize that the majority doesn't succeed; it's always the minority. So I am always looking for a minority view.'

His investments and deals are extensive, and it is known that he has involvement in companies such as Vivas Health, Datalex, BETDAQ, Daon, Intuition Publishing, Barlo, Unidare, Golden Vale, Biotrin, Greencore and, years after he left, NCB Stockbrokers again. He has an extraordinary record in successfully providing finance for high-risk financial technology companies, and the basement of his IFSC building served as a hothouse for e-commerce start-ups. He pocketed about £15 million from the sale of Quay Financial Software, one of the early companies he championed, and an estimated £55 million profit from the sale of shares in Baltimore, the internet security firm, which he realized was overvalued; it crashed and burned shortly after joining the FTSE100. He made about €6.5 million in 2001 from selling his shares in Today FM, then the only independent national radio station.

His international investments include a one fifth share in the Newfoundland and Labrador Refining Corporation, which has permission to build a $4.6 billion oil refinery – North America's first in decades – in Newfoundland's Placentia Bay. In 2005 he paid an estimated €100 million for a 33.1 per cent stake in Latvia's fourth-largest bank by assets, Rietumu Bank, although this may be a doubtful investment, given Latvia's economic collapse. His plans with the Donegal-born developer Pat Doherty for a €1.5 billion regeneration of the Titanic Quarter in Belfast – where, pre-credit crunch, it was planned to build more than 3,300 residential units, around 180,000 square metres of offices and leisure facilities – have been revised.

Like McManus, Desmond offered to part-fund a major project for the state. He wanted to build an 'eco-sphere' at the Custom House Docks as Ireland's Millennium project and had a scale model and designs assembled in 1995. The eco-sphere was to be a giant glass pyramid containing a tropical forest on top of an aquarium, filled with exotic vegetation, animals and fish (and was quickly dubbed 'Gorillas in the Mist'). The building would have been eighty-one metres high – about twenty-five metres higher than nearby Liberty Hall. He offered to contribute millions towards assessing and designing the project – and something towards its construction, which would be mainly paid for by the state. He also promised it would be self-financing soon after its opening and personally offered to make up any shortfall. He even offered to pay for a new bridge across the Liffey to assist in access. He believed that his original vision for the IFSC included a significant element of urban regeneration that the authorities had failed to execute and that this would provide a major tourist attraction as well as giving a non-commercial life to the area.

He presented it to Taoiseach John Bruton, who decided not to back it; neither did Ahern subsequently. 'Unfortunately, we didn't have a Charlie Haughey in power who'd say let's get it done. It would have been built by 2000. It takes a man of vision to recognize it. No other politician in Ireland would have built the IFSC but Charlie Haughey,' he said.

Desmond has been consistently disappointed by what he regarded as the failure of IFSC to fulfil its original remit of being an 'exciting people place'. He has lamented its lack of life outside of office hours. He has argued in favour of levies being placed on the occupants of space at the IFSC, with the money being put towards the construction of leisure amenities and other facilities to make it a more pleasant place to work. He has objected to other buildings in the IFSC, near his own South Block, on the basis that they are not of sufficient stature. While he wants things to be big, he doesn't want them to be too big, and he has advocated this throughout other parts of Dublin.

Over the last decade Desmond has been particularly active in making submissions to An Bord Pleanála fighting major developments.

He was central to defeating controversial plans for a Spencer Dock development on Dublin's north quays because he believed it conflicted with his vision for the IFSC. Desmond was easily the best funded of the eight opponents to the idea for a massive development of six million square feet that had been proposed by a coalition of Treasury Holdings (the property development company led by Johnny Ronan and Richard Barrett), Point Depot-owner Harry Crosbie and state transport company CIÉ, which supplied the fifty-two acres of land.

The proposed plan included a National Conference and Exhibition Centre, two hotels (a four-star and a five-star), and 5.3 million square feet of retail, office, car parking and residential development. The high density of the development was in conflict with the Dublin Docklands Development Authority (DDDA) master plan but Desmond's objections were unmatched in their vigour. He spent up to €200,000 in hiring consultants who argued publicly to demolish the plan.

Desmond claimed the size was 'driven purely by economic consider-ations of maximizing commercial floor space within the site'. He warned of the 'frightening' impact of 'a fortress-type development' and described the building's design as 'inspired by American corporate architecture' and 'inappropriate in the context of an historic European city'.

He even made a personal appearance at the planning hearing for the Spencer Dock development. Desmond said he was not opposed to high buildings as such, but he did not want to see a concrete jungle. The objectors won and the construction of the national conference centre was delayed for years.

A scaled-down version is presently under construction, again by Treasury, but when in late 2007 Treasury Holdings sought permission to build a 152-metre-high, 427-bedroom hotel adjacent to the new centre, Desmond again joined An Taisce and the DDDA in object-ing. The plan was refused on the grounds of excessive height, and the council said it would 'be contrary to the proper planning and sustainable development of the area'.

Desmond did not confine his planning objections to the docklands. He objected to a plan by developer Ray Grehan for a fifteen-storey tower on the former UCD veterinary school site in Ballsbridge, describing it as an 'incongruous spike'. Desmond accused Grehan of being concerned with 'the maximization of profit'. He laid a similar charge at the door of developer Seán Dunne's even more ambitious plans for Ballsbridge, where Desmond has his largest Irish home.

Dunne had his revenge in 2008 when news of Desmond's possible appointment to the Aer Lingus board appeared in the newspapers. Dunne, as a small shareholder in the airline, wrote to Sharman, as outgoing chairman, to complain about Desmond's suitability as his replacement, bringing up the two major pieces of controversy involving Desmond that had featured at the Moriarty Tribunal.

Dunne's letter said that 'no hint of controversy can attach to the chairman of one of our most important public companies.' Knowing Desmond's Achilles heel, he decided to kick it hard. Dunne recommended that the board of Aer Lingus should 'familiarize' itself with the findings of the Glackin report. He also warned against the possible consequences of an adverse finding from the Moriarty Tribunal into the circumstances of the awarding of the second mobile phone licence.

Dunne said that he did not allege any 'turpitude' against Desmond but warned that an adverse finding from the Moriarty Tribunal would make his position as chair of Aer Lingus 'untenable'. 'The findings of that report remain extant. It would seem to me, therefore, to be an act of some concern that the board's members, with the apparent tacit approval of the government and unions, who between them control over 40 per cent of the shares, are considering inviting Mr Desmond to become the chair of our company, when a High Court judge's report on a tribunal, as authorized by Dáil Éireann, has not yet delivered its findings.'

Not stopping there, Dunne also said that Desmond 'could not hope, in my respectful submission, to secure the support of ordinary working people . . . and in particular in our company, Aer Lingus.'

Desmond decided early in August 2008 that he wasn't interested in being offered the position, saying that 'work commitments' would not allow him enough time to do the job. But it was far from the end of his involvement in Irish public life. He would be vocal in debate about the future of Irish banks.

PART V

Bringing down the house

19

House of cards

The first credit crunch-inspired meltdown in Irish financial services received little attention outside the business pages of the newspapers. But the meltdown of International Securities and Trading Corporation (ISTC) in late 2007 was an extraordinary event that dragged in many of the biggest names in Irish business, resulted in nearly €1 billion in losses and presaged many of the problems that were to crucify the Irish economy over the following two years. There has never been faster corporate growth, or a faster subsequent demise, in Irish financial history.

ISTC was the brainchild of Tiarnan O'Mahony, an affable banker who had been Sean FitzPatrick's number two at Anglo Irish Bank but who left in early 2005 with compensation of over €3.75 million when David Drumm beat him unexpectedly to the job as FitzPatrick's successor. O'Mahony had spotted an opportunity to invest in banks: not in their shares but in what is known as their 'Tier 1' capital.

Tier 1 capital is defined as the 'book value' of the shares in a bank, plus whatever profits are kept within the business after dividends to shareholders and tax are paid. Banks are required under international standards to keep a sum equivalent to at least 4 per cent of the total loans advanced to customers as Tier 1 capital. It is meant to be a buffer if things go wrong and loans are not repaid when they fall due. In practice many banks like to have twice as much, but, rather than issuing new shares, which dilutes the profits that can be attributed to existing shareholders and which is more expensive, banks prefer to issue bonds. These are considered Tier 1 capital, even though it is effectively a posh way of naming a form of borrowing.

In 2004 international banks issued €20 billion worth of such banking instruments to boost their reserves, bringing the total of capital on the balance sheets to over €400 billion. Banks are not allowed to trade in the capital of rivals, so this is where ISTC saw an opening for the development of a new business.

O'Mahony's idea was to create an investment fund that would trade in Tier 1 capital: by trading in existing bonds; or by buying them on their creation by the banks and holding them until they matured and had to be repaid; or by selling them again. Effectively, ISTC would be a lender to the banks who were raising capital, or a 'banker's banker', although it would not hold a banker's licence, as it was not allowed to do so if participating in this game.

His idea was that he would raise capital and then borrow a multiple of this to create a fund that was of a big enough size for investment. The interest he paid on the borrowed money would be his cost of doing business, but by making the right investments in higher-yielding bonds he thought he could make profits for his new company. According to O'Mahony, his profit margins on the deals would vary from as low as 75 basis points, or 0.75 per cent, to as many as 500 basis points, or 5 per cent, over interbank rates, depending on the risk attached to the bank in which the investment was made. All he needed was a certain degree of stability in the banking market and adequate liquidity of funds.

'The real attraction of this business is that you are lending to the highest-quality borrower that there is. Banks are highly regulated, with the regulator ensuring they are in a position to meet their obligations. That's why I think it's such a safe form of business. You can't say that banks don't fail, but everybody agrees banks are a fairly safe bet,' he said in a 2005 interview.

O'Mahony had no problem raising money from investors. He originally planned to start with €50 million in 'equity', €5 million of which he would put in himself. So interested were high-rollers like Seán Quinn, Denis O'Brien, Sean FitzPatrick, Seamus Ross, Paddy Kelly, Johnny Ronan, Gary McGann and many others that he raised €165 million. It is not known how much of that money was itself borrowed by those individuals rather than coming from their spare cash. AIB's stock-broking subsidiary, Goodbody, went through its list of private client investors, as did Anglo Irish Bank's wealth-management division. As many as 220 'high net worth' individuals became involved.

ISTC borrowed a multiple of that 'equity' to build its own balance sheet, providing the finance that could be used to run the business. On top of the equity, it attracted a multiple of that again in so called 'mezzanine finance', through the issue of bonds sold to investors by the likes of Friends First and First Active. The investors were not the super-rich millionaires but the merely well-off, and some put most of their savings into this supposedly conservatively managed idea. ISTC also borrowed over €2.6 billion from a variety of Irish and international banks, including the likes of ABN Amro, Bank of America, Credit Suisse, Merrill Lynch, Morgan Stanley and Royal Bank of Scotland.

O'Mahony now had about €3 billion to use in making investments in the capital of banks all around the world. 'There is only one objective and that is to make money,' said O'Mahony. 'This is unashamed capitalism. There is no debating the issue. This is about making money. When John Teeling taught me in college, he used to say, "make money". I still live by that principle.'

At first all went very well. ISTC achieved €6.5 million in profit in its first full year of trading, to year-end September 2006. By May 2007 the company had about 165 customers in twenty-five countries and did about 6 per cent of its business in Ireland. O'Mahony predicted full-year pre-tax profits of €15 million to year-end September 2007.

ISTC's shares were trading at €328 each in a 'grey', or unofficial, market operated by Goodbody Stockbrokers, having been issued at €100 each in July 2005. With 1.9 million shares in issue, that gave the company a market value of about €623 million. O'Mahony had taken 15 per cent of the equity, valuing his stake at €93.4 million. He intended to join the stock market during 2008, and in a note to clients in November 2006 Goodbody Stockbrokers estimated that the company could be worth up to €835 million by then.

The word was so good that O'Mahony was invited in March 2007 to address the Leinster Society of Chartered Accountants luncheon. In advance of that year's general election he warned against Sinn Féin's 'Long Kesh school of economics', as it posed a major threat to the future economic stability of the state. O'Mahony warned that Sinn Féin would bring 'old-fashioned Marxism' to Ireland if allowed access to power by the electorate. He described Sinn Féin's policies as economic terrorism, and said they would nationalize industry and increase taxes, particularly corporation tax.

O'Mahony held an important position, given to him by government.

As finance minister Brian Cowen had appointed O'Mahony as chairman of the Irish Pensions Board, to oversee the performance and regulation of pension funds and to recommend ways of preparing people for their retirements. In one of his few public comments about the role, O'Mahony said that he did not believe that employers should be forced to contribute to pensions – but he emphasized that he had said that in a purely 'personal capacity'.

Pensioners were investing in ISTC by this stage, so hyped had it become. Insurance investor Friends First got clients to invest in subordinated loan notes: thirty-seven of them invested €15 million in the Creative Bond product in December 2006 and another eighty-eight put €28 million into the Creative Step-Up product in June 2007.

In August 2007 everything suddenly went wrong. Global panic about the exposure of banks to bad-debt risks led to a freezing in capital markets, and it was discovered that ISTC had invested in subprime bonds. It packaged these high-risk US mortgages under the title SIVs (Special Investment Vehicles).

A small sum was enough to bring down the house of cards. German bank Dresdner Kleinwort gave ISTC twenty-one days to repay a €176,250 debt in September 2007. The Irish institution couldn't raise the cash and sought protection from the courts through the examinership process to avoid immediate bankruptcy. Although Dermot Desmond initially expressed interest in investment, he withdrew after examining the books. British stockbroker Collins Stewart eventually took over the business for a nominal sum, but only after the majority of ISTC's debts had been written off.

The losses amounted to €820 million, creditors being owed €878 million with assets of only €57.8 million to offset against this amount. The capital of the wealthy shareholders was eliminated entirely; nor were the purchasers of bonds repaid. Lenders to the company received only a fraction of their money and had to write off €435.6 million as bad debts.

ISTC had traded profitably until the credit crunch, which was caused by the US subprime mortgage crisis. Even though O'Mahony insisted that the company's SIV assets represented just 7 per cent of its total loan portfolio, which stood at €3 billion, it was still enough to bring his bank for banks down.

O'Mahony continued as chair of the Irish Pensions Board. In 2008 he applied to the Wicklow County Council for permission to demolish his home near Enniskerry, to be replaced by a brand-new build of 15,000 square feet. It could all have been worse: he could have stayed at Anglo.

20

The bank of the boom

Tiernan O'Mahony had been able to raise money easily for ISTC because he had been one of the senior figures at Anglo Irish Bank and had been endorsed by his old boss Sean FitzPatrick, who became an investor in the new venture. If Anglo was the bank of the boom, beloved by entrepreneurs who needed cash to fund their dreams, then FitzPatrick was their hero, the man who backed them when others dithered or rejected. Where they went, he provided.

FitzPatrick was what's called a 'relationship banker'. He got to know his biggest clients and encouraged them, while nailing them to reasonably tough terms and expensive fees for their loans. He offered something that the big banks often failed to: personal attention and support. The bank offered not just money but a form of partnership; its size allowed it to provide a personal touch.

He was a salesman, as well as a qualified-accountant-turned-banker. Unlike many of his rivals he hustled for business. He targeted those with high incomes or surplus capital. He understood ambitious and expanding businesses because he ran one himself. Small, brash and thrusting, but welcoming and perpetually on the go, all the things that you noticed about 'Seanie', as he was widely known, suggested that Anglo was constructed in his image. FitzPatrick was always talking things up, even during dismal days, telling you what his bank had done and what it could do.

As Anglo was quoted on the stock market, he held twice-yearly press conferences in his Stephen's Green headquarters in which he bubbled and fizzed. Years later, as his bouffant hair greyed, there was a passing resemblance to Riverdance's Michael Flatley: FitzPatrick could talk as speedily and passionately to investors and the press as his lookalike could dance. Barack Obama's mantra 'Yes, we can' could have been written for FitzPatrick in the 1990s.

The name Anglo Irish was one he'd inherited but kept, as it sounded like the name of an old establishment bank with a list of old-money clients, mainly from the Protestant landed classes. It was, however, created in the mid-1980s, when a number of small private banks were brought together as one, offering a relatively limited range of services to a small customer base, with the name chosen deliberately to make it seem grander. FitzPatrick's family were Catholics of modest means who were not from a traditional professional background. Many of those who were to become his clients came from similar backgrounds and indeed revelled in a perceived anti-establishment attitude.

It wasn't always easy for FitzPatrick, particularly in the early years of the 1990s when a deteriorating international economic condition suggested that the economic reforms introduced by the Charles Haughey-led governments from 1987 might not succeed. The stock market listing was a benefit and a burden. It gave him access to capital but it also required transparency in reporting performance. It also gave him a 20 per cent shareholder who almost destroyed him early on.

That was an Englishman called John Clegg who was linked, wrongly, in newspaper articles to the IRA; and, had the accusations been true, the implications for Anglo would have been dreadful. But, while allegations of money-laundering by Clegg were incorrect, Clegg had engaged in serious insider dealing at a British waste company called Wace that was quoted on the stock market. In a foretaste of what was to come many years later with Seán Quinn when Anglo had to reduce the size of his shareholding and move some of his shares elsewhere, FitzPatrick had to get Clegg off the share register by finding new buyers for his stock. Rumours swirled that Anglo was running out of money and would close. At one stage FitzPatrick confronted his Bank of Ireland counterpart Mark Hely Hutchinson to demand that his executives stop spreading gossip about his bank. FitzPatrick saved Anglo when he persuaded a group of institutions and wealthy investors to buy Clegg's shares, but the currency crisis of late 1992 and early 1993, when interest rates rocketed, created another burden that required imaginative action on his part.

FitzPatrick embarked on a series of issues of new capital, bringing in cash from a variety of prominent Irish businessmen who subscribed for shares. In some cases they were offered deals whereby they borrowed from the bank on an interest-only basis, covering their repayments with the generous dividends that Anglo still managed to provide out of profits. At a later stage, after the bank's share price had gone up, they were able to sell and repay the loans, pocketing sizeable profits. Anglo did this three times over two years and worked hard to ensure that loans it had issued would be repaid. The discipline involved in making sure loans did not 'go bad' was an education that would serve them well for many years to come.

In the year-end to 30 September 1995, Anglo had just €1.36 billion in loans to customers and made an after-tax profit of €18 million. Its stock market value was less than €150 million. But it was on the way to benefiting from the rise in the economy. In FitzPatrick's last year as chief executive, to year-end 30 September 2004 it returned after-tax profits of €396 million, advanced €25 billion in loans to customers and was valued at almost €6 billion.

Anglo Irish Bank was in full flight, much to the amazement and distress of its competitors. As the property and construction boom – fed by McCreevy's tax policies – took off, FitzPatrick became extraordinarily powerful. While the tax breaks were important, as were the lower interest rates during the late 1990s and then lower again once Ireland became a member of the euro, little would have happened had banks not been willing to take big risks in making money available to business ventures and property investments.

FitzPatrick claimed a disproportionate amount of business for his still small, by comparison with AIB and Bank of Ireland, but fast-growing bank. He continued to attract the professional and business classes and the developers. While Anglo insisted on security for its loans – including the usual personal guarantees – it gained its reputation for assessing projects or investments quickly and giving a decision while rivals dithered. The extra charge for this service was regarded as worth while by those who didn't want to hang around or who feared an opportunity would be lost by procrastination. Anglo was not afraid of risk, although this was mitigated by the value of the property and other assets that it demanded as security moving in a seemingly upwards-only direction.

Almost all of the most prominent figures in the country's growing property development sector sought borrowings from Anglo, even if they also used other banks. Rugby fanatic Seanie became a fan of the Wicklow under-21 Gaelic football team because developer Sean

Mulryan's son got on to it. Derek Quinlan banked some of his biggest investments with Anglo. Seamus Ross, Gerry Gannon, Paddy Kelly and various other property developers all had substantial or occasional relationships with Anglo.

Nor was it just property developers. Dermot Desmond and Denis O'Brien were long-standing customers, as was Seán Quinn, which explains why so many loyally came to FitzPatrick's defence as his world collapsed in 2008.

In retrospect, this proximity to billionaires and multimillionaires created something of a problem for FitzPatrick, as it often does for many bankers. Without his bank's money at an early stage of their business adventures, many of their cash-generating projects would never have happened. FitzPatrick watched as the men he helped became extraordinarily rich. The temptation for all bankers is to ask why they can't have some of that. It wasn't like FitzPatrick to be jealous, but, while his own shareholding in Anglo made him a very wealthy man and provided him with an excellent annual income, he could see the potential for making more for himself.

In February 2004 FitzPatrick sold €27 million worth of Anglo shares, giving himself equity for new investments. He took nearly €2.7 million in pay, bonus and pension contributions in his final year before moving to become part-time chairman. He said he was 'taking a bit off the table' so he could 'pursue personal interests'. FitzPatrick had been helping himself for many years to tens of millions in personal loans, quietly, as was discovered in late 2008 to some amazement – and with spectacular consequences, because he had been secretly using Anglo as a form of personal piggybank.

Meanwhile, the baton in Anglo Irish passed to an eager young executive called David Drumm. He was a surprise choice as FitzPatrick's replacement. Many had expected it to be either O'Mahony, the chief operating officer, or Tom Browne, the head of Irish operations and wealth management, both of whom had been with FitzPatrick since the early 1990s. Significantly, both were somewhat more cautious in their projections as to how quickly Anglo could continue to grow. In 2002 O'Mahony, in an *Irish Times* interview that may have betrayed that he was not ambitious enough to suit the demands of the board, said 'the days of double-digit national growth are over' and that this meant slower growth in profits for Anglo. 'We certainly see it slowing to the region of earnings-per-share at 15 to 20 per cent, as compared with 40 per cent last year and indeed the year before.'

Browne stayed for another three years before leaving with the same generous package as O'Mahony enjoyed. In that time he tried to reduce the bank's exposure to the Irish property market: as far back as early 2005 he told me that it had become dangerously overheated and too dependent on tax breaks; there was limited value left for investors. However, while he had some success in reducing the bank's exposure, it continued to do new business in Irish property, both as a banker and as an investment organizer.

Drumm was on a dash to prove himself FitzPatrick's equal or better. The dramatic growth under FitzPatrick not only continued but accelerated now. Drumm boldly stated his intention to double profits within five years, a target he achieved in just two. If ever a bank symbolized the inflation of valuations in the Irish economy, it was Anglo. By 2007 it was the decade's best-performing share on the Irish stock market, valued at over €13.3 billion at its peak, with the shares trading at €17.60 each. It received the accolade of the world's best-performing bank of the previous five years.

Drumm received massive bonuses – about half of his total remuneration took this form – so the greater the bank's lending, the greater the potential to make profits and the more his bonus increased. Drumm received €4.65 million in 2007, making him the best-paid public company executive in the country, beating the money received by Bank of Ireland boss Brian Goggin. Few people outside of the bank complained at the time.

FitzPatrick, as chairman, watched approvingly. He had kept 4.5 million shares in Anglo, worth €83 million at their peak in May 2007, and pocketed over €500,000 annually as chairman. Finance director Willie McAteer's shares were valued at €57 million.

At face value it all seemed a wonderful success. No wonder Seán Quinn was interested in being a major part of this. After all, his insurance group was making massive profits, he had become a 25 per cent shareholder in NCB Stockbrokers, and he had invested €2 million in O'Mahony's ISTC, which seemed to be flying.

21

The man who booby-trapped the bank

Denis O'Brien was prepared to point the finger and apportion blame. Bemoaning the demise of Anglo-Irish Bank and rueing the public's demonization of his friend Sean FitzPatrick, O'Brien decided that he would call out one man who, as far as he was concerned, had much to answer for and was getting away without public opporbrium much too easily: his fellow billionaire Seán Quinn.

While the collapse of Anglo's share price had many interlinking causes – and FitzPatrick was central to them – O'Brien was none the less correct to highlight Quinn's role. If Anglo's foundations had been shaky, Quinn's actions in secretly buying an extraordinary large shareholding in the bank had the effect of booby-trapping those foundations from within and then exploding them. Though Quinn kept his counsel, the financial markets assumed, correctly, that he was the person assembling the very large and expensive shareholding in Anglo. As most of his purchases were taking place in a falling market, he was placing himself in a vulnerable position. Short-sellers, who make money from betting on falling share prices, aggressively targeted the shares. Quinn's stubborn persistence with his investment strategy, in the face of all the signals that it would not succeed, gave the short-sellers further encouragement and allowed them to benefit even more as the spiral continued. It wasn't only Quinn who lost, of course, as the share price fell. Every other shareholder in Anglo looked on aghast, but many, instead of cutting their losses, shared Quinn's belief that the shares would rebound. O'Brien was right: although many other factors caused Anglo's share price to collapse, Quinn's strategy played an important part.

Yet Quinn had not become a figure of public ridicule or contempt. Indeed, he carried on, seemingly almost regardless. In early 2009 he was allowed the platform of a short and none-too-incisive interview on RTÉ television's news in which he complained he was being 'victimized'. It ended with the 'human interest' revelation that he was about to become a grandfather and added to the myth of the ordinary Quinn, no different to the rest of us, even though this was a man whose wholly owned company had been landed with the biggest fine for financial misconduct in the history of the state – €3.25 million – and who had been required to pay a €200,000 personal fine as well.

But the romantic rise of Seán Quinn was a story that many people loved during the era of the Celtic Tiger and seemed reluctant to surrender. How Quinn played to it. In a rare television appearance in late 2007 – for a 'rich list' programme on RTÉ television – Quinn gave a very brief interview in which he modestly confessed to playing cards with older friends from Cavan every Tuesday evening for a maximum stake of 50 cents a hand. The most anyone could win in a night was €10, the most he could lose a fiver. This measured man emphasized his modesty: the house at which he played had only an outside toilet.

This apparent humility came despite claims that he had become not only the richest man in Ireland – with a net worth of €3.9 billion, according to the April 2008 edition of the *Sunday Times* rich list – but one of the 200 richest men in the world.

How he had done this in just thirty-five years seemed extraordinary, as he built his businesses from nothing; a doughty opponent of establishment monopolies and a creator of vast new wealth, he came from a family without wealth in an area traditionally blighted by poverty. That he did all this in a border region, where smuggling was rife and the activities of the IRA made high-profile wealth creation dangerous, added to the tale. His ambition and can-do approach, despite the handicap of geography, was rightly held up as a great entrepreneurial success, especially when thousands in the Cavan–Fermanagh region in particular benefited greatly from his vision by getting jobs.

However, that brief and innocuous lifestyle television interview told us very little about the true Quinn, a man who travelled by helicopter around Ireland and who also had his own $24 million Dassault Falcon private jet to take him outside of the country. And, while he may have emphasized the ordinary nature of the businesses in which he invested – starting in construction and, with the exception of his lucrative foray into insurance, staying with construction-related activities – the truth was many of Quinn's achievements were down to extraordinary optimism and fearless gambling.

The state's authorities seemingly judged him too big to be allowed to fall, such were the numbers he employed and insured. Quinn's vulnerable position may not have been the government's primary focus as the banking crisis unfolded – and there was little enough commentary on Quinn's responsibility and subsequent weakness – but there isn't much doubt that it influenced the actions taken by the Central Bank, Financial Regulator and government. Extraordinary proof came in December 2008, when Tánaiste and Minister for Trade, Enterprise and Employment Mary Coughlan took the calculated and deliberate decision, despite what was known to the government at that stage about Quinn's extraordinary recklessness and its catastrophic effects, to praise Quinn lavishly during a visit to the company's new Cork insurance operations. Quinn promised to create 450 new jobs, and Coughlan congratulated Quinn Insurance on its 'continued success and most importantly for their [sic] investment in Ireland in these difficult economic times'. Coughlan's comment might have been appropriate in other circumstances, but, given that the regulator had fined Quinn for his insurance company's involvement in the Anglo debacle, it was a very doubtful political judgement.

In September 2007 Quinn gave one of his rare speeches when he addressed the Cavan County Enterprise Board at his own Slieve Russell Hotel. Speaking off the cuff, he admitted that 'I suppose I was always very greedy. Whatever we had, I was never happy with what we had. And I was always looking for new opportunities. We always followed the bigger return. We build and buy assets we feel we are going to get double-digit returns on. Some people go for the safe return – we go for the bigger return. We don't like the 3, 4 or 5 per cent returns. Any of the properties we ever bought, we only bought them on the basis that we'd receive a 10 per cent return, with one or two exceptions.'

Despite his reputation for careful evaluation, he revealed that 'we came from a very simple background and we try to make business always simple. We don't believe in too much fuss. We have never had a feasibility study done in our lives.' Much of this, including his use of a private jet, was ignored in populist reporting about his not having a mobile phone, living a simple life and giving his brain 'much more time to do what it's best at doing'.

He explained his diversification strategy. 'Some people, whatever field they're in, they would try to expand in that field – whether sand, gravel, blocks, readymix or whatever – rather than having one or two or four or five areas. We never took that view: was there any better business that we weren't in, and who was in that business? If it was David Drumm of Anglo or Michael O'Leary of Ryanair that were in that business we would try to avoid it. If there was somebody else in it, we might take that to be a healthy challenge – and we always welcome a healthy challenge.

'When we started in 1973, we set ourselves a target of 20 per cent annual growth in profits. We achieved that. On average, we've had 30 per cent growth, so we feel we can do that again over the next five years.' These were very ambitious targets, given that fears about the continued expansion of the global economy abounded by that stage.

In retrospect, the Drumm comment was especially interesting, as rumours were growing that Quinn was quietly assembling a sizeable shareholding in Anglo, that he was losing money by doing so and that he was continuing to chase his losses. I met a friend of Quinn's just before Christmas 2007 and asked if it was true that Quinn was down about €400 million on his rumoured investment. 'Probably,' came the answer, 'but that's nothing to somebody as wealthy as Seán.'

Quinn was always a gambler and – like many other businessmen – he could not have succeeded in building up his vast wealth if he had not been willing to take the type of enormous chances that eventually led to the massive losses that humbled him.

Quinn grew up on a small farm of twenty-three acres in Derrylin, County Fermanagh. He left formal education at fourteen because he didn't like school and began working as an agricultural contractor, rotavating soil for local farmers. He once said that he was the worst farmer in Europe, so in 1973, the year he met his wife, Patricia, he borrowed £100, sank a well on the family farm, extracted the gravel, washed it on site and sold it to local builders, using just one truck to start.

He expanded into roof tiles, thermal blocks, tarmac, insulation products and, most importantly, readymix cement. In the late 1980s he opened a cement plant in Fermanagh to compete with the monopoly supplier Irish Cement, owned by the Irish multinational Cement Roadstone Holdings. Quinn later complained that his efforts were 'confronted with strong systematic and sophisticated industry opposition'. Without providing evidence, he accused some unnamed parties within the industry of bringing pressure on banks not to support him; objecting to his planning applications; preventing some major international cement plant suppliers from selling him technology; and making representations to the Northern Ireland Industrial Development Board to restrict his grant aid. He still managed to raise £25 million in borrowings and was so successful that within less than a decade Quinn Cement could afford a new €80 million plant in Cavan, within sight of the Shannon–Erne waterway, producing one million tonnes of cement each year.

He built a glass-making factory near Derrylin that would use the sand from his quarries. The £70 million Fermanagh glass plant, which had a capacity of 170,000 tonnes a year, had the capacity to supply all the glass that was needed for food and drink products in the whole Irish market and had the currency advantage of dealing in sterling into the British market, as well as a lower cost base.

Quickly, Irish Glass, based on a massive site in Ringsend, Dublin 4, beside the river, was out of business as its owner Ardagh moved operations to Britain. It used part of the proceeds of the sale of the site to finance the purchase of a British glass-maker called Rockware, pitching Ardagh into a bitter conflict with Quinn in Britain when the latter built a new £300 million container-glass manufacturing plant in Chester. Relations between Quinn and Ardagh's multimillionaire controller Paul Coulson soured during this period, especially when Coulson claimed that Quinn had broken all of its planning permissions by building a far-bigger-than-allowed plant, helped by British government grant aid of about £300 million. Subsequently, Quinn had to fight an attempt by the local council in Chester to close and demolish the plant.

Building in scale became a Quinn hallmark as he sought not just to take on established companies in sectors he felt needed competition but to smash them. He was ruthless in dealing with competition.

Considerable embarrassment was caused to Quinn by public disclosure of its attempts to stop Lagan Cement of Belfast from building a €50 million production plant near Kilbeggan in County Westmeath to produce 450,000 tonnes of cement per annum and create 200 jobs.

Quinn took legal proceedings against the planning permission granted to Lagan, but in October 2000 Mr Justice John Quirke in the High Court said the action was mounted in 'a cynical, calculated and unscrupulous fashion . . . I am satisfied that the sole purpose of the proceedings is to inflict damage upon its competitor, Lagan. I am satisfied that that is an improper purpose for the commencement of proceedings and an improper use of the process of the courts.'

Underhand efforts to stymie the project had been discovered, such as covert payments totalling nearly €40,000 from the Barge pub in Dublin, which Quinn owned, to the Ballinabrackey Residents' Action Group that had fought the planning application. Mr Justice John Quirke said the Quinn group had not come to court with 'clean hands' and was involved in 'doubtful practices' in funding the protest group.

Quinn subsequently explained his actions by reference to a history of personal disputes between him and Kevin Lagan of Lagan Cement. 'We have never objected to planning permission before in our lives,' he said. 'This is the first thing I've done to him [Kevin Lagan] that I am not proud of.'

But Quinn remained defiant, and indeed saw himself as something of a victim, as a statement from the company to the editor of the *Irish Times* emphasized. 'We believe Seán Quinn as an individual and the Group in general has suffered more than any other Irish company in its efforts to enter markets controlled by monopolies in the various industries which it operates . . . The Group's history shows that we have never been afraid of competition, not afraid to break the mould in Irish business by taking on well-established players.'

In August 2005 the Labour Court instructed Quinn Cement to place workers on a 39-hour week and implement other benefits, saying that the company had failed to honour commitments made previously to the court when unions had complained about its failure to engage in collective bargaining with members represented by trade unions. The company had promised in March 2005 to implement the shorter working week, review its grievance and disciplinary procedures, utilize the machinery of the state in appropriate industrial relations cases and to introduce a sick-pay scheme, but within months the Labour Court decided that Quinn had not honoured its commitments.

Yet much of this was ignored because he continued to invest in Ireland and to create jobs. He opened a landfill in Armagh and 18.5-megawatt wind farms in Derrylin and Ballyconnell to sell electricity into the national grid. Quinn Packaging specialized in the dairy spread and margarine container sector in Ireland, with a facility in Cavan beginning operations in 2006.

Not everybody has had praise for him, though. In 2008, just four years after Quinn scuppered a planned management buyout of the Barlo radiator plant in Clonmel, County Tipperary, by buying the company, he closed the plant, at the cost of ninety jobs, and moved manufacturing to the new £300 million plant he had constructed in Newport in Wales, with enormous British government financial assistance. Quinn argued the efficiencies associated with the replacement of four old and inefficient radiator plants by one new one in Wales had proved very effective in preserving margins in a slowing market: the new plant produced more than four million radiators annually, or one every fifteen seconds.

The Clonmel plant had operated for over forty years, and local Fianna Fáil TD and junior minister Martin Mansergh angrily asked why Quinn had denied the Irish plant investment and whether he had bought it merely to close it. 'It has often been said, and very often unfairly, that multinationals are footloose with no commitment to their current locations. It is deeply disappointing that an Irish-owned group, Seán Quinn, should close down a manufacturing plant here to transfer it to Wales,' he said. The scale of the new Welsh plant, however, may now be haunting Quinn during the recession.

Quinn's expansion in recent years has been spectacular. He has established radiator and plastic manufacturing plants in Germany, Belgium, France, Spain and Slovakia as well. He has also planned a €300 million chemical-production facility in Leipzig, Germany, which is being developed by Quinn Chemicals, but opening has been delayed until 2010 at the earliest, apparently because of cost overruns in its construction.

But if construction-related manufacturing remained essential to him, it was his investments in property and insurance that were mainly responsible for catapulting him into the super-rich league.

22

Going for growth

Quinn's first big diversification out of cement came as early as 1990, into what he called the 'hospitality' sector.

In 1990 he bought Parkes Hotel in Dublin, the Kilmore Hotel in Cavan and a few very large pubs in Dublin, including two that went under the family name: one in Drumcondra, near Croke Park, and one at Harolds Cross. He bought the Barge pub on the Grand Canal near Portobello, before later establishing Messers Maguire and the Q-Bar in the city centre. He liked the cash flow of the pub business: getting paid as soon as drink is sold but before the supplier gets his money. This was when the pub trade was still highly profitable, before the smoking ban, high prices and a societal shift to home drinking undermined the business.

He bought Buswells Hotel opposite Dáil Éireann, a favourite with rural TDs, and then took his biggest gamble – building the landmark Slieve Russell in west Cavan, almost in the middle of nowhere apart from the lakelands, at a cost of around £14 million. It proved a remarkable success. He anticipated the rise in popularity of fitness centres and established the Iveagh Fitness Club in a converted listed building near Christchurch in Dublin city centre.

He foresaw the downturn in the Irish pub trade and sold some pubs in the early part of this century. However, he simultaneously became a massive investor in hotels outside of Ireland and paid some very high prices. His most eye-catching acquisition in Britain was the £186 million Belfry, a property near Birmingham that included a 324-bedroom luxury hotel with leisure and conference facilities alongside three golf courses, including the internationally famous Brabazon, which has hosted the Ryder Cup four times. The Belfry had a turnover of just £34 million in the year before purchase and operating profit of just £12.2 million, but Quinn saw the prospect of better-than-average capital appreciation due to the trophy status of the property – the thinking behind many of the high-profile commercial property purchases made by Irish buyers in the UK. Even then this rationale seemed doubtful, long before the property crash.

His 2004 purchase of the Prague Hilton for €145 million was cited as the largest-recorded single-asset transaction in Czech Republic history. He embarked on a €50 million expansion and upgrading of the property, bought the Sheraton in Krakow in Poland and the Hilton in Sofia in Bulgaria. He bought a number of business centres and shopping centres, such as the Prestige mall in Turkey, the Caspiy business centre in Moscow and the Leonardo business and retail centre in Ukraine. He developed an enormous fascination for India and has sought property acquisitions there too.

The funding for much of Quinn's expansion came from his entry to the cash-generative insurance business in Ireland in 1996, apparently based initially on his frustration at the price his businesses had to pay to others for insurance.

Founded at the end of 1995, Quinn Insurance (QIL) had fifty-six staff and a turnover of €15 million in its first year. By 2007 QIL's turnover was almost €1.1 billion, with a workforce of over 2,000, based in Cavan, Enniskillen, Dublin, Cork and Manchester. It was the second-largest insurer in Ireland and had more than a million customers. It had gone from providing non-life assurance, concentrating mainly on motor, home and liability insurance, into all types of cover, including life and pensions and, with the takeover of Bupa Ireland in 2007, healthcare, all under the Quinn brand name.

The Bupa takeover was not without controversy, causing a major row with the government. Quinn took control of Bupa Ireland, and the 475,000 contracts with its customers, in January 2007 after Bupa's British owners said the imposition of risk-equalization compensation payments to the dominant, state-controlled VHI meant their Irish business was unviable. Risk equalization, in this context, means that other insurance companies must compensate VHI because its customer base is much older than those of its competitors, and therefore likely to make bigger and more regular claims; VHI's profits would thereby be reduced. Rivals claim that the end effect of the compensation will be an unfair advantage for VHI, allowing it to maintain 75 per cent of the market.

Quinn reckoned that, as a 'new entrant' to the market, he would be able to avoid making those payments to the VHI for three years, as allowed by the law. But the company hedged its bets, doing its €150 million deal with Bupa subject to a reduction in price should the three-year exemption not be applied and should it not be able to keep its subscriber base. It was a wise decision: the government felt that avoidance of the payment would be contrary to the intention of the laws, as Quinn was buying such a large existing operator. It introduced emergency legislation to stop him by abolishing the three-year exemption for equalization payments for new entrants. In turn, Quinn was allowed to cut the purchase price by a 'radical' amount, which later turned out to be more than €100 million. Quinn argued that he was doing the state a favour by saving 300 jobs, providing competition and continuing cover for Bupa members who might not have wanted to join the VHI or the other competitor, Vivas. He met Minister for Health Mary Harney, but even when he promised to maintain community rating – the system whereby everybody paid the same irrespective of their age and the likelihood of having to use their insurance – she didn't change her mind. He claimed he offered to buy VHI, which she wouldn't entertain on competition grounds.

Harney's refusal prompted him to issue a personal statement to the press, although he was not available to take questions about it. Quinn attacked VHI strongly, arguing that

the VHI is in our opinion trading illegally without the required solvency, is charging far too much for their products and is being propped up by the Irish taxpayer without any accountability . . . The existence of the VHI in its current form, with no solvency margin and being subsidized by its competitors, is totally at odds with any definition of fair play.

In our view, the position taken by the VHI and now backed by this legislation, is untenable. We completed a contract with Bupa based on existing legislation and now the government brings in emergency legislation to make us subsidize their own business, which we believe to be trading illegally. How can we be expected to run a business if government can change legislation retrospectively which changes this business from a profitable activity to a loss-making one?

He pointed out how the Quinn Group was a private company that met all Irish and international solvency obligations, employed over 4,000 people in the state and contributed over €100 million annually in taxes (this would include PAYE on wages, PRSI and VAT, not just corporate tax). 'We have reduced the price of general insurance in Ireland by 45 per cent over the past five years and have more than trebled our market share.'

He claimed that 'our intentions at all stages in this process have been to bring much needed competition to a dysfunctional health insurance market', although a cynic might have said that profit was his main concern, an argument buttressed by his asking 'the public to support us in that commitment by moving your business immediately to Quinn and giving a clear message to VHI'.

Quinn's venting amounted to little more than the letting off of hot air. Harney and the VHI denied his accusations and were vindicated by Supreme Court judgments confirming the legitimacy of the risk equalization legislation and VHI's actions.

Clearly, he saw an opportunity to make money, just as Dermot Desmond did when he entered the market in 2004 as an investor in Vivas. Quinn Healthcare – as Bupa Ireland was later renamed – has continued in business ever since.

Quinn made significant profits from insurance, as the annual publication of profits revealed, at least until 2008. In the five years between 2003 and 2007 Quinn Insurance had performed well enough to 'gift' €570 million to its owner, although this could perhaps be better described as dividends.

It was an extraordinary recovery from the performance of 2000 and 2001, when the business incurred not just heavy underwriting losses but, in a sign of things to come, also heavy investment losses from punting on dotcom stocks. Quinn famously sacked himself as investment manager after losses understood to have amounted to €70 million and then provided that amount in new capital to the insurance company, from both group and personal resources. Again, he was defiant. 'The only time that Quinn-Direct will be in trouble is when Seán Quinn is in trouble,' he stated.

Rivals in the insurance industry were scornful of Quinn's business practices. What really seemed to upset competitors was the Quinn policy of undercutting their prices, all of which was to the benefit of consumers. However, competitors alleged this had serious consequences, claiming that Quinn pressed customers to make settlements for low amounts of money too quickly.

Quinn appeared very conscious of the media by this stage: in his 2009 RTÉ interview he complained about an 'outlandish, outrageous media frenzy' and an agenda against his group that he couldn't understand. It is likely that he put coverage of the case involving Dubliner John Deegan into this category, although it was a shocking story that received much attention and for good reason.

The High Court heard early in 2009 how Deegan, a father of five, had been a passenger in a car that crashed in 2003. He had spent a month in intensive care after his accident and, because his injuries had left him a paraplegic, he had been incapable of independent living since. The driver admitted fault and Deegan claimed against the driver's insurance, which was with Quinn. The company refused to pay. It claimed that Deegan had sustained his injuries in a fall from a third-storey balcony. It was six years after the time of the accident before the case was heard.

Mr Justice John Quirke then learned that there was no evidence to support the claims by Quinn and furthermore that the company was in possession of a Garda report stating that there was no such evidence. Quirke said it was a 'very serious' matter that such grave allegations were made in open court by 'a very substantial and well resourced company'. Quinn promptly offered a settlement of €1.75 million, which was accepted.

Once the glitch of 2000 and 2001 was covered, the company prospered financially during the subsequent stock market and property boom. Again, however, the company played with fire, taking a riskier approach to investments than its competitors, most of which traditionally held about half of their assets in government bonds, which pay a lower level of return but which are at far less risk of loss.

In 2006 QIL held just 33 per cent of its €1.25 billion of investments in cash and bonds, while almost 50 per cent was held in shares of companies that could be traded on the stock market, known as 'equities'. The rest was held in 'loans and investments' to subsidiaries of the Quinn Group, including a €123 million investment in the 100 per cent ownership in the group's hotel and property company and €73 million to other property investments in Britain and Ireland.

By 2007, 46 per cent of QIL's €1.5 billion investment portfolio was tied up in 'loans and shares' of the Quinn Group's companies, meaning that the insurance company's dependence on Seán Quinn's investment strategy was becoming more pronounced. More detailed figures supplied to the Financial Regulator showed that 40 per cent of its assets were invested in shares and property; with dreadful timing, between 2006 and 2007 it had doubled its exposure to property to €574 million, which amounted to over a quarter of its total assets of €2 billion. Throughout 2007 the company reduced its holdings in shares from €600 million to €175 million, though this may have represented the falling value of the shares held as much as the sale of those shares to raise cash. It seems that the movement of a landfill site and a wind farm on to the insurance company's balance sheet may have been some compensation. Thankfully, Quinn retained €783 million in cash, but, unlike other insurers, Quinn had no government bonds.

An investment strategy that did not undermine Quinn's ability to finance the payment of legitimate claims to customers was crucial, not just for the company itself but for the Financial Regulator, which had to oversee this in order to avoid any possible failure that might undermine the entire industry. At the end of 2006 it did not seem that there were any real problems, however. Quinn Group had made profits of €432 million, €322 million of which was attributable to the Quinn-Direct insurance business. The group turnover in 2006 was €1.4 billion and more than 5,000 people were employed. But Seán Quinn was about to engage in what would prove to be a dangerous escapade with enormous consequences. He secretly began investing in Anglo Irish Bank, but did not do so with his own or borrowed money, instead depending on a complicated and excessively risky alternative method.

23

The St Patrick's Day massacre

The story of prudent Seán Quinn's five-euro gambles at Tuesday-evening card games was rendered ridiculous by the manner in which he bought shares in Anglo Irish Bank and suffered horrendous losses. Quinn's full losses may never be revealed officially, but they have been estimated at more than €1 billion – which made his survival an extraordinary feat.

Quinn's initial investment in Anglo was confirmed in January 2007, although he offered no comment about his purchase of 36.6 million shares. Newspapers quoted 'sources close to Quinn' as describing the purchase as an investment and not part of any strategic stake building or a prelude to a takeover. The Quinn stake was valued at €574 million, with the Anglo share price not far short of €16. The purchase was a surprise, as Quinn had said he planned to invest almost exclusively in opportunities in Russia, Eastern Europe and India.

In early September 2007 Anglo made very encouraging noises about its performance, promising it would exceed profit expectations when it reported for the year ending that month. It boasted of having increased its volume of lending, and stock market analysts anticipated an increase in net new loans of more than €17 billion for the year. Anglo said asset quality – in other words, the security upon which loans were advanced – was 'robust' and that interest margins – the profit it made on the difference between the cost of the money it used and the price customers paid for it – remained 'stable'. It described its liquidity position – the availability to the bank of the money it needed to do its business – as 'excellent'.

That may have been gobbledygook to most, but its accuracy was very important to investors and should have been to the Financial Regulator. Anglo said it had increased its customer deposits by close to €15 billion, an increase of 40 per cent, which would help in financing its lending. The bank said it had raised more than €1.8 billion in additional capital, to provide a buffer against any unexpected losses. 'Our Tier 1 capital position is strong, at in excess of 8 per cent, leaving the bank very well placed for the future.' Group chief executive David Drumm said: 'We believe that the current uncertainty in markets demonstrates the attractiveness of our relationship-driven model.' Anglo's shares fell by 2.5 per cent, closing at €13.80, although this was blamed on the trend in global stock markets.

Quinn decided that he could buck the markets. He believed in Anglo and bought more shares, albeit secretly. Rumours grew – and were reported in the media – that the 7 per cent shareholding held by Credit Suisse was effectively a proxy for Quinn and that he had more shares by way of Contracts for Difference (CFD), the mechanism by which an investor could take effective ownership of a share but pay to take title for it from third parties at a future date.

CFDs are usually described in financial circles as a 'derivative instrument'. They enable an investor to take a position on a stock and its likely performance, without actually owning the shares. The gambler merely buys an entitlement to the gains (and the losses) on the share in a particular period, although he may be required to take title to the shares earlier than he had intended and at the behest of the CFD provider, even if he does not want to do so, usually because something has gone wrong with the investment. When it all works out, and the buyer has bought the rights to future ownership of the shares before they increase in value, it means he has to put out the serious money only once he's already in profit. The buyer, whose identity remains secret, avoids the 1 per cent stamp duty that applies to the transfer of shares, at least until such time as ownership of the share certificates changes.

While the tax saving may be attractive, avoiding stamp duty isn't the main reason for the use of CFDs. The more significant advantage is the number of shares in a company that can be controlled by their use, without having to put up all of the money to buy the shares immediately. CFD providers typically looked for investors to put up 10 per cent of the value of the shares and charged a fee for providing the rest of the finance. Quinn could buy the right to ten times as many shares as he could buy himself with cash at any one time. In some respects it was applying the principles of the property market to the stock market. An investor has a limited amount of equity so he borrows the remainder to purchase the asset.

If Quinn had €100 million to use in buying shares, the use of CFDs allowed him to buy the right to the future ownership of €1 billion worth of stock instead. The profits from doing this were potentially enormous. If the shares went up by 10 per cent, Quinn's shares would have been worth €1.1 billion. He could sell the shares, repay the CFD finance and make a profit equal to his initial equity in the process. Or he could convert the CFDs into shares at the old share price, meaning that he had made a big immediate profit, on paper at least.

Imagine, though, that instead of going up the shares go down by 10 per cent. The provider of the finance for the CFD will demand its money back, which has to be raised by the sale of the shares for €900 million. All of Quinn's equity – €100 million – is gone and he will have paid fees as well for the use of the CFDs. But, worse, if the share price falls too fast to get the sale made in time, say by 30 per cent, then the shares cannot be sold for enough money to repay the loan in full. Suddenly, Quinn has lost his €100 million, has sold the shares and still owes the bank another €200 million. Whereas with property or land, an asset with some residual value remains; with shares all that remains is paper. If Quinn wanted to hold on to the shares in the hope that they would recover value, as he did with Anglo, then he had to make payments to the CFD holder to cover its risk in supporting that strategy.

The Financial Regulator should have acted at the stage when rumours about Quinn effectively owning the Credit Suisse-held shares in Anglo were circulating. EU banking rules state that a country's domestic regulator must approve the purchase of an interest of 10 per cent or more in a registered and regulated bank. The regulator is required to step in when there is 'a direct or indirect holding in an undertaking which represents 10 per cent or more of the capital or of the voting rights, or which makes it possible to exercise a significant influence over the management of that undertaking'. When the 10 per cent limit is reached, the regulator is required to assess issues such as the reputation of the purchaser of the shareholding, its 'financial soundness' and whether the acquisition would hinder its ability to comply with its 'existing prudential requirements'.

As Quinn was already a major player in the financial services industry through his insurance business – the second biggest in Ireland – the regulator's inaction became even more important – even if the claimed reason for inaction was that Quinn's identity was not apparent because he was hiding behind the use of CFDs.

While Quinn's net worth was estimated at close to €4 billion during 2007, this would not have been nearly enough to buy a bank valued at close to €13.3 billion during the summer of 2007. It did give the potential to borrow, however. Some with long memories remembered how Tony Ryan had purchased a 5 per cent stake in Bank of Ireland back in 1988 for about £30 million and how this had led to speculation that he or GPA, the then highly profitable aircraft-leasing company he controlled, would make a bid to buy the bank. It didn't happen – and Ryan barely recovered his money when he subsequently sold his shares – but that didn't stop speculation that Quinn might be braver.

Anglo had alerted the Financial Regulator about its suspicions, knowing that the size of Quinn's holding had significant consequences for the trade in the shares – and the potential to influence the performance of the share price. It is not known what action, if any, the regulator took. Somehow Quinn got to increase his interest in Anglo to 25 per cent, which raises the most serious questions about the performance of the regulator while Quinn increased his involvement in CFDs.

It should also have acted because of the failure of Northern Rock in Britain. It had to be rescued from collapse by way of nationalization: the taking of the bank into state ownership by wiping out the ownership of its shareholders. Although they had different origins – Northern Rock being an old building society – there were many similarities between the two in how they funded their business, even if the Irish bank was focused on commercial development rather than on residential mortgages.

Northern Rock floundered because it had lent an amount of money that was too large in relation to its deposit base. It was reliant on raising money on interbank markets that it then lent to its customers. When the price of money on interbank markets suddenly shot up, because of the effects of the credit crunch, Northern Rock suddenly could not fund its business. Anglo's emphasis on the perceived strength of its deposit base in its September report was now more understandable.

Anglo had two concerns to address if it was to retain the confidence of shareholders: its own method of financing its business; and the possibility that the loans it had made would not be repaid, given that many commentators were talking increasingly about the likelihood of the construction boom coming to a shuddering halt. Anglo's exposure to the property and development sector was known to be huge and the potential for losses on loans that could not be repaid was looming.

When Anglo's full-year results for the year-end September 2007 were released in mid-November 2007, they assumed an enormous importance for investors in the Irish stock market – and for those interested in the economy overall. The results appeared to be spectacular and seemed to put fears to rest. In the year up to 30 September 2007 profits reached €1.2 billion, making Anglo only the fourth Irish company ever to break the billion profits mark in a year. Its total loans had grown to €67 billion, although over 80 per cent of that was related to commercial property.

An ebullient Drumm conducted interviews with the print business media. He was determined to show that Anglo lent more to other banks than it borrowed, that it never had to rely on emergency funding from the European Central Bank or other lenders of last resort. Anglo emphasized that its €56 billion customer deposit base funded two thirds of its lending and that it never did anything that could be equated with subprime lending. He called the deposits a 'sticky' form of funding that would not dry up overnight in the way that interbank funding can. 'We are local lenders,' Drumm told Brian Carey of the *Sunday Times*. 'When we loan it, we own it – it stays on our balance sheet. We never break the chain of ownership and responsibility. That is exactly what happened with subprime. If we make a mistake on a loan, it is our mistake, nobody else's. We know the deals, we are close to the customer.'

The shares went up 15 per cent initially on those results, going up to €11.58 and giving the bank an overall stock market value of €8.8 billion. Quinn – who was sitting on major undisclosed losses by this stage – increased his bets. But not everybody was convinced, and it was a temporary bounce before the slide resumed. Drumm's strategy of growing the loan book aggressively, increasing the amount advanced to borrowers from €50 billion to €67 billion in just one year, didn't impress everyone. Merrill Lynch warned of Anglo's 'higher than expected' proportion of loans to fund speculative property development projects. Although this was the story that gained traction, Anglo was not helped by Quinn's still secret but widely speculated upon trade in CFDs and the decision of massive international hedge funds to bet against his judgement. Short-sellers knew it was most probably Quinn that they were betting against – which meant they were up against an extremely rich adversary – but they also knew that his exposure was too large and that his judgement on Anglo's health was most probably wrong.

In using CFDs, Quinn had gambled heavily that the share price would rise. He continued to do so even as the share price fell, believing it would rise again, instead of giving up and cutting his losses.

He engaged in a battle of wills and judgement with short-sellers, who sold shares expecting to buy them back later at a lower price. If they didn't have the shares to sell, they borrowed them from someone else. They sold the borrowed shares and then repurchased those shares, or shares from someone else, at a later date so they could return them to their original owner. The difference in price was their profit. The lenders of the shares were paid a fee for this, although it was a doubtful practice because if continued for too long it could drive the shares down to a point where they no longer had any value.

Quinn could hardly complain about their behaviour in hoping that the share price would fall, given that he had secretly assembled his shareholding through the mirror-image device of CFDs – which were based on the hope that it would continue to rise. Anglo effectively became the battleground between Quinn and the hedge funds. Their target was Quinn, but the victim was Anglo. However, these short-sellers would never have succeeded had there not been good reason to doubt the Anglo story that all was well; the company was vulnerable because of its underlying problems.

Many of the problems came to a head on St Patrick's Day in 2008, when the Irish stock market was shut but trade in Irish stocks continued in London. Anglo started 17 March with a share price of €6.90 – already a 60 per cent fall from its peak – but this then fell by what was at that time an extraordinary 23 per cent in just one day.

This was attributed mainly to hedge funds profiting from the international fear caused by the near-collapse of Bear Stearns in New York: they sought out weak banks and engaged ruthlessly in short-selling. Anglo angrily pointed out that Bear Stearns had a massive subprime exposure that the Irish bank didn't have. It claimed that hedge funds and Irish brokers were spreading malicious and untrue rumours. It complained to the regulator and wrote bitter letters to Davy Stockbrokers – to whose management it had provided finance for its own management buyout – and Merrion stockbrokers, accusing them of undermining it. The regulator – in conjunction with the Financial

Services Authority in the UK – issued a statement on 20 March, saying that it was concerned by 'false and misleading rumours' linked to the trading pattern in shares (there was no criticism, however, of Davy and Merrion, which had done their job as brokers in advising clients). Though it didn't mention Anglo, everyone knew who was meant.

In retrospect there may have been more substance to the short-selling than mere opportunism. What Anglo concealed from the markets was relevant information about its own funding. Anglo faced a crisis that month because of the shrinking availability of ready cash on the money markets and its higher price. Just as bad was the fact that corporate depositors withdrew or reduced their funds, or put them on shorter terms. This may have been a reaction to the rumours of bad-debt problems circulating, but, whatever the reason, it caused a real problem.

It wasn't revealed until nearly a year later, when Anglo was in state ownership, that Irish Life & Permanent's insurance division, Irish Life Assurance, had made an emergency deposit of €750 million in Anglo at Anglo's request, and with security provided by Anglo, on 31 March 2008. The route by which the money was transferred to Anglo artificially inflated the deposits figure shown in Anglo's interim results for the six months that ended that day. Anglo, having claimed it was the victim of 'market skulduggery' less than two weeks earlier, was engaged in activity that could be said to have misled shareholders.

No one has ever been sanctioned after the investigation by the regulator into the alleged manipulation of the Anglo shares on St Patrick's Day. There may have been a lack of evidence, but this could also be because the regulator has conceded that the short-sellers acted rationally, correctly sensing that Anglo was massively overvalued and was having problems that others in the market had not at that point yet assessed.

This meant Quinn's position, still not confirmed publicly, became more important – and had to be sorted. It created a false market in the shares. Had the extent of his investment been known, it might have persuaded many existing and potential investors in Anglo shares to have behaved differently. The presence of a shareholder with a large stake reduced the amount of shares considered freely available for trading. The size of the so-called 'free float' of Anglo stock was important to its weighting in the ISEQ index – and would influence the size of holding by some institutional investors.

The extent of Anglo's share price fall now terrified many investors, especially multimillionaire developers who had put a significant part of their property profits into Anglo shares and who were now seeing the loss of much of that profit. They worried that a weakened Anglo would not be able to provide the finance for their future ventures. But they continued to believe the stories that Anglo was fundamentally sound and the victim of devious attack by short-selling hedge funds who wanted to profit by ruining the bank.

In April and May 2008 two separate meetings were held at the Shelbourne and Citywest hotels by groups of property developers: they discussed establishing a 'revenge fund' that would buy the shares, send the price upwards and rout the short-sellers. The investors would contribute €500 million of their own money, borrow more and buy enough shares to make a significant impact.

It might have worked had Quinn already not been beaten by the short-sellers. A new crisis had crystallized for Quinn, for Anglo, for the regulator and, ultimately, for the state. Quinn had lost the biggest bet of his life. He would have to close his CFD position and take a huge loss by admitting ownership of the Anglo shares.

24

Losing the biggest bet of his life

In early July 2008 Seán Quinn finally admitted what many people had believed for a long time: that he owned a substantial number of shares in Anglo Irish Bank. But it wasn't presented like that: his admission was partial and did not answer some crucial questions that were posed then and also emerged subsequently. Indeed, the statement concealed some very important facts that, had they been known, might have led investors to look at Anglo's shares very differently.

Quinn said that his family was taking control of 15 per cent of the shares in the company and each family member would be allocated a parcel of just under 3 per cent. While he admitted that he was converting CFDs, nothing was said about how much this had cost him. Far more importantly, nothing was said about a substantial amount of other shares in Anglo that Quinn had held the rights to via his CFDs – another 10 per cent. Why had he not taken ownership of them? Who owned them now? In what circumstances had they bought them? Was he unable to afford to buy the shares himself or had the regulator stopped him?

Quinn's brief statement said 'the family regards these shareholdings in Anglo Irish Bank as long-term holdings, with significant opportunity for capital growth over such a period.' The bluff and guff continued: 'In recent years, we have been highly impressed with Anglo's ability to outperform the banking sector in terms of profit growth, and we are confident this trend can be maintained over the longer term, notwith-standing the current difficulties being experienced in international banking.'

Those 'difficulties' drove the share price down from its peak of €17.85 to just €4.36 on the day Quinn's shareholding was confirmed. It was reckoned that Quinn bought the rights to most of his shares at prices of between €13.25 and €17 but hadn't taken delivery because of the nature of the CFDs. The CFD providers forced 'margin calls' on him – demanding cash – as the share price fell. Eventually, Quinn realized that this wasn't going to stop and he regularized matters. He spent €500 million on taking formal control of 15 per cent of Anglo's shares by converting most of the CFDs but spent an estimated €1 billion in additional payments to the companies that held the CFDs for him.

The Financial Regulator was notably silent in public comment after the formal confirmation of Quinn's investment. It was assumed that the regulator had been informed about the purchase of the shares out of the CFD position and given its approval for the Quinn family, as connected parties, to own these shares, as was required under the so-called 10 per cent rule (the regulator had to decide whether someone owning more than 10 per cent of the shares in a financial institution was fit and proper to do so). But what did the regulator know of the information contained in a genuine scoop on the front page of the *Sunday Business Post* ten days after Quinn's announcement?

It revealed that the Quinn Group had taken out a loan – for an undisclosed amount – with Anglo and had secured it on assets within the Quinn group just two weeks before the public announcement of the share purchase. Details of a charge over preference shares in Quinn – security for provision of the loan – had been lodged with the Companies Registration Office six days before the Anglo announcement.

Quinn had already engaged in a complicated ownership restructuring that involved the establishment of several offshore finance companies in Jersey, one of which had become involved in a mortgage deal with Anglo the previous January for an undisclosed sum. This restructuring was to prove highly significant because the main element essentially moved control of the group south of the border, and the Quinn family was now restricted in what it could do with its assets by the security offered to Anglo. It could not sell or otherwise transfer those shares in the holding group while the loan was outstanding, unless the bank agreed first. It appeared that an enormous amount of the Quinn assets were covered by the charge given to Anglo: the holding company owns the subsidiaries that control the insurance businesses Quinn Healthcare and Quinn-Direct, as well as the Quinn concrete and quarrying operations, property interests, and glass, radiator and plastics manufacturing businesses. That suggested the loan was an exceptionally big one, possibly running into billions of euro.

Around the time Anglo gave Quinn his loan, the bank's chief executive David Drumm said publicly that the credit crunch had resulted in Anglo becoming far more selective about its lending, as access to funding was tight and 'you cannot lend what you do not have'. It emerged later that Drumm had personally approved the loan to Quinn. What confidence, for example, could Drumm have had that the Quinn Group would survive the major losses on the investment in Anglo, given that he must have calculated these amounted to well over €1 billion by this stage? How did he intend to deal with Quinn the borrower as distinct from Quinn his largest individual shareholder? Actions to protect Anglo's loan could cause problems for Quinn that would in turn cause problems for his own bank, in a corporate Catch-22.

There was a more serious and immediate legal issue. Section 60 of the Companies Act 1963 expressly stopped companies from making loans to third parties that would be used to buy shares in the lending company. Although the documents lodged with the CRO said the loan was for 'general corporate purposes', it was clear that it was needed because of Quinn's losses on Anglo shares. A potential loophole in the legislation allowed the advance of money to buy shares if it is lent as 'part of the ordinary business of the company'. This seemed to be a useful get-out for a bank, although, as emerged subsequently, there was nothing ordinary about this particular transaction.

The bank supplied the regulator with legal advice about the appropriateness of the loan. It argued Anglo was allowed to lend money to Quinn because it was not for the specific purpose of buying shares in Anglo. Astonishingly, the regulator apparently accepted this opinion without independent verification. However, it is hard to believe anything other than that Anglo's loan to its new biggest shareholder helped Quinn to pay for shares bought through CFDs.

Quinn carried on as if all was normal. A month later – he wrote an article for the *Irish Times* as part of a series by business people offering their views as to how Ireland could recover from the economic downturn – Quinn confirmed that he and his family had suffered equity losses 'as a result of the stock market downturn over the past year'. With dry understatement, he said these were 'not pleasant'. He added, however, that the losses were 'not the most important thing to me'.

It wasn't until the October bank holiday weekend that the regulator and the company finally disclosed more details, issuing brief statements, with sensational impact. The regulator announced that it had reached a 'settlement' with Quinn personally and QIL over its 'failure to notify of the provision of loans to related companies'. Quinn was being fined €200,000 personally and was stepping down as chairman of QIL. The company itself was fined €3.25 million.

Quinn, as part of his gambling in Anglo shares, had taken €288 million from QIL's reserves as a loan. He hadn't asked the regulator for permission, which is not surprising, because it is hard to see how the regulator could have given it. The regulator said it accepted Quinn's 'confirmation' that 'no consequences have arisen for any of the firm's policyholders as a result of the suspected breaches'. Fortunately, it seems that most of the money had been repaid to Quinn Insurance.

It was extremely serious and raised all sorts of questions as to whether the punishments were severe enough – even if the fine was by far the highest ever levied in the history of Irish financial regulation. QIL, one of the most important insurance companies in the state, with well over one million customers, had been used in this instance as a slush-fund by its owner. QIL had been put at risk for as long as the €288 million loan was unpaid. It wasn't enough for Quinn to say that it was his company and that he would make good the debt. His failed investment in Anglo meant his financial capability should have been for regulators to decide.

For good reasons there are strict rules as to what insurance companies can do with their money. Insurance companies must maintain sufficient cash balances, or investments that can be turned quickly into cash, to meet the solvency ratios and reserves required by the regulator. They must have enough money to pay legitimate claims to customers promptly. The loans advanced by QIL to its owner 'materially reduced' the solvency margin in 2007, a note to the accounts of QIL revealed. The recovery of the €288 million was 'subject to significant uncertainties including future investment performance and material credit risks', although this was negated by the repayment of the bulk of the loans.

Quinn resigned from the board of the insurance company but in his statement admitting mistakes he could not resist the temptation to claim that he was being victimized. 'I accept complete responsibility for this breach of regulation. While I accept that I made mistakes, I feel that the levels of fines do not reflect the fact that there was no risk to policyholders or the taxpayer, but are a result of the pressures existing in the current environment. However, we will pay the fines and move on,' he said.

He remained as chairman of Quinn Group and disclosed he would 'spend more time on family assets outside the group, particularly our exciting property portfolio, which is now active in ten countries.'

Scrambling to reassure its customers, QIL wrote to insurance brokers within weeks of the regulator's announcement, seeking to address concerns over its reserving policy. Insisting on Quinn Insurance's 'financial strength', the letter told brokers that it continued to trade profitably in 2008, possessed €2 billion of assets and had shareholders' funds in excess of €500 million.

Revelation of the fine and of the transfer of money put a new significance on the announcement the previous July that QIL had withdrawn from the international credit-rating system. Many leading international brokers recommend that their clients do not place business with an insurance company if it is unrated or if its financial strength rating is below a certain grade. Experts said that QIL was risking hurt to its business reputation.

Fortunately, pre-tax profits at QIL remained healthy in 2007 at €245 million, compared with €323 million the previous year, but the group's dependence on stock market investments for profits meant that it would face continuing financial pressure. Throughout all of this the Financial Regulator remained silent publicly.

Quinn Group sought also to reassure its customers about its financial strength. It claimed that, despite 'making one-off losses on equity investments in 2007', it was valued at €3.85 billion in its 2007 financial statements, net of debt, and had very strong cash generation and a low level of debt relative to earnings.

The scale of the losses on the investment in Anglo became somewhat clearer. Quinn Group said it was writing off €829 million advanced in 2007 to firms within the group and others who had made stock market investments for the Quinn family. This turned what would have been a €403 million pre-tax profit into a loss of €426 million for the year – one that, ironically, can be set off against corporation taxes in Ireland in future years.

The group suggested the possibility of a further €130 million write-off for 2008 but said it would not exceed that amount – meaning combined losses to the group of not far short of €1 billion in two years as a result of Quinn's gambling on CFDs. Quinn may have had further losses on

Anglo that he had to fund out of personal resources. He took losses on investments in other companies too, such as stock market-quoted Irish house-builder McInerney Properties, which suffered a collapse in value during the stock market crash.

The shares that had been purchased in July would eventually prove to be worthless, as the bank was taken into state ownership.

So where did that leave Quinn, a major employer in this country as well as owner of many insurance businesses? Would his exposure to construction, tourism and property severely dent the profitability of his empire at a time when he needed its cash to repay loans to Anglo for the purchase of worthless shares? What about the investment performance of his insurance business?

If Quinn had been unable to get the loan from Anglo to close out his CFD position, his entire business empire could have been brought crashing down. The CFD supplier would have demanded that he purchase the shares but he would not have had the money to do so. He would have needed to liquidate assets to raise the money.

Admittedly, Anglo Irish can take control of the Quinn Group should it default on the repayment of its loans, which means that the state would own it, but the nationalization of Quinn's many businesses throughout the globe is not something the state would want to contemplate.

Quinn remains defiant and has insisted that his financial position is far healthier than others would paint it. Early in 2009 he posted a 'new year message to staff and customers' on his company's website that accentuated the positive as he sought to boost morale. He boasted of investment worth €2 billion in new production and service-delivery facilities during the decade, with a significant proportion of this in world-class manufacturing technology. He said the group enjoyed the highest margins in all of the business sectors in which it operates, better than any of those of its competitors, and that he had 'resisted the temptation to reduce prices to below economically sustainable levels'. 'In each of the trading periods 2007, 2008 and 2009 the Quinn Group has and will comfortably generate cash profits of between €400 million and €500 million, before exceptional items,' he said, giving a hostage to fortune about 2009. He said profits would improve in 2010.

He admitted to poor stock market investments – which he said were outside the group – as clearly ill timed, costly and very much regretted. 'While these equity investments were clearly a mistake, I think it is also worthy of note that other investments made outside of the Quinn Group in recent years have been extremely successful, including the creation of a very significant property portfolio spread over ten countries incorporating a large element in the emerging economies.'

While saying he understood the negative media coverage he had received, he expressed surprise that 'some of the group's undoubted strengths have not been recognized.'

He hadn't mentioned Anglo since that remarkable short television interview with RTÉ on 30 January. Describing the Anglo investment as a 'bad mistake' and the loss as 'hurtful', he said he believed others had experienced worse investment outcomes than he had. 'I suppose in hindsight we were too greedy by . . . being so much involved in stocks and shares. We don't owe anybody any great apology. If we owe an apology to anybody it's our staff. Maybe we slowed up the growth of the company and maybe the reputation was tarnished . . . We never at any stage put our company in any undue risk. Any money we put into shares was money we could afford to do without.'

He finished the short interview by declaring 'there's no impropriety in anything we've done in that bank.'

As bravado and hard neck went, it was beaten only by some of the stuff Sean FitzPatrick had come up with over the years.

25

'Fair play to you, Willie'

Under the approving eye of chairman Sean FitzPatrick and the board of directors, the new Anglo Irish Bank chief executive David Drumm ratcheted up the bank's lending at a pace previously unimagined. As wealth in Ireland apparently grew unabated, Anglo sought to take advantage by lending as much as possible to the newly rich, often to invest abroad. As the business grew, so did the share price.

While the company's overall valuation of €13.3 billion caught the eye of investors like Seán Quinn and others, and frightened competing banks, it was the amount of the loans advanced by 2007 that should have worried the regulators. The bank supplied loans of more than €73 billion to customers.

Normally sane men had gone mad, caught up in the speculative bubble, believing the economy and property prices would continue to roar ahead, and that if the boom did end, which they believed it wouldn't, there would be a 'soft landing'.

Anglo managed to be both a conservative bank and an entrepreneurial one simultaneously, even if that appears contradictory. While it supported imaginative and big projects – and had a reputation for offering loan approval quickly – it charged customers more expensive fees for this service. It was also known for getting the best security on loans.

Indeed, when PricewaterhouseCoopers was sent into the bank in late 2008, as part of a review by the government to see what it had guaranteed on 30 September, it initially found itself to be reasonably impressed by Anglo's way of doing business, particularly by its management of its loan book. It noted how it concentrated on proven operators and got first security on assets with strong cross collateral, including personal guarantees on other assets in case payment could not be satisfied by the sale of the first security. It seemed to 'stress test' rigorously the ability of borrowers to repay should their circumstances change adversely. About 65 per cent of its loans were categorized as investment lending to the likes of hotels, offices and shops, most of which generated rental income to help pay off loans. The amount of development lending for land speculation in Ireland had been reduced deliberately in previous years, although it still amounted to nearly €13 billion, and this included newer, and therefore riskier, loans such as the one provided to the consortium that planned to redevelop the Irish Glass Bottle site in Dublin's docklands.

However, it soon became clear to PwC that all was not as well as it first seemed. While Anglo may have been unlucky at the speed of the property market collapse, one that occurred across international markets that hadn't seemed as exposed as Ireland, it was the author of its own misfortune by having such a large exposure to property. Its model worked fine as long as property values continued to rise – or even if they stagnated – but as prices fell many of the previously cash-rich clients suddenly found themselves unable to make repayments.

The concept of interest roll-up – whereby a developer was able to defer all repayments, both of principle and interest, until such time as he sold his units and got the cash in, which would then be used to repay the now larger amount of debt – no longer worked well. It couldn't in a seriously falling market or when the developer couldn't make sales at any price. If houses or apartments couldn't be sold, as increasingly became the case during 2008, or if commercial units couldn't be let or became vacant, developers had massive cash-flow issues – and so too then did Anglo. In August 2008 the bank had claimed that over 99 per cent of all its loans were generating income – and the market didn't believe it.

The PwC report revealed that near the end of 2008 Anglo had about twenty unnamed customers – some individuals, some companies, some consortia – who owed the bank €11.4 billion in total, an average of €570 million, which implies that some owed more than €1 billion. These twenty customers made up a quarter of the bank's Irish loan book. The loans were not exclusively for the property sector. Some had borrowed for investment in assets other than property. These assets also collapsed in value because of events on the stock markets.

The circumstances in which people got loans had become a major issue. Just what were the lending policies at the bank when it came to friends and associates of FitzPatrick and other senior executives and indeed its own staff, many of whom were encouraged to borrow to buy shares in their own bank?

Sometimes Anglo provided loans for gambling on the stock market (in a practice not too far removed from the CFD nonsense that brought Quinn into Anglo). These loans appeared to be good business as long as share prices were increasing and dividend payments on the shares covered all or part of the annual interest on the loan. However, in a falling stock market this lending became crushing for both the borrower and the bank, especially if the loans had been secured on other assets or personal guarantees (although repayment terms may have been relaxed if the borrower enjoyed a special relationship with senior Anglo figures). The problem became worse if a company removed or reduced the dividend on the shares purchased, because this affected the borrower's ability to repay, even before the loss in capital value came into play.

Questions also emerged as to the proportion of equity that was put up by some borrowers in relation to the size of overall investments and how much was borrowed. How many of the loans were provided on an interest-only basis, with interest repayments to be covered by rental or dividend income and the principle paid later when the property or other assets had been sold, presumably at a profit? How much of the profit being claimed by the bank was the rolling over of unpaid interest as if it were a new, profitable loan?

The volume of Anglo's new lending was enormous. After 2000 the Anglo loan book grew by over 300 per cent to €73 billion, with its lending in the US going up 750 per cent to nearly €10 billion. Anglo and the state treated the property boom in much the same way, as if it would never end. And just as the state treated the boosted tax revenues as permanent and spent accordingly, so Anglo assumed that it would always have enough money to support its lending. In retrospect, it was a reckless assumption.

A bank's deposit base is a key clue as to its true health. This gives it the money to lend, although it can be topped up with borrowed money. While it is not possible to do all lending out of deposits, as much lending as possible should be done this way. That protects a bank against what happened in 2008, when much of Anglo's deposits suddenly migrated and its own ability to borrow money evaporated. The international credit crunch played its part in both, but things were made worse by investor fears about Anglo's massive exposure to potential bad debts in the property market.

On 30 September 2007, its financial year-end, Anglo had customer deposits of €53 billion available to it. A year later it looked as if the comparable figure would be just €46 billion, a fall of 13 per cent, as money had suddenly flowed out of the bank. PwC subsequently revealed that in one week in late September 2008 Anglo had lost corporate deposits of €5 billion and retail deposits of €440 million, bringing its total loss that month to €10 billion. Had that trend continued, it is possible that without government intervention Anglo would have had negative net cash of €12 billion by the middle of October. Anglo was still solvent, having an excess of assets over liabilities, but it was becoming illiquid, which would bring on a collapse.

Any announcement of Anglo's loss of deposits would have severely damaged whatever remaining confidence there was in the bank. The problem was immediate, and Anglo had to find money from somewhere. Rumours about a flight of money were all over financial markets in Ireland and London.

This was crucial to the government decision of Tuesday, 30 September 2008, to offer a state guarantee to all six Irish-owned financial retail institutions – one that was subsequently extended to five other smaller institutions, bringing the government's total exposure to €485 billion.

Meanwhile, Anglo was doing its best to protect itself, both immediately and with an eye to a few months down the road, assuming it got over this speed-bump. How it did so was to cause enormous trouble when it was revealed.

One of its main competitors, Irish Life & Permanent, came to its assistance in creating the impression that Anglo's deposit base was stronger than it actually was. IL&P made five deposits totalling €3.45 billion in the three days leading up to the bank guarantee but refused to give more money despite three requests from Anglo Irish.

The government was told on 29 September that Anglo could raise only overnight money, such was its liquidity crisis, and that other banks were frightened to give it more in case it wouldn't come back. On 30 September, after the guarantee had been announced, IL&P sent another €4 billion on deposit to Anglo. This was the last day of Anglo's financial year-end and the combined €7.45 billion deposited by IL&P

made Anglo's position about one sixth better than it would otherwise have been.

However, there were twists. It wasn't really IL&P's money at all: it was Anglo's – money that was being returned to it under the guise of something else entirely, which was what Anglo had had in mind when it gave IL&P the money in the first place. Yet it wasn't treated in Anglo's year-end statement as the return of its own money. It should have gone down as an interbank loan rather than as a corporate deposit, which would have made everyone – authorities, investors and counter-parties – look at the Anglo balance sheet differently.

When this finally emerged, in February 2009, both Anglo and IL&P denied any impropriety. Apparently, this was a normal way of doing business: banks did it all of the time. Indeed, €750 million had been transferred temporarily from IL&P to Anglo on 31 March to make the Anglo balance sheet look better for its interim statement.

Not only that, IL&P later claimed that it had implicit support from the Financial Regulator for its September actions. The board said it had been supporting the policy objectives of the Financial Regulator and Central Bank, which had requested that institutions 'support each other in the face of an unprecedented threat to the stability of the Irish financial system'.

While Anglo and IL&P differed on their interpretations of the nature of the transaction, Anglo too claimed that it had regulatory support. The relevant authorities swiftly and vehemently denied that they had requested or authorized any such window-dressing of the Anglo accounts.

Anglo claimed that its former finance director Willie McAteer had a phone conversation with Pat Neary in September 2008 in which he informed the regulator that Anglo would be 'managing' the balance sheet. He reported that Neary replied: 'Fair play to you, Willie.' Phone call records for the following month apparently include a comment by an Anglo executive telling a regulator's official that it was 'manipulating' its balance sheet and that the €7.45 billion from IL&P was 'not a real number'.

IL&P had stepped in where AIB and Bank of Ireland would not on those fateful days at the end of September. At the instigation of the relevant state authorities, both of the bigger banks had apparently agreed to provide deposits of up to €5 billion each, but their terms had been unacceptable to Anglo. If the authorities knew this, and encouraged such deposits, how did they think the money would have been handled on the Anglo balance sheet? If they were to go down as interbank deposits, they would not have made any difference to the strength of the balance sheet. If they were to go down as customer deposits, they would have had the same apparently positive effect as the subsequent IL&P deal.

If so, it is easy to understand why IL&P was so upset about the flak it took when its role emerged and why it fought so hard to protect chief executive Denis Casey and finance director Peter Fitzpatrick (no relation to Sean) when Brian Lenihan demanded their resignations. IL&P chairman Gillian Bowler insisted that, while mistakes had been made, the intention had been to support the 'policy objective of the Financial Regulator'. The clear innuendo was that IL&P thought that it had been asked to 'don the green jersey' and was now being punished for it.

There were other puzzling aspects to the whole affair. In mid-January, Lenihan ordered the nationalization of Anglo, having decided to abandon the planned €1.5 billion investment by the government in its capital. It was only then that the minister was told about the IL&P transaction by his officials.

Curiously, Lenihan did not make this public or call for resignations at that stage. He waited weeks and subsequently justified his decision by saying he did not want to interfere with ongoing investigations. Unfortunately he had to admit that he hadn't seen the information in the PwC report when it had first been given to him, causing a major political storm as to whether he was on top of his job. The storm moved elsewhere, though, as Lenihan and others had much else to worry about.

The minister and his officials also had to worry about the legality of a massive share deal in Anglo, the regulator's knowledge of this transaction and the public's reaction to an easily understood scandal.

While Seán Quinn talked up all the positive reasons for his purchase of 15 per cent of the shares in Anglo when this was finally confirmed in July 2008, some highly material information was not disclosed to the stock market by him, Anglo or the Financial Regulator. What wasn't disclosed was that Quinn had been due to take the title to a further 10 per cent of Anglo shares, via conversion of all the CFDs he had accumulated, but that he had not done so.

There has never been an explanation as to why he didn't buy the shares, especially when he publicly expressed such confidence in the stock: perhaps he didn't want them, or he couldn't afford them, or the regulator had secretly imposed a limit on his family shareholding of 15 per cent, believing that it would be dangerous for the bank to allow Quinn to have any more.

This left Quinn, Anglo and the authorities the problem of what to do with the other 10 per cent of Anglo shares. Putting such a large amount of shares up for sale publicly in one go would have been potentially disastrous for the share price. It would have threatened to further undermine the already declining investor confidence in the bank, with potentially wider consequences for the entire banking system.

It is not known what efforts Quinn made to find a buyer but Anglo most certainly tried, even approaching Middle Eastern sovereign wealth funds – investment funds on behalf of rulers in Arabic states – to see if they would like to buy those Quinn shares.

Eventually, Anglo managed to put together a consortium of ten trusted customers who were offered what seemed like a fool-proof deal: they were to be given loans of €451 million – although not in equal amounts – to buy the shares in Anglo that Quinn could not or would not buy. If the shares went up, they could sell and take the profit; if the shares went down, they could sell the shares in order to repay what they could and the bank would shoulder the balance of the loss.

It is reasonable to speculate as to why the ten invested in Anglo shares. There was an emotional component: this was their bank, the one that had supported them in their business dealings over the years and in which they had invested time and commitment as well as money. There was also a better financial reason: many had invested millions, even tens of millions, in the Anglo shares when they couldn't find property deals that would offer good returns. These shares were losing money fast and they wanted to reverse the trend, rather than selling and taking a loss.

At first the arrangement seemed to be working fine, with Anglo shares bought at about €4, rising to €6.40. But it was a temporary phenomenon, and by January 2009 the shares were worthless, after the state took ownership of the bank via nationalization.

This made the security offered for the loans to buy the shares very important. Three quarters of the money advanced had been secured on the value of the shares themselves; it was only for the other quarter that the borrowers had to provide security independent of the bank shares.

These loans, of a type known as 'limited recourse', went totally against the safeguards Anglo said it always took with its lending. It emerged that the borrowers had repaid about €83 million and that the state was now caught for the balance, which these borrowers were not obliged legally to repay. Not surprisingly, there was outrage when news of this emerged in late 2008 and even more in mid-2009 when it was confirmed that €308 million had been written off as unrecoverable.

Aviation entrepreneur Ulick McEvaddy, who had hit the headlines in 1999 when providing free holiday accommodation at his French villa for Minister for Finance Charlie McCreevy and Tánaiste Mary Harney, and who was a prominent anti-Lisbon Treaty activist during the 2008 referendum, was one of the few who explained and defended what happened. 'Anglo is a great bank and I make no hesitation in saying I would have supported it in a heartbeat,' he declared. He lamented that he hadn't received the phone call to make the investment and said the ten 'should be proud of what they did because they were supporting the bank in its hour of need'. He said Ireland would 'go down the tubes' if it didn't stop 'vilifying' the bankers, who were 'the architects of the Celtic Tiger'.

FitzPatrick's even more influential defender, Denis O'Brien, told his Milltown golf club audience that he blamed Seán Quinn for the millions in Anglo Irish investor losses.

The deal looked like a straightforward breach of Section 60 of the Companies Act, which stops a company lending money to third parties to buy shares in itself. Again the loophole used to justify the loan to Quinn – that it was a normal part of business – possibly could be advanced. However, in reality, there was nothing normal about it.

The regulator knew that Anglo had lent money to Quinn at the time of its purchase of the 15 per cent – even if it was for general corporate purposes – so it is reasonable to say that it should have occurred to the office to ask if loans had been made to the buyers of Quinn's entitlement to another 10 per cent of the shares and on what terms. It would have made sense for the regulator and the Central Bank to have sought to find out how the buyers had financed their purchases, especially if borrowings were involved, how this sat with stock exchange rules, and how it complied with company law. It must be presumed that this was done and that all the right boxes were ticked because otherwise it would imply that the authorities had not done enough.

Since the public announcement of the existence of the Anglo Ten it has been revealed that the Office of the Director of Corporate Enforcement investigated whether the terms of the loans to some of the ten were altered soon after the government announced its bank guarantee scheme. And the Financial Regulator asked the Gardaí to investigate on the basis that the deal concluded may not have been the one presented to the regulator and that any change may have affected its legality and normality. If the regulator and ODCE decide that it was a deliberate share support scheme – designed to artificially support the price of the shares – then prosecutions could follow. But who would be included in that?

Donal O'Connor, the accountant later promoted by the government to be chairman of the nationalized entity, said he had been appointed to the Anglo board only shortly before the transaction. He said he had been told that it was happening and that it was legal, which he accepted. In common with the other non-directors he made no further inquiries. His excuse, delivered in May 2009 as he unveiled the real extent of the Anglo debacle, was that he didn't have much knowledge of banking. It seems his predecessors didn't either.

By the end of 2008 Drumm and FitzPatrick had gone from Anglo. Drumm had given an interview to the *Financial Times* in early 2008 in which he opined that the Irish people were sensible about changing economic circumstances and would be willing to 'tighten their belts' if so required. He clearly didn't feel the noose tightening around his neck, because he bought two luxurious houses in the US resort of Cape Cod during 2008. He spent $4.6 million in March and another $2.6 million in September for two 1900s houses that had been restored. He and his wife took out two $1 million mortgages with an American bank to buy the first house and got a mortgage of €1.8 million from the same lender to assist in the purchase of the second on 30 September – the day the government announced the bank guarantee scheme.

He went on 19 December 2008, with the board of Anglo announcing that it had 'accepted his resignation with regret'. O'Connor, who had taken the role of chairman the previous day at Lenihan's request, said: 'David's decision has been made to ensure that Anglo Irish Bank can move forward with new momentum. He deserves great credit for that. We have a high-calibre management team with great strength and depth, in whom the board has confidence and who will serve the bank well in the years ahead. We also have a tremendous and loyal staff who deserve great credit for their professionalism and team work. I would like to thank David for his immense contribution to Anglo over the past fifteen years and I wish him well for the future.'

It may be good manners not to kick a man when he is down, but, given the nature of the problems Anglo was bringing upon the state, it also suggested that the old board, notwithstanding the best efforts of government appointees Alan Dukes (a former Fine Gael leader and finance minister) and Frank Daly (former head of the Revenue Commissioners), had not yet grasped the full realities of the situation. Drumm wasn't the only one to go, however. A day earlier FitzPatrick had gone too.

26

The fall of Sean FitzPatrick

Sean FitzPatrick wasn't just a hero to corporate Ireland; the Anglo Irish Bank chairman was also its unofficial spokesman.

Many businessmen prefer to operate under the radar, making a virtue of privacy. The annual accounts they lodge with the Companies Office are full of information that is often complicated to all but trained accountants, making it difficult to calculate their full wealth. In recent years there was a trend towards opting for unlimited liability status – leaving the owners personally liable for all debts incurred by a business – to ensure that details of profitability and wealth did not become publicly available. Such companies must have their accounts audited and file tax returns, but they are protected from public disclosure by confidentiality rules. Not surprisingly, such businessmen rarely make themselves available for interview with the media, unless it is on their own terms and they have something they want to sell.

The bosses of publicly owned companies, whose shares trade on the stock market, must have a public profile. The extent of this depends on the importance of the company and their desire to engage. They are required to make themselves available to investors at public annual general meetings. In addition, they give regular briefings on company performance to pension fund managers, investment managers and stock-broking analysts, although there is an argument that this gives certain classes of investor preferential access, allowing them a better opportunity to profit. To get around this, most companies hold press conferences or do media interviews to get the message out.

Unfortunately, these interviews are sometimes of little use to the radio listener or newspaper reader. The business leaders often lapse into jargon, sometimes deliberately, sometimes out of habit. They use terms familiar to their ilk but that confuse the general audience. They prefer to deal in specifics about their own company and talk in generalities about the economy – usually to condemn high costs, lack of competitiveness and excessive pay (for workers, not management). They also tend to steer away from criticism of, and confrontation with, the government or other authorities in the state, with the notable exception of Ryanair's Michael O'Leary.

In June 2007 FitzPatrick bucked that trend. He made a speech to a business lunch hosted by a research company called Experian, where he had become a director. Unusually, Experian circulated the text and said FitzPatrick would be available for interview, suggesting that his comments were aimed deliberately at a wider audience.

The content was far from the usual anodyne stuff that usually makes up corporate press releases. FitzPatrick wanted everyone to know about the dangers to prosperous Ireland being posed by what he called 'corporate McCarthyism'. One of the senior figures of modern-day Irish business alleged that Irish capitalism was facing assault from sinister forces. He claimed that excessive regulation was shackling Irish entrepreneurs and bemoaned a culture that assumed guilt on the part of Irish businessmen. 'In my humble opinion, our wealth creators should be rewarded and admired, not subjected to levels of scrutiny which known criminals would rightly find intrusive. We should be proud of our success, not suspicious of it . . . What concerns me greatly is that just at the time when our economic fortunes are on the wane, those who influence the environment within which we trade seem determined to exert much stricter control on us. This move to a more heavily regulated economy needs to be challenged vigorously and challenged now,' he blasted.

'Having developed this marvellous entrepreneurial culture, which is delivering so many benefits in terms of employment and wealth to the country, we must ask ourselves if there is now a danger that our regulatory environment has gone too far. Are we starting to shackle, instead of encouraging, the entrepreneurs who in turn generate more wealth not just for themselves but for the country as a whole?'

And there was the big accusation. 'Among the more insidious aspects of our current regulatory environment is the apparent presumption of guilt on the part of entrepreneurs and business people generally. The whole structure seems to be geared towards something akin to an annual proof of innocence statement. This is corporate McCarthyism and we shouldn't tolerate it. We should be proud of our successful business people, they shouldn't be pilloried. Indeed, we might look at the workings of some of our own public tribunals of inquiry in this regard. We should ask ourselves if it is fair or equitable to allow almost any person with a grudge the freedom to make any allegations, however wild and unsubstantiated, against any other citizen with seeming impunity.'

I asked my radio production team to set up an interview with Fitz-Patrick for broadcast that evening. I suspected that FitzPatrick might not be well known to many of our listeners at the time but his credentials as a senior and influential player in Irish business could be explained easily. FitzPatrick would provide a good barometer of the way big Irish business was thinking.

I wanted to hear what he had to say about two things in particular: his claims about an anti-business agenda being prevalent in Irish society and his willingness to buck conventional thinking by raising fears about an economic slowdown. This, after all, was just weeks after a general election at which those who had expressed fears about a bubble economy were told by Bertie Ahern to stop 'moaning and cribbing', before he mused that he 'didn't know why they didn't just commit suicide'.

The two were linked. If it was true that there was a real threat to the economic success Ireland had come to take for granted – and a danger of a self-inflicted wound, caused by cutting comments against success – then it was worth finding out more.

Having allowed FitzPatrick to pitch his claim during the interview, as outlined in the text to the speech, I asked him for examples to support his complaints. He wouldn't give any, despite my repeated requests. He wouldn't name any victims of this 'corporate McCarthyism' or name any of those who had suffered at its hands. This dramatically weakened his argument. Having raised the hare, he wouldn't chase it, as angry text messages from listeners to the programme stressed. He couldn't put up.

At the time I didn't realize what had upset FitzPatrick so much. In retrospect, it seems he was concerned about himself as much as friends. I learned subsequently that only a month before his speech and interview he had been the subject of a complaint to the state's Standards in Public Office Commission (SIPO). Legitimate questions had been raised by a member of the public about conflicts of interest that he and his friend Lar Bradshaw – as directors of Anglo Irish Bank – might have had in important decisions made by the board of the Dublin Docklands Development Authority, where both he and Bradshaw were also directors. He had to explain himself to SIPO or, as he would have put it, prove to them that he was innocent. And it was not until some time afterwards that, after a preliminary inquiry, SIPO decided not to launch a full investigation on the basis that there was no evidence that either FitzPatrick or Bradshaw had held control of the bank.

Months later FitzPatrick was willing to attack the low standards of others. In November 2007, at a private dinner attended by members of the Royal Dublin Society, he publicly expressed his concerns about a recent 'high-profile' case in the commercial courts but without naming anyone. He criticized the 'silence' of the business community, professional bodies and regulatory authorities on its outcome. Everyone present guessed that he was talking about Jim Flavin's actions at DCC where, the Supreme Court found, he had dealt in shares using inside information.

When I rebroadcast my June 2007 interview with him, after his resignation from Anglo in December 2008, Today FM's computer system was inundated with even angrier text responses from people outraged by the apparent hypocrisy of his earlier comments.

By that stage FitzPatrick's reputation was ruined, not just by the near-collapse of the bank he had built, but by another radio interview, this time with Marian Finucane on RTÉ Radio, and by the separate exposure of his selfish behaviour in running Anglo.

In early October 2008 – the weekend after Anglo was rescued temporarily by the government's provision of guarantees against deposits and liabilities – FitzPatrick went on to Finucane's show. He demurred when asked to say sorry for the trouble to the state his bank and others had caused. 'It would be very easy for me to say sorry. The cause of our problems was global so I can't say sorry with any degree of sincerity and decency but I do say thank you,' he told her.

FitzPatrick defended the performance of his bank: 'Of course banks have made mistakes and Anglo Irish Bank has made mistakes because we're in the business of risk ... But have we been reckless? No, we haven't. We cover all our loans in a belt and braces way.' And yet FitzPatrick had to concede: 'If the Irish banking system collapsed there would have been chaos ... This was the most important economic decision since the foundation of the state ... The taxpayer has lent the government the sovereign name of Ireland ... And we are incredibly grateful.'

Deep in the hole, shovel in hand, he continued to dig. Later that evening he went to a public function at which reportedly he advised Minister for Finance Brian Lenihan, whose premature budget for 2009 was to be delivered just a few days later, where to cut social welfare benefits. FitzPatrick's contribution was summarized by Labour leader Eamon Gilmore in the Dáil a few days later: 'Let us, he said, cut medical cards and child benefit. Mr FitzPatrick's world is the reverse of the *Titanic* – in his world it's women and children last, while bankers get the first and most comfortable lifeboat.'

FitzPatrick's interviews are likely to go down in Irish history as the business equivalent of disgraced former Taoiseach Charles Haughey's infamous 1980 admonition about how we were living beyond our means. Haughey had his skeletons, most notably massive donations from friends and the hiding of income offshore to avoid paying his due taxes. It turned out that FitzPatrick had his skeletons too, albeit of a different kind.

On becoming a part-time banker in 2004, moving from chief executive to chairman of Anglo, FitzPatrick wanted to be a full-time investor. He didn't want to be just a facilitator of deals; he wanted to be a player too. He knew as much as the guys he had helped make rich, so he would be their partner in future rather than their adviser. He didn't simply help entrepreneurs: didn't his development of the bank show he was one himself?

Liberated, FitzPatrick seemingly invested everywhere. It was revealed later that he got stuck into commercial property investments at home and abroad: an oil refinery in Nigeria, a casino in Macau, a hospital in the US and, irony of ironies, a catastrophe insurer.

Tiarnan O'Mahony's ISTC and Barry O'Callaghan's purchase of Houghton Mifflin Riverdeep – the most debt-laden takeover by an Irish company ever, with borrowings of over €5 billion – were among his big investments. He used Domhnall Slattery's Claret Capital for wealth management, entrusting it with €16 million of his money, but placed other money elsewhere. Bradshaw became his partner in many of those investments.

Unfortunately, FitzPatrick used not just his own money but also loans from Anglo, and had been doing so secretly from as far back as 2001.

FitzPatrick had been borrowing ever larger sums from Anglo each year but concealed this from the company's investors, auditors and non-executive directors on the board. Every year, just before Anglo's year-end on 30 September, FitzPatrick would repay or settle all outstanding loans with Anglo so they couldn't be detected by the bank's auditors and feature in the year-end annual report. He would use money borrowed from Irish Nationwide Building Society (INBS) to do this, but, days later, at the start of Anglo's new financial year, would get new loans from his own bank and use the money to pay off the INBS debt. The practice is known as 'warehousing'.

FitzPatrick borrowed €129 million from Anglo at the start of the 2007/8 financial year in early October 2007. Clever use of this 'backwards and forwards' mechanism with INBS meant that only €7 million showed in the Anglo annual accounts. FitzPatrick warehoused €48 million in loans with INBS in September 2006, but the €129 million a year later suggested he made a lot of investments at the top of the market. That wasn't just his own personal business: as soon as Anglo was nationalized his ability to repay the loans and interest became crucial to all of us because any failure would be a financial cost to the state. The only consolation was that we were told that he had been making his repayments in full and on time and that, apparently, he said he would be able to continue to do so, even though the value of his investments must have slumped.

The apology for his actions was qualified. 'The transfer of the loans between banks did not in any way breach banking or legal regulations,' he insisted in a statement he made on resignation from the board of Anglo in December 2008. 'However, it is clear to me, on reflection, that it was inappropriate and unacceptable from a transparency point of view . . . I am fully responsible for my own decisions and actions and I regret that I had adopted this approach. I have always pursued high standards in my personal and professional life and I failed to meet those standards in this instance.'

The limit to his apology met with outrage, but legal advice may have dictated that he say as little as possible.

He did not give any indication whether anyone else in Anglo assisted his deception. Anglo had boasted of its strict credit controls and lending criteria. The bank claimed that normal commercial terms applied to FitzPatrick's loans, but such criteria would have demanded the loans be judged by the bank's own credit committee before being issued. This raised questions as to what other members of the board knew, particularly the full-time ones, and how much work actually passed through the credit committee.

What has never been explained is just how many of FitzPatrick's investments coincided with the interests of Anglo's other borrowers. Was pressure put on Anglo to provide loans to other customers because they were partners with FitzPatrick in the ventures funded by his loans from Anglo? Would the knowledge that FitzPatrick was involved in a venture have persuaded the bank to have taken risks not just with his loans but with those of associates?

Although FitzPatrick's loans made up only a very small proportion of the overall value of loans to Anglo customers – not 'material', as the business lexicon would have it – the fact that he as a director was borrowing so much should have been disclosed. That he went to such lengths to hide his loans proved that. Even if he did not break the letter of the law, he broke the spirit of the relationship any investor in a bank is entitled to demand of the chairman or chief executive. FitzPatrick misled investors, employees and the regulatory authorities about his personal loan arrangements for over eight years and did so in a deliberate and orchestrated way.

At the height of the scandal the *Irish Times* quoted one 'senior banker' as saying that 'directors' loans are a very fundamental thing with banks because they are at the core of finding out the relationship between the executives and the bank.' He said loans to connected parties and loans to dominant figures within banks were two of the four main reasons cited in academic literature for banking collapses. The other two reasons for collapses were treasury problems – the raising of funds with which to make loans – and lending to overheated property markets. Anglo ticked all the boxes.

These are all reasons why it might have been expected that the Financial Regulator would have taken tough remedial action on discovering Fitz-Patrick's chicanery. Unfortunately, the office didn't discover FitzPatrick's activities until seven years after they started, came upon them almost by accident – in the course of a routine inspection at INBS – and then dealt with them in a somewhat ham-fisted way.

The regulator's office received a legal opinion by the bank that FitzPatrick's actions were not a breach of company law. It does not appear to have taken its own independent legal advice. Unfortunately, the regulator subsequently claimed that it lost the letter from Anglo with that legal advice. Incredibly, it seems that the information did not go all the way to the top of the regulator's office, and its boss, Pat Neary, was unaware of what was happening, learning of it only in December 2008. Somebody else, whose identity has never been revealed, apparently decided that, as no breach of the law was involved, there was no sanction that could be applied. No effort was made to get a second opinion from the Office of the Director of Corporate Enforcement. All that the regulator's office asked Anglo to do was to give a quarterly report on FitzPatrick's progress in reducing the size of the outstanding loans, so this could be properly recorded in the Anglo books at 30 September 2008. When that date was reached, the loans had been reduced to €87 million.

Minister for Finance Brian Lenihan noticed this figure when reading a draft of the bank's accounts and raised questions as to why it was so large. Neither he nor his predecessor, Brian Cowen, had been told about what had happened. Lenihan was furious when FitzPatrick's actions and the regulator's subsequent response were explained to him.

FitzPatrick went quickly from his job following the public disclosures. Despite what he had done, the board of Anglo, with two public-interest representatives nominated by the government among its number, decided that, instead of firing him, it was suitable to 'accept his resignation with great regret'.

As it happened, the other directors had borrowed €163 million in the year-end 30 September 2008 – an increase of €65 million, despite the sharp economic downturn. By May 2009 it was decided to write off €31 million of these loans on the basis that they would not be repaid.

In his going-away statement released by Anglo, FitzPatrick said, 'From the beginning, Anglo Irish Bank was based on a set of beliefs which were pro-business and we achieved great success allowing many new businesses and entrepreneurs to realize their potential in Ireland and later overseas. I remain committed to those ideals of access and speed of delivery based on the strength of relationships that should underpin successful banking practice.'

FitzPatrick never lost the faith during 2008, investing €7 million in the bank's shares and bonds during the year. A subordinated debt – a special form of loan that a bank or company can make that carries high interest rates but comes near the back of the queue for repayment if something goes wrong – worth €5.5 million was purchased and has some remaining value, but the shares, bought at €7.70 in June and €3.85 in September, are worthless. The September decision to buy shares was very strange, given that it came at a time when Anglo was supposed to be trying to interest INBS in a takeover.

There was considerable sympathy for FitzPatrick in business circles after his departure was announced. He was a doer, a risk-taker, somebody who defied convention to get things done and who had achieved a lot. As far as they were concerned, he had been unlucky because of the international credit crisis and the gambling of Seán Quinn; they held that FitzPatrick's critics were just begrudgers who had never done anything of note except pass comment. While these factors contributed undoubtedly and significantly to FitzPatrick's leaving, the excessive lending and unstable financing of the balance sheet cannot be ignored or wished away.

In his February 2009 speech that attacked Quinn, Denis O'Brien stood up for FitzPatrick, saying publicly what many business people were saying privately: 'Sean FitzPatrick has been a friend of mine for quite a number of years. He has made mistakes but he continues to be my friend.

'What has been forgotten is that Anglo Irish also lent to a lot of Irish entrepreneurs and business people who created thousands of jobs. And most of these jobs will survive the downturn. Anglo Irish backed people when others wouldn't. It backed me when I wanted to start a radio station [Dublin's 98FM] and nobody else would. Anglo Irish has been blamed for absolutely everything that has gone wrong in Irish banking. This is both wrong and unfair.'

27

The man at the mutual

Sean FitzPatrick needed an accomplice when it came to warehousing his loans from Anglo at each year-end. He needed somebody who would be secretive and who had the required money. He went to one of his competitors, a man who ran, not owned, a mutual building society, and got the funds he needed. His choice was the Irish Nationwide Building Society (INBS) and the man who controlled and ruled it utterly, Michael Fingleton.

What was in it for Fingleton, apart, presumably, from a large facilitation fee and interest payments to his society? The possibility of being cut in by Anglo on future deals, it was claimed later, but that never happened.

Although there was a risk that the regulatory authorities would disapprove or punish, Fingleton was unlikely to be fearful because he had never had too many problems from that source. He was a friend of the political elite, particularly those in Fianna Fáil. Who did Celia Larkin go to for quick finance in 2008 when she needed a €40,000 loan to repay the 'loan' she'd received from Bertie Ahern's constituency organization fifteen years earlier? Fingleton was her choice, of course, for speedy service, with no need for security. He looked after his friends and did so quickly.

That said, Fingleton got security from FitzPatrick for his loans, which were advanced in dollars and sterling as well as in euro in order to facilitate the Anglo's boss's overseas investments. Crucially, Anglo Irish gave an undertaking that it would repay FitzPatrick's loans if the chairman could not, raising more questions as to who in Anglo had known what was going on. FitzPatrick had offered properties and his shares in Anglo as security for the loan, the latter being something that was worthy of a separate notification to the Irish stock market, although it was not always the practice on the Irish market at the time.

INBS denied any 'impropriety' on its part. It said the loans were part of its 'ordinary' business. But how can facilitating such an arrangement to deceive the shareholders of a rival bank, quoted on the stock market, be considered part of INBS's 'ordinary' business? While refusing to answer many legitimate questions, it was able to cover itself by saying that 'there was no reciprocal arrangement with regard to either members of the board or management of Irish Nationwide.'

The scandal cost FitzPatrick, David Drumm and Willie McAteer their jobs at Anglo, but there seemed to be a reluctance by the authorities to chase Fingleton, even though he had provided the loan. When the ODCE and Garda investigators carried out a high-profile raid on Anglo's headquarters in February, it was reasonable to ask why INBS was not raided simultaneously. Fingleton continued at his desk until the end of March.

By the time the FitzPatrick–Fingleton axis was revealed – in late 2008 – relations between the pair were not particularly cordial. As Anglo floundered in September 2008, it tried to interest the government in the idea that it should be allowed to take ownership of INBS, much to the irritation of Fingleton, who learned of this through third parties. It was speculated that Anglo wanted the INBS deposit base, but financial experts wondered why Anglo would want to increase its exposure to the commercial property sector by adding the INBS portfolio of loans, much of which was reckoned to be highly speculative and risky. It emerged subsequently that it was something of a bluff, designed to create the impression that Anglo was a strong-enough bank to be able to take on ownership of a problem case like INBS, even when it knew it had no real chance of doing so.

Many of the public were spooked by rumours in early September 2008 that INBS was on the verge of being declared insolvent. This led first to the government increasing the guarantee on all deposits from €20,000 to €100,000, and then its giving the now infamous blanket guarantee at the end of that month.

On Friday, 5 September, just after the markets had closed, the respected Reuters news agency reported that INBS was holding 'talks with its lenders to avoid insolvency'. It partially retracted the story a couple of hours later, admitting that 'material elements' of the story were incorrect and that it 'contained false information', but it continued none the less to quote an anonymous source that the society was in a 'very bad position'. The story was eventually completely retracted.

Two days later Fingleton told the *Sunday Independent* that the story was 'irresponsible, false and untrue', adding that 'in the present highly sensitive economic, financial and commercial climate, the putting out of such statements is tantamount to commercial sabotage.'

But many people had concerns by this stage about the extraordinary transformation that had taken place at INBS. The society had abandoned its core business of providing home loans to ordinary members of the general public, with the regulatory authorities seemingly unworried. Indeed, in its annual report for 2007 the INBS boasted that its objective was 'to continue to build up significant income streams based on secured property lending, avoiding the distraction of engaging in general retail banking business and unsecured lending operations'.

It had become a high-risk lender to the commercial sector, with about 80 per cent of its loans in this business. More than half of these were attached to British commercial property, particularly in speculative development in London. It had itself become a participant in ventures, often with Sean Mulryan's Ballymore Properties, although the society deliberately provided few details to the public. It never disclosed how many of its loans related to completed developments – office blocks, hotels and shopping centres – or to incomplete buildings and land-banks earmarked for buildings.

Up to this point INBS had seemed a profitable business. It recorded pre-tax profits of €239 million in 2006 and €390 million in 2007, the two years marking the height of the boom. But the warning signs were flashing. The building society wrote off €25.3 million in specific bad loans – which would not be repaid – in 2007, compared to €900,000 the previous year; the bad loans included those to high-profile solicitors Michael Lynn and Thomas Byrne, both of whom were struck off for misappropriating client funds and for taking out multiple mortgages on properties. The impaired loan charge – which covers loans on which repayments are not being made and which are in danger of going bad – increased to €48.8 million in 2007 from €17.6 million the previous year.

Fingleton put a brave face on things. He said the society had 'an exceptionally strong balance sheet' and was 'well positioned to compete strongly in whatever areas of the market challenges emerge'. The society had no exposure to 'subprime or related financial instruments', but that was missing the point: property lending was its problem. Fingleton said developers had reduced prices substantially and buyers were 'slowly coming back to the market . . .We believe that we are not far from the bottom of the market.'

What he didn't disclose was that INBS had less stringent criteria on lending than most of its competitors, who would not give loans for more than 80 per cent of the value of an office block or tranche of development land. The loans advanced to customers soared in the five years to the end of 2007, going up by 171 per cent to €12.4 billion. More than half of INBS's €10 billion commercial mortgages had a loan-to-value ratio of 90 per cent, giving it a heavier exposure to property development as a proportion of overall loans than any other Irish lender. It also had a relatively small number of big customers with big loans, exposing it to horrendous bad debts and write-downs, especially as INBS had become an equity investor, or partner, of some developers too.

Whereas once INBS dealt with ordinary workers who found it hard to get a mortgage elsewhere, the twenty-first-century INBS did things like finance the €130 million purchase of the K Club by Michael Smurfit and property developer Gerry Gannon, and the *Christina O* yacht for the Ivor Fitzpatrick-led consortium. New customers of INBS included the likes of Bernard McNamara, Seán Dunne, Sean Mulryan and Johnny Ronan. Somebody, identity undisclosed, owed €320 million near the end of 2008 and nobody knew if and when repayments would be made.

There was an additional problem that got relatively little attention at the time but that was about to become huge. In its annual report for 2007 INBS declared it had €7.3 billion in deposits, over €5 billion less than the loans advanced at that stage. That funding gap had to be filled on the interbank market, often through the sale of bonds.

Fingleton engaged in a strategy of high-risk lending in the hope of making big profits; he wanted to build profits as high as he could as quickly as he could to bring about a sale of the society at the highest price possible. It was a recipe for disaster.

In 2006 Minister for Finance Brian Cowen finally gave Fingleton what he really wanted, nearly a decade after Bertie Ahern had made a promise to the INBS boss.

Fingleton wanted the law changed so he could sell INBS without having to follow the criteria set down by the state when his rivals Irish

Permanent and First National had abandoned their status as 'mutual societies' – owned by, and working for, the benefit of savers and borrowers, who were offered the best rates of interest possible rather than those that would maximize profits. These mutual societies had changed their status by joining the stock market. The members who voted to 'demutualize' had received 'free' shares in return, which they were able to keep or sell, as long as a new buyer did not exceed 15 per cent of all shares in the first five years after the society had become a bank. Many INBS members wanted the same.

Fingleton's problem was that he didn't want to follow that method. He wanted a clean sale. He argued that INBS was too small to suit a stock market flotation, as it would not have had enough shares to attract pension funds and other investors. It was an argument with some validity but such was the appetite for housing-related stocks during the boom it was a problem that probably could have been surmounted.

There were other good reasons why Fingleton may not have wanted to follow this route. One was the requirements for disclosure that would have accompanied a stock market debut: Fingleton would have been forced to make substantial declarations not just about his own remuneration but also about personal investment in deals associated with INBS, if there were any. The society would have been required to give much greater detail to the public about its activities as an investor as well as a lender. As a company quoted on the stock market more onerous and transparent public reporting requirements would have applied for the following five years. Fingleton would also have had to wait five years for his pay-off, which was not guaranteed to be forthcoming.

Just how much Fingleton expected to get personally was never made clear. A sale of the society would not necessarily have provided a direct windfall for him – as he didn't own any more of the society than any other member – but it might have allowed him to negotiate a facilitation fee of some kind for the transaction, or an extended contract for a couple of more years that could have included a large termination payment. Termination payments for a banker in Fingelton's position could range from €10 million to €20 million, depending on what type of deal he could do. The 120,000 members were unlikely to object to such terms. After all, there was the promise of anything from €7,500 to €15,000 each, depending on what price Fingleton achieved through the sale. There was speculation in early 2007 that the price could be about €1.2 billion.

Fingleton had entered his sixties when he approached Ahern – then in opposition as leader of Fianna Fáil – with his wish to have the law changed in relation to the 15 per cent, five-year rule. Ahern was sympathetic and publicly indicated likely consent but changed his mind when in power. The EBS building society, wedded to the concept of mutuality, opposed any change to the protections that existed for fear of its being taken over.

Fingleton continued to lobby the government privately and created an expectation among INBS members that they would enjoy windfall tax-free profits, as long as the government changed the law. In 2000 he stated publicly that 'building society legislation is outdated. In this day and age we should not be restricted in what we can do or how we can do it, other than prudential supervision of our abilities to engage in services.' Expressing 'no particular affection' for mutuality, he said he would 'dearly love to link up with a European bank which had no network in the Irish market'.

Success finally came as Fingleton neared his seventieth birthday, a crucial landmark as at that age he would be forced by law to step down as a director of the society and, in theory at least, would no longer be in control.

It was now up to Fingleton to sell the building society, and he had just enough time to do so before the bubble burst. While the legislation was passed by the Oireachtas in July 2006 – which allowed for a wholly artificial distinction between INBS and EBS, based on the use of arbitrary criteria to determine membership of each society – the sale process did not begin until October 2007. Goldman Sachs was appointed to handle the sale, but it was too late, as the downturn in the property market had become obvious and the credit crunch had started to bite.

Ironically, he told members at the 2008 annual general meeting that 'one thing is sure, that we're determined to effect a trade sale of Irish Nationwide at the earliest opportunity. We ain't hanging around.' But at that stage two potential buyers had walked away. Iceland's Landsbanki – which bought Merrion Stockbrokers, only to sell it later as it and Iceland went into the type of meltdown that makes Ireland's woes look manageable – came closest to a purchase of INBS. The other possible bidder was a partnership of Bank of Scotland (Ireland) and the Quinlan Private Equity Fund.

In the meantime Fingleton continued to look after himself. On

12 January 2007 INBS transferred a pension scheme from the society into his personal control. It was presented in the annual report in a way that might have led naive people to believe that there was more than one recipient – and new chairman Danny Kitchen told society members in May 2009, to disbelief, that there had been a typographical error. The amount transferred was €27.7 million, enough to provide for an annual pension of €1.5 million for the rest of his life, about twice the value of the pension to Fred Goodwin at Royal Bank of Scotland, something that had caused enormous political controversy in Britain.

At the May 2009 annual general meeting Kitchen explained to members that in January 2007 Fingleton decided he wanted to transfer his pension entitlements to a private pension fund. The society employed an independent actuary to calculate the size of fund necessary to give him an entitlement of two thirds of his final salary. The amount transferred was almost five times the €5.8 million in pension fund assets carried by INBS at the time to cover the post-retirement incomes of its other 399 employees.

When news of this pension transfer first emerged there was relatively little comment; it was not until details re-emerged during the crisis of early 2009 that many people became outraged.

Fingleton's practices at INBS and self-reward were now major issues because the state had guaranteed all of its liabilities. INBS seemed vulnerable to collapse. Funding was one major concern, as it had €2.3 billion in debt to repay in 2009, with only €800 million in deposits to cover this. The issue as to who would lend new money to INBS loomed large, although the government guarantee assisted in the issue of new bonds.

INBS continued to put up a brave face in discussions with the Department of Finance from September 2008, arguing that it had a buffer of €1.5 billion in capital that was big enough to sustain any losses and could remain independent from any government injection of new funds. It said it would sort things out by 'shrinking' its loan book, which would involve demanding repayment of loans, giving a limited number of new ones and asking for improved security from existing borrowers. Few believed this could work.

And then there was the question as to who was going to do it. Chairman Michael Walsh bailed out first, in February 2009. Walsh's long association with Dermot Desmond had led to all sorts of specu-lation over the years as to the billionaire's intentions towards INBS once its status was changed. Walsh sent his resignation letter to the Minister for Finance and the Financial Regulator. In it he said that 'it is clear to me that Irish Nationwide Building Society cannot survive without reorganization and significant government support.' He also may have signalled the end for Fingleton when he wrote that 'the board and ultimately the minister should have the opportunity to provide new oversight and leadership.'

It had been Walsh, though, who, as part of the board, had approved the controversial €1 million bonus for Fingleton that provoked outrage when it was revealed and that dramatically weakened the latter's pos-ition. That bonus put the final nails into Fingleton's coffin. Although it was subsequently repaid because of enormous pressure, the damage had been done. A public perception of greed had been established. Fingleton claimed a 'pre-contracted incentive bonus' of €1 million that had been put in place earlier that year, as an inducement to stay in his job past retirement age. He didn't seem to believe that anything had changed, even though the state guarantee was costing the country a fortune in higher borrowing costs – and came at a time of higher tax rates and lower government spending. Fingleton still thought it appropriate to pocket the money as his entitlement, and not even the realization that his society was losing an enormous amount of money, as his bets on the property market were being torn up, changed his mind.

At the May 2009 annual general meeting Kitchen came to Fingleton's defence on this issue as well. He said that Fingleton had stayed for an extra year only on the basis that he was paid in 2008 at least the same as in 2007. Indeed, the bonus brought his 2008 income from the society up to €2.34 million, a small increase on his 2007 reward. None of the bosses in the rest of Irish banking – all of whom ran far bigger organiza-tions – came close to taking this sort of money during 2008. INBS staff most certainly did not either: the average employee got paid less than €34,000.

Finance Minister Brian Lenihan was furious about the payment of the bonus, but a softly, softly approach was taken to securing its repayment. It seemed that in the end it was the concerted media pressure – with television crews hanging around outside his house in what he called a '24-hour media siege' – that finally got to Fingleton. He may have feared personal attacks, like those on his British counterpart Goodwin, in the days prior to his announcement that he was giving the money back and that he was leaving the society.

Fingleton's departure statement was the usual self-serving guff about standing by the society members whom 'he had served to the best of his ability for the past thirty-seven years'. Kitchen joined in later with a statement from the board eulogizing the man who had left under a cloud, the latest in a trend that seemed to be popular among many financial institutions forced to ditch one of their own. 'What cannot be denied is that in his thirty-seven years of service, he took the society from a minnow to the substantial financial institution it is today. He was focused on maximising benefits from members and brought a shrewd eye to many of the business decisions made by the society. None of us has a monopoly of wisdom and it is unfortunate that his retirement should coincide with the market turmoil we have seen over the last eighteen months or so.'

Kitchen delivered this tribute as he explained the 2008 results to members. INBS made an after-tax loss of €243 million after setting aside €464 million to cover loan losses. This compared to profits of €390 million in 2007. The widespread expectation was that another €3 billion in losses would be incurred, more than twice the society's capital base, as the bad debts charge amounted to 4.4 per cent of all loans, with the prospect of much more to come. The size of the society was contracting, with its loans reducing by 15 per cent to €10.4 billion in 2008, although of this €1.4 billion was due to the decline in the value of sterling. Total assets fell to €14.4 billion from €16 billion and INBS admitted it had lost €490 million in customer deposits.

There was limited sympathy for Fingleton in public; however, the *Sunday Independent* – almost alone – leaped into the fray to defend Fingleton from the 'braying mob'. Much was made of how he had built the Irish Independent Building Society – of which he became secretary in 1972 when it had a staff of five – into a fifty-branch outfit called the Irish Nationwide, of how he came from humble stock as the son of a garda from Tubercurry in Sligo and how he had trained to be a priest but left before taking his vows. Even the three years spent with the aid agency Concern in Nigeria was paraded as if somehow relevant.

What these articles failed to detail were Fingleton's business practices

– and the distinction he drew between helping the elite and the ordinary people he was supposed to serve in a mutual building society. During the 1990s the society specialized in lending to people with poor credit histories, so it was the slowest to pass on interest rate cuts to existing members because those borrowers had nowhere else to go. New borrowers were offered better rates. Sometimes customers were offered interest-only loans, especially if they wanted to buy commercial properties, some of which may have been built in the first place by developers who had borrowed money from INBS; INBS therefore had an incentive to lend to new customers who would buy those developers' vacant units.

Breaking a relationship with INBS was almost impossible once entered. When the Financial Services Ombudsman found that INBS had systematically imposed unlawful penalties on customers who repaid commercial loans early in order to switch to another lender, and ordered refunds for all affected customers going back for six years, INBS responded with a legal challenge to his finding but later settled the case. The ombudsman did express dissatisfaction with the level of compensation paid to customers, however.

Heaven help the ordinary customer who fell into arrears on repayments on his or her home: in the case of some mortgages the society charged 20 per cent penalty interest on arrears for the remainder of the life of the mortgage, a policy that made it very difficult for borrowers who fell behind on repayments to get out of arrears. It is doubtful whether many of the developers who got into trouble in 2007 and 2008 received the same treatment from Fingleton. Members Brendan Burgess and Shane Hogan made complaint after complaint to the regulator about practices at INBS and spoke at AGMs about corporate governance and succession planning. They received little or no encouragement from the society.

On the INBS board was David Brophy, a senior executive at Ballymore Properties, not just one of the biggest developers in the country but one of Irish Nationwide's biggest clients for loans and a co-investor in some major developments. Brophy must have had to excuse himself from meetings that involved Ballymore Properties, to avoid conflicts of interest.

One of the biggest embarrassments to hit the mortgage sector in recent years was the revelation that solicitors Michael Lynn and Thomas Byrne had run up massive debts. In many cases they failed to register the title deeds to Irish and overseas properties. They also took out multiple loans with different institutions on the same property, confident that nobody would check. INBS did not check whether there were other mortgages on the property but are likely to have taken Lynn's word for this in a furnished undertaking.

Brian Fitzgibbon was the INBS home loans manager who took an unfair dismissal action in 2007. He said he had been scapegoated for loans to Byrne and Lynn that Fingleton had approved personally, including one for Lynn's house in Howth for €4.1 million. Fitzgibbon alleged that the credit committee for approving loans of more than €1 million was a device designed to satisfy the regulator. 'While protocols existed, they were never adhered to and the entire ethos of the society when it came to lending was entirely informal and controlled by Michael Fingleton.' He went on to say: 'I am also aware of a significant number of high-value loans which were personally approved of by Mr Fingleton without any recourse to or compliance with the normal procedures.'

Mr Justice Frank Clarke was impressed by Fitzgibbon's arguments, saying that disciplinary action against Fitzgibbon was intended to 'deflect attention away from senior management' and their role in making loans to Lynn and Byrne that were a 'deviation from the society's written lending policies'. He was allowed to proceed with his case and INBS settled quickly.

All of which raises questions as to why the government was so slow to insist on Fingleton's removal. Even if it owned no shares in the institution, it was keeping it afloat by way of the state guarantee. Fingleton was operating on a year-long contract as chief executive up until February 2009 anyway, having resigned as managing director of the building society in January 2008 when he turned seventy. Few doubt that he would have stayed had it been possible to arrange for the profitable sale of the society.

The suspicion must be that, without Fingleton's help, finding out where INBS had lent and invested and on what terms would have been a near-impossible job. And what did Fingleton know about various powerful people, companies, politicians and their investments? As Sean FitzPatrick knew, Fingleton was a good man to keep a secret. Fingleton was determined to ensure that the confidentiality of his clients was protected at all times, which must have been appreciated by many of his society's customers, especially when he received flak personally for acting this way on their behalf.

At the Planning Tribunal he failed to produce documents as requested, claiming flood damage, misfiling and ignorance as his reasons for not doing as told. Tribunal counsel Patrick Hanratty said Fingleton's attitude was 'cavalier in the extreme', which Fingleton denied.

Just as fascinating was his performance at the Moriarty Tribunal when it was investigating financial transactions at INBS's fully owned Isle of Man offshoot involving disgraced former minister Michael Lowry and the estate of the late David Austin. Even though both had given 'waivers' to INBS to provide whatever information was sought, Fingleton's bank said that, while it would offer written statements in response to questions, it would not be possible to send anyone to give evidence in response to oral questions.

The failure of Irish Nationwide Bank (Isle of Man) to cooperate with the tribunal made it extremely difficult for it to investigate accounts in the bank that were used by some taxpayers to evade tax or to make improper deposits. It didn't matter that INB was fully owned by a building society and Fingleton sat on its board: he told the Moriarty Tribunal that he was 'powerless' to direct his Isle of Man employees to turn up in Dublin to give much needed evidence. He claimed he had received legal advice that he could ruin the offshore status of this bank if he were to make such an order. It would be not an Isle of Man bank then but an Irish one. And that might have left the bank, and its customers, open to investigation by the Revenue Commissioners. At the Moriarty Tribunal the chairman expressed his disappointment that the Isle of Man refused to cooperate with the inquiry and told Fingleton to convey this message to the board.

After Fingleton's departure INBS started a process of trying to reduce its commercial property book to half of its overall business. It declared itself open for business to provide home mortgages. At his first AGM, Kitchen, who had not taken up the job of chief executive in succession to Fingleton at the reduced and capped pay of €360,000, as required by the Department of Finance, lashed out at media reporting of events at INBS and at political comments too, while taking care to lavish thanks on the government. He joined the list of those seeking to forget the past. 'Undoubtedly mistakes were made but my own view is that we need to put this behind us and get down to sorting out the problems. Recrimination will solve nothing.'

PART VI

Playing with the big boys

28

The state gets into bed with the developers

The plan for redevelopment of the Poolbeg Peninsula in Dublin's docklands was hatched by what transpired to be a heady combination of Ireland's most entrepreneurial bank, its most active builder, its most high-profile investor, its best-connected firm of stockbrokers and the state itself. The site lies in derelict ruins as one of the most expensive symbols of the insanity of the Celtic Tiger era.

The old Irish Glass Bottle site, on twenty-four acres of land, adjacent to a sewage treatment facility, in an area the relevant state body, the Dublin Docklands Development Authority, described as 'poorly laid out' and 'isolated from any residential areas', became in 2006 one of the most expensive, and subsequently redundant, pieces of development property in the country. The ultimate cost was horrendous.

Bizarrely, if inadvertently, Seán Quinn kicked the whole thing off. His decision to enter glass manufacturing in his native Fermanagh undercut the business that had run in the Poolbeg site for nearly thirty years. Ardagh, the stock market-quoted company that controlled Irish Glass Bottle, decided that it could no longer compete due to the cost advantage Quinn enjoyed north of the border. In another symbol of the economic behaviour of the time, it decided to move manufacturing to Britain, because, in addition to securing cheaper manufacturing, there was the added incentive of profiting from the redevelopment of the land in Dublin.

Although a stock market company, Ardagh's policies were driven by its chairman, Paul Coulson, a multimillionaire businessman who had made most of his money in high-end corporate financial services; he'd also won enormous damages from a legal case taken against a British adviser when a corporate takeover went badly wrong. He split Ardagh into two parts: its original business – in this case glass manufacturing –

and a property development offshoot. The new second company, South Wharf, had the long-term lease to the land on which Irish Glass Bottle had operated.

Coulson knew of a legal loophole that would allow South Wharf to claim possession of the land from the state. As a company that had rented there for thirty years, Coulson sought to take advantage of a previously little-known provision in the Landlord and Tenant Act of 1978 that would allow it to claim ownership. He discovered that an unnamed client company of the Industrial Development Agency had used the loophole to buy a state-owned property in Clonshaugh at a price far less than its true value.

The Minister for Enterprise, Trade and Employment, Micheál Martin, rushed through an amendment of the Landlord and Tenant Act that was meant to prevent future instances of private companies attempting to acquire state-owned lands for substantially less than their market value. However, while the amendment covered the IDA, Shannon Development and Údarás na Gaeltachta, it forgot to include Dublin Port.

Coulson's South Wharf moved quickly to exercise its legal right to buy the land. It tried to buy it for a derisory €750,000. It succeeded, subject to legal action from Dublin Port Authority. It later agreed a settlement whereby it would pay the DPA just one third of the profits on the subsequent sale of the land.

South Wharf eventually sold the twenty-four acres of land, despite its far from perfect location, to a consortium of investors – led by builder Bernard McNamara and including financier Derek Quinlan and the state agency the Dublin Docklands Development Authority – for a total of €412 million. Their idea was to build one of the biggest developments yet seen in Dublin, running to some 3.25 million square feet. There were to be 2,166 apartments – mostly two-bedroom – and 826,000 square feet of retail and commercial space. McNamara planned to sell the apartments at between €500,000 and €850,000 each, apparently believing that these would be attractive to people living near the IFSC, and close to amenities such as a redeveloped Lansdowne Road and the Point Depot on the other side of the river. The issue of what it would cost to protect the area from climate change – given its vulnerability to coastal erosion – didn't seem to feature prominently.

The consortium's plans were highly ambitious: Becbay, as it was named, expected to bring in revenues of €1.76 billion when all the properties were sold, netting a profit of €296 million, to be split amongst the three shareholders. McNamara pitched in €57.5 million as his part of the investment, Quinlan invested €46.3 million and the state-owned DDDA put in €32.175 million. The balance of the price was €288 million, and this was borrowed from Anglo Irish Bank, which was also lined up to provide the loans for the construction of everything, along with AIB. This was scheduled to cost €898 million, which included €142 million in interest and fees for the banks as their guaranteed return.

Risky as all of these assumptions were – based on continuing and rising sky-high prices in the residential property market in particular – the manner in which all of the participants funded their 'equity' stakes made it even more so: the participants used mainly borrowed money.

It wasn't clear if Quinlan's investment was personal or on behalf of a syndicate of his clients. It is not known if he hedged his exposure by getting others into the deal as partners of his at a later date or how much of this 'equity' investment he borrowed.

But it was known that McNamara invested just €5 million of his own money for his 41 per cent share of the project. Through Davy Stockbrokers he borrowed another €52.25 million at a massive interest rate of 17 per cent over seven years. It was a very expensive way to borrow money, but it meant that he did not have to come up with €52.25 million in cash to buy into Becbay. Nor did he have to make any interest repayments during the seven years, as his interest was 'rolled up'. The plan was that he could repay the capital and interest in full after he had taken in all the cash from the sale of the apartments and offices. Effectively, McNamara got a 'free carry' until after the development was completed, funding his repayments out of his profits. He had also agreed with Davy that he could buy out the holders of the loan stock after two years, subject to giving them a minimum return of 40 per cent on their investment. This looked feasible if he could start construction quickly and book deposits.

The deal was so clever and clearly so risky that it should have set alarm bells ringing everywhere. Both McNamara and Quinlan may have had big reputations but both already seemed overstretched, as various non-banking commentators pointed out in the print media.

McNamara's business – which he had inherited from his father and built up dramatically – had been as a contractor, building on behalf of others. While he continued that business, as it was a good generator of cash, he simultaneously morphed into an investor. The examples of his massive speculation in this decade alone are many, because he was a high-profile purchaser of assets when prices were at their peak.

He led the consortium that bought the Shelbourne Hotel on St Stephen's Green for about €140 million and then spent nearly €90 million on a lavish refurbishment of the property. He bought the Burlington Hotel in Dublin 4, between the Grand Canal and Donnybrook, and adjacent commercial blocks such as the Hibernian Insurance, with the intention of emulating Seán Dunne's plans for Ballsbridge by demolishing and reconstructing in greater density. He bought into supermarket chain Superquinn, apparently with property development in mind, but sold early in 2008 as his financial concerns mounted. He purchased loads of shops in the Grafton Street area of Dublin, some of which he tried unsuccessfully to sell around the same time. He bought a 45 per cent stake in the Conrad Hotel, on Earlsfort Terrace, for around €45 million, and the Great Southern Hotel in Parknasilla, County Kerry, the previous summer for almost €40 million. McNamara and another speculator, Jerry O'Reilly, paid €14.2 million for the Jurys Doyle Tara Hotel next to the Merrion Road site but were refused permission for a 25-storey hotel, office and residential tower on the site that would have been twice the size of Liberty Hall. They were also partners in the Elmpark scheme on Merrion Road in Dublin 4, which paid €45.7 million for the 14.5-acre site and which built more than 400 homes, 28,000 square metres of offices and a 168-bed four-star hotel, with plans for a five-storey private hospital.

McNamara also co-owns the Radisson Hotel in Galway, with O'Reilly, which became the place to be for Fianna Fáil people during the Galway Races. McNamara's contacts with Fianna Fáil during this period were legendary. A former election candidate in his native Clare, McNamara was known to have played host to Bertie Ahern on many occasions at his Ailesbury Road, Dublin 4, mansion (including cinema, ballroom and swimming pool), a house built on the site of the former Japanese embassy.

His political connections did not work against him. He led the consortium that won the right to build the public–private prison at Thornton Hall. McNamara was a member of the board of governors of the National Gallery, and previously served as deputy chairman of the National Roads Authority (NRA), before resigning and being allowed to pitch for, and win, major road building projects. He won the right to construct social housing projects in some of the most deprived parts of Dublin, but he controversially abandoned these in the summer of 2008, citing problems with the contracts with the council; most observers believed his well-known cash crisis was the most pertinent factor in the decision.

Before the crisis of 2008 it was no surprise to hear that the well-connected McNamara was getting state backing for projects such as the Irish Glass Bottle site. But was it really the business of a state development agency to be getting involved in such a massively leveraged project? The DDDA was guaranteeing €26 million of Becbay's liabilities. Should it have been putting taxpayers' money – both as investor and as guarantor of the loans of private sector investors – into a venture that was as risky as this one, particularly when Davy's clients were being offered such a high return?

The involvement of the state-run DDDA as investor was crucial to many private sector investors. The DDDA had statutory powers that allowed it to exempt developments of which it approved from going through the normal planning process, which speeded things up enormously for lucky recipients. The process is known as Section 25 of the Dublin Docklands Development Act, but each application requires approval from the Minister for the Environment before the provision can be applied. The Becbay project for the Irish Glass Bottle site was the subject of such an application and it came as no surprise that the minister, Dick Roche, granted it swiftly and praised the DDDA involvement. 'This joint-venture arrangement will ensure that the authority has a major input into the planning and architectural elements of the development, and will be in a better position to pursue their social, community and amenity objectives in Poolbeg,' he said.

But there was another problem: the involvement of Anglo as such a major lender, both in providing part of the purchase price and then the money for subsequent development. There was an overlap between the DDDA and Anglo boards: at the time of the crucial decisions Sean FitzPatrick and Lar Bradshaw sat on both.

The latter was a Dubliner, born in 1960, who had spent twenty years with the blue-chip management consulting firm McKinsey, both abroad and in Ireland, before striking out as a serial investor and part-time board member for hire. He was said to have been apolitical and was made chairman of the fledgling DDDA by the Labour Party's Minister for Finance Ruairi Quinn in May 1997, a position he held for ten years.

Bradshaw was wealthy from an early stage and had been an investor in the Derek Quinlan-led group that bought the Four Seasons Hotel in Dublin, something that was not disclosed at the time of the DDDA decision to become involved with Quinlan in Becbay. Nor was Bradshaw and FitzPatrick's investment along with Coulson, the vendor of the Irish Glass Bottle site, in a separate property project in Sandyford. Bradshaw was a co-investor with FitzPatrick in a number of ventures, including the Nigerian oil refinery and Fresh Mortgages, a so-called 'subprime lender' that charged exorbitant amounts of interest to customers with a poor credit history who could not get funding elsewhere. Most of their joint investments have not been publicized. FitzPatrick said that a chunk of the loans that he moved to INBS were held with Bradshaw, although moved without the latter's knowledge.

Anglo's involvement as lender caused the DDDA some public problems. When the complaint alleging possible conflicts of interest was made to the Standards in Public Office Commission in May 2007, the DDDA stated it was confident that its board had 'operated in accordance with a strict code of conduct' when it entered the Becbay group. It said that Bradshaw and FitzPatrick both declared their conflict of interest (as dual directors) in the meetings about the site in October and November 2006, and absented themselves from meetings that discussed Anglo's role in providing finance.

After a preliminary inquiry SIPO decided not to launch a full investigation into connections between Anglo and the DDDA. 'While it may be that both held substantial shareholdings in the bank, there was no evidence that either held "control" of the bank,' it noted, deciding that the power that FitzPatrick, as chairman, continued to hold at Anglo was not relevant as far as it was concerned. SIPO also declared that there was no evidence that any of the decisions made by the authority 'had the consequence or effect of conferring on either FitzPatrick or Bradshaw personally a significant benefit'.

What SIPO also ignored was the considerable importance of the entire DDDA area to Anglo's profitability. Even before the projected Irish Glass site deal, Anglo appeared to have lent at least €1 billion to developers operating in the DDDA area – most at a time when FitzPatrick sat on the DDDA board and many after Bradshaw joined the Anglo board in 2004. The sums of money risked by Anglo were enormous – which meant that the decisions taken by the authority about size, density and social housing quotas, which did not have to go through the normal planning process, were essential to it. The quicker that units were built and sold, the faster Anglo got its fees and loan repayments.

Most of the biggest builders in the country became involved in the area, such as Paddy Kelly, who ended up with debts of over €700 million to Anglo (much of it linked to development in the Dublin docks), and Johnny Ronan's Treasury Holdings, which borrowed more than €390 million from Anglo for the development of Spencer Dock, reportedly the largest secured property loan in the history of the state. Quinlan, who was partially financed by Anglo in his €1.4 billion purchase of Jurys Inns, was also a major player in the docklands, with some of his private clients owning several sites and the McCormack family of Alanis Capital – partners with Quinlan and Bradshaw in the Four Season deal – having investments in the area as well.

Anglo was instrumental in providing finance for the relocation of the National College of Ireland from Ranelagh to the docklands, on land provided by the DDDA. It opened in 2002 with Joyce O'Connor – a sister of Sean FitzPatrick – as president of the college from the time the deal for the construction and financing of the new campus was agreed in 1997. This was a year before FitzPatrick joined the DDDA board, but Bradshaw was already in place. Old friends, including Kelly, the McCormacks and Ged Pierse, were involved in its construction. At a restaurant function to mark the opening of the college Kelly publicly made a €250,000 donation on condition that O'Connor take to the floor with him for a dance, even though no music was playing.

FitzPatrick's practice of warehousing loans with INBS started back in 2001, at a time when capital allowances were available for the purchase of buildings in Dublin's docklands. Partnerships were allowed to buy buildings and offset the capital allowances against their entire income. Anglo used to provide the loans. What was to stop FitzPatrick being involved with the companies or partnerships on both sides of such deals?

29

Catching the development disease

Controversial Liam Carroll prospered as a builder of relatively low-quality apartment and office blocks in the early 1990s. Though he was roundly criticized, and convicted in the High Court for the shoddy workplace practices that led to the death of one of his construction workers, as he got bigger and braver the quality of some of his developments improved, and all of the banks, including Anglo and AIB in particular, queued to provide finance to his companies Danninger and Zoe Developments.

Before he too was laid low by the collapse in property values – ending up with debts estimated at €2.8 billion by early 2009 and nowhere near enough assets to sell to cover them – Carroll paid €71 million for a five-acre site at North Wall Quay. After waiting a few years he began building a new €200 million headquarters for Anglo Irish Bank in the heart of the North Docks near the O2 concert arena, as part of a €1.5 billion complex he had agreed with the DDDA. However, in late 2008 he was forced to stop work, after spending €87 million, and was threatened with a demolition order, the consequence of an action taken by rival property developer Seán Dunne against the DDDA.

Carroll had been a central player in Dunne's attempts to gain control of the publicly quoted Jurys Doyle Hotel Group in 2005, buying 8 per cent of the shares that Dunne wanted. Instead of selling to Dunne, as the latter had expected, Carroll sold to the Doyle family, who then had greater ability to control the sale of the land at Ballsbridge that was central to Dunne's interest in the hotel chain.

However, that was not the issue here, as Dunne was exercising his legal entitlements on a separate matter: Dunne claimed the permission given to Carroll by the DDDA in July 2007 to build to a greater density than the 2002 development plan for the area had permanently damaged his own plans for the area. He said it would lead to a situation where his own planned apartments would look out on to office blocks rather than on to a garden area. He claimed access to his site would be restricted.

The court discovered the existence of a secret agreement, made in May 2007, between the DDDA and Carroll whereby the developer would cede, free of charge, some land on his site that the authority wanted. The quid pro quo was that Carroll would be permitted to do more on the remaining site than should have been allowed, benefiting from the powers available to the DDDA under Section 25 of the 1997 Act that had established the body.

In her High Court judgment Ms Justice Mary Finlay Geoghegan decided that work carried out by Carroll's company, North Quay Investments Ltd (NQI), constituted 'unauthorized development'; this led to Dunne seeking an order for its demolition. The agreement gave rise to a 'reasonable apprehension of bias' on behalf of the authority in reaching its decision on Carroll's planning application in July 2007, the court decided. Ms Justice Geoghegan found that there was 'a direct relationship' between the granting of Section 25 approval and Carroll ceding part of the site to the DDDA for use as public space.

In early January 2009 Dublin City Council granted Carroll's company retention for the work completed already, but Dunne immediately appealed this to An Bord Pleanála. Then Dunne went to the High Court seeking an order to have the building demolished, but this was adjourned until July to give time for his other appeal to be heard. Since the authority has no power to grant retrospective planning permission, or retention, Carroll had to apply to the Dublin City Council for retention of something it had rejected previously. This implied that the pre-let tenancy deals he completed with Anglo, as well as with AIB Capital Markets and solicitors O'Donnell Sweeney, for office space on the site were unenforceable. Significantly, the DDDA did not appeal the High Court decision to the Supreme Court.

The Treasury Holdings-led Spencer Dock consortium, which also had property interests in the area, took its own High Court action against the DDDA's deal with Carroll, claiming that it had suffered many of the same problems as Dunne because of the DDDA's actions.

Questions as to how the DDDA conducted its business and the level of corporate governance at the body arose again, as speculation mounted that the DDDA might end up paying major compensation to Dunne, Treasury and even Carroll.

By this stage the DDDA was having major financial problems of its own, caused by the Glass Bottle site debacle and other investments it had made in partnership with the private sector on its own lands.

Although planning permission for the Glass Bottle site had been fast-tracked as intended, the discovery of asbestos slowed the beginning of construction work. However, the commercial partners soon started to experience their own toxic financial problems. Was the building work unviable? Who would buy these expensive apartments now if built?

At the Elm Park scheme, a couple of miles away but much better located, McNamara cut prices from €585,000 to €475,000 for apartments and offered loans of up to 30 per cent of the purchase price himself to potential purchasers. It didn't work. In such circumstances, the cost of building apartments at Poolbeg might not be recouped by their sale, and this was without even taking the cost of the land into account.

McNamara, now massively overextended, became the subject of some wild speculation. His decision a few years earlier to opt for unlimited status made him personally liable for all of the debts of his businesses. There wasn't just widespread speculation about his going bust – which culminated on the Marian Finucane radio programme – but also crazy and clearly untrue rumours that he had been seriously assaulted by people to whom he owed money. The rumours got more bizarre with each week and were being circulated by some very senior business people: he could go nowhere without bodyguards; he had been brought to a bank by creditors to cash a cheque and when it bounced he was beaten up in the bank's foyer, his injuries being so bad that he was forced later to go around on crutches; the Russian mafia had purchased his debts from Polish subcontractors and were pressing for payment. I saw McNamara on the street a couple of times during all of this – on his own – and he walked without any difficulty. Although the rumours persisted, it transpired that they were untrue.

Becbay had paid the equivalent of €17.16 million per acre for the Irish Glass Bottle land. If it was now worth just €10 million per acre, and that was generous, the entire site was worth €240 million. That would not even pay off the loan to Anglo, which was owed €293 million before interest, and would mean that every other investor would get wiped out. However, most experts agreed that the site was probably worth about €100 million at best and would not be developed for many years to come. Clearly the state, both through the DDDA and the newly nationalized Anglo, was going to take a massive hit.

Yet the DDDA seemed to be in denial. In February 2009 its chief executive Paul Maloney told an Oireachtas committee meeting that the value of the site was 'is in the order of 20 to 30 per cent lower than the valuation received in 2007'.

Cue an embarrassing session for Maloney, who insisted that the price paid per acre in 2006 was 'good value' when other docklands sites were commanding €50 million an acre. This ignored the poorer location of the Glass Bottle site, the ambitious scale of the development and the fact that just because some other land is massively overvalued doesn't mean that something cheaper isn't overvalued as well.

The DDDA told the Oireachtas committee that Becbay had not paid any interest to Anglo because of 'short-term technical issues', which cynics said meant the private investors had no money with which to do so. The official explanation was that there was a dispute over other undisclosed elements of the contract but significantly the DDDA was said to be the only party seeking to renegotiate the agreement. This was very likely, as it now emerged that the DDDA, in the partnership agreement, had apparently given cross-guarantees, making it jointly and severally liable for its partners' repayments of more than €13 million a year if they defaulted.

There was another twist, as the newly state-owned Anglo started to put pressure on the DDDA to make all of the payments falling due when its other partners could not do so, effectively exercising enforcement of the DDDA's cross-guarantee. Anglo would get its money back, but from an arm of the state, while the private investors would get away scot-free.

Remarkably, the chairman of Anglo by this stage, in succession to FitzPatrick, was Donal O'Connor, a former managing partner of PricewaterhouseCoopers. And he had succeeded Bradshaw as chairman of the DDDA (a position from which he resigned in December 2008 on becoming chairman of Anglo, to avoid 'any conflicts of interest'). While O'Connor had not been chair at the time of the Glass Bottle deal, he had been a board member, and he had been chairman at the time of the secret deal with Carroll that had led to the humiliating court decision for the DDDA. O'Connor had been invited on to the Anglo board during FitzPatrick's time as chairman, further intensifying the cosy relationship between the two organizations.

The Minister for Finance decided he was satisfied that O'Connor's resignation from the DDDA and his retirement from PwC averted any potential problems. Known in business circles as a man of integrity as well as a hard worker, O'Connor came highly recommended, especially as one of PwC's tax partners was Lenihan's cousin Fergal O'Rourke (son of Mary), upon whom the minister relied heavily for advice. The appointment attracted some criticism, as it was suggested that O'Connor was not distant enough from the old regime at Anglo, even though he had joined the board only recently, mainly because of his involvement with FitzPatrick and Bradshaw at the DDDA.

The DDDA had an aim to 'develop the Dublin Docklands into a world-class city quarter paragon of sustainable inner city regeneration' by 2012, but it seems it got as caught up in the property hoopla as any private sector operator. Instead of becoming a facilitator, the DDDA had become a partner in many ventures and had taken on a role as lead developer when it could not interest others. It faces substantial write-downs on a retail complex, CHQ, in Stack A near the IFSC – where Dermot Desmond had proposed to establish his eco-sphere – as well as on other land-holdings in the docklands, and its decision-making process has led to several disputes and about turns.

One involved the long-running saga to develop a national conference centre. Treasury Holdings – the aggressive development company owned by the charmless Johnny Ronan and the urbane Richard Barrett, which Frank Dunlop represented for years – was originally awarded the multi-million-euro project in 1998. However, it fell apart in July 2000 when An Bord Pleanála rejected the massive high-rise office scheme, which the developers claimed was necessary to support the centre, with opposition led by the DDDA itself; Desmond, who spent hundreds of thousands of euro opposing the plan; and Bertie Ahern, the local TD as well as Taoiseach, who described it as 'a monstrosity' in an apparently unguarded moment in front of a television camera. The government finally awarded Treasury Holdings a new contract for the National Convention Centre at Spencer Dock – on a scaled-down basis – and it is set to open for business in 2010.

One of the other big disappointments for the DDDA in 2008 was the announcement of another twist in the long-running saga involving the design and construction of a giant tower on the south quays at Grand Canal Basin.

In September 2005 the DDDA announced that it envisaged two towers – one on each side of the river – forming a 'landmark entry' and 'visual gatepost' for the city from Dublin Harbour. One would be in Harry Crosbie's €800 million Point Village development at the site of the renovated O2 concert venue. It is known as the Watchtower and it has been built. The other would be the so-called U2 Tower, a residential complex with U2's new recording studios to be placed at the very top. The DDDA decided that it was to be 120 metres high, instead of the sixty metres originally proposed, to match the height of the Watchtower. Minister for the Environment Dick Roche approved the DDDA's plans in July 2006, and two months later it invoked the provisions of Section 25 of the DDDA Act 1997 to fast-track the application for an even bigger tower of 130 metres, which was approved within weeks.

Tenders for construction of the tower were invited and a shortlist of five firms was published in February 2007. The winning bid, announced in October, was from Geranger, a consortium made up of Paddy McKillen, Sean Mulryan's Ballymore Properties and U2. The design selected was not the original BCDH design that had been approved, but rather one commissioned by Geranger from Norman Foster. However, bids for the construction of the tower were submitted at the peak of the market and the prices for the apartments that were to be built would have had to drop sharply, making the €200 million price-tag impossible to bear. In late October 2008 the DDDA announced that it was suspending construction plans indefinitely. The members of the consortium had reason to be thankful for the delays, especially as their good friend Harry Crosbie had suffered from bringing the Point Village to market at just the wrong time.

The other consolation for McKillen, Mulryan and indeed Derek Quinlan was that they were thanked by name on the sleeve notes of U2's 2009 album No Line on the Horizon. Proof, it seemed, that for a time property development was the new rock 'n' roll.

30

Loadsa leverage

The Davy consortium that provided the cash for Bernard McNamara's gamble at the Irish Glass Bottle site did something that became particularly popular among well-heeled and well-connected investors during the boom years.

If leverage – the ability to borrow money that increased the amount available for investment – was essential to the boom in the Celtic Tiger years, then syndication was too. Someone who was well-enough connected would be introduced to a small group of similarly wealthy people who could pool their resources, borrow a multiple of that again, and then make big investments that often benefited from favourable tax rules and low interest rates on borrowing. These deals were never advertised. They were for rich insiders.

The first eye-catching syndication deal of the era that came to the public's attention involved what has since become a landmark in Ballsbridge in Dublin 4: the Four Seasons Hotel. Set in the grounds of the Royal Dublin Society, directly across the road from AIB's corporate headquarters, this hotel made a lot of already wealthy people far richer with the help of the state.

In 1997 Derek Quinlan – a former Revenue Commissioner – assembled the Nollaig Partnership, made up of so-called 'hinwris', or high net-worth individuals, who wanted to 'shelter' income from tax as well as making capital gains on investments. Quinlan assembled a twenty-strong group that featured some very prominent and well-connected people in Irish business, some of whom became famous to the general public only a lot later.

Included were many early-stage property developers, including David Arnold and brothers Niall and Alan McCormack, whose family company Alanis had developed Ibis hotels in Cork, Dublin and Galway using tax incentives and who later became significant developers in the Dublin docklands. Mark Kavanagh of Hardwicke Properties, who developed the original IFSC site and retained P. J. Mara as an adviser, was another involved. He later developed a massive office complex, Central Park in Sandyford, County Dublin, with Quinlan, Arnold and Treasury Holdings. The country's most long-standing influential stockbroker, Kyran McLaughlin of Davy – who had advised many of the country's biggest companies, including Elan, GPA, INM and Ryanair – was another participant, as was serial investor Lar Bradshaw. Other members of the group were Donal Geaney, chairman of Elan, the only Irish pharmaceutical company quoted on the stock market, and also chairman of the National Pension Reserve Fund for a period; Dermot Gleeson, Quinlan's next-door neighbour in the nearby Shrewsbury Road, probably the most expensive and exclusive road of private houses in the country; and fellow lawyer Fidelma Macken, a judge in the European Court.

The idea to build a Four Seasons Hotel on a site leased from the RDS in Ballsbridge was put together by estate agent Sean Dillon in the mid-1990s. He got developers involved: two companies called Harvard Properties and Simmonscourt Holdings, who had the responsibility for raising bank finance from ACC Bank, Anglo Irish Bank and Scotia Bank. They contracted to build on the site and sell it to Quinlan's Nollaig Partnership at a fixed price of €60.3 million.

The fixed price allowed the investors to plan for tax benefits on taking ownership of the newly built hotel. The relevant tax laws allowed the partners to claim the hotel's construction costs as a deduction against the tax due on other income, spread out over seven years. The tax saved – or lost by the state – was estimated at just under £20 million. The Nollaig Partnership secured the break just months before McCreevy's changes restricted the relief to rental income by capping it at £25,000.

It got better. Quinlan's investors got a luxury hotel for less than the cost of building it. The target construction cost had been for £51 million, implying a profit to Dillon's developers of £9 million, but, even though they overran on costs and made losses instead of profits, they had to deliver it to Quinlan's group at the agreed price.

The Four Seasons syndicate was the first high-profile example of how those with large incomes – and a willingness to borrow – could come together to buy expensive assets that they would never have been able to buy on their own. If someone had the right connections – essential because these deals were never advertised – membership in a syndicate or partnership provided big opportunities.

An individual could make a contribution to a syndicate, maybe anything from €100,000 to €250,000. The super-rich invested a lot more in later years, as they usually had large profits to reinvest. The investor might have borrowed the money to make his equity contribution, but the syndicate, in turn, would borrow a multiple of what had been raised to make its investment, usually in commercial office buildings in the IFSC in Dublin, or in an approved private hospital, or in a hotel anywhere in the country.

The banks were willing participants as long as investors put up 15 per cent of the cost of a deal. The asset that had been purchased usually provided a cash flow that would cover the interest repayments on the loans taken – and often banks were happy to provide interest-only loans to preferred wealthy clients, in the expectation that the asset would be sold at a later date to repay the loan, or that the money would come from other profitable investments. For many years that seemed a safe bet.

When prominent tax consultant Kevin Warren bought La Touche House in the IFSC for €82.5 million, he assembled a group of nearly eighty investors who each paid around €317,000 to enter the syndicate. The remainder of the required money was borrowed. In return, the investors were able to write off €47 million in capital allowances against any rental income they had from other property investments. This meant that other rental income was sheltered from tax, while they were likely to make a capital gain on the increase in the value of this particular property.

Warren – often referred to as Quinlan's biggest competitor in assembling syndicates and finding investments to buy – arranged finance of €100 million for the construction of the Galway Clinic private hospital. Beef baron Larry Goodman, Louth businessman Brendan McDonald, Blackrock clinic founder Jimmy Sheehan and his brother Joe, a US-based surgeon, were the main suppliers of equity, putting in about €18 million; but another €14 million came from smaller investors who were also part of the syndicate. More money was raised by selling thirty-six suites to the consultants who were to work from there, and €35 million came in loans from Anglo Irish Bank.

When AIB built a new extension to its Bankcentre headquarters complex, it was sold to the Serpentine Consortium, an outfit made up of an unspecified number of unidentified wealthy people and companies, although the rumour was that a single family had undertaken the entire deal. The consortium spent €367.75 million to buy ownership of the new building. AIB committed to renting the development for thirty-one years, for €16 million per year initially, to be reviewed every five years. This implied the investors were accepting a yield, or return, of 4.25 per cent on their investment, which suggested they expected their investment to be justified by an increase in its capital value, as the cost of borrowing was almost certainly more than the rental yield. AIB announced that it would make a profit of over €160 million in just three years by completing the deal and moving operations from other locations to the new building. It also provided the bank loans to the buyer.

Quinlan, meanwhile, kept buying. In 2000 a site fronting on to the Stillorgan dual-carriageway in South Dublin near the landmark Galloping Green pub was sold for €31.75 million to a consortium of investors he led. It included consultant doctors, lawyers and businessmen, all people with high incomes who wanted to save on tax and make investments that would provide big returns. Quinlan got planning permission for 478 apartments, a nursing home and various other facilities on the 11.3 acre site, but then he decided to sell it. Just four years later it was sold for more than €85 million to a company called Glenkerrin Homes owned by Ray Grehan. It was the highest price ever obtained for a development site in Dublin at that time.

It turned out to be a nightmare for Grehan, who failed to sell most of the apartments before the crash of 2008. With banks offering only 80 per cent of the price as a mortgage – at best – Grehan offered a deal whereby he would finance three quarters of the balance – leaving the buyer to find only 5 per cent of the overall price as a deposit – with a seven-year loan at zero interest. That didn't work either, as he was still trying to sell two-bedroom apartments at a price of €535,000. Eventually, he entered into negotiations with Dún Laoighaire-Rathdown County Council with a view to selling the blocks as social and affordable housing – at a deep reduction in price.

Developers misread the foreign market as well as the domestic one. Many of the top developers and their investors had bought overseas for years, in an attempt to diversify their risk. Some of the richest people in Ireland borrowed heavily to buy retail units, office blocks and shopping centres in the most expensive locations in Europe, especially in London. Less well-off people bought apartments in holiday resorts in places such as Bulgaria, at prices that seemed modest to us but that were impossible for locals to afford, which meant there was no real resale market. The Irish-owned banks supplied the bulk of the money. When property values fell in those countries too, albeit by less than in Ireland, it contributed to the crisis at the Irish banks, because the loans they held overseas were not being repaid and the assets there were often worth less than the loans given. It meant that the Irish taxpayer was left to pick up part of the tab for this foreign adventure.

The deal that caught all of the attention – and played somewhat to atavistic national pride – was Quinlan's purchase of the Savoy Group in London for €1.15 billion in 2004. The four luxury hotels included – the Savoy, Claridge's, Berkeley and Connaught – were much favoured by the British establishment, the wealthy and even royalty. The lobby of Claridge's is full of pictures of Winston Churchill and its restaurant is run by celebrity TV chef Gordon Ramsay. In April 2004, when the transfer of ownership was completed, the Irish tricolour was run up the Savoy's flag-poles. It prompted Quinlan to remark that he had cried on hearing this, because his father had been a member of the Irish Army.

Quinlan Private bought the group from Blackstone, the US venture capital group, beating competition from Saudi businessman Prince Alwaleed Bin Talal Alsaud, regarded then as the world's fourth-richest man. Prince Alwaleed was so keen to purchase the Savoy that just five months later he paid Quinlan €300 million for that property alone, providing the Irish with an immediate profit of about €50 million.

The identity of Quinlan's investors in the purchase of the hotels has remained private. There were reports of an involvement – subsequently ended – by Riverdance creators John McColgan and Moya Doherty. As few as six people may have been involved, borrowing at least €30 million each, with borrowings of over €800 million added then to their equity investment. Developer Paddy McKillen was also reported to be one of Quinlan's biggest backers.

Quinlan may have had different backers for each of his many overseas investments, which are too numerous to list. However, his ambitions certainly grew, as he bought in more prominent and famous locations and paid ever bigger prices. In the summer of 2005 Quinlan Private paid more than €730 million for a 3.4 acre site in Knightsbridge, between luxury retailers Harrods and Harvey Nichols on the so-called 'mile of style'. He then began the €300 million project to extend (upwards) and refurbish the luxury Claridge's and Berkeley hotels. He acquired the Jurys Inn chain of three-star hotels in Ireland and the UK for €1.16 billion – the vast bulk of the money a loan from Anglo – and announced plans to expand the brand further with another twenty new hotels. He also bought a 50 per cent stake in a portfolio of forty-seven Marriott hotels, before extending his investments to Spain, Germany, Eastern Europe and the United States. He was part of a consortium that bought the Spanish headquarters of Santander Bank in 2008 for €1.9 billion, purchased the €300 million Diaganol Mar shopping centre in Barcelona and bought a €270 million 'mixed use and residential scheme' in Munich.

His most dramatic, and potentially risky, London investment came in late 2007, when he completed the €1.4 billion acquisition of the landmark Canary Wharf building in London in a fifty-fifty joint venture with Propinvest, a UK-based property company. It was the second-biggest UK property transaction that year. The 42-storey building at 25 Canada Square, which is comprised of 1.2 million square feet of space, was acquired from Royal Bank of Scotland, the much criticized British bank that nearly went bust in 2009 and had to be rescued by the British government. This, however, seems to have been one of RBS's better deals, as it had owned the building for just four years and sold it at the peak of the market. The property is entirely let to global investment bank Citigroup, producing a rent of £46.5 million a year, according to reports, on a new thirty-year lease, with a yield of 4.5 per cent to 5 per cent for the new owners.

But Quinlan struggled to raise the finance for the deal. Even before it was completed Citigroup was planning to sublet about 100,000 square feet of the space, and independent analysts said the buyers had overpaid. Quinlan was said to have invested in a personal capacity, but, in the light of the enormous borrowings that would have been required, he must have sought to sell parts of the ownership to others. If he didn't, Quinlan – or his bankers – faced massive potential losses, given the collapse in London property values, especially in buildings rented to banks.

Quinlan claimed that the total assets under his group's management, at its peak, were worth more than €10 billion. But it was never known how much he had borrowed to make these purchases and the question now is how much they are worth. Unfortunately, the perception is that Quinlan always paid top prices to purchase the assets and that this left him facing large potential losses.

His sale of assets started in early 2009. He put a New York townhouse on the market with an optimistic price tag of €28.3 million. The house – 13,000 square feet on 64th Street – had been purchased in 2005 for €19.8 million. Bernie Madoff, the disgraced and jailed US investment adviser, had been a neighbour. He offered an office building of 10,000 square feet on the same street for sale at €27.3 million, having bought it for just over half that in 2005. He quickly reduced the asking price by nearly €8 million. In May 2009 the *Sunday Times* reported that Quinlan was offering a plot of land for sale in California, where he had planned to build an eco-friendly house next door to The Edge of U2. The Malibu plot, along with three others he advertised, was on a 120-acre estate the duo were developing at Sweetwater Mesa. It also reported that he had hired a dealer to sell much of his art collection, which included works by Jack B. Yeats, Sean Scully and Roderic O'Connor, many of which had been bought at the peak of the market. The *Irish Times* published details and photographs of a house on Eglin Road in Dublin 4 he had bought in 2007 for €7 million and that was now offered for sale at an optimistic €7.5 million. In July 2009 Quinlan suddenly announced that he was retiring as chairman of Quinlan Private, even though he was aged just sixty-one. He would have plenty to occupy him, though, in sorting out his investments.

Quinlan's private interests should in theory be of no concern to anyone. However, it seems that he borrowed massively from Irish banks, among others, which makes them very much our problem. Bank of Ireland, Anglo Irish Bank and Ulster Bank were known to be the main financiers of the Savoy Hotel acquisition, which suggests that they and other Irish banks may have been involved in some of his other ventures.

Quinlan also offered schemes that minimized the tax payments of his investors in Ireland. Typically, his overseas assets were purchased via companies using offshore locations such as Jersey. Investors formed a partnership and invested about 15 per cent of the equity. Banks lent the balance. As Jersey was used, no capital gains tax arose for any of the investors as long as they left the capital gain or profit within the partnership. Gains were used to buy further assets. No tax was paid as long as profits were not distributed to investors, which gave them an incentive to keep making their bets. If they needed cash they borrowed from a bank, using the value of the investments as collateral. It was cheaper to pay the bank interest than to pay tax. In other words, some of the massive profits were reinvested in order to avoid incurring and paying tax at home, but this increased the risk of overpaying for the new investments.

The profile of the acquisitions made in Britain by Irish people, companies or syndicates was extraordinary. Bond Street in London is regarded by many as Europe's most prestigious retail street, and at one stage Irish investors owned about 80 per cent of the properties on it. Apart from Quinlan other investors were the famous bread-making Brennan family, developer David Daly of Albany Homes, young Limerick developer Aidan Brooks (a regular partner of John Magnier and J. P. McManus), and consortia of smaller investors put together by BCP Asset Management and accountant BDO Simpson Xavier. Multi-millionaire Lochlann Quinn of electrical products manufacturer Glen Dimplex, who was chairman of AIB before Dermot Gleeson, also owned units there and an unnamed Irish investor bought the Tiffany building on the street.

On Oxford Street, Irish investors included McKillen and retired book-maker Joe Donnelly, who was extremely close to his racing buddy Charlie McCreevy. Also a major investor there was Cosgrave Property Developments, the highly regarded Dublin house-builder that went very quiet in Ireland a few years ago, believing prices to have escalated too much. Instead, the group, run by brothers Peter, Michael and Joe, paid €415 million for a shopping centre in Romford, Essex, in August 2006, bringing the company's spend on British property that year to €740 million.

There were countless other examples of super-rich Irish investors who wanted to diversify out of Ireland and there were many attractions in buying up Britain. Part of it was visceral pride – colonialism in reverse in some respects – part of it was knowledge of a fellow English-speaking market, part of it was proximity and, even at inflated prices, part of it was that the rental yields were better than those available in Ireland. But considerable amounts of money were also borrowed to invest in

Eastern Europe, apparently the 'coming market', where land and existing assets could be bought 'cheaply'.

The trend of a massive capital outflow was clear from as early as 2004, despite the continued existence of the domestic tax incentives for property investment. Over €3 billion was invested in foreign commercial property in 2004 by the Irish wealthy, with nearly one third of this by Quinlan. It was a combination of newly borrowed money and the profits accumulated over the years by massive tax-efficient investments at home that investors were now trying to protect by reducing the proportion of their assets held in Ireland.

The outflow increased in 2005 to about €4 billion – which was more than was being spent in Ireland – and property consultants estimated that more than one in five British commercial property deals by non-British buyers were by Irish investors. Quinlan's Kensington land grab and the purchase of the Standard Chartered headquarters building by a company called Sloane Capital – controlled by Aidan Brooks, who had enlisted J. P. McManus and John Magnier as investors – hit the headlines.

One estimate was that Irish people and companies spent €6.8 billion on commercial property during 2005 – nearly 1.5 per cent of the world's total spend that year on commercial property. This was extraordinary, considering the population of the country was little more than four million, but it was facilitated by a banking system that seemingly had no fear of regulation and was determined to take enormous risks to make bigger profits.

Estate agents C. B. Richard Ellis Gunne suggested at the end of 2005 that many Irish investors were being squeezed out of the market due to intensifying competition, particularly from Middle Eastern sovereign wealth funds, and diminishing yields. A survey by Jones Lang LaSalle suggested that Britain ranked as one of the largest property markets in the world and attracted, alongside the US and France, the majority of international investor capital, thereby forcing up the prices. Yet the Irish continued to plough in, while investing smaller sums in Paris, Amsterdam, Brussels and Eastern Europe.

By 2006 it was estimated that as much as €9 billion in 'Irish money' was invested in overseas commercial property, about three times the amount invested in Ireland. The warning bells should have been going off everywhere – but nobody wanted to take any notice of the few media commentators and economists who raised questions about the trend or who criticized it.

In the autumn of 2006 Marie Hunt, head of research at C. B. Richard Ellis Gunne, warned the Society of Chartered Surveyors, in a speech that was made available to the media, that investors were creating a bubble. 'The fear is that some Irish investors are ignoring the core fundamentals of investment selection and valuation and paying unrealistic prices to secure product . . . At this point, we urge caution and advise investors to get back to reality and have regard to the core fundamentals of property investment of which the most important indicator is now rental growth prospects,' she said.

Things started to slow in 2007 but that was due to market forces rather than to any government or regulatory intervention. At the end of 2007 estate agents Lisney reckoned that Irish investors had spent €4.3 billion in commercial transactions in Britain that year, despite the clear signs of a slump and the reduced availability of finance. 'As largely debt-funded buyers,' it noted, 'we have found it harder to compete in the last twenty-four months against institutional and sovereign wealth investors, particularly in London.' It appears that some Irish investors began selling in 2007, but unfortunately not in sufficient scale. Lisney estimated that Irish investors sold about half the value of what they bought, leaving net investment for the year at about €2 billion.

Many Irish investors had gone beyond buying established properties in so-called prime locations and with existing 'blue-chip' tenants, whose ability to continue doing profitable business and paying the rent was assumed. Some had started taking development risks in Britain, believing that new properties opening in 2009 and 2010 would provide excellent profits. These turned out to be bad bets that they and their bankers made – with consequences for all of us.

The big problem, though, was that many people had bought property that was now worth less than the money they had borrowed to pay for it. Their 'equity' was gone, but, worse, they still had big borrowings to repay. Suddenly, much of their wealth was gone.

PART VII

Two barons fall to earth

31

The last days of Celtic hubris

If Bernard McNamara's financial difficulties got plenty of media airing in 2008, in the early months of 2009 everyone in business and political circles was waiting for news about the fate of Seán Dunne. Dunne and McNamara had arrived at much the same place in the construction sector but by different routes: whereas McNamara's background was in the family's contracting business, Dunne had prospered as a self-started house-builder. But both had great ambition and, like McNamara, the Carlow-born developer was prominent in taking large-scale gambles at the peak of the boom.

Dunne engaged in a massive high-profile punt in Ballsbridge in Dublin 4 in 2005, buying seven acres of expensive land with the intention of demolishing landmark hotels and other buildings to construct, he said, a Dublin version of London's exclusive Kensington area. It was a plan of awesome ambition – to create an upmarket hub in the city, costing over €1.5 billion, and including a 37-storey spiralling tower (thereby ignoring the fact that Kensington doesn't have high-rises). In early 2009 Dunne faced an anxious wait to see if An Bord Pleanála would accept his appeal against the limited nature of Dublin City Council's planning permission for the scheme. Or indeed if the numerous objectors to the granting of even limited permission would succeed. Everyone else in his sector wanted to see where he would get the money to build his development if he got the permission or how he would cover his debts if he didn't. Interest charges on his bank loans, once they started, could not be covered by income from the reopened hotels or by rent from any existing commercial space, because there simply wouldn't be enough money coming from those sources.

The story gained international attention as a symbol for Ireland on the cusp of a hefty fall. In early January 2009 Dunne was the subject of a remarkable profile that appeared in both the *New York Times* and the *International Herald Tribune* (and has subsequently been reprinted in newspapers around the world). Reporter Landon Thomas Jr followed Dunne around Dublin for a day in December 2008, noting in particular his eating and drinking habits, which included champagne cocktails to kick off a hectic evening, copious wine to wash down a dinner of potatoes and gravy-drenched turkey, followed by five pints of Guinness during a session in Doheny and Nesbitt's pub that lasted until three in the morning. The reporter noted admiringly that Dunne hardly slurred his words by the end of it all.

The article detailed the scale of the massive financial gamble of Dunne's Ballsbridge dream. In the interview Dunne said about himself that 'Seán Dunne as an individual is 100 per cent solvent', but 'there are not many companies in Ireland today that are probably solvent and that's just a reality of life.' Much was made of his stooping to 'pick a penny' off the floor of Doheny and Nesbitt's pub in the early hours of the morning, quoting Dunne as saying he was never too proud to do so. 'I grew up with nothing and know the value of money. The Celtic Tiger may be dead and if the banking crisis continues I could be considered insolvent. But the one thing I have is my wife and children – that they can't take away from me.' He did not say who the 'they' were and why 'they' would want to take people in return for unpaid debts. Dunne later told the *Sunday Independent* that his conversation with Thomas had been off the record and that what he could remember saying was not what had been quoted but that 'with countries, banks in almost every country and legends of the banking world for over 100 years going bust, I would not bet against myself or anybody else being taken out.'

'Jealously and begrudgery are still alive and well in Ireland, and whoever eradicates them should be Prime Minister for life . . . It's part of the Irish psyche, and it is the result of 800 years of being controlled by other people, of watching everything the master or landlord is doing,' Dunne said. 'This is the way God made me, with heavy shoulders and an ability to carry a great load.'

The interview was accompanied by a picture of Dunne 'at home in Dublin' – the luxurious drawing room of what was presumably his Shrewsbury Road mansion (where his neighbours include Bernard McNamara). He was in the foreground, looking dapper in an expensive suit but wearing a somewhat guarded expression, while his immaculately groomed wife Gayle Killilea smiled serenely at the camera from her position in the background. The piece and photograph caused quite a stir in Ireland. Dunne issued a statement from his holidays in Vienna, attacking the article as inaccurate. The *Sunday Independent*, where Killilea had once worked, aired his views sympathetically.

Although he was objecting to the conditions imposed by Dublin City Council, Dunne had in fact received permission for the bulk of his proposed development. And, while DCC rejected his application for a 37-storey skyscraper and a ten-storey office block, it stated that it believed that a landmark building of height was necessary for the development to work aesthetically. It seemed that Dunne's vision was shared to a large degree by the city planners. The Danish architect who designed the development told An Bord Pleanála's hearing that former city architect Jim Barrett had favoured a 37-storey design over the 32-storey tower originally proposed. Senior planner Kieran Rose's report recommending permission, which formed the basis of city manager John Tierney's decision to approve the scheme, even suggested that many people would find the 'diamond-cut' 37-storey tower 'exciting'. He went on to quote Seamus Heaney in praising the tower: he said it could 'catch the heart off guard and blow it open'.

DCC's approach was somewhat surprising, given that back in March 2005 – just six months before Dunne began a land spree that could be justified financially only by building upwards in massive scale – its planners had rejected plans by Denis O'Brien for a 26-storey residential tower in Donnybrook on the grounds that its 'excessive height and scale' would have an 'overbearing' impact.

DCC's planning department approved four blocks containing a total of 294 apartments, a 232-bedroom hotel, an embassy building, cultural centre, crèche and district shopping centre – by Danish architects Henning Larsen – in the Ballsbridge scheme. The tallest building approved would rise to eighteen storeys on the Shelbourne Road frontage, while the lowest would be nine. The three apartment blocks on the Lansdowne Road frontage were allowed to be nine storeys in height – compared to the eleven Dunne had wanted.

However, all this wasn't enough to allow Dunne to cover the cost of his land acquisition and subsequent planned development. The 37-storey tower would have contained 182 apartments, and lowering the height of the Lansdowne Road blocks resulted in cutting the number of apartments in the scheme from 536 to 294. Potentially, that reduced his planned revenues by as much as €200 million. So, while others lodged objections to An Bord Pleanála – the ultimate planning arbiter – against what he had been allowed, Dunne appealed for the right to go ahead with what DCC had disallowed.

Most prominent of the objectors to Dunne's plans was Dermot Desmond. He said Dunne's plan was 'completely incongruous' with the surroundings. 'Grouping embassies together in one tall building would . . . [make them] a sitting duck for a terrorist attack. A cynic might say that the inclusion of the embassy block is purely because it is permissible in an area zoned residential.' Desmond described the plan as 'entirely unacceptable' and 'excessive'. 'The design proposed is reflective of the need to maximize the commercial development of this site,' his official submission stated. 'I have a real concern that the developer, rather than the planning authority, is dictating the planning process.'

To cap it, Desmond argued that the scheme 'seems based on the need to obtain the maximum financial return' and warned against allowing 'the desired financial return of any developer to be a valid planning consideration'.

An Bord Pleanála's decision, announced weeks after the *New York Times* piece, was as bad as anything Dunne could have imagined: the plans were rejected in their entirety. It said the development contravened the Dublin City Development Plan and agreed with its inspector, Tom Rabbette, who, having conducted a month-long public hearing on the development in September 2008, said the scheme was too tall, too intensive, would have a bad impact on the existing area and would contravene the development plan in bringing excessive retail and office development to the site.

However, the board went further than its inspector, who concentrated on the effect of the development on the surrounding area. It said it was not satisfied that the apartments would be a pleasant place in which to live. In a damning judgment for apartments that would have cost at least €1 million each, the board raised issues about wind turbulence, the availability of daylight and the penetration of sunlight.

The board did not refer to the 37-storey building in its reasons for refusal, but said the 'scale, massing and height' of the development as a whole would constitute 'gross over-development and over-intensification of use of the site'. It said it was an 'inappropriate design response' to the established character of Ballsbridge that would make a 'radical change in the urban form of the area'.

An Bord Pleanála also highlighted the decision of the planners at DCC – and its then manager acting at their recommendation – to approve something so dramatically at odds with its own development plan and the public statements of the elected councillors. This was seized upon immediately by the coalition of sixteen residents' associations in the area that had objected to the development.

In the aftermath of his rejection Dunne alleged 'a lack of leadership coming from the planning authorities'. He said, though, that he had no criticism to offer of DCC. 'They're trying to implement the development plan as they see fit but they seem to be met with a stone wall with An Bord Pleanála, for example,' he said.

'Development is not about greed; it's about building a country, building an economy. Somebody's got to do it. I was the man who decided to buy this site. I had a vision for it.'

Dunne's foiled plans for Ballsbridge will be remembered as one of the classic examples of Celtic hubris: massively ambitious in its physical scale but also based on the most optimistic – and ultimately flawed – of financial projections.

This is not a case of being wise after the event. In 2005, as Dunne neared taking control of the seven-acre site in Ballsbridge that housed, among other things, the Jurys Hotel and Berkeley Court hotel sites, I wrote in the *Irish Examiner* that 'in years to come, if and when the story of the madness of Ireland's property boom is told, then the saga involving the ownership of this high-profile piece of land in Dublin is likely to figure prominently.'

The price Dunne paid for the land was enormous, in the light of the precedent set by the O'Brien case and the need for a material contravention of the local development plan, should his plans be permitted. This would have been the case even if Dunne had paid only marginally more than the other developers had bid. The enormous price-per-acre was later outdone by others who looked to piggyback on Dunne's vision for the area, paying as much as €83 million and then a ludicrous €125 million per acre for adjacent properties. At least Dunne had kept his costs to €55 million per acre. He paid €260 million for Jurys and €119 million for the Berkeley Court and then did a deal with Irish Life to buy Hume House – across the road from Jurys – for around €130 million by partially bartering a new office block of 150,000 square feet in the Dublin docks as part of the deal. Then, with an eye to later development, he personally bought part of the AIB headquarters on two acres further up Merrion Road for €200 million on the basis that AIB would vacate it by 2011.

Dunne received plenty of bad publicity after his land purchase, most prominently in the *Irish Times*, which criticized both his closure and reopening of the hotels. In fairness to Dunne, he bought the properties, not the hotel operating companies, which had been closed by the previous owner, and he had other plans for the site. In what was probably the longest letter to the editor ever published in the *Irish Times*, he accused it of being wrong in attacking his plans before he had even applied for permission, describing it as being akin to judging a beauty contest in the dark. 'The business of property development involves risk-taking, and, in this case, a belief in the sustainable success of the Irish economy,' he wrote. 'While others have chosen to sell up now while the going is good and depart with their profits, I have chosen to put my trust, faith and money in the future of my country and its economy.'

Showing a surprisingly thin skin for a man who later boasted of strong shoulders, Dunne concluded his missive by charging that 'one change I would personally welcome is a change in the current trend among certain members of the media of blaming property developers for the ills of all society, a fad the *Irish Times* is now championing.'

The €710 million Dunne spent on buying all the land was not the end of his costs. He got repayments deferred for a period as he sought permission for development and he spent €15 million in professional fees. After An Bord Pleanála's decision Dunne criticized the planning process as 'lengthy, expensive, confusing and unworkable' and a 'game of roulette'. Bertie Ahern as Taoiseach often quibbled with the length of time it took to get decisions on major planning projects and Dunne certainly suffered in this way. Despite his close association with Ahern (something else he had in common with Bernard McNamara), Dunne's applications were in no way fast-tracked through the system.

Dunne's financial position became a matter of much conjecture, as Ulster Bank registered its legal charges against DCD Builders, Dunne's main company, for €556 million in order to secure its loans. But it has never been clear what security Dunne offered on the loans, other than the land itself, and whether he has given personal guarantees for the repayment of either the capital or the interest.

Accounts for DCD Builders filed in November 2008 showed property assets of €477 million – a figure that must now be in doubt following the property slump – and liabilities of €624 million. Dunne had lent DCD Builders €176 million himself but it is not known how much of that he had borrowed elsewhere. It has been rumoured that Dunne put up between €75 million and €150 million himself, borrowing the rest, although the *Sunday Independent* put a definitive figure on it, saying that he had personally provided €135 million of the €510 million acquisition spree (i.e. excluding the separate purchase of AIB Bankcentre).

Ulster Bank became his banker because, apparently, it was eager to do a high-profile deal – almost as advertising to other developers – after missing out on the financing of a major transaction involving another big developer because its parent company, Royal Bank of Scotland, was somewhat anxious about the level of risk involved. Ulster's bosses vowed that they would not miss out on the next big deal. It just happened that Dunne's Ballsbridge deal was the next one to come along. Ulster battled off other banks who wanted to provide finance to Dunne, although not long afterwards rumours circulated that RBS was highly anxious about its exposure to any failure on Dunne's part to secure the planning permission required.

When he lost his An Bord Pleanála appeal, Dunne blamed a 'snobbish element' in Ballsbridge for opposing his high-rise scheme for the Dublin 4 site. He claimed the construction of the scheme would have created 970 on-site jobs and about the same number off-site for seven years. 'A lot of people have said to me, and a lot of friends have said to me, if an American or a foreign multinational company was coming to Dublin and relocating anywhere, including Ballsbridge, and creating 5,400 full-time jobs, I think it's fair to say there would be a queue of Mercedes back from D4 hotels all the way back to Government Buildings,' he said.

That was pretty rich coming from Dunne, a man who has enjoyed better access to Government Buildings than most. There is no doubt that he is one of the few men outside of Bertie Ahern's Drumcondra circle to have become very close to the former Taoiseach.

Examples of that closeness have become legendary. When Ahern became the first Taoiseach to address the House of Commons – in the run-up to the 2007 general election – Dunne was there. According to a government spokesman he just happened to be in London and Ahern tried to get tickets for whoever he could. But it undoubtedly must have impressed and reassured RBS.

And when Ahern gave his oration to the Joint Houses of Congress in April 2008, Dunne and his wife were there. Not only that, but Killilea wrote a gushing piece for the *Sunday Independent* describing the experience. In the piece she castigated members of the media she felt had not been suitably deferential to Ahern.

The relationship goes back further. In 2002 Dunne provided return flights to Cardiff for Ahern so he could see the Heineken Cup final between Munster and Leicester. In accordance with state rules, Ahern later refunded the €1,480 cost to Dunne's company, DCD. Ahern is believed to have been a regular at private dinner parties in Dunne's home, and unconfirmed reports have had it that a tap of Ahern's favourite drink, Bass, was installed in the bar in Dunne's house. Dunne was a regular at the Fianna Fáil fund-raising tent at the Galway Races (where he met Killilea, his second wife) and at Ahern's annual constituency fund-raisers in the Royal Hospital Kilmainham or Clontarf Castle. Ahern was at Dunne's son's twenty-first birthday celebrations in 2008.

Most notably, perhaps, Ahern and his then finance minister Charlie McCreevy were invited in July 2004 to the Dunne–Killilea wedding celebrations on board the luxury yacht / floating tax break, the *Christina O*. Had Ahern and McCreevy turned up, they could have partied with Irish rugby internationals Ronan O'Gara and Mick Galwey, Irish Nationwide's Michael Fingleton, fashion designer Karen Millen, P. J. Mara's son John and theatre impresario Michael Colgan. The party went on for days.

They did end up there in voice – via speaker phone during the speeches. McCreevy, whose Kildare mansion in Straffan was built by Dunne, was the first to speak, followed twenty minutes later by Ahern. According to the *Sunday Independent* in a full-page report the following Sunday, Ahern started by saying: 'Dunner, you and I go back a long way. I wish I could be there. I'm sorry I couldn't come but I would have been more trouble to you than I'd be worth.'

Killilea, who was quoted at length in Anne Harris's piece, said that Ahern was concerned that he would draw the media to the event, much as had happened at the wedding in France of his daughter Georgina to Westlife singer Nicky Byrne some weeks earlier. The Irish media were furious that they could not get photographs because of an exclusive deal with *Hello!* magazine and tracking down Ahern as he tried to avoid them became a big part of the story. 'He didn't want our wedding to turn into all being about him. Then Charlie McCreevy said he better not come either,' Killilea explained.

All of which raises the question as to how Ahern became so close to Dunne, a man who has stated publicly on many occasions that he is not a member of Fianna Fáil. The answer is Des Richardson. Richardson and Dunne used to live near each other in Foxrock; when Dunne moved to Shrewsbury Road, Richardson moved to a property in Sandymount adjacent to Dunne's AIB Bankcentre acquisition and it is not clear if he bought or rented his new address from Dunne. Richardson lobbied for Dunne's Ballsbridge plan, putting his name to planning submissions and even arguing the case at a residents' meeting organized by Fine Gael. And Richardson was with Dunne at both of Ahern's major international speeches.

This closeness may go some way towards explaining comments that Ahern made about Dunne's failure to win planning permission for the Ballsbridge adventure. The *Sunday Independent* headline – 'Developer Dunne gets full backing from Ahern' – somewhat oversold the content of a report the paper published on 8 February 2009, little more than a week after Dunne's scheme had been rejected by the planners. As the paper was pitching it, Ahern had not just come out in support of Dunne but was the first prominent person to do so publicly. However, the only thing quoted in the article underneath was the former Taoiseach saying, 'An Bord Pleanála seems to think that Ballsbridge is unique but I never thought so.'

With Ahern it was usually possible for a newspaper to endow his seemingly innocuous comments with great significance. This was one such time. Dunne had argued that there was nothing positively unique about Ballsbridge that made it beyond change and improvement and Ahern's comments could easily be read as a tacit endorsement of that view. If so, then this was the former Taoiseach disparaging a decision An Bord Pleanála had come to after careful consideration and a one-month public hearing at which hundreds of representations had been made.

But Ahern was not so naive as to endorse Dunne publicly, given that his friend was a developer of the type so readily maligned by the public for contributing to the inflation and subsequent bursting of the Celtic Bubble. However, it was another indication that when Ahern could do something for a friend, even if it was just a shrewdly placed word, he would.

32

The battle for the Independent

In April 2008 Ahern announced that he would step down as Taoiseach the following month. Tony O'Reilly desperately needed two favours before Ahern left office, to help each of his biggest investments, Waterford Wedgwood and Independent News and Media. Ahern had to convince the government that the actions required by O'Reilly would be in its continued interest even after Ahern had gone.

O'Reilly's Waterford Wedgwood group – owner of the iconic Waterford Crystal company – was in such deep financial trouble that it was having difficulty securing loans from its bankers. It needed more money to continue manufacturing both at Waterford and abroad. Without it, the entire operation was threatened with closure. It needed €39 million immediately, but probably even more would be required later. O'Reilly asked the government to provide a guarantee to the banks that it would make repayments on the latest loan if the company couldn't.

It was an extraordinary request for Ireland's apparently richest man to make. Only the previous month O'Reilly had bought additional INM shares to the value of nearly €20 million, in an attempt to fend off the possibility of a takeover bid by rival Denis O'Brien, who was buying more and more shares. However, O'Reilly was nowhere near as rich as was widely assumed, and almost certainly not a billionaire when his debts were subtracted from the value of his assets. He was under pressure – not just financially but to maintain management control of both companies.

Waterford might as well have been burning O'Reilly's money in the fierce furnaces used to mould crystalware for all the good his investments there were doing him. Between 2004 and 2008 the luxury goods group – which also owned the ceramics manufacturers Wedgwood and Royal Doulton in Britain and glassware company Rosenthal in Germany –

raised about €775 million through share sales, bond issues and asset disposals. Over €300 million of the money came from O'Reilly and his brother-in-law Peter Goulandris, the Greek shipping magnate. They ended up with a majority shareholding in the business almost by accident, when other investors refused to contribute further to seemingly endless rounds of new fund-raising. They provided personal guarantees over at least €100 million in loans. The group's accumulated losses headed for €1 billion and debts mounted to nearly €500 million.

The company's assets were no longer sufficient in number or value to guarantee that their sale would generate enough money to meet the repayment of the loans if it proved impossible to do so out of profits. Nor did it help that consumer demand for the expensive products was falling, even before the recession had really hit and left luxury goods at the bottom of consumers' shopping lists. Unfortunately, too, the strength of the euro further reduced the profit margins on Waterford's exports from Ireland to Britain, the United States and Asia.

In the absence of even more equity investment, the banks were not prepared to advance further credit without getting guarantees of repayment. Waterford Wedgwood emphasized to government that it was not looking for a cash grant or gift from the government. It did not want to have to call on the money at all, if possible. But that didn't lessen the substantial risk that the government's pledge would later be converted into the transfer of hard cash.

The government wanted to protect the 800 remaining Irish jobs but it couldn't be seen to be helping O'Reilly openly. He was still publicly regarded as one of the wealthiest men in Ireland, and many people believed him to be non-tax resident, which didn't help matters, though in fact he has never clarified whether he is non-tax resident or not. Ahern's government would find it hard to escape criticism that any bailout was motivated by the exceptionally soft coverage Ahern's tribunal dealings had received in the *Sunday Independent*.

Waterford Crystal had put the city of Waterford on the map economically and there were also major ancillary tourism revenues associated with the visitors' centre: hundreds of thousands attended it annually, especially from the US. They might not have gone to the south-east of Ireland at all were it not for the opportunity to see the incredible skills of the glass-blowers and their handicrafts.

But by this time the importance to the country of this supposedly iconic Irish brand was debatable. Contemporary tastes had changed and the appeal of the elaborate old-style designs suited to manufacturing in Waterford had diminished. Also, most buyers neither knew nor cared exactly where glass came from as long as it served its function. The use of international celebrities to promote the brand – people such as Sarah Ferguson, the Duchess of York, designers John Rocha, Jasper Conran and Vera Wang, chef Gordon Ramsay and American lifestyle guru (and jailbird) Martha Stewart – was an attempt to counteract this development. However, these marketing initiatives did not stem the loss of custom.

There were practical issues too. The European Commission might block any guarantee as anti-competitive – unfair state aid that would disadvantage glassware-makers in other member states. Even if allowed, it might have created a dangerous precedent, with other Irish and multinational companies looking for similar support. The reality was that propping up an ailing, privately owned company, especially when it had already shed about three quarters of its workforce, would only postpone the eventual closure of the Irish manufacturing operations and that the money might be lost.

There was also the question of 'moral hazard', of bailing out O'Reilly for his own poor business and investment decisions. His strategy of building a four-pronged luxury goods group – Waterford Crystal, Rosenthal, Wedgwood and Royal Doulton (the latter two operating in ceramics) – had gone badly wrong. Not only had the financial failures of the ceramics companies weighed down the performance of crystal divisions, but there was a worry that the latter were profitable only because of what was made outside of Ireland. A more ruthless man than O'Reilly might have closed the Irish manufacturing base a decade earlier and shifted production to far cheaper locations in Asia or Eastern Europe. The company could employ 1,300 staff in Indonesia for the cost of fewer than 100 people in Ireland.

Despite all the criticisms of his reputed tax status and use of a British title, it seemed that a form of economic patriotism contributed to O'Reilly's mistakes. 'If you cut him open, his blood runs green. He's an Irishman before anything. And perhaps that goes some way to explain his commitment to Waterford Wedgwood,' said David Palmer, an Englishman who had a spell running Independent's Irish operations before handing over to O'Reilly's son Gavin.

In any case, Ahern's cabinet colleagues were in no mood to help. 'There was no way we could do it,' one senior government minister told me, on condition of not being named for fear of the consequences to him in the O'Reilly-controlled media. 'It was impossible to be seen to set such a precedent and especially for somebody like O'Reilly.'

If his problems at Waterford weren't bad enough, O'Reilly was distracted by a growing threat to his control of INM. This was another company to which he was not only emotionally attached, but also on which he was financially dependent.

O'Reilly had done an extraordinary job in growing INM. From a company with annual sales of £12 million and an exclusive focus on Ireland when he took control of it in 1973, it now had annual sales of nearly €1.7 billion and in 2007 had reported profits of €286 million, with sizeable operations not just in Ireland but in Britain, South Africa, Australia, New Zealand and India. O'Reilly did enormously well out of all of this personally, controlling INM despite having a shareholding of just 27 per cent. At the company's peak value, O'Reilly's shareholding was worth about €650 million.

But he took out enormous amounts of money too. In the six years since the turn of the millennium, O'Reilly took €110 million in cash from INM. That figure represents only his dividend income, salary, bonus and perks, and not the extra shares that he was able to purchase at favourable prices. In 2006 alone he received dividends of over €25 million and more again in 2007. The last dividends that O'Reilly received were in November 2008, an interim payment of more than €10 million from that year's profits; the amount had been decided earlier in the year before the sudden economic downturn. In January 2009 INM announced that the final dividend for 2008 had been cancelled.

The company had embraced a strategy of paying a large proportion of its profits in dividends. In 2005 INM made after-tax profits of €229 million and paid out dividends of €72.9 million. The after-tax profits fell to €198 million the next year but the dividends increased to €84.6 million. In 2007 the after-tax profits fell by another €3 million but the dividend went up by €13.1 million, to just a couple of million shy of €100 million. It was money that could have gone towards paying off borrowings instead of to the shareholders.

The company engaged in ruthless cost reductions among ordinary staff. O'Reilly declared that INM had to become the 'Ryanair of the newspaper sector' – the industry's low-cost operator. The highly profitable Irish operations were targeted for redundancies and outsourcing, although there was relatively little coverage of this in the Independent titles. Many of the clerical and production staff were either made redundant or shifted off, albeit with some compensation, to outside companies that provided lower-priced contracted services to Independent and offered new jobs on inferior terms, especially when it came to pensions. Then the same happened with the majority of sub-editors, the people who edit the content of the papers and design and lay out their pages. There was hardly a murmur from other media as their bosses contemplated following what seemed set to be the new industry norm.

O'Brien's presence provoked O'Reilly into mistakes that were to have serious consequences for both. O'Reilly failed to realize the importance of reducing group debt quickly because his focus was on keeping O'Brien at bay. This led to his decision to endorse a share buy-back scheme, whereby INM used its money – or rather borrowed money – to buy its own shares in the market. This is a perfectly legal mechanism, designed to allow a company to use its cash to reduce the number of shares in issue, thereby making the remaining shares more valuable. It is best suited to a company with excess cash, however, not one that is in debt. INM spent €130 million in 2007 and 2008 buying its own shares at prices ranging from €2 to €3.50, all apparently to prevent O'Brien buying more shares.

It is not hard to see why O'Reilly was spooked by O'Brien. Like O'Reilly, O'Brien was regarded as a billionaire and his ambitions were not yet sated. O'Brien's first successful business investments were in radio, but he hit the big time when he got involved in the evolving telephony market during the 1990s. He was instrumental in forcing the government to deregulate the sector, breaking the monopoly of the state-owned Telecom Éireann by cleverly using European legal rulings to his advantage. When he sold the Esat group (which included the shareholding in mobile phone operator Esat Digifone) to British Telecom for over $2 billion at the height of the dotcom bubble mania, he received a personal windfall of €250 million.

That achievement turned O'Brien into the poster boy for the Celtic Tiger entrepreneurs, his 'can-do' attitude and ready smile making him an appealing antidote to the seemingly more traditional stuffy business classes. Even though O'Brien grew up in Dublin 4, the son of a successful businessman, had been GPA boss Tony Ryan's personal assistant, and had a range of prosperous contacts to approach for capital, he portrayed himself as an outsider who had prospered by bravely taking on and defeating establishment forces always rallying to deny him. But in 2000 even establishment Ireland recognized him: Bank of Ireland invited him to join its court (its board of directors). He started firing money at political parties, Fianna Fáil, Fine Gael, Labour and the Progressive Democrats receiving £50,000 each, although Labour didn't cash the unsolicited cheque and returned it.

He was not about to relax. 'Entrepreneurs never know when to leave the casino,' O'Brien said in an interview not long later. 'An entrepreneur always wants to start another business. It's part of your make-up. If an entrepreneur sells their businesses, within a couple of months they're off setting up a new business.'

In early 2001 O'Brien decided to try to buy his old nemesis, Eircom, as it struggled on the stock market. However, in the middle of his campaign O'Brien was dragged into a controversy that was to dog him for years to come.

In late January 2001, when the *Sunday Tribune*'s political correspondent Shane Coleman and I co-wrote the lengthy report that detailed extensive information about Dermot Desmond's involvement in the Esat Digifone consortium (see Chapter 17), it was the first the public had heard of it. We followed this initial piece with further reports about the Esat Digifone £50,000 payment to Fine Gael six weeks after Minister Michael Lowry announced O'Brien's consortium as winner of the competition for the second mobile phone licence in 1995.

I reported how the payment had been made by Telenor, but that the Norwegian company said it had been made at O'Brien's request and that it was repaid subsequently by Esat Digifone; how the late David Austin, a close associate of Michael Smurfit and an unofficial Fine Gael fund-raiser, had been the conduit for the payment; how the payment got 'stuck' within Fine Gael, which didn't know what to do with it; and how the party tried to return it to the donors, who didn't want to take it back.

O'Brien denied that he had ordered the payment, saying it was a Telenor initiative that it was trying to blame on him. He was furious about the story because, correctly, he expected that it would lead to investigation by the Moriarty Tribunal into how the licence had been won (an investigation that eventually went on for over eight years). He gave interviews to the media in which he disputed the accuracy of the *Tribune* story. He also rang Gavin O'Reilly to complain.

This led to the only occasion during my time as editor of the *Sunday Tribune* that a director of Independent rang to find out why a story about a third party had been published; if it was correct; if it would stand up to legal scrutiny; and whether there was more to come. O'Reilly apologized for doing so, but admitted there was sensitivity because of Independent's part in a losing consortium. I told him that I would not have published a story of such obvious sensitivity unless I was convinced it was correct and that all subsequent reporting would continue to be fair and accurate and not designed to cause O'Brien deliberate damage. O'Reilly said that he could not tell me as editor what to do, but asked that I be careful to protect the *Sunday Tribune* from unnecessary legal expense.

I had no personal agenda against O'Brien. I knew him reasonably well and felt that I'd always got on well with him. I first met him in late 1989 when he was launching 98FM; at the same time the *Sunday Business Post*, where I was a reporter, was being launched. We kept in reasonably regular contact over the years – sometimes meeting for lunch – and he provided information about what was going on in radio and telecommunications, some of which provided interesting stories for the *Sunday Business Post, Irish Independent* and, indeed, the *Sunday Tribune*. My wife and I were guests – along with about 700 others – at the launch of Esat Digifone in the Point Depot in March 1997. He was entertaining company, irreverent about other people, always looking to do new things and had an infectious energy. But that didn't mean that I was going to bury a good story about him if it was important and accurate. I was doing my job, delivering a story of considerable public interest, while also boosting the *Tribune*'s profile as the kind of newspaper that could break a big story.

O'Reilly senior subsequently won the battle for Eircom. O'Brien affected not to care, saying there was far more money to be made in developing a mobile phone network in the Caribbean than in owning a small bit of Eircom. However, the experience of defeat clearly rankled, and in March 2004 O'Brien made a formal complaint to the Office of the Director of Corporate Enforcement and the Stock Exchange Takeover Panel about the manner in which the Eircom ESOT had received the crucial secret tax changes (detailed in Chapter 1) that gave O'Reilly's Valentia an advantage over O'Brien's e-Island. This complaint, in which he asked for further investigation, fitted into an emerging pattern as O'Brien struggled to cope with a mounting list of troubles arising from the Moriarty Tribunal, all of which were reported across the media, not just in INM outlets.

In the summer of 2003 Gavin O'Reilly wrote to O'Brien offering his personal congratulations on O'Brien's highly successful chairmanship of that year's Special Olympics World Games in Ireland. O'Reilly was mistaken if he expected the conciliatory private letter to repair what had become an increasingly fractious relationship.

O'Brien responded with a letter that made it clear he was in no mood for reconciliation. He recited a list of perceived injustices against him, carried out by newspapers in the INM empire. Ominously, he warned: 'I am waiting for the appropriate time to rectify the damage.' He offered no indication as to what he meant by this or how he would do it.

Soon afterwards – on 23 October 2003 – he gave an interview to the *Irish Times* in which he made reference to O'Reilly's 'ragbag of investments' and complained about his newspapers making 'outrageous allegations against me and my companies'.

He appeared to blame O'Reilly personally for not curtailing the commentary in the newspapers – although at this stage the vast bulk of the coverage was based on nothing more than evidence given at the Moriarty Tribunal as it progressed. It was the tribunal that brought forward the allegation that O'Brien had told his former Esat Digifone managing director Barry Maloney that he tried to make a £100,000 payment to Lowry, but that it got 'stuck'. O'Brien later said he was only spoofing when he made the comment to Maloney during a run in the Wicklow mountains and that he did so because he wanted Maloney to release payments to P. J. Mara and other consultants that Maloney didn't want to pay. O'Brien insisted to the tribunal that he had never paid the money to Lowry and indeed it emerged that he had convinced his fellow directors at Esat of the same thing privately some years earlier. According to documents brought to the tribunal's attention, O'Brien had told Esat directors that while he had thought of making a payment from a personal Woodchester bank account to assist Lowry in some business issues, he had thought better of it because he feared it could be misconstrued if ever revealed. The tribunal uncovered evidence of Austin giving a loan to Lowry for the purchase of a house in Dublin, with the money coming from a bank account in the Isle of Man into which an agent of O'Brien had deposited almost the same amount of money. The tribunal disclosed O'Brien's explanation that the money was payment for a house in Spain he'd bought from Austin and that O'Brien had no idea what Austin did with it afterwards. The tribunal revealed that Lowry had repaid the loan to Austin on the day the McCracken Tribunal (the forerunner to the Moriarty Tribunal) was established to investigate Haughey's and Lowry's actions. It drew together evidence of O'Brien's money being used by associates of his for property deals in Britain in which Lowry was to be a partner, although it also acknowledged that O'Brien said this had happened without his knowledge or consent.

O'Brien angrily denied any wrongdoing and demanded that the tribunal cease its work because it was casting unreasonable doubts over his success in winning the licence. He was deeply concerned about the tribunal's modus operandi and insisted that it had produced nothing to suggest that Lowry had influenced or corrupted the licence award. On one red-letter day he stormed out of a hearing at Dublin Castle saying, 'That's my reputation they've torn up in there.'

Tony O'Reilly had been a good loser over the mobile licence competition, initially at least, even if it later emerged that he had complained privately to the government. He wrote to O'Brien in 1996 to congratulate him on his win. 'My dear Denis,' it began, 'many years ago at Blackrock Baths I watched your father in the national championships, I think against a certain Eddie Heron. The multitude of the Kavanagh brothers were there flexing their pectoral muscles and I was sure your father would win an Olympic Gold. In fact, he didn't and you did, and I think your achievement in securing the second digital network is your equivalent.'

Having been disappointed subsequently in his attempt to buy Eircom, O'Brien headed for the Caribbean, where he was to enjoy enormous financial success. O'Brien built a mobile phone business very quickly, focusing on supplying low-priced services to countries and customers that richer companies had ignored or dismissed. Digicel – as the new company was named – went into thirty countries and impressed investors so much that when O'Brien decided to refinance the business in 2006 he constructed a remarkable deal.

The business in the Caribbean was owned by Digicel Ltd, of which he owned 78 per cent. Now that the business was considered to be successful and had value, O'Brien wanted to take some of the riches for himself. He considered selling the company by way of a stock market flotation, in which he would keep a percentage for himself but raise cash for other things by selling a proportion. Instead, he came up with another solution, complicated but with the ability to give him full ownership of the company and lots of cash to spend on other things. What he did was to set up a new company in Bermuda called Digicel Group, which he owned 100 per cent. It paid $2.4 billion in cash for Digicel Ltd: $1.4 billion of this came through the issue of high-yielding junk bonds on the US capital markets, and he paid the balance himself. He got the money he needed from the sale of Digicel Limited to his new company, his share of the $2.4 billion being $1.87 billion. (Although it may seem confusing that he was paying himself for his own shares and using the payment to fund the deal in the first place, such transactions are signed off on simultaneously, so a deal can be structured in this way.) O'Brien reinvested $1 billion of this into Digicel Group, the new owner of the mobile phone business. That left him with $870 million in surplus cash. This was the point of the exercise: to restructure his business in a way that enabled it to remain properly funded but that also enabled him to leverage its value and generate a fund that could be used for other investments.

However, there was a catch. As 100 per cent owner of Digicel Group, O'Brien was liable now for the repayment of the junk bonds, for the annual interest repayments and for the other debts in the business. It was a bold statement of belief in the quality and profitability of the business he had developed and suggested that he expected to be able to sell it at a later date for an even larger sum of money, repaying the bonds and other debts and having another massive profit to enjoy. It was indicative of O'Brien's willingness to gamble on something in which he believed he could make big profits, an attribute that set him apart from others, taking risks where others perhaps wouldn't.

'This is a great time to do an LBO [leveraged buyout],' he said at one business conference in late 2006. 'Money is cheap and there is the opportunity of raising fresh capital in the bond markets. A company with earnings of €10 million or €15 million could raise a bond of €100 million today and go and do something really mega. Obviously, you bet the ranch, but the rewards are there.'

And now he was buying shares in INM and disclosed as having a 3 per cent shareholding in January 2007. It raised legitimate questions as to whether this was his seeking to 'rectify the damage', as he had written to Gavin O'Reilly. Observers recalled an interview he gave a decade earlier in which he said money was never his main motivation. 'I spend my time thinking of ways to create a downfall for my competitor, particularly if they are big,' he had said.

Clearly O'Brien had cash and the willingness to use it as leverage for further borrowings. O'Reilly had an unexpected and unwanted problem. Suddenly there were all sorts of unanswered questions that were not just interesting to outside observers but crucial to O'Reilly's continued stewardship of his prized asset. There was speculation that O'Brien wanted outright control and that he would seek to buy O'Reilly out to make himself the single most important and powerful figure in Irish media. There was talk of 'greenmail' – forcing O'Reilly to buy him out, thus providing O'Brien with massive profits on his investment and the enjoyment of making mischief for O'Reilly.

People wondered if he would be happy to continue as a minority shareholder – putting pressure on O'Reilly both to change his behaviour as chief executive and to sell prized assets, all to help the share price rise further as the company's potential was better realized – but without formal input. Investors, staff and customers asked if O'Brien would be content to remain without board representation, just so he wouldn't have to sit on the same board as the O'Reillys and friends.

If O'Brien had aspirations to win full control of INM, however, O'Reilly's shareholding remained a major obstacle to the financing of a deal. To take control of the assets of a publicly owned company it is necessary to get a minimum of 80 per cent of the shares; once this is done it is possible for the company to raise borrowings against its own assets, which the new owner can then use to cover the cost of the purchase of the shares. However, with his 27 per cent (later increased to 28 per cent), O'Reilly could block such moves. In other words, if O'Brien was to secure loans to fund the purchase of the 72 per cent of the company O'Reilly didn't own, he would have to offer both the shares and other assets of his outside of INM as security for the loans.

That looked unlikely, given the probable size of the deal – something in the order of over €3 billion, as it seemed then in advance of the credit crunch.

While continuing to buy shares – eventually giving him one quarter ownership of INM – O'Brien launched a very public and high-profile strategy of denigrating both O'Reilly and INM. In a series of print and television interviews, mainly in London and New York, he described O'Reilly as an 'old-style media mogul', implying that because of his age he was out of touch, particularly with the potential and importance of developing an internet strategy. He hit hard. He called for the sale of the loss-making London *Independent*, calling it a 'vanity' investment, and also at various times for the sale of the group's highly profitable Australian radio interests and South African newspapers. At no stage did he call for the closing or sale of the Irish perennial loss maker the *Sunday Tribune*. He questioned the cost of the corporate jet at O'Reilly's disposal and the expensive parties regularly held at O'Reilly's home – which Independent may have partially funded – and various sponsorships. He sought to clear out the large board, filled with family members, family friends and long-standing members whose independence could be questioned. He sought a disbandment of INM's international advisory board, which was filled with high-profile international figures (such as, bizarrely, the actor Sean Connery) with whom O'Reilly liked to associate.

O'Brien's assault on corporate governance was the subject of reports prepared for the annual general meetings of shareholders in 2007 and 2008; and, even if most other shareholders continued to side with the board, his criticisms got plenty of attention and some sympathy too. Leaving aside O'Reilly's stewardship of INM, the controversial style of journalism engaged in at some of Independent's papers over the years – particularly at the *Sunday Independent*, and that paper's favourable coverage of Bertie Ahern – meant that many figures in business and politics were upset by what Independent titles had printed. Even if O'Reilly had no direct involvement in the content of his papers, he was blamed for not reining in some editors.

The prospect of a battle for control of Ireland's most powerful print company meant that both were likely to be looking to other pillars of Irish society, particularly in banking, for support. All sorts of relationships would be called into play. Both men were powerful but not necessarily popular. Some people would be forced to choose sides. Some might have preferred to take none. O'Reilly's age was also counting against him – in his seventies he might have found that many of his old supporters and friends were no longer in a position to help him. But he did have his relationship with Ahern.

O'Brien's decision in mid-2007 to buy the Irish radio assets of the UK publicly quoted company EMAP had raised all sorts of competition issues and given INM the opportunity to cause its own mischief – as well as raising legitimate questions. So, just at the time the government wouldn't help O'Reilly on the Waterford Crystal issue, it gave him the less contentious of the two favours that he sought – the appointment of a special investigating commission into media ownership.

The irony was enormous: having berated the Competition Authority in the mid-1990s for declaring that Independent Newspapers had a monopoly position, the company was now hoping for the same body to limit O'Brien's shareholding in INM because of his extensive and growing number of important Irish radio assets.

EMAP had owned the national commercial broadcaster Today FM (where I present and edit the drive-time show *The Last Word*), the Dublin local radio station FM104 and Highland Radio in Donegal. Today FM was the prize O'Brien's Communicorp really sought, a successful national station that could partner and help the struggling national station Newstalk, where he held a controlling majority stake. As well as Newstalk, O'Brien also owned Dublin pop station 98FM, Dublin youth station SPIN 1038 and regional station SPIN South West. The Broadcasting Commission of Ireland (BCI) had to decide whether the acquisition of EMAP's Irish assets would give O'Brien too much control of the commercial radio sector. The commission is legally charged with promoting the plurality of media ownership. It is supposed to guard against any single person or group having control of, or substantial interests in, an undue amount of communications media.

The commission decided that ownership of FM104 on top of his existing Dublin assets would be too much, so he was ordered to sell it. He decided to sell Highland too, leaving him just Today FM to add to his existing stable of radio assets. But that wasn't good enough for INM.

Final approval for the purchase of Today FM lay with the Minister for Trade, Enterprise and Employment, Micheál Martin. In December

2007 he received a delegation from INM made up of Gavin O'Reilly and the chief executive of the Irish operations, Vincent Crowley. INM objected to the deal on grounds of cross-media ownership, arguing that O'Brien was becoming too big and powerful in Ireland. It demanded changes to competition legislation, including restrictions on any single person, or company, controlling large sections of both print and broadcast media.

INM made the same representations to the Competition Authority, but the authority, which decides on media mergers within and outside the broadcasting sector, told the government it did not have the expertise to decide on the need to maintain plurality of ownership in the media. All it was interested in was measuring the impact on competition in the advertising market.

O'Brien's purchase of Today FM was approved by the minister and completed in late March 2008. The timing was significant because this was when INM decided to go public in its fight with O'Brien, whose shareholding had grown to 21 per cent. It issued a public statement in which it labelled O'Brien a 'dissident shareholder', a term that has no status in law and that it withdrew some time afterwards. At this point the slagging match really started. INM issued a statement asking, 'What experience does Mr O'Brien have of ever managing a broad-based and internationally diversified media group with the complexities and sophistication that INM demands? What experience, if any, does Mr O'Brien have in publishing – the core competency of INM?' It accused O'Brien of trying to destabilize INM and then questioned his business prowess by pointing to losses at his radio group Communicorp.

O'Reilly senior entered the fray personally a couple of days later when he told the *Sunday Tribune*, 'O'Brien has had great success. He has also had periods where he was not successful, but criticism goes with the turf. One day you are the greatest player in the world, seven days later you are the villain of the peace. That's the way life is.'

In early April – the same week Ahern announced his departure – Martin established an inquiry into media ownership rules by appointing a special advisory group, chaired by barrister Paul Sreenan, to investigate and make recommendations. The timing was merely a happy coincidence: the government said its decision followed a call for guidance from the Competition Authority when it found itself lacking the expertise to examine the Today FM deal. Martin's department was also able to cite an internal report from 2006 that pointed to a 'clear recognition that there comes a point at which concentrations of media power in the hands of a small number can injure the marketplace of ideas'.

By this stage O'Brien's stake in INM had reached 25 per cent, which required the BCI to examine his ownership of radio assets again. It decided that the size of the stake in INM did not breach its media ownership and control policy, which considers factors such as the ability of an investor to influence media content. It did not explain how it came to that decision, although O'Brien's continued non-representation on the INM board may have played its part.

Meanwhile, the sniping between the parties went on. 'The dissident shareholder can't beat something with nothing and, frankly, that's exactly what he's offered shareholders,' Gavin O'Reilly said of O'Brien in a *Sunday Times* interview in June 2008. 'He has offered no alternative vision, strategic or otherwise – no directors, no bid, nothing. All he's done is pursue a Don Quixote-like campaign in an area where he has no experience and, to judge from his less-than-stellar Communicorp results, no expertise either.' O'Brien continued to press on the corporate governance issues and the lack of strategy for new media.

Soon it would all be redundant. The warring parties were to be forced into a truce and then more.

33

Testing times for Tony O'Reilly

The long-anticipated collapse of Waterford Wedgwood came early in 2009. O'Reilly tried all he could to persuade its banks to continue advancing credit, and when they wouldn't he couldn't find replacement finance, not even from his remaining contacts in the big US banks he knew so well from his time at Heinz. The Sunday after Christmas 2008 he visited Taoiseach Brian Cowen at Government Buildings to enlist his help: Cowen phoned a senior executive at Bank of America at O'Reilly's request, pleading for it to continue rolling over loans for the Irish company, but to no avail. Eventually, the receivers were appointed. O'Reilly and his brother-in-law lost all the money they had invested, estimated at more than €400 million. It was an ignominious end to a well-intentioned adventure, and there were many losers beyond the shareholders: eventually only a couple of hundred jobs were saved when a new investor came along, but the pension entitlements of workers were decimated.

As if one crisis was not enough, O'Reilly had to cope with another simultaneously, this time at INM. Whereas Waterford had been a basket-case for years, nobody foresaw the disaster at INM, and most certainly not the investors who had purchased its shares so eagerly. Despite the emergence of the credit crunch in late 2007, and growing fears throughout 2008 that economic slowdown would hurt advertising, both O'Reilly and O'Brien were buyers of the shares in the first half of the year, as the sniping between the warring partners intensified and O'Brien edged closer to matching O'Reilly's 28 per cent shareholding. O'Brien's accumulation of shares had sent the share price of INM rocketing throughout 2006 and 2007, reaching a peak of €3.80 at one stage, producing a value for the company of €1.8 billion.

Many others bought shares in the hope of profiting should one of the titans buy full control of the company, something that would have sent the share price upwards again. It seemed that all they had to do was follow the example of these supposed masters at making money. Although he had bought the majority of his shares decades earlier at a fraction of the price, O'Reilly had followed up his €20 million purchase of shares in March 2008 with another €10 million in June, at an average of over €2 per share, in an effort to copper-fasten his position. The company that these two men valued so highly had to be good.

The shares started to slide dramatically from August 2008. Observing the fall in the INM share price was like watching a car crash in slow motion. Down they sailed towards €2 and, once through that, to €1 each. Then, when that floor was breached, they continued all the way down to as low as nine cents each – giving one of the giants of Irish corporate life a value of just €80 million – before staging something of a recovery. The consequences for the wealth of both O'Reilly and O'Brien were catastrophic. Both owned shares worth as little as €20 million at the low point – had they been able to find someone to buy them.

It mainly cost O'Reilly 'paper money' – as he'd bought most of the shares ages previously – but he still had a problem with the loans that were secured on INM shares when they'd had a much higher value. It was more expensive for O'Brien, as he had recently bought the shares for cash at much higher prices than those O'Reilly had paid for the bulk of his. Although never confirmed, O'Brien may have spent up to €500 million on his accumulation of INM stock, implying huge losses.

The loss in capital value was one thing; the loss of dividend income quite another. The hefty dividends paid by INM would have been useful income for any shareholder and the expectation that they would continue on an annual basis would have been a factor in other investment decisions; in O'Reilly's case they must have been useful in financing his almost annual investment in Waterford Wedgwood. O'Brien may have invested partly on the basis that the high dividends would cover the interest costs on any borrowings he had incurred to buy the shares, but he declared himself satisfied by the January 2009 decision to stop paying the dividend as a way of repairing the balance sheet.

It shouldn't have come to this. The group had a wide range of businesses across geographic areas but all began to suffer simultaneously from an advertising slump caused by the global recession. Revenues began to crash. Yet the group remained highly profitable at an operating level, achieving pre-tax profits of €211 million in 2008, before it had to make a provision of €371 million for exceptional and unexpected items. The consequence was that it sent the company tumbling into loss.

And the big problem not anticipated by either of the two major shareholders, or indeed by anyone else: the €1.4 billion in borrowings that INM was carrying and the realization that sizeable chunks had to be repaid in short order went largely unnoticed. While the interest repayments were just about manageable, the principle repayments were not. The company had over €200 million in bonds to repay in May 2009 and INM was not generating enough cash to do this. In normal circumstances the bonds would be repaid by issuing a new set and using the proceeds. But these were not normal times and it might not be possible to sell a new bond; or, if it was, it would come at an enormous price, with a hugely increased rate of return. That would put the pressure on INM to achieve higher profits in order to make higher interest repayments, at just the wrong time. The company's decision to spend €130 million buying its own shares, using borrowed money, now looked even worse.

The company's troubled financial position enabled its bankers to enforce radical change, beyond insisting that the cash dividend be abandoned. The first indication of the new powers of lenders to INM came in August 2008, when the group announced that it had 'succeeded' in securing a new €105 million bank facility to replace a bond that had matured in December of that year. But success is relative because the company paid a high price for this new money: the group of banks, led by AIB, granted loans secured by a charge over INM's main Irish newspaper titles, specifically the *Irish Independent*, *Sunday Independent* and *Evening Herald*. It provoked memories of what had happened to the Irish Press titles more than a decade earlier, when a profitable business with established and successful titles was dragged into the mire by rows between shareholders and mounting debts. AIB, as lead banker in providing the facility, was also granted a charge over the *Independent* newspaper title in London and the company that owns a controlling stake in the *Sunday Tribune*. This requirement to gain effective control over the central assets showed the fear the banks now had about INM's ability to repay its debts.

Suddenly INM needed to raise money and fast. There was little fat to be cut from the business – although Irish employees took pay cuts late in 2008 – because INM had been ruthless in slashing the costs of producing its titles, outsourcing advertising sales and sub-editing of its Irish titles to cheaper service providers. While the Irish newspapers operated at profit margins that were the envy of the global industry, the company did not use its profits to pay down debt sufficiently: too much of the money went towards feeding the voracious appetite of the shareholders for cash through dividends.

The group hasn't made a major acquisition since its purchase of the Belfast Telegraph Group in 1999 for the extraordinary price of nearly €500 million. After that deal the group had debts of €1.6 billion and was put under pressure to reduce them. O'Reilly sold the profitable British regional newspapers and the New Zealand newspaper business to the Australian group APN, in which INM had a 39 per cent shareholding. But once the short-lived economic downturn in the early years of this century passed, the pressure to reduce debt eased too and borrowings of €1.4 billion were regarded as a not unreasonable amount. Investors were happy as long as the dividend payments remained generous; the presence of O'Brien served to help boost the share price too.

INM did try to conduct one major initiative at the end of 2007 that might have made everything different, although not necessarily any better. It tried to sell APN and then, in conjunction with venture capitalists such as the Carlyle Group, repurchase it. But this failed when the other shareholders in APN regarded the price offered as too low. A year later, in October 2008, INM took the decision to put APN up for sale, something that would have ended O'Reilly's twenty-year involvement in the business, of which he was inordinately proud. The idea was that a sale might have halved INM's debt.

INM claimed that it had received unsolicited approaches for its shares in APN. If INM had sold APN, it is thought that the proceeds of such a sale would have substantially reduced INM's debt. It was a seminal moment. The purchase in 1988 had been the first overseas by Independent, announcing O'Reilly's arrival as a major international media player. It was facilitated by the Australian citizenship of the O'Reilly children courtesy of O'Reilly's first wife, thereby giving it an additional emotional component. Executives within the INM argued hard against the decision. The one thing that should not be sold was this asset, he was told. O'Brien was also spooked, believing much the same, even if its sale would help reduce debt. But few people realized how straitened O'Reilly's position had become and how he would have to look to do things that only months earlier would have been anathema to him.

O'Reilly's problem was that, having given away so much in security to raise loans to cover the November 2008 bond repayment, he had little ammunition left to deal with the €200 million repayment falling due in May 2009 or, almost as pertinently, the €590 million bond repayment due in September 2010, a debt of such a massive size that refinancing had to be organized well in advance.

O'Reilly and O'Brien were suddenly facing the ruin of INM together. O'Reilly desperately sought outside help, going so far as to approach his old nemesis, Rupert Murdoch of News Corporation. He offered to sell him new shares that would have given INM cash and News Corp, publishers of the *Sunday Times*, a 5 per cent stake in INM, but Murdoch's people refused. In an extraordinary and previously unimaginable bid to save money, INM did a deal with its arch-rival Associated Newspapers to supply non-editorial administrative services to the *Independent* in London in an effort to cut costs. Associated was the publisher of the *Daily Mail*, which was damaging circulation of INM's domestic newspapers through publication of cheap Irish editions of its papers. INM looked to sell other assets overseas but could find no buyers.

Realizing that his own investment could be enormously damaged if he didn't act to protect it, O'Brien decided to initiate peace talks. In early November 2008 O'Brien wrote to INM's chairman, Brian Hillery. In return the one-time so-called 'dissident shareholder' was quickly offered a meeting not with his foe but with his one-time social friend Gavin O'Reilly, at City West.

O'Brien, his adviser Paul Connolly and stock market strategist David Sykes met with O'Reilly, chief financial officer Donal Buggy and the head of its Irish operations, Vincent Crowley. It was such a cordial meeting that, significantly, the visitors were given a tour of the plant, news of which quickly found its way into non-INM-owned newspapers. The INM executives outlined to O'Brien and his people what the company would do to stave off ruin.

According to Gavin O'Reilly, this led to months of productive meetings, but it culminated in an announcement in March 2009 that still came as a significant shock: his father was to step down as chief executive of INM in May on his seventy-third birthday.

It didn't end there. Gavin's own two brothers would leave the INM board too, along with long-standing loyalists such as Ivan Fallon, Ivor Kenny and Vincent Crowley. The board was reduced from nineteen to ten, in accordance with O'Brien's long-standing demands about improved corporate governance, and O'Brien nominated Lucy Gaffney – chairman of his Communicorp radio group – and his friends Leslie Buckley and Paul Connolly to the INM board. The only consolation for the O'Reilly family was that Gavin would replace his father in the role of Chief Executive.

Suddenly everyone spoke well of each other in public as the enormous changes were announced. O'Brien was generous in his comments on O'Reilly's departure. 'I would like to thank Tony O'Reilly for his long-standing contribution to the company. I welcome Tony as president emeritus and also take this opportunity to wish him well on his retirement,' he said.

One can only imagine was what said between O'Reilly and O'Brien when they met for the first time ever, in the upstairs drawing room of O'Reilly's five-storey townhouse in Fitzwilliam Square on the Saturday lunchtime of the Ireland versus England rugby match in February 2009. While O'Reilly had always been careful not to engage in public insults of his young rival, the circumstances of their business dispute, as well as other perceived affronts, must have created a great degree of nervousness and friction. But both have an incredible ability to charm others when it suits them, the groundwork for the meeting had been laid, and they had a common purpose. Gavin insisted that the meeting was highly cordial, motivated by the fact that they had more interests in common than not, although he was unlikely to say anything else.

Most importantly, they both had the banks and bondholders on their backs. INM announced in January that it intended to sell €100 million in assets – in Germany and South Africa and elsewhere – but had failed to find buyers, which was unsurprising, given the extraordinary state of world markets, the loss of popularity of the media sector and the difficulties in raising finance facing any potential buyers. In addition, the collapse of the share price brought about another major problem. The fall in the stock market value of INM to below €200 million meant that, under company law, any attempt to sell assets for more than a combined amount of €100 million would have required approval at an extraordinary general meeting. The banks could not afford O'Brien using his shares to block any initiative.

Gavin O'Reilly insisted that the banks had not sought the clear-out; nor had they said his father should go. With the type of overstatement that had sometimes been noticed from his father, Gavin said that suggestions that the banks had forced the deal were 'the greatest conspiracy since Kennedy got shot'. Gavin said it was a 'win-win' for all shareholders and that there were 'no losers' in the shake-up. The power shift within INM was enormous, with his own promotion the only concession to O'Reilly family interests.

Tony O'Reilly had a line he often liked to use in interviews and speeches. Whenever two great rivals in business ended up helping each other, he would joke that it was the most unlikely alliance since the Stalin–Hitler pact. Gavin conceded that both sides had 'thrown grenades at each other' and that this had been foolish. 'I'm very happy to say that it's water under the bridge. We've been working with and talking to Denis and Denis's colleagues for quite some time now. This is a triumph for common sense and in the interests of all shareholders.' And as for himself: 'It's a fairly humbling position I find myself in, with very big shoes to fill. I have the endorsement of both Tony O'Reilly and Denis O'Brien, which is pretty good, especially when they represent 55 [sic] per cent of the company.'

On the day that it was announced that O'Reilly senior was stepping down, O'Reilly junior joined me on the phone for a live interview on *The Last Word*. He listened patiently while Richard Curran, the deputy editor of the *Sunday Business Post*, who had written perceptively about the mounting crisis at INM, explained to listeners what had happened. O'Reilly must have been tired and stressed after a long day of media interviews – in which he was batting off a poor wicket – because he was uncharacteristically narky. His polished demeanour disappeared when he didn't like my line of questioning, particularly when I asked him how confident he was about INM's ability to repay its loans. 'You have to presume that I know a little more about this than you do,' he replied acidly. 'I think I could say that I'm very confident.' I refrained from pointing out that, given his €1 million plus annual salary, I would expect him to know more about his company than I did; nor did I mention the 97 per cent fall in the INM share price between its peak two years earlier and news of this restructuring.

I moved to finish the interview by asking about his father's legacy. The answer was perhaps more revealing about the son than the father. He spoke of his pride in the scale and reach of the business empire that his father had developed. 'I think creating Ireland's first media multinational, flying the flag very, very high for Ireland in markets as far-flung as New Zealand, India, Indonesia, South Africa, I think that's probably his greatest achievement. He set out back in 1973 with a very clear vision of how he wanted the company to expand and largely that has been achieved.'

I had expected that he might express some pride in the quality of some of the newspapers that INM owned and sponsored, and his father's role in ensuring that the editors and journalists had sufficient freedom to do as they felt necessary in the honourable pursuit. When I asked him about his father's editorial legacy, O'Reilly paused and coughed and then spoke briefly of his pride in his father's 'non-interventionist policy', which had been enshrined since he first invested in the company back in 1973.

We had arranged for Senator Eoghan Harris to join us on the programme, to give us his assessment of Tony O'Reilly. I asked Harris how significant a figure O'Reilly had been in Irish cultural and political life. 'The important thing is that he was a huge force for peace for thirty-five years at the head of Independent Newspapers,' he said. 'There was a dictat, an unwritten, informal one: no truck with terrorism . . . he played a huge part in keeping this society stable for 30 years . . . he was the biggest single presence apart from Jack Lynch, Garret FitzGerald and Bertie Ahern, he shadowed them. He was a huge force for liberal democracy and his Ireland Fund played a huge part in getting people together – Catholic and Protestant – on the ground with hard cash behind them.'

He said there was no editorial interference, which differed from his experiences in working with the *Sunday Times* and RTÉ. 'I've never worked for anyone who has interfered less . . . all that stuff you read, he meets Cowen, he meets Ahern, it's all rubbish . . . I genuinely, hand on heart, have never encountered any evidence that Tony O'Reilly interferes with the political agenda of any newspaper. I know that is hard to believe but I would know if he did and there were sometimes over the years I would have wished that he'd interfere with the political line. He would stand behind me or Gene Kerrigan or Alan Ruddock or Robert Fisk and I know that there are times when he would violently disagree with what we would write but we never heard anything back.'

Harris contended that O'Reilly was 'the victim of jealousy at every level and not just commercial. He's tall, he's glamorous, he's good-looking, he's witty, a very good speaker, he has that rugby background, very handsome, incredibly successful, naturally people are going to be begrudging ... There is also a political agenda about some of the people who obsess about him, particularly his radical socialist republican enemies, because he was the single biggest media influence, a colossus, standing in the way of the Provisional IRA and any other threat to Irish democracy. He was a core figure in defending threats to Irish democracy, as I know Gavin will be too.'

There were remarkably few tributes to O'Reilly from outside of his own company, with political statements about O'Reilly personally notable by their absence. INM chairman Brian Hillery, a former Fianna Fáil Senator and one of those to stay on under the new regime, said, 'Tony's retirement marks one of the most remarkable executive careers in Irish history. Tony has been a significant business leader for more than forty-five years and has been a key figure in the making of modern Ireland.'

Despite the work that had been done on concentration of media ownership a year earlier when O'Brien came into the INM stable, little was said about these events, initially at least. There was barely a word from anyone in the political system, despite the significance of what was happening. Everyone seemed to have more important things to worry about, because of the way the economy was collapsing.

O'Brien had apparently got much of what he had wanted in INM: a degree of control, although at a substantial financial cost. Some months earlier, when O'Brien's shareholding in INM passed the 25 per cent threshold, the Broadcasting Commission of Ireland concluded that there were no cross-media ownership issues. It didn't change its position immediately when O'Brien got his three seats on the board, although some months later it announced another review into his level of media ownership, which concluded in late 2009 when it declared there was no problem in maintaining the status quo.

However, it was also clear that while O'Brien was now in the driving seat at INM, this did not automatically confer control. In mid-March 2009 INM announced that it would no longer be proceeding with the issue of a new private subordinated bond, which it had intended to use to pay the investors in the €200 million bond that was maturing in May 2009. It said it was ending its 'recent marketing efforts' and that the new bond would not proceed due to 'current market conditions in credit markets'. This set alarm bells ringing. It either couldn't raise the money or the terms being demanded were too expensive.

Instead, INM hired Davy Stockbrokers and Rothschild to engage with the owners of the 5.75 per cent guaranteed bonds. The bond owners were in a powerful position to extract new terms and conditions for the extension of the deal. What assets could INM sell? What loss-making businesses would it close? In mid-May the company reached a six-week 'stand-still' agreement with its bond holders, during which they wouldn't take legal action to press for repayment, while negotiations continued about a new deal. This was later extended into August and INM sold part of its Indian investment in an effort to raise cash.

The government, consumed by its own many problems, watched but did nothing other than seethe at the regular criticism of its performance in the INM titles. There had been a meeting between O'Reilly and finance minister Brian Lenihan at the Fitzwilliam Square house in late 2008, at which nothing of any help to O'Reilly and Waterford Wedg-wood was forthcoming, and then the late 2008 meeting between Cowen and O'Reilly. In a sign that things were changing, O'Reilly went to Cowen's office. Apparently, O'Reilly was very impressed by Cowen's intelligence and authority, as displayed in this private meeting, and regarded him as a fitting successor to Ahern.

O'Reilly's decline put paid to one of his unstated ambitions. Sources in both the O'Reilly and O'Brien camps have told me that they believe O'Reilly was interested in appointing Ahern to the board of INM once a suitable period of time had elapsed after his stepping down as Taoiseach. Former taoisigh, such as Jack Lynch and Garret FitzGerald, and former Minister for Finance Ray MacSharry had taken corporate directorships on leaving politics and, while INM did not have a track record of appointing former Irish ministers, O'Reilly had appointed many promi-nent foreign former politicians, including prime ministers, in recent years. Given their relationship, Ahern was an obvious choice, notwith-standing the inevitable controversy it would have caused.

In the summer of 2008 that would have been possible, notwithstanding O'Reilly's need to reduce the bloated size of his board to fend off criticism from O'Brien. However, the swift collapse of the share price and O'Reilly's loss of control put paid to the idea. Both men were experiencing a degree of powerlessness that only a couple of years earlier had been unthinkable.

PART VIII

The failures of regulation

34

The high price of giving investors what they wanted

The only consolation to Becbay, the consortium that spent €412 million on the Irish Glass Bottle site in Ringsend in Dublin 4, was that the deal could have been much more expensive. Fortunately for the parties involved, the government had provided legal opportunities for the buyers of big properties or sites to reduce their taxes on purchases dramatically and Becbay benefited accordingly.

Becbay was one of a large number of companies to benefit from a generous tax relief known as sub-sale relief that allowed a builder/developer to avoid stamp duty on certain transactions. The normal rate of stamp duty for an investor would be 9 per cent on the transaction price, a rate that applied to the sales of all property valued at more than €317,000, but this could be avoided legally. The duty was the price of the stamp that must be applied to the piece of paper claiming title to land when it is being transferred to a new owner. There were, however, several tax reliefs that could be availed of to avoid the stamp duty.

One was to keep the deeds of ownership of land in a company and to trade the company instead of the property it owned. The transfer of the shares attracted a stamp duty of just 1 per cent. The new owner had both the company and the land or asset it wanted. Instead of paying €37 million to the exchequer at a 9 per cent stamp duty rate, Becbay paid just a little over €4 million, saving itself nearly €33 million. It was an idea that didn't just work for development land. It could be applied equally to an office block, a warehouse or a block of apartments.

This was just one of the tactics that developers used to avoid the payment of stamp duty during the boom years. Other variations were practices known as 'resting on contract' and 'building licences'.

In the resting on contract technique, the builder/developer entered into a contract to buy the property and paid the purchase price to the land owner immediately, but delayed taking a deed of conveyance to the land at that time. Instead, it was not until the development was completed that the deed of conveyance was executed. That meant the conveyance was between the original land owner and the purchasers of the ultimate units, be they houses, apartments or office blocks. In other words, while the final purchaser ended up paying the stamp duty, the builder / developer in the middle legally avoided it.

With a licensing arrangement a developer obtained a licence from a land vendor to build on the land. The developer did not take ownership of the land. At completion, the builder who had previously paid a contract or licence fee to the owner of the land sold the units to the new purchasers and stamp duty based on the purchase price of each unit was paid by the buyer of the constructed unit.

Another measure to help a developer avoid paying stamp duty involved an agreement for a long lease. The vendor granted a power of attorney to the developer, then the vendor executed a conveyance of the legal title to the ultimate purchaser without further recourse to the developer. If these generous tax arrangements – which were to the benefit of developers and not ordinary consumers making the end purchases – had not been written into law, the state could have received two tax payments instead of one.

Although the use of the above tax reliefs was perfectly legal, the Revenue Commissioners took the view that significant amounts of tax were being lost – €40 million was the estimate for 2006 and over €200 million between 1999 and 2006. The Revenue Commissioners suggested to the Minister for Finance, Brian Cowen, that the relief be removed from the legislation. He agreed and made late changes to the Finance Act of 2007, just before it was passed by the Dáil, to end these practices, on the basis that full stamp duty would have to be paid if the builder / developer was receiving more than 25 per cent of the value of the land at the first stage of the process.

But then, following lobbying from the industry, Cowen did not sign the necessary commencement order to put the measure – Section 110 – into law. Instead, five months after announcing it, he hired Goodbody Economic Consultants, owned by AIB, the country's biggest bank and biggest property lender, to examine the potential effects of closing the loophole.

Cowen's handling of this amazed many people, and Joan Burton, the

Labour Party spokesperson on finance, alleged the minister had 'caved in to the power and influence of the building lobby'.

Cowen justified the delay and the review when answering questions in the Dáil in July 2007 by saying he had 'to consider the state of the property market before the provision comes into effect, to ensure that it does not have an unforeseen negative effect on the market'. This raised questions as to why that had not been considered five months previously.

One defence put forward by Cowen's advisers was that just bringing the law on to the statute books had had the desired effect, even though it had not been implemented. They claimed that banks and financial institutions were no longer lending to developers who used the loophole. Why they wouldn't have done so was not explained, and it seemed far more likely that the true cause was the slump in bank lending and the fall in property market prices.

Goodbody produced its report in March 2008 – and its findings and conclusions were remarkable. It discovered that it wasn't just private sector developers who were using the schemes. The report stated that as many as sixteen public–private partnership (PPP) agreements between local authorities and private companies availed of the licensing loophole. The National Roads Authority also used it in building major infrastructure projects. It found that allowing the measure was costing the state far more in unpaid tax revenues than anticipated. In 2006 alone the loophole cost the exchequer approximately €251 million, more than six times the figure quoted by Cowen at the time of introducing the new law.

Yet Goodbody's proposal was that nothing should be done about implementing the law. 'To do so would run the risk of exacerbating the downturn in the property market,' it claimed. Goodbody said that if Section 110 were to be implemented, 'the cost of PPP road projects would rise, as operators seek to cover the perceived risk.'

Goodbody argued that the Irish property market was experiencing a downturn and that the government should not compound the situation by acting in case already dwindling confidence was undermined. It claimed that developers had become 'very price sensitive' and might 'withdraw from the market, rather than shoulder the tax burden'. 'Section 110 will reduce the liquidity of the land market to some extent by raising the cost of land transfer, the cost of entry to the market, and site assembly and break-down,' Goodbody argued. It claimed that the stamp duty money could not be easily borrowed and would have to come from the buyer's equity – as if that should be a concern for government.

Although the Goodbody report estimated that about 40 per cent of all land transactions were structured to dramatically reduce the amount of stamp duty paid to the exchequer, it qualified this by stating that 'the use of Section 110 arrangements is widespread but is far from universal.'

The Department's choice of Goodbody to conduct the review was surprising, if only for the difficulty it created with optics. Although Goodbody is an autonomous subsidiary of AIB, it was still 100 per cent owned by it. AIB was revealed subsequently as having the largest exposure to development land in the country by far, although there is no suggestion that its subsidiary was unduly influenced in any way in reaching its conclusions in the most professional fashion.

Cowen continued to defend his unwillingness to bring his own measure into law and denied that €250 million was the annual loss to the taxpayer, despite Goodbody's contention. Cowen said that this figure was 'not indicative of the revenue gain' if the government moved to close off the loophole and that €50 million was more likely to be the available return once the new law was implemented. He said this despite further new information that had come from the Revenue Commissioners. They had conducted a survey of just 100 developers that revealed a €234 million loss to the exchequer in 2006 by way of legal avoidance of stamp duty. This was less than the Goodbody figure, but was indicative of a larger loss because of the number of developers not covered by the survey.

An opportunity to dampen down the insane prices paid for development land had been simultaneously missed. Buyers may have paused, or not borrowed as much, if they had faced a 9 per cent tax on transactions.

The ball passed to Brian Lenihan on his succeeding Cowen, and in his Finance Bill for 2009 he drafted new legislative provisions in order to curtail the relief. His new anti-avoidance provisions bore a strong similarity to the 2007 ones but, crucially, they did not apply to certain transactions involving public–private partnerships and certain incentive schemes for capital allowances. In other words, builders were still to be allowed to legally avoid tax, apparently in the belief that it would get them to use land. The idea that all construction had to be good, because it provided building jobs, employment taxes and VAT, was allowed to hold sway.

If Cowen's failure to implement reforms on commercial stamp duty could be partly explained by a desire not to further depress the property market, his decision in relation to the stock market gambling allowed by the use of Contracts for Difference had far less rationale to support it. Yet again, Cowen buckled in the face of lobbying from vested interests. The consequences for the economy were disastrous, as the absence of the tax contributed to reckless speculation in stocks and shares.

CFDs were the popular choice of wealthy investors in the stock market between 2004 and 2008, being at their peak in 2006 and 2007. Sometimes they were used by people who were trying to diversify out of property so that they would not be overexposed to any fall in values in the sector. CFDs made for some very risky investing, akin to gambling. (Just how risky we saw in the case of Seán Quinn's punt on Anglo shares – see Chapter 24.) Using the CFD mechanism, if an investor had €1 million to invest – a not uncommon sum for someone who had made big returns on property – he could spend a much bigger amount on shares. There was a second advantage to investors: they had effective ownership of the shares but did not have to pay stamp duty because the transaction was not completed. Stamp duty only became applicable if they took possession of the shares. Typically, the investor sold the CFD to take the profit and never actually owned the underlying shares.

If somebody bought shares worth €1 million and they went up by 10 per cent in a year, that investor could sell and make €100,000 in profits (minus the initial stamp duty of €10,000 and capital gains tax charged at a rate of 20 per cent). However, the use of CFDs meant that the investor with €1 million to spend on shares could borrow an additional €9 million, secured on his equity, and have €10 million to invest. The same 10 per cent rise in the value of the shares would provide a profit of €1 million on the sale of the CFDs. The same 20 per cent capital gains tax would apply to the profits but the buyer would not have to pay the €100,000 stamp duty charge that a €10 million share purchase would have required because stamp duty did not apply to CFDs. In effect, the €1 million equity would have realized an after-tax profit of €800,000, less the fees paid to the CFD provider and the interest on the €9 million loan.

Fortunes were made this way until about the middle of 2007, when the stock market began to fall. From that point on many CFD investors in the Irish market began to 'blow up', to use the broker parlance. It is believed, for example, that one wealthy farmer who had built up a CFD portfolio worth over €80 million suddenly found himself with debts of over €30 million – and no way to make the repayments.

Lenders did not offer a one-way bet: they put 'loan to stock' ratios into their contracts with investors. This meant that if the price of the shares fell below a certain level, the investor/borrower had to write a cheque to bring the new value of the security into line with the value of the loan, rather than waiting for the share price to improve again. There were many anecdotal examples of CFD counterparties – the institutions providing the finance – making late-night phone calls to the homes of investors, delivering so called 'margin calls': a demand for money to support the value of the loan. If the investor could not provide the money, the shares were sold into the market by the CFD provider, forcing the CFD investor to take the loss.

The main supplier of CFD finance into Ireland was the American company Cantor Fitzgerald, the firm that tragically lost hundreds of staff when one of the planes that crashed into New York's Twin Towers on 11 September 2001 went straight into its dealing floor. The main broker through which it dealt was Davy Stockbrokers.

The use of CFDs was the talk of the wealthy classes through the middle years of this decade, as various people boasted of all the money they were making. A survey of Irish Stock Exchange member firms indicated that the aggregate value of trades in Irish shares associated with CFD contracts in 2005 represented 30 per cent of the overall value of trades on the Irish stock market. For about three years the Irish stock market was regarded as one of the most 'turned over' in the world, which meant that people were not investing for the long term but making short-term speculative bets on the shares of one company, taking profits and moving on to another company to do the same thing again. In particular, the share prices of the cider and soft drinks company C & C, the pharmaceutical company Elan and Anglo Irish Bank were driven forward and downwards by the use of CFDs, causing havoc at each. The same happened to a more limited extent with Ryanair.

While this suited investors, who were profiting enormously, it also suited the stockbrokers, who were trading in the underlying shares and who were getting fat commissions connected to the rising share prices. It has been calculated that at one stage about €60 billion was pledged in CFD positions on a small number of popular shares on the Irish stock market. It was estimated by brokers that the net loss caused by the bets was more than €6 billion.

It wasn't until very late in the day – after August 2007, when it became known that many CFD traders had incurred substantial losses – that the regulators became involved. The touch was light: brokers were merely asked to force credit checks on customers and to provide more information about the risks involved.

On St Patrick's Day 2006 the Revenue Commissioners had announced that stockbrokers were going to have to start paying stamp duty on shares they bought to underpin Contracts for Difference. There was panic among those who profited from supplying the service. Cowen and his officials were lobbied immediately by the Irish Stock Exchange, the London Investment Banking Association, Davy Stockbrokers and PricewaterhouseCoopers. Apparently, some stockbroking firms claimed they could be put out of business if they were forced to make payments of back taxes, plus interest and penalties on the shares they had bought, even though retrospection had never been mentioned. More importantly, perhaps, the argument was put forward that if the tax treatment was changed, investors would flee the Dublin market and the taxpayer would lose on the capital gains tax haul from share transactions. Tax on the profits from the sale of shares was reckoned to account for about 40 per cent of the state's annual capital gains tax take of around €1.5 billion.

Just five days later Cowen undercut the position of the Revenue Commissioners. He announced that he would review the whole issue of stamp duty on shares – not just CFDs – in order to ensure that 'the market in Irish equities would continue to be a liquid market, conducive to capital acquisition by Irish firms' and that he would make an announcement on his findings at the next budget. After Cowen's announcement the Revenue Commissioners were left with little choice but to withdraw their compliance notice. Notably, they did not indicate that they had changed their view, but the Finance Bill 2007 confirmed the tax-free status of shares bought to cover CFDs.

Cowen's declared reasoning in relation to helping Irish firms use the stock market raise capital was incredible. There was no shortage of money, either domestic or international, available at the time to good companies that wanted to raise new capital by way of the issue of new shares. CFDs had nothing to do with that. They merely facilitated speculation and gambling in existing shares.

Cowen's decision came back to haunt him nearly three years later when he faced serious questioning in the Dáil in February 2009. He claimed that he had 'followed official advice in relation to the reversal of the proposed change', as if that excused his bad judgement. 'On the basis of submissions received from my officials at the time, I considered carefully the representations made as they seemed to have substance, taking account of the international nature of stock markets.'

Although it is not known whether the tax reliefs were a major consideration in the decision by Seán Quinn to buy CFDs in Anglo, it was his purchase of an underlying stake of about 25 per cent in shares through this mechanism that contributed significantly to the fall in Anglo's share price. And the collapse of Anglo led to its expensive purchase by the state by way of nationalization.

35

Two humps on the same camel

The Fianna Fáil–Progressive Democrats coalition and the Fianna Fáil–PD–Green Party alliance that followed it got plenty of support for the fiction of an economic 'soft landing'. The phrase came into vogue in the mid-2000s as a rebuff to a number of economists and commentators, such as David McWilliams, George Lee, Alan Ahearne, Morgan Kelly, Richard Curran and Brendan Keenan, who warned that the country was losing competitiveness against its trading partners and, more importantly, inflating a property bubble that could burst with disastrous consequences for wealth, jobs and tax revenues.

For everyone who made those arguments there seemed to be a dozen others – either politicians or those with vested interests because of banking and property links – who denied the dangers angrily and said that while a slowdown was inevitable, it would be managed. The commentators who feared that the bubble would burst were accused of undermining economic confidence; of being unpatriotic; of wanting to be proved right. The idea of 'talking the economy into recession' became widespread. Some of these concerned realists were bullied into near-silence, or had to mitigate strongly held opinions for fear of the odium they would attract by expressing themselves freely.

But while commentators, columnists and pundits can influence public opinion and decision-making, they do not have real power. That rests with people like Central Bank governor John Hurley. In late January 2009 Hurley went in front of an Oireachtas committee and declared himself firmly among the number who had warned sternly and consistently about the dangers of a property crash. Central Bank reports had tried to warn about excessive house price growth and credit growth (lending by banks, borrowing by customers). Unfortunately, he said, 'in the context of an unprecedented period of expansion and wealth-creation, this proved a difficult message to get across.'

He said that he had pointed out Ireland's vulnerability to an international shock, that our debt levels had grown too fast and that we built too many houses. He highlighted the regular publication of financial stability reports, in conjunction with the Financial Regulator. 'I regularly gave press conferences, speeches and interviews in regard to these risks but behaviour did not change,' he said.

It was an extraordinary claim to make. The citizens of the country, its businesses and its banks were being blamed for not having paid enough attention to his statements. They hadn't modified their behaviour so as to keep in line with his warnings.

It would have been hilarious had it not been so serious. While it was true that there were warnings about the economy 'over-heating' in many Central Bank reports, it also liked to indulge in the 'soft landing' fantasy. What it did in its reports was to assess various scenarios and then make predictions about further economic growth, while making reference to potential problems. In other words, it may have been attempting to be balanced but there was an element of having its cake and trying to eat it. For example, in his 2007 stability report, amid the usual impenetrable clichés and jargon terms of such reports, Hurley wrote that 'the underlying fundamentals of the residential [property] market continue to appear strong. The central scenario is, therefore, for a soft, rather than a hard, landing.' In other words, house prices remained high because there was a large demand for new property while money remained cheap and incomes remained high; and, while that might come to an end, it wouldn't happen so fast as to cause an economic crash. He used the words 'soft landing' himself; he endorsed the optimists and failed to put the bank's warnings anything like forcefully enough.

If Hurley was as worried about substantial threats to the economy as some of his comments suggested, he really shouldn't have been reducing their impact by making references to soft landings, which politicians were bound to seize upon because it suited them. He should have been knocking at the doors of Ahern and McCreevy, and when McCreevy went Cowen, demanding that they implement different fiscal / budgetary policies to restrain the economy – something he couldn't do because of his lack of monetary powers. If they wouldn't listen, and if he felt sure that they were following dangerously wrong policies, he could have made direct criticisms of the government in public and in plain language, although clearly this isn't the done thing for civil servants.

Hurley should have argued more strongly with the political bosses because that was one of the few options available to him. The Central Bank had few other powers left to it after our entry to the Economic and Monetary Union. Before entry into EMU the main purposes of the Central Bank were to control monetary policy and mint the currency. It moved interest rates according to economic circumstances to affect the demand for borrowed money and to have some influence over exchange rates. But post-EMU neither Hurley nor his predecessor Maurice O'Connell had control over fixing interest rates – this being the preserve of the European Central Bank. It was the loss of a key tool and it took away one of the main reasons for the existence of the bank.

Much of what the Central Bank did was to conduct research and recommend policy, although it also had a role in discussing implementation of prudent measures with the Financial Regulator. Hurley was in possession of analysis conducted internally, and by the ECB and European Commission as well, that told him how to deal with an economy that had inappropriately low interest rates, as Ireland had. The only worthwhile measure was in the hands of the government, through control of fiscal policy. As that was not his direct responsibility, it was up to him to make the case to the government that it needed to cut its spending to stop the economy from overheating. If he did make this argument, nobody heard him or paid any attention.

The other major thing left for Hurley to do was to influence and support the performance of the Financial Regulator. It's not hard to imagine that Hurley has asked himself often in recent times if he could or should have done more to encourage the regulator to enforce the powers that it had to deal with bank lending and to have done so at an earlier stage than it did.

If two heads are supposed to be better than one, then the regulation of banking and other financial services in Ireland proves the exception to the rule. Since 2003 the country had had two public servants in charge of banking – with apparent confusion as to their respective roles. After Ireland's entry into EMU, finance minister Charlie McCreevy wanted the Central Bank to retain responsibility for financial regulation, but enterprise minister Mary Harney demanded a consumer champion. The solution was the establishment, in May 2003, of the Irish Financial Services Regulatory Authority (which later started to refer to itself as the Financial Regulator). Some of the powers of the Central Bank were assigned to the new authority. The Central Bank retained responsibility for monetary policy, financial stability, economic analysis, and currency and payment systems; the Financial Regulator was given a consumer protection job, as well as banking supervision duties. Although the regulator was a nominally independent entity, it still worked under the legal remit of the Central Bank. Seven Central Bank directors sat on the nine-person board of the Financial Regulator. When McCreevy established the new body, he said the Central Bank and Financial Regulator were two humps on the same camel. In the light of the economic debacle and the criticism levelled at the new structure over its failures, it is not surprising that the institution described as a camel came to be dubbed an ass.

One of the areas where the Central Bank and the regulator both had a role was in monitoring the level of lending by banks. They could have insisted on a clampdown on excessive lending. For most of this decade there was stark evidence that the banks were lending far too much money and had become over-reliant on property-related lending. Monthly Central Bank figures showed an explosion in private sector credit – or lending – often increasing by about 30 per cent year on year. Most of the media focus was on how individuals and businesses would be able to repay this money if interest rates went up or incomes went down, but there was another issue that should have been of equal interest to the authorities. The money being lent had to come from somewhere. As it was being borrowed from abroad, there were serious questions to be asked as to what would happen if that source of funding slowed down or dried up, given the size of the commitments into which the banks had entered. The bank balance sheets were expanding at a pace that was a multiple of the real growth in the Irish and global economies. Because sufficient deposits were not available to them, the banks relied far too heavily on borrowing from interbank markets. Anglo Irish was not the only bank that was overtrading.

It would be unfair to say that the Central Bank and the Financial Regulator did nothing. The problem was that they waited too long and did not act firmly enough. In 2006, at the height of the boom, the regulator required banks to increase the amount of capital they set aside for certain categories of higher-risk property lending, particularly for commercial lending and high loan-to-value mortgages. The regulator also insisted on tightening the stress-testing criteria, which measured a borrower's ability to repay if economic conditions deteriorated. However, the regulator and Central Bank were reluctant to put a cap on lending by Irish-owned banks because they would be unable to apply it to foreign competitors, which they did not regulate; they seemed to fear that the problem of over-lending in the domestic market would have continued, albeit not to the same extent, only with Irish banks at a disadvantage. Though the Irish banks' profitability would have suffered, hurting their capital base, that would have been a short-term problem, and such a cap would at least have mitigated some of the pain that was to follow.

In July 2007 a new liquidity regime for the banks was enforced, with the emphasis on internal controls and systems, stress testing and contingency plans increased. However, the 2007 financial statement report from the Central Bank showed that 85 per cent of all new lending was still going to commercial property. This suggested that the moves were coming too late or were not having the desired effect. Any success the measures had may have been mainly due to the belated realization among investors that the bubble had been inflated to its maximum and their subsequent unwillingness to borrow more. The damage had been done.

The excellent RTÉ programme *Future Shock: Property Crash*, broadcast just weeks before the 2007 general election, highlighted all of the excesses in the property market that had been going on for years and about which nothing had been done. The programme infuriated Bertie Ahern, who told me that it was 'irresponsible and inaccurate' and that he disagreed 'with almost everything in it'.

Throughout 2008 and early 2009 Hurley and Neary publicly defended the lending policies of the Irish banks on many occasions, endorsed the strength of their balance sheets and decried suggestions that the banks might have walked themselves into trouble. They were either every bit as much to blame as the banks in underestimating the scale of the problems or they took a conscious decision to understate their worries in public discourse in the hope of protecting the overall 'national interest'.

It was part of a gigantic and failed effort to instil and retain confidence. Sometimes it appeared that these state officials regarded it as their duty to present a positive face when asked for their opinions. If they expressed doubt or concern about the stability of the Irish banks, it would spook the markets and become a self-fulfilling prophecy.

Almost everyone in every walk of business does this, pretending that things are better than they are for fear that admitting the truth will make things much worse. It is human nature and often pragmatic. It's understandable. It's what politicians do all the time, so it's hard to blame public servants for doing the same. The problem, though, is that when this approach fails – and its practitioners are caught out in doing it – it cannot be tried again.

Hurley held the party line throughout 2008, insisting that the banking sector's 'shock absorption' capacity remained strong, despite widespread speculation that the banks had serious mounting problems in getting repayment of the loans they had advanced. Hurley and Neary waffled on about the security of loans, the low likelihood of default, the more-than-adequate capital available and the steady flow of liquidity in the banking system. In the summer of 2008 Hurley told an Oireachtas committee that Irish banks 'are weathering a very difficult situation well'. It is a pity they did not issue public rebuttals of the self-serving guff from the banks in front of the Oireachtas committee, although they may have been afraid that to do so would have undermined even further the already declining confidence in the banks, as shown in falling share prices, and have contributed to a loss in deposits.

Neary in particular failed to offer convincing arguments. On 17 September, two days after the collapse of US investment bank Lehman Brothers, he told the Institute of Directors that 'Irish banks are resilient and have good shock absorption capacity to cope with the current situation.' But he wasn't so confident as to not announce a ban on the short-selling of bank stocks almost immediately. He appeared very much out of touch during an incredible interview two days later on RTÉ's *Primetime*, when he said bad lending practices had little or nothing to do with the banking crisis being experienced. He said that Irish banks had plenty of capital, irrespective of any property crash. Again, his priority may well have been to try not to undermine confidence in the banks any further, but, given the circumstances and the level of information and rumour that was circulating, that was becoming an almost impossible task. Like the government, he blamed the international credit crisis for the shortage of liquidity, while steadfastly refusing to accept that there was an extra, essential factor at play: the Irish banks couldn't get enough money because they had engaged in high-risk borrowing and lending, and counter-parties had lost confidence in them.

If Neary knew it, he did not want to admit to the under-capitalization of the banks – the problem implied by large, unaccounted-for bad debts – because the authorities clearly feared it would have increased the pressure on the banks to find fresh capital at a time when it was not available from anyone other than the government. Maintaining his credibility in this situation was going to be difficult for him because he was denying what everybody else could see: the banks' lack of strength.

The pair were at it even after the introduction of the state guarantee. In October, Hurley supported the banks trenchantly, saying their bad debts had not increased materially, they were not under pressure to raise fresh capital and they had a negligible exposure to the subprime market. He said that the Irish banks were 'well-capitalized with good asset quality'. The Central Bank had stress tested the ability of the banks to weather a serious economic downturn, and the preliminary results suggested that 'the banking sector's shock absorption capacity remains strong'. Neary seemed to believe that his actions had helped the banks escape the worst of the crisis. In January 2009 he told an Oireachtas committee that 'while we could not see around corners and did not anticipate the market events of recent times, it was certainly useful that these practices were already embedded in the system when market issues arose.'

Unfortunately, it was a classic case of locking the stable door after the horse had bolted. About 60 per cent of €400 billion in total private debt related to residential mortgages and loans to builders, developers and property investors. The consequences of the bursting of the property bubble were to be catastrophic.

36

A carrot rather than a stick approach

Not dealing with bad lending was one thing, but the failure to deal with bad and irregular practices by some bankers and investors in banks was another. Unfortunately, the Central Bank and, in particular, the Financial Regulator adopted and engaged in a practice known as 'light-touch regulation', which, given what happened, can be described as disastrous, even if the intention was good and the decision to adopt the model was political. It is not surprising that some critics made jibes about hands-off regulation, even if this exaggerated the case somewhat. The idea was that those under supervision would 'observe principles' and 'codes of practice'.

Light-touch regulation is a carrot, not a stick, approach, based on trust. The belief is that too many laws encourage the exploitation of loopholes, as if the absence of laws fosters better behaviour. It is also a low-cost way of doing things, which partly explains why so many companies are based in the International Financial Services Centre, contributing enormous tax revenues to the state. The idea is that a more highly regulated financial environment might be so expensive as to deter foreign financial institutions from locating in Ireland. So light-touch regulation was a politically inspired policy.

Given the track record of some banks, culminating in four of them making settlements totalling €225 million to the Revenue Commissioners in relation to the wrongful use of bank accounts to avoid payment of deposit interest retention tax (DIRT), the decision of the regulators to allow for a policy of self-regulation was extraordinarily trusting, to put it mildly. The banks had to be monitored because this country has had a culture of the rich and poor trying their best to hide their income from the Revenue Commissioners in order to reduce or eliminate the payment of tax and of sometimes using the banks to do so. Ansbacher allowed the elite – those with the best political and business connections – to evade tax by depositing large sums of money offshore. Still, they could retain the convenience of accessing the money at home through the device of taking out 'loans' from an Irish bank. Taoiseach Charles Haughey was one of those who used this service. It was run from the offices of his financial adviser Des Traynor, the chairman of one of the biggest companies in the country, CRH. Nobody ever went to jail for the corruption involved in the scam.

Financial corruption and tax evasion were embedded in our culture. Ireland was a country where 53,000 residents had salted away £600 million in offshore bank accounts, usually in collaboration with the Irish resident banks, such as AIB, Bank of Ireland, National Irish Bank and ACC. While the ultimate responsibility lay with the individuals who actively sought to evade the tax they were due to pay on their savings, they were facilitated by the banks and, in some cases, encouraged to engage in this bogus behaviour.

The worst offender among that lot was AIB, the country's biggest bank. In 1999 AIB made the biggest tax settlement in the history of the state when it paid €114 million in unpaid tax and penalties to the Revenue Commissioners arising from its liabilities from DIRT evasion.

While AIB was 'helping' its customers in this way, it was ripping them off in another. In 2004 it emerged that the bank had been overcharging personal and corporate customers for foreign exchange transactions for more than a decade. As well as charging a commission for exchanging money, the bank took a margin between the buy and sell rates, to give it a profit as well as a fee. The margin rate keyed into the system was 1 per cent, while the rate authorized by the Office of the Director of Consumer Affairs (ODCA) was 0.5 per cent. Nobody within AIB noticed. AIB's response to customers was to tell them they were victims of a 'systems failure'. In fairness to the regulator, once it was alerted to the matter by a whistle-blower it managed to get AIB to refund €65 million to customers.

Internal controls at AIB were so shoddy that a so-called rogue trader called John Rusnak at All First, a US subsidiary of AIB, was allowed to lose $691 million by betting wrongly that the yen would weaken against the dollar and then hiding his trades from his superiors. Rusnak was quickly convicted and sent to jail: how he must have wished that he had offended in Ireland, where there was a very good chance, based on track record, that he would not even have been prosecuted, let alone sent to jail.

Knowing all this, the regulator continued to rely on principles, and the light touch, and the honesty of the banks with whom it was dealing.

In 2005, four years after it was set up, the head of the Office of the Director of Corporate Enforcement, Paul Appleby, asked for twenty more staff, believing his office to be 'wholly under-resourced'. Two years later he got eight people, after Bertie Ahern told him he would have to 'wait his turn', despite the mass recruitment taking place in other parts of the public sector.

The body, charged with investigating corporate malfeasance, had to outsource some of its work: for example, securing High Court approval for the appointment of respected barrister Bill Shipsey as an inspector tasked with investigating the offshore share dealings in Fyffes involving Jim Flavin. It often found the going tough, as well-resourced targets spent big money on high-flying lawyers. The Bailey brothers of Planning Tribunal fame won a High Court action against the ODCE in 2007, preventing it from using materials, such as the reports of the Planning Tribunal, in actions against them to disqualify them as directors. The ODCE budget for 2009 was a modest €5.47 million and it employed just forty-six people, despite the massive and increased workload. That was how seriously the state wished to investigate corporate wrong-doing.

Over the same period much was made of the need to give regulators more powers. However, the need for the powers of the Central Bank and Financial Regulator to be reinforced or replaced was not entirely convincing. The Financial Regulator had powers, but was often criticized for not using them enough, which suggested there was truth to the old maxim that 'over time regulatory agencies come to be dominated by the industries that are being regulated.'

The regulator's first public levy of a fine was on the Irish Nationwide Building Society: it was ordered to pay €50,000 after Michael Fingleton Junior sent out an e-mail seeking deposits soon after the state's bank guarantee was issued, despite firm direction by the government not to engage in such activity. The fines against Seán Quinn and Quinn Insurance had been made earlier but were not disclosed until later.

In such circumstances it is not surprising that the New York Times described Ireland as the 'Wild West' of international finance as far back as 2005, because of our lack of regulation. The state made the 'stability' of the system – its ability to continue functioning – more important than its probity. Ironically, it would be lack of probity that would destabilize the entire system.

These experiences suggested that regulation in Ireland should have been adversarial, with regulators conducting surprise visits and challenging what they were told. Instead, in 2007, the regulator carried out just fifteen on-site inspections of the fifty banks under its remit and in many cases gave advance warning that it was coming.

Much was made of the high-profile February 2009 raid on the premises of Anglo Irish Bank by members of the ODCE and the Financial Regulator, as if this finally showed proof of a clamp-down. In the same month a letter from ODCE head Paul Appleby to the Dáil finance committee said that in his opinion 'circumstances suggesting prejudice, misconduct and / or illegality are present with respect to the company's affairs.' However, while the raid on Anglo's Stephen's Green headquarters looked good for the television cameras, it soon emerged that Anglo had been told the investigators would be coming. The officials didn't make a public raid on the offices of Irish Nationwide Building Society to find out more details of the loan arrangement it had with Sean FitzPatrick. And if Irish Life & Permanent was raided to find out the truth about the extraordinary transfers of cash that inflated the true worth of the Anglo balance sheet at its 30 September 2008 year-end, the media weren't told about it.

Neary's approach to dealing with events at Anglo had been somewhat baffling. His statement in October 2008 on Seán Quinn's involvement told us only as much as we needed to know without emphasizing the seriousness of the affair. But it raised all sorts of important questions. Quinn said he was resigning as a director of Quinn Insurance but had he been required to do so by the regulator? And even if Quinn was no longer a member of the Quinn Insurance board, what influence would he have as its owner?

If the position on Quinn was doubtful, his approach to FitzPatrick's hiding of loans with INBS was almost unbelievable. Neary was far too fast to concur with FitzPatrick's contention that the loans, while inappropriate, were not illegal, especially as an investigation was ongoing.

When Neary said this it appears that he might not have been aware that Section 194 of the Companies Act 1963 states that 'it shall be the duty of a director of a company who is in any way, whether directly or indirectly, interested in a contract or proposed contract with the company to declare the nature of his interest at a meeting of the directors of the company.' That would have covered the loans. It is also a criminal offence under Section 197 of the 1990 Companies Act to make a 'misleading, false or deceptive' statement to the auditors of a company. This is punishable on indictment by a fine of up to €12,700 and, crucially, up to three years in prison.

The regulator was supposed to apply a 'fit and proper' test to the directors of financial institutions. They were supposed to meet standards of probity and competence, and to be 'honest, fair and equitable'. So why wasn't FitzPatrick removed about a year previously?

As if that wasn't bad enough, Neary says he was kept out of the loop about what was going on, and his underlings had not briefed him about it. Finance minister Brian Lenihan had to tell his own Financial Regulator about what had happened.

Lenihan's public disclosure of FitzPatrick's loans and the regulator's inept handling of the issue brought about Neary's early retirement as Financial Regulator. He was encouraged by the payment of an accelerated pension lump sum of €400,000 and compensation of €200,000 for the loss of the earnings he had the right to expect before his due retirement date.

Neary's retirement also meant that he was off the stage by the time the IL&P deposits scandal emerged – which was helpful to all involved, since Anglo alleged that not only did Neary know what was going on but had raised no objections to it (his office, however, claimed not to have approved it). These movements of money were crucial to maintaining the 'stability' of Anglo, in giving it the appearance of greater financial strength than it had, but it misled shareholders, credit rating agencies and potential new investors.

The revelation that Neary's office had supplied the Minister for Finance and his officials with only partial information before 30 September – and that they even did so again afterwards, when the recapitalization of Anglo and other banks with state money was under active consideration – was deeply worrying. Would different decisions have been made if Lenihan, Cowen and their officials had been given more information?

Even after Neary left, Lenihan defended the board of the Financial Regulator in February, saying they were not 'industry insiders' and had 'no connections' with banking and, as such, were not directly culpable for the sins of the banking sector. But could it be said that some of them were asleep on the job? Several of the non-executive members of the Central Bank and Financial Regulatory Authority were appointed by the Minister for Finance. The decision to reintegrate the two – in a new Central Bank Commission, as announced in the April 2009 supplementary budget – was an implicit acknowledgement of failure. The intention to look outside the civil service for a head for the new commission – for the first time in the history of the state – was occasioned by the need to show the watching world that the old way of doing things was over.

PART IX

After the boom is over . . .

37

Guaranteeing the banks

Ultimately it fell to Taoiseach Brian Cowen to make the decision as to how to save the Irish banks and, by extension, the economy on the evening of 29 September and in the early hours of the morning of 30 September. He took counsel from plenty of advisers before making the decision to offer a blanket guarantee on all deposits and liabilities for a two-year period. In other words, even if a bank got into difficulty the state promised to make good on whatever arrangements depositors and creditors had come to with them. Though much has been made of the circumstances in which ministers gave their approval, being roused by phone calls in the early hours of 30 September to attend a so-called incorporeal cabinet meeting via conference call, they really had little choice. The decision was approved because it was the one Cowen told the cabinet he wanted.

It was an enormous moment for Cowen, whose record to that date both as Minister for Finance and Taoiseach suggested a deep caution and conservatism. This added to the degree of nervousness being experienced by others: was he up to it? Nobody doubted Cowen's integrity, but he had been a largely passive Minister for Finance throughout his four years in the job. He allowed the property bubble to inflate largely unchecked, taking few initiatives to reduce it. At times he seemed prepared to just sail along on the seemingly unstoppable tide of rising tax revenues and unchecked economic growth – as his leader expected when he appointed him to replace the more maverick McCreevy.

He dithered when it came to confronting Ahern about his continuing leadership of Fianna Fáil, although he was appalled by the revelations about Ahern's financial misfeasance and angered by the number of times he and others had been required to publicly go to Ahern's defence. It was not until Gráinne Carruth's evidence to the Planning Tribunal fatally undermined Ahern's authority that Cowen visited Ahern in his Drumcondra office and told him that the time to go had come. Cowen denied afterwards that this was what had happened, but that denial was motivated by his loyalty to the party and his desire not to be seen as someone who would remove a leader. It was not that Cowen was not prepared to act; it was merely that he had to be utterly convinced that it was the right time to do something before he did it. Out of a sense of decency, he allowed Ahern the indulgence of the long goodbye, which turned out to be the wrong decision when a fresh focus was required urgently.

Worse, he was perceived to be struggling with the demands of being Taoiseach. Cowen had been elevated for political reasons: for his perceived ability to lead Fianna Fáil, with the secondary assumption that it would automatically render him suitable for the bigger, more important job of Taoiseach. While he had a reputation for readily understanding what was going on, he did not have a name for making tough and brave calls; his moves were too often dictated by his assessment of likely political outcomes and public reaction. He had performed strongly in the 2007 general election campaign, but some critics pointed out quietly that his performance as a minister had not matched those perceived political strengths and that different skills were required of a Taoiseach.

For these reasons, a night like 29 September was an enormous test. To do what he did that evening – to guarantee the deposits and liabilities of the nation's main banks to the potentially catastrophic amount of €440 billion – was a monumental step and a clear indication of just how desperate the situation had become for the state. It also put him in a situation where he had to emphasize the sovereignty of the state and the role of the government. Insiders say that Cowen was decisive that evening, when some wobbled about whether they were doing the right thing and others had little to say. Cowen decided upon what he considered to be the least worst of all the bad options and demanded that the action be taken.

At first it appeared that he had done the correct thing, but hindsight has not been kind. It is not clear whether Cowen and Lenihan had been informed about the full nature of the crisis that fateful evening. It appears that the politicians thought that they were dealing with an Irish liquidity crisis caused by international events. In reality there was an added dimension that should have been factored into the eventual decision: the imminence of a major solvency crisis at the banks caused by their excessive and often careless lending. The dreadful state of the loans carried by the banks meant that the giving of the blanket guarantee – and the potential liability to the state – was even riskier than it first appeared. If the people 'in the room' had known how badly undercapitalized the banks were, that there was a major asset quality, as well as a liquidity, problem afoot, it is possible that different conclusions might have been reached and other decisions made, particularly in relation to Anglo Irish Bank and Irish Nationwide Building Society.

The public statements of the Central Bank governor and the Financial Regulator in advance of 30 September – and indeed afterwards – were along the lines that the banks did not have a capital problem and that as a result whatever bad debts emerged would be manageable. This suggested that neither was best placed to perform the job of informing or advising Cowen and Lenihan. It could be that they were presenting this position in public, in the belief that they were serving the national interest by not undermining public or international confidence in Ireland any further, while giving the full unvarnished facts in private.

However, the public has not been told what options were up for serious discussion that night. The government refused to make all relevant documents and notes available under the Freedom of Information Act, as, under the Act, the state does not have to hand over documents or records if they are deemed to pose a serious threat to 'the financial interests of the state' or could lead to 'undue disturbance in the ordinary course of business generally'. This meant we were asked to take a lot on trust.

The proper use of power requires the availability of the correct and relevant information, and it appears that the politicians may not have had sufficient information about the lending behaviour of all the banks and the extent of their exposure to economic meltdown. It wasn't made known to them until later that Anglo's chairman, Sean FitzPatrick, had engaged in secret practices that, upon revelation, not just destroyed the credibility of his bank but also seriously damaged the country's economic reputation and stability. This was known to the regulator's office on the night of the guarantee, but not apparently to its boss, Patrick Neary, and it was not relayed to the decision-makers. The full circumstances of Seán Quinn's share transactions in Anglo – and the sale of

10 per cent of his shares – were relevant too, but we do not know whether they featured in discussions. It was disclosed eight months later that the National Treasury Management Agency had been so concerned about the quality of lending done by Anglo that it refused requests to deposit large sums of money with the bank, for fear that it wouldn't get it back. The NTMA was not represented in the room that night, which raises questions as to what information it had given to other institutions of the state previously about its view on Anglo and whether its opinion would have made a difference to the decision to offer the guarantee.

On 29 September the politicians may not have known that many developers had stopped making interest repayments on their debts, particularly on development land, because the Central Bank or Financial Regulator may not have been aware of the extent to which the banks were gambling that things would pick up. Alternatively, they may have known but were afraid to admit it, because that would have raised legitimate questions as to why they had allowed things to reach such a pass and what they had tried to do to rectify the situation.

There were other options available that night. Anglo could have been allowed to fall, leaving its investors to pick up the tab during a liquidation of its assets. Not everybody is convinced by the government's arguments that Anglo was of 'systemic' importance, that its fall would have created a domino effect that would have taken everyone else with it. Alternatively, Anglo could have been nationalized there and then, three months earlier than it was, with guarantees offered over the deposits in all the other banks. That would have wiped out the investments of all the existing shareholders, including Quinn and many other well-connected and powerful people. It might also have wiped out domestic and international holders of subordinated debt, something that might have affected confidence in Ireland as a place to make investments. This was considered absolutely the worst of all outcomes by most interested parties.

In an opinion piece published in the *Irish Times* some months later, Professor Morgan Kelly of University College Dublin – who had predicted accurately the implosion of the property bubble – continued his strong campaign against the rescue of Anglo. His view was that many of the developer clients of Anglo were going bust anyway and should not have been rescued. Kelly argued that Anglo had no real importance to the Irish banking system. He believed that the hit should have been taken by investors in subordinated bonds, who held about €22 billion in such investments. These were professional investors who had known the risks when they bought the bonds, received high interest payments in return and insured against possible losses through the purchase of credit default swaps. The insurers would have taken the hit if Anglo had been allowed to fail, but instead the Irish taxpayer had done so by investing all of the required new capital.

If Kelly is correct – and many economists and opposition politicians have come round to his view – the decision to indemnify the subordinate debt carried by the banks was one of the biggest mistakes made that fateful night. Others, however, maintain that Kelly's approach might seem fine in theory but, had it been implemented, it would not have worked in practice.

The events of 29 September did not come out of the blue. Department of Finance officials, along with their counterparts at the Central Bank and the Financial Regulator, had been working on disaster scenarios from August. This preparation contradicts the consistent argument of government that the crisis really hit only after the Lehman fall on 15 September.

However, 29 September was an extraordinary day. It had begun with the news that Dutch financial giant Fortis, UK mortgage lender Bradford & Bingley and German commercial property bank Hypo Real Estate had all been rescued with state bailouts. As outlined in the introduction to this book, Ireland did not escape the carnage on world stock markets. Without some form of protection it was feared the share prices of the Irish banks would collapse the following morning. While the government feared the impact of such losses on pension funds and individual investors, that was not their main concern; what worried it most was the likelihood that deposits would evaporate and short-term loans on the interbank market would not be available, bringing about a domino effect as the banks fell one by one. When the country's main bankers made their pitch Cowen and Lenihan were told apparently that if Anglo 'died', the other banks could follow 'within minutes' as deposits were withdrawn and loans recalled. 'They came to the room and we heard what they had to say and we asked them to leave the room,' said Lenihan. 'It is very important when representations are being made to you – by whatever source – that policy is not discussed with them.'

The central group of seven sat in a large meeting room beside the Taoiseach's office. Others who were asked to contribute included Tony Grimes, the director-general of the Central Bank, Kevin Cardiff, the Department of Finance's second secretary general and William Beausang, its assistant secretary. The Taoiseach's advisers, such as Joe Lennon, Peter Clinch and Eoghan Ó Neachtain, went in and out as required. Cowen was adamant in his refusal to countenance nationalization. He apparently feared that it would spark legal action by the bank and its shareholders and that the government did not have the necessary evidence to justify the action, no matter what it suspected.

Instead, the decision was taken to set up the guarantee scheme. A calculation was made that the worst-case scenario was a €20 billion hit, a little more than was in the National Pension Reserve Fund at the time. The government hoped that choosing this method would cost little or nothing.

Early on Tuesday morning, 30 September, Lenihan began a series of media interviews in which he said there had been a 'number of triggers' for the dramatic announcement he was making. He criticized the US government for wrongly letting the Lehman Brothers bank collapse and said Ireland could not have risked the same. 'We have to have faith in ourselves as a nation and a people that we are capable of having a viable banking system,' said Lenihan.

The government's announcement was met with shock by most and opinion divided sharply as to whether the chosen method of protecting the banks was the correct one. When Cowen went into the Dáil that day he declared that 'I have not handed over money to any bank . . . I have provided the reputation of the state to those banks in a position whereby they can gain access to funds to continue in a stable financial system so the economy and financial life of this country can continue.'

Cowen insisted that the decisions he took were in the national interest. 'How far back do people think this country would be if we were to wake up this morning and we were to find a failed banks system on our hands?' he said.

While Fine Gael reluctantly supported the plan, citing the national interest, the Labour Party refused to do so, highlighting in particular the impact on the cost of borrowing for the exchequer and the risk that the banks would profit from the scheme.

The first worry proved to be correct, as a combination of the bank guarantee and an explosion in the exchequer deficit sent the nation's borrowing costs much higher. However, the second was the least of our problems, as bad debts at the banks mounted. The government decided in its public comments afterwards to focus on the liquidity issue and to deny problems about solvency or the capital adequacy of the banks. 'The risk of any potential financial exposure from this decision is significantly mitigated by a very substantial buffer made up of the equity and other risk capital,' said Lenihan. Unfortunately that confidence in the banks' financial strength proved to be unfounded, as many had predicted as early as October 2008.

'They [the banks] made it clear to us that liquidity was drying up in the Irish banking system and the maturity dates for the various loans they need to fund their businesses were shortening all the time and reaching dangerous levels of exposure in terms of time limits,' Lenihan told the Seanad later that week. 'This legislation is not about protecting the interests of the banks. It is about the safeguarding of the economy and everybody who lives and works here.'

He got support from Denis Casey, then chief executive of Irish Life & Permanent: 'The oxygen supply for the Irish banks was being cut off, and healthy banks were starting to gasp for breath. This guarantee turns on the oxygen supply.'

In acting as it did, the government struck something of a blow for national sovereignty but took the risk of further damaging our fragile relationship with the European Union, which had already suffered because of the rejection of the Lisbon Treaty. Rather than asking for permission to act, our government told the European Central Bank and European Commission that it was becoming the first Western economy to openly underwrite its entire banking system.

The movement of money to the Irish banks as a response to the guarantee was the main reason for Britain's incensed reaction. Its banks feared the mass transfer of funds. Chancellor Alistair Darling twice remonstrated with Lenihan – accusing him of 'economic nationalism' – while Prime Minister Gordon Brown berated Cowen. The Irishmen held firm, saying it was their job to protect the Irish national interest. Nor did the British get any joy from the complaints they made to the European Commission. Fortunately, Lenihan had got to the relevant politicians – Jean-Claude Juncker, the Prime Minister and Minister for Finances of

Luxembourg, as well as chairman of the euro zone finance ministers' group; and the French Minister of Economic Affairs and president of Ecofin, Christine Lagarde – before them.

Critics wondered why the guarantee hadn't been restricted to the four main financial institutions – AIB, Bank of Ireland, IL&P and the EBS Building Society – omitting Anglo and Irish Nationwide. The government told the European Commission that they had to be included because of their 'systemic importance' and the need to provide protection against 'irreversible damage to the financial system'.

The existence of the guarantee initially attracted billions of new deposits to the Irish banks, greatly strengthening their balance sheets at a stroke. Although the initial purpose of the two-year guarantee was to cover Ireland's six main banks, this had to be expanded to eleven banks and €485 billion in liabilities.

However, it proved to be only a temporary respite: the money started to leave again, as investors began to fear that the guarantee would have to be invoked, such was the dire state of the balance sheets of the banks; there simply was not enough capital to cover mounting bad debts on loans. The actions on 29/30 September had been taken to prevent 'serious disturbance in the economy' – the phrase used in communications with the press and the EU. Those actions were not enough.

38

The price for drinking too deeply from the national cup of confidence

The AIB implosion did not involve Anglo-style skulduggery. Its key decision-makers were not obsessed with self-enrichment and did not engage in the type of behaviour that will require investigation by the Office of the Director of Corporate Enforcement and the involvement of the Gardaí. We should be thankful for such small mercies. But, despite the absence of disgraceful behaviour by senior executives, akin to that of Sean FitzPatrick, AIB is none the less culpable: not just for almost ruining itself but for contributing massively to the overall economic downturn and requiring the state to spend billions of euro it could ill afford in shoring it up. It remains to be seen how the National Asset Management Agency will affect the fortunes of AIB over the coming year and beyond. AIB may not have created as large a need for capital investment by the state as Anglo did but that does not excuse its behaviour: it was so much bigger, and so much more embedded in the fabric of the Irish economy and society, that its responsibility ran deeper.

During the era of the housing bubble, everybody took leave of their senses and the authorities did little or nothing to stop it. The availability of cheap money as interest rates dropped in the euro zone was one of the key drivers of speculative lending. Borrowed money had never been so cheap in Ireland. Of course, the banks didn't have to make money available in such vast quantities, but those banks that didn't feared they would lose market share and profits through being over-prudent.

This is where what might be called 'the Anglo effect' came into play. That bank adopted an aggressive approach to growing its loan book, made big profits out of doing so (in the days before borrowers were unable to make repayments) and saw its share price soar as a result. The bigger banks watched aghast. Whereas once the main banks tolerated Anglo as a competitive nuisance, it now had a stock market value that neither AIB nor Bank of Ireland could bear. Under David Drumm's stewardship, even more than when Sean FitzPatrick was at the helm, Anglo ate seriously into the market for large profitable loans, which the two big banks assumed was theirs almost by right. On top of this Anglo was not encumbered with a costly branch network like the main banks. It was the favourite of investors.

AIB, in the company of its main rival, Bank of Ireland, decided to respond to this increased competition. It sought out the developers and builders aggressively, offering them loans for the purchase of development land and then for the construction of houses, apartments and, particularly, commercial developments. It always had plenty of this business, but as the pie became bigger it was determined not only to keep hold of its share, at the very least, but to expand it. It is ironic to note that it did this just as Anglo decided that the Irish market was turning into a bubble and moved much of its new lending outside Ireland.

In AIB's case, branch managers were urged to go for growth; their bonuses were linked to the introduction of new business and the expansion of existing customer lending. Bank lending was predicated on grandiose assumptions as to the valuations applied to land and properties. The era of the conservative branch manager was at an end, albeit only temporarily. Those who said these valuations were crazy, particularly when the rental yield was examined, were dismissed as cranks or 'doom and gloom merchants', or as wanting to talk the country into recession.

The amounts that banks lent to developers for the purchase of land contributed greatly to the inflation in prices for residential and commercial accommodation. Whereas in the early days of the boom many builders were able to use land they had hoarded for years or had been able to buy cheaply, now demand was such that this was no longer possible. The regulators watched as banks provided the finance for developers who were paying as much as €50 million an acre for land and sometimes even more. Even where prices were much lower they were still too expensive in some cases because of where the land was located. This over-borrowing meant that the builders had to charge higher prices to recoup their costs. This in turn gave the banks an incentive to lend bigger and bigger mortgages to the end purchasers so their original clients, the developers, could repay their loans.

In the residential property mortgage market AIB and Bank of Ireland saw Bank of Scotland (Ireland), part of the UK giant HBOS, become a noisy nuisance. Also in the field were Ulster, which had bought First Active to increase its presence in home mortgages, and Irish Life & Permanent, which had a traditional strength there. It was this competition that led to some wild practices: the introduction of 100 per cent mortgages for first-time buyers in 2005, which in many cases resulted in a negative equity trap – where their loans were greater than the value of their properties; mortgages that lasted for thirty, thirty-five or even forty years; and loans that were a multiple of six, seven or eight times real incomes. The regulator must have heard the anecdotes about some purchasers who, desperate to have a place of their own, falsified income statements by claiming fictional rental income from a bedroom or including a bonus as part of annual salary, as well as the allegations that some mortgage brokers turned a blind eye when confronted with evidence of this or even sometimes encouraged it. Meanwhile, newspaper advertisements hyped the provision of interest-only loans for property investments, particularly to older people who wanted to 'release equity' from homes that had increased greatly in value and had small or no mortgages attached. Amateur investors began to develop 'portfolios' of investment property, not worrying that the rent would not meet the monthly repayments because they believed the capital value would continue to increase.

Both of the main banks claimed to have been responsible enough when it came to providing home mortgages. On a number of occasions when I interviewed Eugene Sheehy, the AIB chief executive, he insisted that his bank would not advance more than 92 per cent of the value of a property, even when prices were at their peak and customers were having great difficulty in raising the 8 per cent deposit.

Yet what the media didn't notice, and the regulator should have but didn't, was that so much of the shockingly fast rise in AIB's lending was due to its facilitation of property speculation. In 2006, for example, when the madness was at its height, AIB added €10 billion of loans to its property portfolio in a single year. Just under a third of AIB's overall loans in Ireland at the end of 2008 were in property and construction, valued at more than €33 billion. Lending to that sector grew by 124 per cent over four years. In 2008 the bank's lending to property developers and construction was ten times the size of its loans to the manufacturing sector – and this at a time when the party clearly was over. If AIB couldn't stop itself, the regulator should have done the job for it.

Some of AIB's most highly paid senior personnel got things wrong during the boom; as the bust hit they arguably made things worse by denying the extent of the problems and therefore failing to act quickly enough to shore things up. The bank may not have understood how far the crash in the economy would go or anticipated its own problems in getting repayment of its loans; or it may have tried to put a good face on things in the hope that everything would work out better than it had feared.

At the 2008 annual general meeting chairman Dermot Gleeson told shareholders that the bank had no need to ask them for extra capital. He said the capital, asset quality and funding at AIB were all robust. The provision – or the amount of money set aside by the bank out of its profits – against loans not being repaid was just 0.2 per cent. He spoke of the bank's 'diversity and resilience' and boasted of a 'carefully chosen spread of businesses'. As recently as February 2008 AIB spent €216 million on buying a half-share in Bulgaria's BACB bank and said it was looking to make more purchases in Eastern Europe.

In August 2008, to widespread amazement, the board decided to increase AIB's interim dividend by 10 per cent, costing AIB €270 million in cash. This was insanity and many people said so at the time, knowing that the bank needed to conserve cash, even before September's Lehman Brothers crash. Instead of inspiring confidence it had the effect of raising serious questions as to how detached AIB was from the new reality.

In October, weeks after the granting by the government of the guarantee, a defiant Sheehy declared that he would 'rather die than sell equity to the state', but his bravado failed to inspire any confidence in AIB's ability to assess and deal with its situation. Over a period of nine months AIB consistently underplayed the mounting problems it faced. It did so time after time, until it finally had to admit that things were far worse than it had believed or said.

PricewaterhouseCoopers, having begun a post-guarantee examination of the books at all the banks covered, discovered what it considered to be undue optimism on the part of AIB as to its likely losses. There began a series of lively confrontations between the Department of Finance and Ireland's biggest bank as the former emphasized that the latter needed more capital, in the national interest as much as in its own. AIB fought and resisted, but eventually just before Christmas in 2008 conceded that it needed an additional €2 billion in capital. It accepted an offer from the government for €1 billion and pledged to raise the rest itself.

That didn't work either, as investors shunned the Irish bank, partly due to its own perilous state but also because of the damage to Ireland's reputation caused by that month's revelations about FitzPatrick's share deals at Anglo. The nationalization of Anglo on 9 January 2009 sounded the death-knell for AIB's intention to raise its own capital, and on 12 February it announced that the bank now needed €3.5 billion and that it would all come from the government. However, under the deal that had been struck the government would hold only 25 per cent of the voting shares in the bank, with more capital invested by way of preference shares, so as to reassure international investors that it had not passed into state control.

War continued between the Department of Finance and the bank as to AIB's future. In March 2009 AIB said that it could write off up to €8.4 billion in bad loans between 2008 and 2010 and still have enough capital to survive, once the government's €3.5 billion injection was taken into account. Unfortunately, the government's advisers then estimated that the likely losses would reach €12 billion. Meanwhile, Sheehy tried to rally staff by sending them an e-mail to tell them that 'it is very important that the staff know the bank has done nothing to be ashamed of, that it is going to support its customers through this downturn.'

Sheehy was living in denial: his overconfidence about the strength of the economy and AIB's ability to withstand a severe downturn, endorsed by Gleeson, had severely undermined the bank. The figures were frightening. The top fifty customers at AIB owed €19 billion, about 15 per cent of all its global lending. The average net debt per client was €380 million, although clearly some had larger debts. The situation was made worse by the fact that big clients also had major debts elsewhere, which could lead to rows as to who had first entitlement to security. Property developer Liam Carroll had debts of €2.8 billion by early 2009, but, while AIB may have been his largest lender, about a half-dozen others had major claims to his assets too.

Sheehy and Gleeson's attitude became a major source of annoyance to the Department of Finance. AIB's top executives rated themselves highly; their predecessors, such as Gerry Scanlan, Tom Mulcahy and Michael Buckley, were among the smartest and most impressive men I've encountered in twenty years of business journalism, but behind their charming demeanours was the clear message that they knew best. Gleeson's precise and painstaking attitude to every issue infuriated some in the department, who felt that his long-standing experience as one of

Ireland's leading barristers encouraged him to look at things too often from a legal, rather than a business, perspective at a time when speed was needed. His protection of Sheehy was regarded as admirable but perhaps somewhat misplaced.

By April it became obvious that AIB needed even more capital than it had admitted. The government's stress testing suggested that €5 billion would be required and even more might be necessary depending on the price at which AIB's property loans were compulsorily purchased by the new National Assets Management Agency (NAMA). NAMA was a government initiative to rescue all of the Irish banks: the agency would take ownership and control of the mortgages they held in return for bonds to compensate them for the loss of the loans from their balance sheets. It would buy them at market value, however that would be defined. It was estimated that NAMA would have to buy about €30 billion of property loans carried on AIB's balance sheet. If NAMA paid 80 per cent for these loans, the resulting €6 billion reduction in AIB's balance sheet would require more capital to be injected again, giving the state a majority of shares or even control. AIB was angry that the government would not make the details of the PwC stress testing available to it, but it was not in a position to put up much of an argument. It agreed that it would have to sell assets and buy back its own debt at less than its face value to raise this latest batch of capital. It was the latest in a long list of humiliations. It was to signal the end for Gleeson, Sheehy and group finance director John O'Donnell.

The Department of Finance did not want to be seen to be in total control at the bank and did not order the trio's removal. But it did apply pressure by refusing to commit its 25 per cent of votes in the bank to their re-election at the 2009 annual general meeting. In the end, the three men decided it was best that they stood down.

By taking manners to a ridiculous level, the government did not give the public what it needed: a reassurance that it was punishing AIB as well as rescuing it. Instead of making its exercise of power obvious, the government allowed AIB to manage the departures. Gleeson announced that he was to 'step down' in June, O'Donnell was to 'retire' in August and Sheehy was to 'retire' when his replacement was appointed. It was all very gentlemanly and a touch unsatisfactory. The government and the investment institutions that own the bulk of the stock then actually voted for their re-election.

The trio were brave enough to face the music at AIB's May 2009 AGM and they did apologize for and admit their failures. Just days before the meeting AIB had set aside €4.3 billion to cover losses on loans, mainly to Irish property developers, on top of the €1.8 billion it had announced for 2008. It had put an upper limit of €4 billion on such losses as recently as March.

Gleeson, who was paid fees of €475,000 during 2008 for a job that was supposed to be part time but that had become virtually full time in the second half of 2008, admitted he had been wrong and said: 'In common with the European and US banking systems, in common with our customers, Irish people and businesses, and in common with the Irish state, we believed the momentum in world economies, including Ireland, would continue for some time, and would slow gently, rather than abruptly. Regrettably, we were wrong in that view . . . We drank too deeply, I suppose, from the national cup of confidence.'

By the day of that meeting AIB's value on the stock market had fallen by over €20 billion. Shares that had traded at a high of €23.95 in 2007 changed hands at just 87 cents that day. 'If you look at the tipsters for yesterday's racing, one in ten of the tipsters is right and nine are wrong,' Gleeson opined. But when investors buy shares in a bank they don't believe they are gambling. The majority bought for stability and safety, for the annual dividend and the security of a nest egg, rather than in the hope of turning capital gains that could be realized.

The throwing of two eggs by 66-year-old pensioner Gary Keogh at the podium – one of which splattered the arm of Gleeson's jacket – may have been a cheap shot, but it was apt, considering what AIB's mismanagement has done to the savings and investments of so many older people. Keogh was ejected by bouncers. Arguably they got the wrong man. That Eugene Sheehy committed €2 million of his own money to buying AIB shares at €15 each during the boom may be of some small consolation to others who lost money.

There was no doubt that AIB is of such a size that it had to be rescued. The consequences of AIB's madness were catastrophic: to its shareholders, its customers, the government and the general economy. Staff wouldn't escape either, as eventually a less active and smaller bank is going to shed workers; the pension fund is short of money too. The increase in income taxes for the general public can partly be blamed on financing the cost of this rescue.

Finding a successor to Sheehy was not an easy job. In normal circumstances, there would have been a raft of internal candidates. Not now. There was a pressing need to make an external appointment, to show a clean break from the past. Not doing that was a mistake that Bank of Ireland had made months earlier.

Richie Boucher first came to the attention of the general public when he attended the Oireachtas finance committee on 2 July 2008 on behalf of Bank of Ireland, as head of its retail operations in Ireland. He was bullish that the bank would be able to weather whatever economic storms were brewing. 'We are often wrong but we have a strong belief that we have significant and sufficient capital to meet even worse scenarios than we envisage. If bad debts and the economy get worse, we believe we are sufficiently capitalized.'

A week later his boss Brian Goggin told the Bank of Ireland AGM, 'We have been prudent in our stress testing and it has proven to be robust.' By early 2009 Goggin was gone from this job, to be replaced by Boucher. This amazed many observers: while Goggin clearly had to take the blame for the many mistakes made at Bank of Ireland, how did his right-hand man not only escape but get promoted?

Goggin had taken charge at Bank of Ireland in somewhat unusual circumstances in 2004, when his predecessor Michael Soden was rumbled looking at a web-site offering escort services in Las Vegas just before he was due there on a work trip. Goggin had been passed over for the job initially because he was regarded as too conservative; Soden's brief had been to head off the growth of Anglo. Goggin decided that he had to be aggressive. He was overly so.

Bank of Ireland was guilty of many of AIB's sins, and, though these were not on the same scale, its situation was no less serious. Its customer loans went from €68 billion in March 2004 to €145 billion in March 2008, an extraordinary and unsustainable level of growth. Of this €13 billion was to developers of commercial and residential properties. For a time, Goggin was one of the hear no evil, see no evil brigade. 'It's not beyond the bounds of possibility that we could actually talk ourselves into a recession and I think that would be absolute sacrilege,' he told reporters in May 2007 at the announcement of the bank's profits of €1.9 billion for the year ended that March.

Goggin eventually managed to talk himself out of his job. Bank of

Ireland went through the same process of detailed examination by the government and was offered state investment at the end of 2008 on the same basis as AIB. It also failed to raise €1 billion from its own resources. On 12 February 2009 the government announced that Bank of Ireland too would have to take €3.5 billion in new capital from the state.

The Department of Finance was actually relatively happy with the way Goggin and chairman Richard Burrows quickly realized the extent of their problems and were willing to accept help, which was contrasted with the more difficult negotiations with AIB. 'They held their hands up quicker, realized and admitted their mistakes and agreed to doing something about them,' said one of Lenihan's advisers. But then Goggin made a mistake that made his position, already highly tenuous, imposs-ible to maintain.

On 13 February, Goggin was giving an interview to RTÉ radio about the recapitalization when he was hit with a surprise question about his salary. 'I can tell you for a fact that it will be substantially down on what I earned last year,' he said. Asked what that was, he said the annual report showed it to be €2.9 million. 'What would you expect to take home this year?' reporter Christopher McKevitt pressed. 'It will be less than €2 million.' As it happened, it was 'just' €1.1 million but the damage was done. Lenihan rang Burrows and chewed him out of it. Goggin wanted to stay until a replacement was found but he ended up going quickly, with €1.1 million in compensation and his six-figure pension to come a year later. He suffered ill-health shortly after his departure, but recovered from a triple bypass heart operation. Goggin was replaced quickly by Boucher.

While most investors in the bank did nothing, one shareholder did. Dermot Desmond was furious, phoning Burrows to complain. (He knew Burrows from their encounter at Irish Distillers twenty years earlier: Burrows had been Distillers' chief executive when Pernod Ricard, advised by Desmond, took it over.) Boucher himself then phoned Desmond to ask what his problem was. The matter was not settled amicably and Desmond sent a letter to Burrows that quickly found its way into the public domain.

Desmond had become a shareholder in both AIB and Bank of Ireland early in 2009, just before the government's nationalization of Anglo Irish Bank and its decision to spend €7 billion in trying to recapitalize the two main banks. This led some commentators to speculate that

Desmond could somehow come to the rescue of either AIB or Bank of Ireland, while others questioned whether he had the wherewithal to do so. This ignored the fact that nobody knew just how rich Desmond actually was or what he had done with the proceeds of the sale of London City Airport. He was known to have a one third share of a Latvian bank; and, while the losses there might be limited by the scale of the operation, nobody knows what losses he may have made by investing in other banks. His good friend Joe Lewis lost about $1 billion when Bear Stearns collapsed, but nobody knew if Desmond had followed Lewis into that bank. If he had invested in other banks, in Britain or elsewhere, he likely would have lost heavily.

The AIB share register showed Desmond's IIU nominees acquired €5.1 million AIB shares on 2 January, giving Desmond 0.58 per cent of the bank's shares at that time. The Bank of Ireland's share register shows IIU nominees buying 8.9 million shares on 6 January, just under 1 per cent of the bank. The combined investment cost €16 million. In just over two months it was worth less than a quarter of that, leaving IIU nursing a €12 million paper loss amid growing speculation that the banks would have to be nationalized, wiping out all shareholders. Subsequent gains for the shares reversed that notional, and unrealized, loss.

In his letter to Burrows, Desmond asked the chairman to 'clarify whether Mr Boucher had a major involvement in the bank's exposure to property lending'. Detailing Boucher's senior roles within the group since joining it from Ulster Bank in 2004, Desmond argued that Boucher 'must have been responsible for fatal errors of judgement, including advancing loans to developers on the strength of overstated land values and insufficient security.' He pointed out how by September 2008 there were €38 billion of loans to property and construction. 'There has to be a direct correlation between Mr Boucher's appointment to these senior positions and the excess lending policies of the bank. How did Mr Boucher and others within the bank view the warnings of the Central Bank in 2004 concerning the overheated residential property market?'

Saying that the appointment sent out 'completely and utterly the wrong message', Desmond argued that 'credibility and confidence need to be restored . . . this will not be achieved by promoting existing management further up the chain.'

In his letter Desmond went to bat for 'people who invested their pensions and savings in Bank of Ireland shares [who] have been put under extreme financial pressure through absolutely no fault of their own. People are quite rightly angry. A clean break is needed. The people who got the bank into the mess are not the people to get the bank out of the mess.'

Desmond has a profile of such prominence that the leak of a letter like this made for headline news. In his letter he didn't refer to Boucher's close friendship with his adversary Seán Dunne. Boucher was a public supporter of Dunne's Ballsbridge development against which Desmond had argued so fervently. In his letter to Dublin City Council on 2 October 2007 Boucher wrote: 'I write to confirm my strong support for this landmark proposal, which I believe will significantly benefit the City of Dublin and its citizens through helping enhance the concept of a living city and providing buildings of significant architectural merit befitting Ireland of the 21st Century.'

When Dunne appeared on the Marian Finucane radio programme on 15 March 2008, he singled out Boucher as 'a very good friend of mine' and said he had advised him on raising finance for the Ballsbridge project, although it was Boucher's old employer, Ulster Bank, which provided the bulk of the loans after Bank of Ireland had been among those to decline to do so.

Burrows came to Boucher's defence, saying he was the 'unanimous choice of the board ... having the required leadership qualities and banking experience' for the role of chief executive. He said Boucher was selected for his 'expertise, determination and pragmatism'. It was no surprise that Burrows defended him, having just appointed him, and having received the endorsement of the government.

Desmond and the board of Bank of Ireland were left in agreement on one thing, however: neither wanted the bank to be nationalized, because that would have meant all shareholders being wiped out. Like AIB, things continued to get worse. Bank of Ireland announced in May 2009 that it expected to write off €6 billion in loans in bad debts over the following three years, compared to its previous estimate of €4.5 billion. The bank made a loss of €7 million for the year-end March 2009, which may seem like a small figure until it is compared to the profit of €1.9 billion made the previous year. In June 2009 it got a new chairman. Pat Molloy, a 71-year-old who had retired as chief executive eleven years earlier, was appointed by the government. His track record was excellent, and he had won kudos for rescuing Bank of Ireland from an ill-fated foray into New Hampshire and Britain in the early 1990s. Nobody objected to this return to the future, not least Desmond: he had recommended publicly that Molloy should be recalled as chief executive in succession to Goggin, notwithstanding his age. Clearly, Lenihan was listening to him.

The extraordinary surge in lending by Ireland's two biggest banks led to many questions about the failure of both the Financial Regulator and Central Bank to stop them, as well as Anglo.

Both John Hurley and Pat Neary watched in July 2008 as a procession of leading bankers advocated the financial health of their establishments – in the national interest of course – or displayed absolute denial. 'I reject the suggestion that banks have been foolhardy in recklessly lending and driving up values. We are in competition right across the board and I cannot think of a bank that has been reckless,' Willie McAteer of Anglo told the Oireachtas finance committee the same day as Boucher attended. (It emerged nearly a year later that McAteer had borrowed €8 million from Bank of Ireland himself to buy Anglo shares. When he couldn't repay it, Anglo repaid it on his behalf and hoped that he would repay it.)

Not surprisingly, after the introduction of the state guarantee on 30 September, Neary was called upon to attend the Oireachtas committee on finance, where he would be expected to answer questions from elected politicians on this and other things. Incredibly, the date was set for Tuesday, 14 October, the day of the 2009 budget, brought forward by two months by the government in an effort to maintain public confidence. This meant that media scrutiny of his performance was not as detailed as it would have been otherwise. Fortunately, Neary was still put under enormous pressure to justify himself. He reassured members that the six Irish banks covered by the guarantee had regulatory capital – or a buffer to protect against bad debts – of €42 billion, giving a capital solvency ratio of 11 per cent, as compared with the European average requirement of an 8 per cent minimum. He told the members that speculative lending to the development sector was €39.1 billion, of which €24 billion was supported by additional collateral or alternative sources of cash or reasonable security. Only €15 billion was secured directly on the underlying property and nothing else, he said. While that was not good in itself, questions also had to be asked about the quality of the security for the remaining loans. Worries were not assuaged by Neary's confidence.

The pantomime continued after Christmas. In the same January 2009 Oireachtas committee performance at which he said he had tried to warn about the dangers facing the economy, John Hurley also claimed that the share prices of the main Irish banks quoted on the stock market were 'not really indicative' of their actual situations. It has to be presumed that he meant that the shares were undervalued rather than overvalued, because he said they were 'strong institutions' and 'solvent institutions'. Calling the institutions 'strong' was overstating it, in the light of their desperate need for new capital and their failure to raise it from sources other than the government. Hurley's comment that AIB and Bank of Ireland had 'a very good opportunity' to raise €1 billion each from private investors, as was being attempted at that stage by the then government plan, and that efforts should be allowed to run their course, was predictably undermined within days and Hurley's authority suffered the more for it.

Meanwhile, Anglo began to disappear from sight. In the run-up to its nationalization, Lenihan heard from a variety of senior businessmen, not all of them tax resident in the country, about how important the bank was to the country – and not just the bank but also its chairman, Sean FitzPatrick. Lenihan admitted to surprise at just how many people were willing to pitch for their man. The government, however, had to be sensitive to perceived favourable treatment to Anglo, especially when it came out that Cowen had had dinner with two Anglo executives on 24 April 2008, just before he became Taoiseach. He said such dinners were normal for an outgoing Minister for Finance.

In late May 2009 the full enormity of Anglo's implosion became clear. Things were even worse than anyone had imagined. After a full review of the period between the previous financial year-end and 31 March 2009, it was decided that, of all the loans that had been given to customers in the past, €4.1 billion of this money was lost and would never be recovered. All sorts of stupid things had been done, including buying properties in the hope that it would subsequently be able to sell them to its own private banking clients, who would have borrowed from it to buy them. As if that wasn't bad enough, the loss of another €2.6 billion in loans was considered likely and, should things go even more wrong, another €3.5 billion could be lost. Out of a total loan book of nearly €72 billion, only little more than half of these – 54 per cent – were regarded as 'good' (in other words borrowers were making repayments on schedule).

This meant that the government was required to provide €4 billion in new capital immediately and was warned that the bill to keep Anglo alive could top €10 billion. It also emerged that the incredibly generous provision of deposits by the European Central Bank and our own Central Bank – more than €23 billion – was keeping the show on the road.

Immediately, the pressure was on to kill Anglo. What was the point in keeping the bank alive, especially as it was no longer lending money? O'Connor argued that it would cost even more to close the operation – and in that he was backed by state-appointed non-executive directors Alan Dukes – a former Fine Gael leader and Minister for Finance – and Frank Daly, formerly head of the Revenue Commissioners. Their fear was that the announcement of Anglo's closure would cause an immediate run on the deposits that were being used to finance the outstanding loans – and that the infamous government guarantee would be called upon, at a cost of more than €60 billion.

Politicians and officials 'pulled on the green jersey' again. Nobody believed O'Connor's contention that Anglo would operate as a going concern, just in a different way. It was understood that the government would close it down slowly without ever admitting it.

The bill for saving the banks just kept rising – and the burden for a generation of taxpayers did too.

39

The NAMA cure . . . as bad as the banking disease?

'There will be no NAMA tent at the Galway Races,' finance minister Brian Lenihan told me forcefully in an interview for *The Last Word* in April 2009, two days after his supplementary budget speech included details of the new plan to sort out the bad debt mess in our banks. 'We will pursue these borrowers to the ends of the earth. There will be no hiding place for them because they owe the state, all of us, this money.'

Lenihan's declaration conjured images of developers moving money secretly to Swiss bank accounts and of agents from the new National Assets Management Agency seizing houses, cars, helicopters, airplanes and whatever else these people had purchased during the boom years.

Lenihan was acting on the advice of economist Peter Bacon – who formerly worked for Sean Mulryan's Ballymore Properties – in setting up the new state-owned agency to take control and ownership of the mortgages that the banks held over commercial properties, development land-banks, and occupied and unoccupied houses and apartments. Nobody was to be given an exception, no matter how well connected they were if they were a developer who had a loan with an Irish bank, although it was later decided that a size threshold would be introduced of about €5 million. All property loans were going to be included, good, bad and doubtful, whether the borrowers were meeting repayments or not. In return, NAMA would issue bonds to the banks as a compensation for the loss of the loans from their balance sheets, where these loans were still treated as assets. The borrowers would be put under pressure to make their repayments to the new agency.

Taking control of both banks and developers would give the government power over a huge swathe of the economy. NAMA meant the state was virtually to control the entire property sector – from ownership of land, to control of planning permission, to owning the banks that advance finance. It was painted as an alternative to nationalizing the banks, but in reality it was the nationalization of the property sector, as the title to all land assets would be held by the state for as long as debts remained to be paid. If borrowers failed to make their repayments to NAMA, the state was entitled to seize the land and properties on which the loans had been secured. If the subsequent sale of this was not enough to cover the size of the loan, the state could, in theory, force those borrowers to hand over other assets or cash to make up the difference. These were to include the luxury mansions in which they lived. It was decided that the right to a family home enshrined in the constitution did not mean that they had the right to a family home with a swimming pool and a home cinema. Developers would be required to buy somewhere smaller in which to live.

It constituted the end of an era: the end of the power of the property developer, in conjunction with the destruction of their wealth. NAMA was a proposal for an extraordinary transfer of power. It was also an idea loaded with the potential for massive problems.

The biggest issue of all was the price at which the loans would be purchased from the banks. NAMA was to buy the loans from the banks at a discount. The size of an outstanding loan is known as its 'book value'. The state was taking the view that the security for these loans – the properties – was worth less than the banks were admitting and would therefore not cover the full book value amount if sold. This application of a discount was a protection for the state, assuming of course that it correctly estimated the new values of the assets behind the loans. Even with a discount in place there was a risk that it was going to overpay. Given that there would be up to €90 billion in loans involved, it could suffer horrendous losses, which would have been borne by the banks had NAMA not taken over. The idea that the state could recoup any overpayment by way of a special levy on the banks at a later date seemed an unrealistic aspiration.

Lenihan emphasized that even if NAMA bought the loans at a discount, the size of the debt owed by the developers was not written down accordingly. The original borrower was still required to pay off the debts in full, although this would be easier said than done.

Complications abounded. What prices would be obtained for the sale of distressed property assets in a market short of buyers, especially when those assets were so large that buyers needed loans to finance their purchase, and banks were not making new lending available? Would it all happen transparently, to convince the public that action was being taken and that erstwhile donors to Fianna Fáil were not being let off the hook? A number of developers had opted for the status of unlimited liability, to hide their profits from the prying eyes of the public. However, this meant that when things went wrong they could not limit their exposure to meeting their debts. Would NAMA be prepared to bankrupt such previously powerful and well-connected people?

How would NAMA deal with those who had secured loans on a so-called 'non-recourse' basis? This meant that their loans were secured merely on the assets purchased. If the value of those assets failed to meet the size of the repayment, the bank, or now NAMA, would be left to cover the loss. There was legal precedent to protect those who had taken loans on that basis. In 1993 Bank of Ireland sought to freeze nearly £500,000 in an account belonging to former GPA executive Colm Barrington (now chairman of Aer Lingus) to offset against a loan for £1.5 million he had taken to buy shares in GPA, which had become worthless. Barrington argued successfully that the bank could take the shares and sell them and that any loss as a result was not his concern.

What would happen in the case of investor syndicates, where some borrowers were able to make their repayments but others couldn't? What would happen if there were foreign banks – which were not subject to the compulsion to transfer their assets to NAMA – amongst those in a bankers' syndicate? What would happen if borrowers had pledged the same security to different banks, à la solicitor Michael Lynn at Irish Nationwide and other institutions?

Fortunately, although the banks got it wrong far too many times in their loan approvals, they weren't always totally stupid when it came to getting reasonably adequate security. The problem with non-recourse loans occurred only in a limited number of cases. Ironically, given that it was the first to be nationalized, Anglo probably had the most stringent policy in relation to securing personal guarantees and charges over other assets in addition to the property or development land for which the loan had been provided. Other banks had sought what was known as cross-collateralization: a charge was put over other pieces of property owned by the borrower in case the sale of the main security did not provide what was required to repay the loan. This proved to be very important to the banks as the downturn came and was the source of major irritation to borrowers, who found that cash from other investments had to be used to finance an asset gone bad or, worse, good investments were sold out from under them. Ultimately, this was going to be to NAMA's benefit, but it still didn't make its job any easier.

Unfortunately, Bacon believed that most of the property development companies did not have 'the depth of management skills to engage in the kind of portfolio sales and work-outs which ultimately are required to resolve the impairment issue'. Boiled down, this implied that unless they had other assets to sell, they would not raise all the money required.

While the government's April announcement was designed to reassure the markets that it had a plan to deal with the banking crisis, implementation of NAMA was going to take months because of the complexity of drafting legislation, hiring staff and deciding exactly how it should be run. The potential for lobbying by vested interests during this period was immense, especially as so many questions remained to be answered.

The Construction Industry Federation in particular was keen to exploit any opportunities to protect its members. Its director-general, Tom Parlon, a former junior minister, argued that there was a 'clear distinction between the professional property development companies represented by the Construction Industry Federation and the groups of property speculators who became active at the height of the market in 2005 and 2006' – cheerfully and wilfully ignoring the fact that some of the most outrageous speculation had been conducted by some of his most high-profile members. 'A sizeable proportion of the land and property that changed hands at the peak of the market in 2005 and 2006, and which is considered now to be the most impaired, was purchased by individuals and consortia (often groups of solicitors, barristers, accountants and bankers) with no history of building or delivering projects.' Parlon argued that NAMA might have no option 'but to incentivize more experienced developers to get involved through joint venture or other partnership arrangements'. This led to speculation that the full force of NAMA would not be used against the bigger players, for fear that the receivership or liquidation of one could have a domino effect.

Another big fear was that banks would stop providing working capital to developers before the establishment of NAMA, on the basis that it would be wasted money if these new loans were to be sold to NAMA only months later at a reduced price.

What about the 'rolling over' of loans, as often happens, meaning that if a development is not completed or unsold, the loan is extended or reissued? As NAMA was not established to be a bank, but an asset management company, who would provide the fresh loans that are often required to finish a development, especially as the titles for properties, as security, would rest with NAMA? Would the banks get involved again at this point and, if so, what security would be offered to them?

Indeed, who would finish developments or use the land-banks? Would the developers be allowed a way back in as partners in the newly established special purpose vehicles (SPVs) in which NAMA is the controlling shareholder? What would the public reaction be, even if it could be shown that these builders have the specialist expertise to do the required job? Would the builders who had caused the mess be given management contracts or licences to build on behalf of NAMA, getting paid a fee or a percentage of the profits or both? There has to be an opportunity for property companies to make some profit; human nature is such that these people would not want to work for what in their eyes was next to nothing. But how could that realistic aspiration be accommodated, without it seeming like the latest chapter of cronyism?

It was front-page news when it emerged that Bertie Ahern's old friend Seán Dunne was trying to make himself central to the action. But Dunne got a muted response when he tried to set up a new body called the Irish Property Developers Federation, with each applicant expected to stump up just €500 to join. Instead, most developers opted to stick with the Construction Industry Federation, which established a special subcommittee that would deal with the Department of Finance, banks, planners and NAMA, raising about €2,000 per member with the ambition of establishing a €2 million fighting fund. On it were developers such as Joe Cosgrave, Michael O'Flynn, developer of the landmark Elysium apartment complex in Cork and much else, Matt Gallagher of Earlsfort and Ravenshall Developments, Ray Grehan, John Bruder of Treasury Holdings, Alex Brett of Maplewood Developments, and Paul Sheeran of Park Developments.

Then there was the issue as to who would work in NAMA, a commercial semi-state body under the governance, management and director of the National Treasury Management Agency (NTMA). Would it hire from the same banks responsible for playing their part in the mess? What about the cosy relationships that some of those lenders enjoyed with the developers? Would these be continued by bankers now in the state employ? But if they weren't hired, who else would be? What would happen to employment in the banks? And what would be the pay and incentives? Would the type of limits on salaries being imposed in the banks be applied in NAMA, when the best approach might be to pay big to get the best results?

Much would depend on the quality and integrity of the people appointed to value assets and negotiate discounts with banks, but, as former Central Bank chief economist Michael Casey warned, 'if there is even the slightest taint of cronyism or political interference the entire exercise could end in disaster.' The risk was that however the government decided to price these assets – using accountancy firms, overseas auctioneers or economic consultants – the process was going to be arbitrary, potentially leading to all sorts of rows.

Possibly the best way for the state to deal with this would have been to take the banks into state ownership through nationalization. That way, there would be no need for any cumbersome or expensive messing about with regard to how much the loans were worth, as the state would just be buying from itself. Admittedly, the state would still have to spend billions on recapitalizing the banks, but once that was done those banks would be in a much better position to resume a semblance of normal lending – which, presumably, was the whole point of the exercise.

Just as overpaying for the banks' loans would be a disaster for the state, underpaying would be a disaster for the banks and ultimately for the state too. The property-related loans made up an enormous proportion of the assets at nearly all of the banks. If these were removed from their balance sheets, to be replaced by government bonds worth far less than the book value of the departing loans, the banks were going to face massive losses that could wipe out their capital. The government was warned by a number of sources that a discount set as high as 25 per cent could do that and that it would then have to step in, spending billions to replenish that capital, because otherwise the banks would go bust. Economists Professor Brian Lucey and Constantin Gurdgiev from Trinity College Dublin did estimations based on the state paying between €63 billion and €76.5 billion for the loans, at a discount of between 15 and 30 per cent. With the total capital of Irish banks standing at €35 billion, their worst-case scenario of a €27 billion discount suggested that the banking system would be massively undercapitalized and that the government would have an enormous gap to fill. But the government would have no choice but to fill it because it could not allow the banks to go bust – should the infamous 30 September guarantee be exercised, the country could be bankrupted.

But there was another twist: if the government supplied too much capital, it would end up fully owning the banks. It had set its face against total nationalization of the banks, whereby they would be fully owned by the taxpayer and under the control of officials nominated by the government, although it conceded that majority ownership was something it would undertake if necessary.

There were a number of reasons for that. Surprisingly, given what has happened at privately owned banks this decade, many respected international studies suggest that banks perform even worse when in state ownership. The potential for corruption is enormous, the type of lending advanced is overly conservative, and losses are as likely as profits. The fear was that banks would operate according to political exigencies, with decisions taken to curry favour with the overall electorate – such as releasing people on fixed interest rates from their loans without penalty – or on the basis of who you knew or supported politically.

It was all spelled out by Dermot Desmond in April when he told a gathering at the National College of Ireland that nationalizing the banks would leave the economy in 'dire straits for several decades' and open to 'political interference, skulduggery and cronyism'.

In addition, the government did not want to extinguish the hopes of shareholders – be they individuals who had put their savings into bank shares, pension funds or other investors – that at least some of the wreckage would be salvaged to their eventual benefit.

There was another very important reason for not going down the nationalization route: the European Central Bank had indicated informally that it didn't want full nationalization and the government was not going to do anything more to risk the ECB's wrath. Indeed, the ECB knew that Irish banks were going to use the government-backed bonds issued to them by NAMA as the security for their raising of fresh funds for new lending.

The other practical problem cited by government was the claim that government borrowing would become more expensive if the banks were

to be included on the state balance sheet – a requirement of full ownership – dramatically increasing the size of the national debt. Critics said
this was the de facto position anyway because of the bank guarantee.

Few were convinced that NAMA covered the angles as thoroughly as
the government wanted. In mid-April twenty academic economists from
a range of universities put their names to a piece for the *Irish Times* in
which they said it was impossible to simultaneously '(a) purchase the bad
loans at a discount reflecting their true market value; (b) keep the banks
well or adequately capitalized; and (c) keep them out of state ownership.

'These three outcomes are simply mutually incompatible, and we are
greatly concerned that the NAMA process may operate to maintain the
appearance that all three objectives have been achieved by failing to
meet the first requirement,' they said. They argued that a situation where
'a dripfeed of recapitalization is required would be the worst of all
possible outcomes'. 'We believe that the correct action to take now is
nationalization of the banking system, or at least that part of it that is
of systemic importance.' They suggested that once the banks had been
'cleaned up, recapitalized, reorganized with new managerial structures
and potentially rebranded', the banks could be sold back to the private
sector. 'We consider that nationalization will better protect taxpayers'
interests, produce a more efficient and longer-lasting solution to our
banking problems, be more transparent in relation to pricing of distressed assets, and be far more likely to produce a banking system free
from the toxic reputation that our current financial institutions have
deservedly earned,' they argued.

'A government that needs to be seen to purchase the bad assets at a
reasonable discount and that does not want to take too high an ownership share may end up skimping on the size of the recapitalization
programme. Thus, rather than create fully healthy banks capable of
functioning without help from the state, this process may continue
to leave us with zombie banks that still require the state-sponsored
life-support machine that is the liability guarantee.'

They admitted that nationalization would not change the underlying
loan losses on the bank balance sheets. 'However, what it does change
is who owns the equity and also who has first claim on any increase in
value in the new banks after they have been recapitalized,' they said.

What the academics did not address was who would perform the management functions, given the failure of the state, in the form of the Financial Regulator and Central Bank in their oversight capacity, to take effective measures to prevent the crash.

After this engagement by the academic economists in April, May saw an extraordinary event: the appearance by Michael Somers, the head of the National Treasury Management Agency, at the Dáil's Public Accounts Committee, and his decidedly less-than-ringing endorsement for the new agency.

Somers is one of the country's most powerful public servants, a fact reflected in a confidential salary believed to amount to at least €1 million annually. He had been in charge of the NTMA since its establishment in 1990 and was regarded as having done an excellent job in helping to reduce the national debt dramatically through clever use of the new funds available to him and smart manipulation of the existing debts. So impressed had the politicians been with the performance of the NTMA that it gave it the National Pension Reserve Fund, the State Claims Agency Fund and the National Development Finance Agency to run too, on a staff of just 170 people.

Now, however, as retirement approached, Somers was in charge of the difficult task of borrowing about €60 million each day to keep the country's economy afloat. 'It does say something about the state of public administration in the country that the NTMA, which was set up originally as a boutique specifically to deal with national debt, had become involved in a range of activities. We are trying to keep the whole thing on the road and this is becoming increasingly challenging, particularly in the present environment, where we are in a disaster scene the likes of which we have never seen before,' Somers told the committee.

Bad enough as that was, the NTMA was now to have a role in running NAMA. 'I do not know whether NAMA will be a function of the NTMA or whether it will have a separate board and we will just carry out the management. I do not know what NAMA is going to be,' he said. 'I know very little apart from what has appeared in the newspapers.'

Asked if the NTMA had clear directions from the minister on what was to be done, Somers replied simply, 'No.' He said he had not made any arrangements because he did not have a clear brief. Asked about the appointment of one of his staff, Brendan McDonagh, as interim managing director, he said, 'I was asked whether I had any objection and I said no.'

Somers said that the NTMA didn't have the staff or experience to deal with either the operation of NAMA or the bank restructuring. Somers created the impression that the NTMA was not deeply involved in the creation of NAMA, although the involvement of McDonagh suggested that it was and that Somers, the country's highest-paid public servant, was not being given the prominent role that a man of his talent and experience might have expected, had he wanted it.

Somers also failed to provide Peter Bacon, the consultant credited with developing the idea of NAMA, with a ringing endorsement. 'We hired him into the NTMA on the direction of the Minister for Finance. He was brought in as a special adviser working directly to the minister. He was not preparing this report for us. I am not trying to wash my hands of this but it is well to know where we stand on this issue.' He said he had been instructed by government to use the advisory services of the global financial services company Merrill Lynch, which cost €6 million. 'We do not feel comfortable about paying €6 million to these people but we were asked to get the advice and this is unfortunately what it will cost.'

Somers was also worried about the potential for legal challenges to the transfer of assets. 'I see great potential for arguments down the courts if we don't get this right,' he said. 'The implications of this are enormous and the legislation will be very complex.' He said he was 'aghast' at the scale of the development loans advanced to a small number of borrowers and called it 'a huge eye opener for us'.

The type of plain-speaking that he displayed in front of the Dáil's Public Accounts Committee was of the kind we sadly lacked during the boom years, although the government may not have been too happy to have it coming from one of its top civil servants. When the committee expressed concerns about the ability of the Department of Finance, Somers said, 'I do not want to drop Mr Doyle into it, and I would prefer not to comment.'

These criticisms from the economists and Somers stung the government into response. Lenihan did a number of radio interviews, and Alan Ahearne, the NUI Galway economist who had established his reputation by being one of the first economists to predict the bursting of the property bubble, and who had been seconded to join Lenihan as an adviser in February 2009, defended NAMA in the *Irish Times*.

He rebutted claims that NAMA would add greatly to the country's national debt because of the issue of new bonds. He argued that while this would add greatly to one side of the country's balance sheet, it would be matched on the other side by the value of the loans that the state was taking from the banks. That assumed, of course, that the two matched: that the price NAMA was paying for the loans matched their actual value – which threatened to be an assumption of heroic proportions.

Ahearne argued that the evidence from property busts in other countries showed that the longer that bankers and developers were allowed to avoid the reality of their situations, the bigger the ultimate cost to the taxpayer and economy became. 'Decisions about which development projects are viable and which are not should be made in the taxpayers' interests, not in the interests of developers and bankers. After all, additional funds will be required to bring viable development projects to completion. Troubled developers should not be allowed to use taxpayers' funds to gamble for resurrection,' posited Ahearne.

It was not going to be his job to make it work, however. Brendan McDonagh, a 41-year-old career civil servant, emerged as one of the most powerful men in the country when he was nominated as NAMA's chief executive. The Kerryman had been among a small group of key advisers to Lenihan in previous months, along with John Corrigan, the man who oversees the National Pension Reserve Fund within the NTMA, and had been given a role in negotiations with the banks over assessing the size of their debts. McDonagh's job in the NTMA had been to establish risk limits for its investments, as well as assessing its spread of investments and measuring its performance. He provided financial back-up to all NTMA operations and was responsible for all IT projects. Some asked if this provided relevant experience, but the advantage of appointing McDonagh was that he had no conflicts of interest with the domestic banking or property sectors. What he did have, however, was experience of dealing with the banks post-guarantee.

Time will tell if NAMA is the right idea – but something had to be done. The banks had to start lending money again. Despite their claims to be doing so, nobody believed them. They were unable to get as much money as they needed on international interbank markets, because fears remained that they would not be able to repay.

'The key issue for the economy and for Ireland is that we have to force the banks to take the losses now because if they intend to trade their way through this recession it will inflict further damage on the economy,' Lenihan insisted. 'Without a viable banking sector we will not have a viable economy.'

Paradoxically, although the credit crisis and capital shortage meant that banks had never been any weaker, they may never have had as much power over their customers – or ever have used it more ruthlessly. The economic disaster of 2008/9 was made worse by the lack of available finance to businesses already suffering from declining sales, adverse currency movements and higher taxes. While the banks may not have been repossessing homes – and claiming to be responsible citizens on that basis – they were, however, failing to make finance available for investment by businesses and sole traders. Worse, they were making it very difficult for many customers to get even small sums of money to use as working capital for the normal day-to-day running of operations.

There was some understanding, if not sympathy, for the position of the banks. Having been pilloried for excessive borrowing and lending over the years, and being in possession of many loans on which they were not receiving payment – from beyond the property sector too – the incentive to rein in was obvious.

This created an appalling vista for the government. Even if the banks offloaded their toxic property assets on to NAMA and received fresh capital, there was no guarantee they'd improve their attitude towards lending to business and consumers. In an era of falling prices and reduced demand, such lending might not make much sense. It was another argument for the government to exercise its power by nationalizing the banks, but it waited instead.

40

The view from abroad

Just because Charlie McCreevy may have sounded paranoid didn't mean that what he said wasn't true. When McCreevy addressed the annual dinner of the Association of Higher Civil and Public Servants in March 2009, he alleged that Ireland was the victim of a deliberate campaign by the British media designed to damage the standing of the country. 'There is nothing very new about this,' he charged. 'These campaigns used to be designed to titillate readers of their tabloid press. But their wider press has now joined the fray. We all know that at some vulnerable moments in our history, our immediate neighbours have tried to take us out. Let's make sure they never will.'

There was some evidence to support McCreevy's contention – just as there was plenty of evidence to justify some of the apparently damaging claims being made by British newspapers, publications further afield that McCreevy didn't name, the foreign broadcast media and, of course, on the internet.

One of the most irritating jokes, one that found its way on to BBC 2's influential *Newsnight* programme on a night Brian Lenihan was being interviewed in January 2009, went like this: What's the difference between Ireland and Iceland? The answer: One letter and six months. The implication was that we were the next sovereign state to go bust and presumably our government would fall too after riots on the streets.

Lenihan put up a valiant display in denying the extent of this country's problems as detailed by *Newsnight*'s short report – which exaggerated the extent of our unemployment, for example, and also included several other factual errors. The BBC was not alone in comparing us to Iceland. The *Economist* scornfully referred to 'Reykjavik-on-Liffey', conveniently ignoring that the *New York Times* had first coined the phrase 'Reykjavik-on-Thames' to describe London.

Ireland was not a 'glorified hedge fund', as Lenihan pointed out to the BBC, which is what Iceland effectively became: a country that borrowed on a massive scale to make bets on business investments throughout Europe. While we were culpable in that regard, the scale of our indulgence was nothing like that of that other little island in the Atlantic.

However, Lenihan somewhat undermined his argument by describing the Irish economy as 'vibrant'. With domestic retail sales contracting, unemployment soaring, tax revenues collapsing and overall confidence shot to pieces, Lenihan's choice of adjective rang somewhat hollow.

The influential Lex opinion column in the *Financial Times* lumped us into a group called the PIGS, pointing out how this country's debt ratings – along with those of Portugal, Greece and Spain, the other members of this group with the offensive acronym – had suffered from downgrading by international credit agencies. There was a time when Italy would have taken Ireland's place among the PIGS.

The first thread running through British coverage of Irish woes was *Schadenfreude* – a sense of enjoyment from our misfortune. There had been an undercurrent of resentment in some British circles at the Irish getting above their perceived station. One article on Irish people getting high-profile jobs in the UK (former Aer Lingus boss Willie Walsh heading up British Airways; John Fingleton taking charge of the Office of Fair Trading after his stint running Ireland's Competition Authority) referred to them as 'Micks on the Make'. Some of this might have been a reaction to the extraordinary prices paid by many Irish individuals and consortia in buying land and commercial properties in London and other parts of Britain. Their actions could be said to have contributed to the inflation of the asset bubble in Britain, and its bursting had affected all. But, put simply, some British people did not like the Irish turning into the new Arabs through their purchase of traditional London addresses. This element believed that the jumped-up Paddies were a bunch of free-spending self-indulgent fools who didn't know how to handle their new-found wealth. Early in 2009 the left-leaning *New Statesman* magazine claimed 'a cocksure and hedonistic generation is getting a small taste of the hardship and anxiety its ancestors endured'.

The *Mail on Sunday* wrote of how Ireland 'transformed itself from a priest-dominated, sclerotic, agrarian economy to a place where some of the most powerful companies in the world chose to make their headquarters', before predictably calling our continued future as an independent state into question. Having to claim the latter would no doubt have hurt the newspaper, given that its owner had lost at least €60 million in trying to establish a foothold in the Irish newspaper market – previously it must have considered that this was a good place to invest.

This tendency to cover the fall in our economic fortunes as though it were a chastisement of a people who had got above themselves went beyond the UK. The *New York Times* piece on property developer Seán Dunne is a prime example. And in a piece in *USA Today* in January 2009, entitled 'Ireland Stands United in Hatred of Banker Sean Fitz-Patrick', an unnamed elderly Anglo shareholder was quoted as saying 'the whole place has been founded on a lie.' The same article alleged that FitzPatrick 'now symbolizes the crony capitalism that was an essential, if unacknowledged, aspect of the nation's economic ascent.' It didn't need to say *and subsequent fall*.

A second thread in the coverage of our woes was a deliberate attempt to blame them on our membership of the euro, a tack taken by those in Britain who feared that the outcome of its own financial crisis could be British entry to the euro. Although it seemed most unlikely that the British people would be persuaded to give up sterling, some had started to argue that there would be economic benefits for Britain if it were to join the euro when its currency had a low value. The strong euro-sceptic element of the British media was determined to persuade public opinion that this shouldn't be allowed to happen, and selective interpretation of Ireland's woes was useful in this regard.

They had never liked the fact that the Irish were able to use the strength of the euro to increase their purchasing power in Britain – to splash the cash ostentatiously at the horse racing at Cheltenham. It suited them to push the idea that Ireland would be ejected from the euro – which would leave us perilously close to being another Iceland – or that our financial woes would lead to the currency's implosion. 'So much for the theory that the single currency is going to be a safe haven in these troubled times,' a *Daily Mail* columnist noted gleefully.

The truth was that the euro did provide a massive protection for Ireland, something even those who had initially been worried about our membership had to admit. There had been a scandalous lack of political and public debate about Ireland's entry to the euro in the first place – with the elite insisting that it was unquestionably a 'good thing' and wilfully ignoring the many disadvantages it could bring us. One of the big lies, repeated consistently by politicians of almost all hues prior to our agreeing to join the euro, was that sterling's entry to the currency was inevitable and that therefore we had no need to worry about currency fluctuations with our main trading partner. We were also told that if Britain didn't join – for political reasons about sovereignty – it wouldn't really matter because sterling would become a satellite currency, effectively tracking the movements of the euro and varying from it only by very small amounts. This was shown to be totally wrong during 2008 and 2009, when sterling fell in value against the euro by over 25 per cent, decimating profit margins for exporters to Britain and leading to the shopping exodus over the border.

The other big selling point from the elite was that the euro would bring us permanently lower interest rates and that this would always be a good thing. Former Taoiseach John Bruton – now EU Ambassador to Washington – was a particularly strong proponent of that line, saying that Irish business would be able to expand greatly with access to a larger pool of cheaper money. Unfortunately, for the best part of a decade interest rates were too low for us and access to cheap money was the major driver in the pump-priming of the property bubble; this signally failed to facilitate an appropriate increase in productive investment.

Added to that was the failure of successive Fianna Fáil-led governments to introduce appropriate budgetary policies to counter the boom cycle and prepare for the inevitable fall – a key requisite of economic planning for a country that had lost control over its monetary policy and that saw interest rates being set according to the needs of the much larger continental Europe. Our problem was not the euro per se; it was how we had handled it.

Yet by the time our economy imploded we were lucky to be part of the euro. The paradox is that while membership of the euro wounded our economy badly, it also stopped it from nearly being destroyed. While the strength of the euro was an additional problem for our hopes of a return to export-led growth, the currency also provided a protection against what would have happened – a run on the pound and sky-high interest rates – if we hadn't been part of it. The euro provided a protection for our banks, which would otherwise have faced a run by dollar and sterling bond-holders.

Even if we hadn't been part of the euro, we may very well have gone mad anyway: being outside of the single currency didn't prevent economic insanity taking hold of Iceland and Britain.

Another advantage of our membership of the Economic and Monetary Union was that it made it more likely that we would be bailed out of our difficulties by the European Central Bank (although those who voted 'no' to the Lisbon Treaty would have to swallow their pride in return). Indeed, much of the money deposited in our banks during 2009 came from the ECB, and the bonds issued by NAMA would also be used by the banks as collateral to raise further money from the ECB.

Lenihan used the 2009 St Patrick's Day holiday – and the unique marketing opportunity it affords Ireland each year – to launch another offensive to protect Ireland's name abroad. Brian Lenihan told German newspaper *Handelsblatt* that 'the downright obsessive view here in London that Ireland is like Iceland is simply bizarre. Some of this can be explained by the English media, who are sceptical, for the most part, about the euro.' Interestingly, he emphasized that the bank guarantee was effectively endorsed by the ECB, saying that it guaranteed the stability of the entire Irish banking system and the solvency and liquidity of it.

However, Lenihan found it very hard to move foreign opinion. On 25 March 2009, just a week after the minister and a delegation had love-bombed the *Financial Times*, its Lex column opined that 'Ireland is running out of options as fast as its coffers run dry.' A damning piece concluded that 'investors in Irish debt are exacting a fat penalty for Dublin's poor grip on its boom-bust economy.' After April's supplementary budget, which put the emphasis on tax increases, the *FT* opined that Ireland had little chance of reviving its export-led economy and predicted a return to mass emigration, with the loss of our best chance of recovery. A furious Lenihan lashed out at 'the unnamed scribes in Lex who hide their identity' when I spoke to him afterwards about this.

Wisely, Lenihan remained quiet when the highly respected Nobel Prize-winning economist Paul Krugman turned his attention to Ireland in April 2009, with a column entitled 'Erin Go Broke'. Krugman offered a succinct and accurate assessment of what had gone wrong in the Irish economy, with particular emphasis on our property bubble – describing Ireland as Florida without the sun and snakes – and on the dangers involved in the government's approach of raising taxes by more than it cut in spending. Minister for Trade, Enterprise and Employment Mary Coughlan, much criticized for her performance in a job for which she had very little relevant experience before Cowen appointed her, made the mistake of criticizing Krugman when asked to comment by the *Irish Times* a few days later during her visit to Washington. 'There has been comment which has been neither helpful nor, in my view, appropriate, and I would like to move on from that and give the view that we collectively as a government have, yes, difficult times, but we have the capacity to deal with these issues and we would like to revert back to the international reputation we had and continue to have,' she told the newspaper.

The policy of denial extended to trying to muzzle domestic commentators who expressed honest opinion to foreign newspapers. A Department of Finance official contacted the investment company Friends First to complain about comments made by its economist Jim Power to the *Financial Times*. Politicians and businessmen alleged that those who spoke critically about Ireland to the foreign media were somehow anti-patriotic. The problem, however, much as we might not have liked it, was that there was substance to what was written and said. Indeed, if instead of just reacting to it we had considered it, it might have helped the country.

For example, the *FT* focused on our loss of competitiveness, about which there has not been nearly enough debate in Ireland. The newspaper reinforced something that many in Ireland had been saying for years – to be shouted down as unpatriotic by politicians, trade unions, business leaders, banks and their economic cheerleaders: that the low cost of money not only unleashed the credit boom and the surge in asset prices to unrealistic prices, but also contributed to a surge in wage rates. Higher wages were needed by people to afford the rising price of property, even with lower costs in borrowing. The productive sector and the public sector paid up, all to give people more money to pay to the property developers and property sellers.

Since 2000 Ireland's relative wage costs rose by 20 percentage points against Germany's, whereas Greece's, for example, went up by just

5 per cent. 'Export performance has been further hurt by the weakening currencies of two of its major trading partners, the US and the UK,' the *FT* noted. 'The quick solution would be for Ireland to devalue too. As a euro member, it cannot.'

All of this mattered. An international portrayal of Ireland as an economic basket case – and the consistent reinforcement of that perception – was powerful in its potential to undermine confidence in Ireland as a location for foreign direct investment (FDI). It gave competitors for FDI a stick with which to beat us. It also affected the state's ability to repay its rapidly growing borrowings, driving the price of our exchequer borrowing upwards, as well as making it harder to get.

The power of the press is real, and in the internet era what's written in the newspapers cannot be merely dismissed as tomorrow's fish-and-chips paper. Such material moves quickly and widely online and it is sticky. It has a sense of permanence because archives are accessible through Google and other resources. Talking heads on specialist television business channels and newswires spoke about our supposed inability to meet our national debts and save our banking system; their credibility rarely mattered, as long as they could provide an ear-catching and authoritative sound-bite. It may have been 'soft power', in that it merely influenced opinion, but it was power none the less.

After all the negative coverage in late 2008 and into 2009, just about the only positive acknowledgement of Ireland as a changed country – mainly because of foreign direct investment – came, appropriately enough, on St Patrick's Day, in a special episode of the massively popular American animated comedy *The Simpsons*. It showed Homer and his father on a visit to Ireland, bemoaning the fact that all of the pubs were empty – because everybody was too busy working to fulfil the traditional Irish stereotype. We were treated to images of American multinational factories – with names such as Hewlett Fitzpackard and Mickrosoft – dotting the countryside.

It so happens that this depiction of a nation that was too hard-working and technologically advanced to have anything to do with cheesy old stereotypes was more a matter of timing than of anything else. When I interviewed executive producer Al Jean about the special episode – and why it showed such a positive image of Ireland at a time when our unemployment was soaring – he told me that it had taken a year to make. It had been scripted when the boom was still apparently under way; had it been made a year later, it would have been different. Sadly, *The Simpsons* is unlikely to influence the international investment community.

41

Doing the right thing to impress the global financial community

The 'supplementary' budget of April 2009 was a shocker to almost everyone in Ireland. It delivered savage tax increases, to raise an additional €1.8 billion in revenue, and great cuts in public spending – amounting to €1.5 billion. More misery was promised in December 2009 and in the budgets that were to follow.

These were extraordinary measures for a government to take just two months before local and European elections, but they indicated the depth of the financial crisis. They also showed how power over decision-making in Ireland had shifted to the international money markets, to the European Commission in Brussels and to the European Central Bank in Frankfurt. The government had been forced to make the budgetary changes: while it had succeeded in getting permission from the commission to lift exchequer borrowing to 10.75 per cent of national output, as against a limit of just 3 per cent, the only way to achieve this target would be by cutting spending and hiking taxes. The sole discretion allowed the government was the decision as to what it would prioritize. As if it didn't already have enough bad news to deliver, it also had to outline its plans to rescue the Irish banks if it was to regain a modicum of international confidence.

There were sound financial reasons for regaining that confidence. By April slumping tax revenues dictated that Ireland was going to have to borrow about €25 billion for 2009, just to meet the government's bills. This was going to happen every year, if tax revenues did not increase and spending was not cut. Getting this money was no longer cheap or easy. 'Capital markets are not driven by sentiment but by fundamentals. It doesn't matter why they like the Irish or not, it's a matter of getting money back with a return,' Charlie McCreevy had warned just a few weeks earlier, in the same speech in which he lashed out at the British media. Michael Somers, head of the National Treasury Management Agency, the body charged with borrowing on behalf of the state on the best terms possible, now paid 1.5 per cent more for our borrowed money than Germany did, even though as part of the same economic union we'd previously paid only a whisker more.

Economist Peter Bacon, the man who had come up with the plan for NAMA, also warned that deposits were flowing out of Irish banks, despite the state guarantee. The foreign financial markets dismissed Ireland's chances of escaping a rout. Comparisons with Iceland became common again.

In particular, the government worried about the comments by the international ratings agencies, to which investors look for advice as to the likelihood of being repaid by countries seeking to raise finance through borrowings. The likes of Moody's, Standard & Poor and Fitch have enormous soft power as a result. While their judgements are often far from perfect – as their failure to appreciate the risk of subprime lending to the stability of international banks graphically illustrated – those who invest in financial markets continue to regard them as informed. There was uproar in April 2009 when comments by an S&P analyst in a radio interview were interpreted as an attack on the government's policies and as a call to change its personnel. Even the Labour Party, to the forefront in criticizing the government, got patriotic and told S&P to butt out of internal sovereign affairs. The same analyst swiftly backed down, but it didn't go unnoticed that many of these ratings firms felt comfortable assessing the political and managerial competence of a country as part of their judgement on its financial standing.

While the method chosen to fill part of the exchequer deficit – concentrating more on increasing taxes – was motivated by domestic political judgements as to what the electorate would find less unpalatable, the ratings agencies were unimpressed by the decision to go for tax increases rather than public-spending expenditure cuts. Moody's warned about 'the severe economic adjustment taking place in Ireland, which threatens to undermine the country's low-tax, financial services-driven economic model'. It was much the same type of criticism that Krugman had offered.

The government's exchequer position was one thing; our exposure to the banks another. Moody's downgraded the credit ratings of twelve

Irish banks after NAMA was announced, citing concerns over their exposure to residential property and commercial loans. The creation of NAMA – and its announcement months before it could ever be implemented – was designed to allay market fears as much as anything else. It didn't succeed because suddenly the market feared that the losses would be far higher than previously anticipated. Moody's concluded the state would emerge from the crisis with relatively weak growth prospects and a much higher debt burden, although it waited to follow its counterparts in downgrading the country's top-notch status as a borrower.

The bogeyman of the International Monetary Fund (IMF) first raised its head in January 2009; it hadn't threatened to run our finances for us since the late 1980s. The IMF is the lender of last resort, the place where a country goes for money when it can't get it anywhere else. The price extracted for this money is huge: high interest rates must be repaid on top of the capital, and numerous things must be done, under instruction from the IMF, to make sure that the flow of repayments is consistent. The state would be forced to cut its costs dramatically, which would mean a savage reduction in public spending. The government would be made to sack tens of thousands of public servants and reduce pay, whether it wanted to do so or not. Change would not be negotiated with the unions; it would just happen. We would lose the remaining control that we have over our own economy and how we spend money within it.

The spectre of the IMF was raised almost by accident, because of comments a union leader made, but it may have done the government or public little enough harm to face up to the possibility. Taoiseach Brian Cowen had to react immediately to dismiss the likelihood of this as extremely low and nowhere near imminent, and moreover had to do so from a press conference in Japan, where he was on a trade mission. However, the doomsday scenario was not impossible to envisage. The combination of the bank guarantee, the cost of taking control of the banks and the widening public sector deficit illustrated that starkly, particularly as the economy had entered into a further tail-spin.

The likelihood of having to go to the IMF was considered remote, if only because the European Union, and specifically the European Central Bank, would intervene first, to protect the euro. However, just like the IMF, the price extracted for such support would be huge. Merely ratifying the Lisbon Treaty meekly by way of a 'yes' vote in a second constitutional referendum, following the 2008 rejection, would not be enough. The terms demanded could be along IMF lines. Our much coveted corporation tax rate of 12.5 per cent, correctly regarded as highly important to attracting inward investment, would be under threat, regardless of its importance to aiding economic recovery: much of the rest of Europe saw it as Ireland taking an unfair advantage and it could be imposed as a form of punishment.

Europe was good to us during the crisis, however, despite its anger at the initial rejection of the Lisbon Treaty, the unilateral decision to implement the bank guarantee and the favouring of tax increases over spending cuts to raise money. In February, Jean-Claude Trichet, the president of the ECB, declared that 'Ireland is certainly not the weakest link of the euro area.' He continued: 'there is no weak link. The euro area is a very intertwined, single-market economy with a single currency. Speaking of any particular country in the euro area as a weak link is an error of judgement.'

While it was nice to hear, it did not fully reflect the reality of the Irish situation: our dependence on trade with the sterling and dollar areas was greater than that of any other country in the euro. The statement was phrased so as not to undermine Ireland any further.

Almost out of sight, the ECB was engaged in practical and important measures to save us. It was providing our banks, via a circuitous route, with the money they needed to keep going. About one third of the bonds issued by the Irish government during the first five months of 2009 were purchased not by international investors but by the cash-strapped Irish banks. The Irish banks then used these bonds as collateral for borrowing from the ECB. This added to the hope that the ECB would be favourably, if quietly, disposed towards Irish banks doing the same with the bonds they were due to receive from NAMA. The ECB was acting as the lender of last resort – and for that we had reason to be truly grateful, because if it hadn't the consequences would have been appalling.

Europe was none the less angry with us, particularly the careful Germans, who had given and lent us so much money and watched us waste it. In September 2007, even before the crash, it emerged that German Ambassador to Ireland Christian Pauls had cut loose at a meeting of visiting German industrialists and pulled no punches in criticizing the excess he felt was endemic in the country, particularly our way of spending our new-found money. Pauls focused on how Irish junior ministers were paid more than the German Chancellor and how hospital consultants had refused a new salary offer of €200,000 per annum as 'Mickey Mouse money', even though the health system was 'chaotic'. He made unfavourable references to property prices and the rush to buy new cars, contrasting this with the Germans' habit of driving their cars until they were eight or nine years old before changing them. He said the question being posed in Ireland was whether the new prosperity had made Irish society a 'rougher, less caring one'.

He said that 'very many Germans, including politicians and high-ranking civil servants, believe that it was EU money, including a large portion contributed by the German taxpayer, which was responsible for the Irish success story.' He went on to say that this was 'rubbish' and that '95 per cent of the success was owed to the work of the Irish people', but some interpreted this as simply politeness on his part.

Instead of taking the criticism on the chin and doing something about addressing the issues he raised, the Irish government complained to Germany about their ambassador's breach of protocol, publicly reprimanding him for the comments, which it said were 'inaccurate, misinformed and inappropriate'. But a surprisingly large number of Irish people wrote letters to the Irish media in support of Pauls.

Pauls returned to the fray in 2009 when comments he made at an event in Kerry were reported days later in local newspapers and then found their way into the national media. This time he spoke about the Lisbon Treaty referendum rejection of 2008 and the anticipated re-run of the vote: 'A second "no" vote would have horrific consequences for Ireland and the Irish, and I am not the first to say it,' adding that Ireland would 'throw away its future' if it repeated its first decision. Pauls said that in the run-up to the first referendum on the Lisbon Treaty, foreign diplomats based in Ireland had 'stayed quiet' because they did not want to be perceived as interfering. 'We are in a different stage in the ball game now . . . Everybody seems to be forgetting that this is a family issue involving twenty-seven family members. I find the prospect of a second "no" frightening and I am going to continue making that case.'

He said Ireland could not have an à la carte approach to Europe and simply pick and choose what it liked. He reportedly made pointed references to those who 'complain about other nations fishing in their waters . . . and forget who pays their milk subsidies'. Asked subsequently if his views were undiplomatic, he replied: 'They are not. I am simply conveying what my government thinks. That is my job.'

If anyone harboured the hope that Pauls did not reflect the official German position, Michael Somers of the NTMA demolished that in his contribution to the Oireachtas Public Accounts Committee in May when he declared he had 'taken a lot of flak' from German investors following the rejection of the Lisbon Treaty. 'Fritz and Günther and Heinz want their money back,' he said.

The supplementary budget was also aimed to reassure the multinational corporate sector, particularly those from the United States. Ireland has been one of the biggest beneficiaries of globalization and the movement of capital, for all the hand-wringing that's heard about it from the left. Our country was the largest recipient of foreign direct investment (FDI) in the OECD in the period from 1993 to 2003, recording a balance of inflows over outflows of €48.5 billion. The International Financial Services Centre played a major part in achieving that. Foreign multinationals employed over 100,000 people directly and were indirectly responsible for around another 200,000 jobs in the smaller Irish firms that supplied them. FDI accounted for €2 billion in productive investment in Ireland during 2008, with 130 project announcements, three quarters of which were from American firms.

US investment in Ireland alone exceeded €87 billion. No wonder 'neutral' Ireland – or at least Bertie Ahern's government – was so willing to make Shannon Airport available to the US military as a transportation point during the Gulf War. Not only was the airport most grateful for the paying business, but it was pragmatism writ large: keeping American interests in Ireland happy.

It wasn't enough to keep all of the Dell manufacturing operations in Limerick open, however, as 1,900 jobs were lost at the start of 2009 in one of the most symbolic examples of the economic crisis. Dell found it cheaper to open a replacement facility in Poland and the government seemed oblivious to the threat, although it was spoken about widely in Limerick for up to two years beforehand. It may have been that the government felt powerless to stop the rise in labour costs, possibly because of the Faustian pact entered into with the trade unions. But when Dell went, it raised fears as to who else might follow.

The episode suggested that the American Chamber of Commerce

should be considered as one of the most powerful economic groups in Ireland, and whatever economic policies are formulated by this state should be based upon attracting and keeping investment from the United States. After all, Irish subsidiaries of multinationals were competing against subsidiaries in other countries for investment from their global parent. That had made cost competitiveness a crucial issue. Almost as fast as property prices rose, Irish labour costs increased – because workers needed increased incomes to help pay for more expensive property. We fooled ourselves with jargon such as 'going up the value-added chain', which was just a way of pretending that we had skills commensurate with more expensive remuneration. We made ourselves uncompetitive.

Multinationals looked for reduced costs and higher productivity and, in most cases, got it from people happy to have jobs. They were not pleased to find their workers hit with savagely higher taxes, especially when the public sector was not reducing its numbers or its pay rates, making jobs in that sector more valuable. The average salary in the multinational sector, according to the last available statistics, was €45,000, which was €4,000 lower than the public sector average. The latter also had guaranteed pensions, even if they complained bitterly about an increased contribution towards these as introduced by the government in early 2009. There were also major differences in flexibility of work practices.

The main attraction for FDI remained our low corporation tax rate of 12.5 per cent, and this infuriated the British government as much as its media (the *Guardian* ran a week-long series on the issue) because of its own 30 per cent rate. In April 2009 the *Sunday Times* discovered that all of the advertising revenue generated by Google in the UK was taxed in Ireland, where Google had headquarters. It estimated that Google's £1.25 billion in revenues in Britain during 2007 led to a corporation tax payment of just £600,000. It was estimated that by clever accounting, and the use of Ireland as its European hub, Google had legally avoided paying over £100 million in taxes in Britain. Allowing major British firms to headquarter here for tax reasons – availing of our corporate tax rate – was not necessarily a clever move, because it was regarded as unfriendly tax competition.

It was a concern for the American tax authorities too. In 2005 the *Wall Street Journal* discovered the existence of an Irish-registered company called Round Island One. It turned out to have more than $16 billion in assets, to have earned $9 billion in profits and to have been able to save its parent more than $500 million in annual taxes. It was owned by Microsoft.

Both Google and Microsoft are massive employers in Ireland. Indeed, Google provided one of the rare bits of good news in 2008 by substantially increasing the size of its operations in this country. These companies provide well-paid jobs, usually to graduates. Ireland likes to think of itself as providing a highly educated English language workforce (which it does, although standards are slipping), and of having excellent infrastructure, though this is not true of its broadband communications and road transport. Ireland also has access to the euro zone, which is very important. But it shouldn't fool itself as to the real reason why these foreigners are here: to reduce the tax they pay on European profits. And at the IFSC, light-touch regulation was the major attraction.

The government pointed out that the highly regarded OECD has never called Ireland a tax haven. The benefits to the state from having these companies here were obvious. Those that came to Ireland to cut their global tax bills may have paid a very small proportion of their tax in this country, but it was better than nothing at all. In addition, they created jobs that provided good incomes for people who didn't have to emigrate and they provided payroll taxes for the government too.

The Irish government was terrified by the possibility that Barack Obama's new administration would live up to its pre-election promise to crack down on American multinationals that deliberately reduced their domestic profits through the use of foreign subsidiaries in order to avoid tax. It was therefore no surprise that Brian Cowen's government placed such store on his meeting with the US President on St Patrick's Day – and was pleased that it seemed to go so well.

However, early in May President Obama announced his intention to crack down on American companies that were avoiding the payment of their fair share domestically – and he named Ireland as one of three major locations for American companies engaged in practices, albeit lawful ones, that aroused his displeasure (the Netherlands and Bermuda were the other two). These countries accounted for nearly one third of all foreign profits reported by the foreign subsidiaries of US multinationals. After lobbying by the Dutch – who were left by the Irish to do it on their own – the names of the three countries were removed from the official statements, but the implication was clear: we were being targeted. Obama also promised a crackdown on the system known as 'deferral', whereby foreign profits made by US companies are taxed in the US only once they have been repatriated. Any changes to the tax laws are not due until 2011. They have to gain the approval of Congress, and already some Democrats, who are in the majority, have joined with the Republicans in expressing concern. The Irish government and officials will lobby in Washington and watch anxiously. There have been a few good omens: some US companies have opted to move from Bermuda to Ireland, with the giant consulting firm Accenture the most prominent of a number of such companies. Irish politicians and officials have claimed that the threat has been exaggerated, but that could be another example of donning the green jersey. The experience of recent years suggests that any complacency would be most unwise.

42

The end of the affair

Social partnership was like a good marriage turned bad: the end had become inevitable, but when it came, it was still a shock, to one of the parties at least, and a cause of considerable regret to both.

The Irish Congress of Trade Unions had become so used to getting most of what it wanted from government – even if it occasionally had to throw a strop to get it – that it hadn't seen the blow coming. It was 1.30 a.m. on the morning of 3 February 2009. The parties discussed their differences before the government tabled its proposal: it wouldn't cut the pay of public sector workers but they would be expected to make a much greater contribution towards their guaranteed pensions. This had been signalled through deliberate media leaks in previous weeks but it was the extent of the cut that floored the trade unions.

Dermot McCarthy, the secretary general to the government and the Department of An Taoiseach, and a constant presence at these talks for over a decade, delivered the news that a pension levy would be imposed on the country's 380,000 public and civil servants, at an average of 7.5 per cent of pay. The unions had not expected the extent of the change; nor had it been very well explained, because it didn't emerge until later that tax relief would reduce the effective level of the hit to an average of about 4 per cent.

Participants in the talks said there was a momentary stony silence before ICTU president David Begg, SIPTU's Jack O'Connor and Impact's Peter McLoone started to ask for explanations. There was an air of finality to the proceedings. Nobody treated this news as a bargaining ploy, an opening gambit that would lead to agreement later on a much smaller sum, if any. The government had already committed itself to telling the Dáil later that day what public sector spending cuts it would implement to deal with a rapidly deteriorating situation in the public finances. There wasn't time for negotiation. This was a dictat. That wasn't the way things were usually done in this marriage. This was a move to end it.

Begg said as much afterwards. 'The government and IBEC [Irish Business and Employers Confederation] have derogated from social partnership. We're the last man standing in this partnership – and it's hard to have a partnership arrangement with yourself,' he said, almost more in sorrow than in anger.

It had been coming, although the unions must have thought that they were still dealing from a position of some strength, given Cowen's weak political position. His vulnerability had delivered them a national pay deal the previous September that nobody had thought was possible.

When talks had broken down in August 2008, Cowen's stock was low, especially as this occurred so soon after the referendum on the Lisbon Treaty. He was now said to be the man who couldn't continue social partnership, the process regarded by many – although more usually by those within the process than by objective observers – as having been central to the economic progress of the previous twenty years. Others outside the process saw it as a lucky break – the pace of the downturn in the economy being obvious to most and the idea of a commitment to pay increases looking crazy.

However, Cowen came back and agreed a new deal that, while it had the benefit of an eleven-month pay freeze in the public sector, committed the government to paying increases thereafter. Incredibly, IBEC agreed to the terms and a mere three-month pay freeze for its members. It did this to the consternation and bafflement of the bulk of its members, and of those who weren't affiliated to IBEC but who feared now that their employees would seek the increase.

Cowen was heavily influenced by McCarthy and also by Joe Lennon, a former Ahern insider who, after spending time with the HSE, was asked by Cowen to return as a special adviser. Although Lennon's experiences at the HSE had made him a little less tolerant of trade union inflexibility, he and McCarthy believed that it would be easier to get other things done if there was agreement on future pay increases, particularly if public sector reform and redundancies were going to have to be part of the agenda. By signing a national deal Cowen wouldn't be the focus of unfavourable comparison with Ahern, who had been regarded as the main glue in the marriage of social partnership, at least for a temporary period.

Although his name had become synonymous with social partnership, it hadn't been Ahern's creation. That honour fell to Charles Haughey. He got the idea from German Chancellor Helmut Schmidt when he was at a European summit in 1982, but he didn't get the chance to introduce it in Ireland until 1987. It was a time when the crisis in the economy was as deep as it is now, with unemployment reaching a sky-high 17 per cent; the only mitigation was the annual emigration of about 1 per cent of our workforce. Tax rates were set at punitive levels to support excessive public spending and evasion was widespread (even by the likes of Haughey, who was, corruptly, in receipt of millions of pounds at the same time as demanding sacrifices from others). Haughey decided to apply a discipline to the public finances that he would signally fail to apply to himself. He wanted to cut public spending but to avoid massive industrial unrest, so he had to provide some guarantees on living standards for workers. The unions and employers agreed, and pay restraint, accompanied by a tougher stance on the public finances, was followed some years later by a progressive reduction in taxes.

In its early years social partnership had undoubted merits. Ahern was central to the process, first as the Minister for Labour who forged a reputation for building consensus at difficult partnership meetings, and later as Minister for Finance.

Social partnership became of even greater political importance during Ahern's time as Taoiseach. Once Ahern gained power in 1997, partnership was elevated to suit Fianna Fáil's needs: public money was used to buy political popularity and to enhance Ahern's standing. McCreevy, for all of his right-wing rhetoric, and indeed actions, was regarded by some trade union leaders as close to Ahern in his level of support for partnership, something that was borne out by the warm tributes he received from union leaders on his exile to Brussels in 2004.

In retrospect, it is easy to see why Fianna Fáil was so keen on the process. Social partnership instilled the false confidence that we were planning our economy properly, whereas we were only dividing the proceeds of the illusory boom according to who, apparently, had the most influence. It was a cosy relationship between government, business and trade unions that meant hard decisions weren't made because tradeoffs and compromises prevailed instead. It was another variation of crony capitalism, but this time the unions were the willing participants.

It provided cover for the tax breaks for the wealthy and all the other pork-barrel projects, because at the same time the public sector – where industrial unrest was far more likely to surface because of the high union membership – was getting regular pay increases and lower income taxes. Nothing was done to ruffle the unions unnecessarily, so, although reform of work practices and staffing numbers was always suggested and promised, it was almost never implemented. The public sector unions suspected they were being played, but as long as they were getting something from the booming economy they were happy enough.

Indeed, they were getting plenty out of it. A process called benchmarking saw to that. The first benchmarking exercise in 2000 – conducted in secrecy and apparently designed to ensure public sector workers did not continue to feel they were being left behind in a booming economy, irrespective of what the evidence would produce – delivered pay increases averaging nearly 9 per cent on top of what they were already getting from the normal pay deals. Senator Joe O'Toole, then prominent in the Irish National Teachers Organization, described it as being akin to a bank's ATM: his members would simply go to a hole in the wall and withdraw cash.

Benchmarking didn't just add €1 billion to the following year's public sector bill as a one-off payment; it was a permanent addition to the wage bill on to which all further increases were added and which provided a new higher level of pay for those entering the system. It also meant bigger pensions for the retired. Over 80,000 additional people were added to the public sector payroll between 2000 and 2008, and the overall pay and pension costs soared from €10 billion to €19 billion, with disastrous consequences when tax revenues plummeted.

One of the big issues benchmarking created for the unions was the need to defend the retention of the people who were added to the public sector pay bill during this time. With the country needing to cut €15 billion from its spending over four years, this was bound to cause considerable strains between government and unions – although the unions' position was helped by the reluctance of the government to increase the size of the dole queues and its own social welfare bill, which was already more than €20 billion.

To the frustration and disappointment of the unions, the second benchmarking exercise – completed in 2008 – delivered only for a very small number of highly specialized employees. Some public sector unions responded by talking of double-digit increases for members to 'compensate' for the 'failure' of the exercise to further reward those with the most secure, pensioned employment in the country.

But that should not have come as a surprise. In December 2008 the ESRI reported that there was a '23.5 per cent public–private sector wage gap in Ireland in 2006, with senior public service workers earning approximately 10 per cent more than their private sector counterparts and those in lower-level grades earning between 24 and 32 per cent more'. Benchmarking did not produce an adjustment of such disparities.

Cowen's government baulked at pressing for reform, notwithstanding the work done investigating spending in the public sector by independent economist Colm McCarthy, a man given charge of rerunning a cost-cutting exercise of twenty years earlier called, colloquially, An Bord Snip. This time around it was dubbed An Bord Snip Nua.

The government's task would have been difficult at the best of times but now that deep cuts were required it became almost impossible politically. In the good times – when there was enough money to pay for it all – it wasn't necessary to seek confrontation. Unions had become used to getting much of what they wanted. The bulk of the extra tax revenue gathered during the boom had gone towards expanding the size of the public sector and rewarding those who worked in it; there was no reform in the provision of public services that added greatly to the cost burden of the productive sector. It was near impossible to change that culture now.

The government did not want to provoke strikes by public sector workers who controlled utilities, such as the ESB, and vital public services such as teaching and medical care. This gave the trade unions real bargaining power. Some attempted to use this power to promote political priorities based on left-wing political philosophies that do not attract popular support when championed by parties at elections and that their own members don't necessarily share.

In 2006 – a year before the general election – Begg set down various preconditions for entering talks. He identified healthcare, care of children and the elderly, pensions, up-skilling of workers and the role of the state in the economy – by which he meant an anti-privatization agenda – as items for discussion. Ahern agreed to the discussions, even if he didn't give them all they wanted at the end. While everyone may want better healthcare and improved provision for children and the elderly, public sector delivery – as the unions demanded – was not necessarily cost efficient or effective. However, the regular access to the airwaves enjoyed by public sector unions allowed them to dictate the terms of the debate on such issues, sometimes by making emotional pleas, and gave them arguably more influence than elected politicians who sat on the opposition benches in the Dáil.

Despite all of this access and apparent power, trade union membership as a proportion of the workforce fell dramatically during the boom years. In an economy that added over 800,000 new workers in a decade, trade union membership went up only marginally, even though a tax credit was provided against the cost of an annual subscription. SIPTU's Jack O'Connor told me in 2008 that union membership was at a record high and would have been higher were it not for the refusal of many companies, especially multinational ones, to negotiate with legitimate union-organized workforces.

This told only part of the story. The bulk of membership tended to be in the public sector or in long-established traditional private companies. It is reckoned that only about 15 per cent of private sector employees were union members. An age profile of this membership would most likely show them to be middle aged and upwards. There are also some jobs and professions where people are obliged to be union members even if they would prefer not to be.

Younger people, interested in job mobility, were not easily impressed by the rhetoric of the unions and their politics. They were clued into the damage done by the payment of undeserved increases, and by the provision of overly generous working conditions to workers on the basis of service and seniority rather than merit. They were not interested in veiled threats about militancy, in securing jobs for life or in putting up barriers to workplace change.

The modern generation – the million new workers of the last decade, and many of those who had become workers in the decade before them – saw the boom as a chance to build a career, not to find a job for life. They looked to move around and to seize opportunity. For a while it seemed that they could do better by joining non-union businesses that rewarded flexibility in work practices and provided greater job challenges.

The downturn provided an opportunity for the unions to exercise power – but not at social partnership level, where economic conditions dictated that their demands could not be accommodated. Instead, the opportunity to add numbers came at local level, among workers who were now looking for certainty rather than opportunity. The unions had to demonstrate that they could provide effective negotiations for members while not scaring away jobs. The failure of the Impact trade union to get the required two thirds majority for a day of action on 30 March 2009 showed that many members were less interested in old-fashioned militant tactics than their leaders had anticipated.

Still in the unions' favour – and thus a source of power – was the government's fear of provoking strikes, which would be very damaging for the country's ability to attract investment.

The April 2009 supplementary budget was dictated by that fear. The government was badly rattled by the reaction in the public sector to the introduction of the pension levy in January; it did not have the courage to risk reducing its massive costs there again, choosing to cut current spending by just €800 million for the rest of the year. It did this by reducing overtime, cutting projects and releasing part-time or contracted employees. More was needed, hard though that would have been to achieve. Instead, the government opted for the political lesser of two evils by ramping up taxes, despite warnings from most economists that this could make the depression even worse, reducing domestic consumer spending further and lengthening the dole queues.

Cowen and his government – rattled by the surprising belligerence of old-age pensioners the previous October when they refused to give back their automatic medical cards – had a fear of near-anarchy and the damaging loss of public services due to strikes. It didn't want to get into a fight with the unions, especially since it would need their support in the rerun of the Lisbon Treaty referendum. At the same time, however, the government felt its choices were limited. Channels of communication were kept open, but gradually, if reluctantly, the government faced the inevitable. A union ultimatum that a deal had to be struck by 1 May passed, much to the unions' frustration. Cowen had decided that he had other priorities.

43

Getting the country back on its feet again

If taking virtual control of the property sector and the banks wasn't enough of a burden for the government, it faced further issues as to the role the state should play in other areas of the economy to help effect the nation's recovery. The political 'right' suggested that the sale of state assets should be considered, to raise billions of euro that could be used to pay off national debt, although perhaps not until markets recovered and better prices could be obtained. The political 'left' not only rejected that option but even wanted certain formerly privatized companies brought back into public ownership, even though that would have resulted in large payments to existing shareholders and an increase in debt on the national balance sheet.

The state's role in economic life had changed somewhat during the boom; the historical function of the state as the only provider to sectors starved of capital became redundant. Financial services companies such as Irish Life and ACC Bank were sold to the private sector, as successive governments believed that the state should play no part in influencing lending or the sale of savings products. Irish Sugar was sold as far back as 1991, and eventually Greencore (as the company was called after it joined the stock market) gave up sugar processing in Ireland entirely, shutting all of its four factories. Bizarrely it proposed massive property developments at Carlow – involving the creation of virtually a whole new town – and Mallow as replacements for its closed factories. That didn't happen, and instead it concentrated on ready-made sandwiches made abroad and other businesses that had little relevance to the Irish farmer. The B&I shipping line was sold to Irish Ferries, which years later behaved disgracefully by paying off its staff and replacing them with cheaper foreign-based agency workers to whom the Irish minimum wage of €8.65 per hour did not apply.

The state companies that excited the most debate were Eircom and Aer Lingus. Eircom was valued at €8 billion – with almost no debt – when it joined the stock market in the summer of 1999, giving the state a massive cash windfall with which to start the National Pension Reserve Fund. It was a very successful company at the time, having reported pre-tax profits of €119 million and sales of €1.8 billion. Its value plummeted over the next decade. The low value placed on the company was explained by debts of €3.6 billion, a pension fund deficit of over €440 million and losses of €464 million on sales of €2 billion in its most recent accounts.

This was because the company had been ravished by its investors. The bewildering list of owners all used borrowings to buy the company and then took the company's cash flow to repay debt and profits when possible. This use of the company's money meant there was massive under-investment in expensive infrastructure, including the much needed roll-out of an extensive broadband network. The geographic availability of broadband was patchy and compared very poorly with that of almost all other developed countries, the speeds available were low, and the prices charged were dear. It was a major issue when it came to attracting foreign investment to the country and a serious impediment to domestic businesses trying to develop trade, especially from rural locations.

While calls for the renationalization of Eircom became more common throughout 2008 and 2009, the trade union movement was not as vocal as might have been expected. It might have been hypocritical for them to be so. The workers, through the ESOT, had shared in profits of about €700 million tax-free over the decade, having received free shares from the state in the first place. They had acquiesced in every decision to change ownership of the company. The former Communications Workers Union boss Con Scanlon had been among those to benefit greatly from the distribution of money. The person who had negotiated the original ESOT deal was David Begg, now head of the ICTU. Begg had not benefited personally from the deal, since he had gone to work for the charity Concern before the company joined the stock market and he had no responsibility for what happened to the shareholding subsequently.

Another company where the workers got a substantial free shareholding was Aer Lingus. The formerly state-owned airline seemed to hold a special place in the affections of politicians. However, Aer Lingus had long been the problem child of the state-owned commercial sector, with some costs caused by an amount of employee inflexibility that would not be tolerated in the private sector and suffering heavy losses whenever there was an economic downturn. It was not alone in the airline industry in this, but the unions' dominance at the airline restricted management's ability to deal with these issues. Unsurprisingly, Aer Lingus has had a dozen chief executives since the early 1990s, if you include chairmen who've had to do the job on a temporary basis while the company searches for the next victim.

Aer Lingus joined the stock market in 2006 after a lengthy campaign finally broke Taoiseach Bertie Ahern's resistance to the idea of a sale. The state retained a 25 per cent stake in the company. In retrospect, the decision to sell the company saved it from immediate ruin. Aer Lingus raised about €500 million from the sale of shares, which gave it cash to see it through the recession and to contribute about €200 million towards the gap in the employee pension fund. The government got €206 million out of the deal. Had this not happened, it is arguable that Aer Lingus would have been destroyed by the losses it incurred during 2009; instead, it did not have interest costs and had cash to cover these losses.

Yet how Aer Lingus got to that position is an intriguing story of the use of power. Aer Lingus almost collapsed in the aftermath of 9/11 but inspired leadership from chief executive Willie Walsh – a former pilot – saved the company. Walsh halved the workforce to 3,500 and changed working practices dramatically. He was resented for doing the right thing and it made him a target.

The unions claimed that the company had been saved by the workers' acceptance of a reduction in the number employed and new working practices. The truth, however, is that none of it would have happened without the vision and leadership of Walsh, whose track record shows that he was by far the best of the company's former managers – an opinion confirmed by his subsequent recruitment as chief executive of British Airways, one of the largest airlines in the world.

However, Walsh left Aer Lingus because he was frustrated by political interference in his attempts to bring the company to the next stage of its development. He believed the airline had to raise money to expand if it was to protect itself against further cycles of economic downturn and intense competition. The only way to do that was by selling shares via the stock market or to a rival airline. He asked for a decision. He begged.

He cajoled. All to no avail. Ahern wouldn't say yes and he wouldn't say no – apparently because he didn't want to offend those trade unionists opposed to a sale; the desire to keep companies such as Aer Lingus in state ownership was based not necessarily on what was best for the consumer or for the owner but included considerations that amounted to feather-bedding employees and meeting unions' requests.

Ahern left Aer Lingus hanging. While politicians sometimes benefit from putting things on the long finger, no business can prosper in such uncertain circumstances. Not surprisingly, Walsh got frustrated. He made a big tactical mistake. He tried to call Ahern's bluff by publicly asking to explore options to raise money, including the possible purchase of the airline by himself and two other senior executives, Seamus Kearney and Brian Dunne.

There was a wholly predictable outcry that this was inappropriate. The idea of Irish entrepreneurs purchasing an iconic state company – especially given that Walsh had an inside track on the company in his position of chief executive – was anathema to our self-styled 'socialist' Taoiseach and his mates in the unions. They accused the trio of greed, but envy appeared to be at the heart of their reaction to the proposal: it seemed that they did not want to see Walsh become rich. The government had conveniently ignored the fact that the employees had received a gift of 15 per cent of the company in return for little more than a few productivity concessions. There was nothing to stop the state from charging Walsh a fair price, the same as anyone else would pay.

Walsh's proposal was subjected to a most unfair, misleading and vitriolic attack by Ahern from the safety of the Dáil chamber, where the laws of libel do not apply. Ahern accused Walsh of trying to 'steal' the assets of Aer Lingus and of planning to 'shaft' the workers. He never withdrew the allegations. His spokesman said afterwards he didn't mean to say 'steal', and Tánaiste Mary Harney said he probably meant to say 'strip', as if that was any better. It was all patently untrue but it was grist to the mill for a certain constituency.

Walsh had little option but to go. Ahern allowed one of the most talented executives in the world aviation industry to leave one of the most important state-owned companies, as if it was of no consequence. He said he was not irreplaceable. Ahern's government appointed people such as his friend Des Richardson, solicitor Ivor Fitzpatrick and banker Sean FitzPatrick to the Aer Lingus board as part-timers.

Two years later the company was sold via the stock market because the new chief executive, Dermot Mannion, insisted he would take the job only if he was allowed to raise money for expansion by the sale of shares to the public. Walsh's track record would have commanded investor interest if he had been allowed to lead the sale to any other party, but his request was granted to someone else. And here's the rub: Ryanair, also detested by Ahern, swept in to buy nearly 30 per cent of the company, giving it a bigger share than that retained by the state.

When British Airways experienced turbulence in the opening of the new Terminal Five, Walsh set an example for all other executives by forgoing a £750,000 cash bonus as a punishment for the losses the airline had incurred. Mannion suddenly went from Aer Lingus in April 2009. His position had been undermined a couple of months earlier when it emerged that he and chairman John Sharman had agreed a secret €2.4 million 'golden parachute' for Mannion in the event of a rival's takeover causing his departure. The board had not been informed and ICTU's David Begg, who serves on the board (and gives his director's fees to congress), insisted that the deal be revoked.

It didn't always suit the trade unions to scorn those who were dipping their noses in the trough, especially when it happened in the public sector.

The departure of FÁS chief executive Roddy Molloy from the state-run training agency might not have been required a few years earlier, when waste was tolerated more readily. However, he badly misjudged the public mood in late 2008. Molloy had been the subject of an exclusive report in the *Sunday Independent* that detailed the extraordinarily expensive travel jaunts he had engaged in: he had taken sixteen overseas trips in just three and a half years and, endearingly, brought his wife with him to Brussels, Boston, Washington, New York (twice) and Orlando (twice) at the taxpayers' expense. Indeed there were flight costs of over €380,000 between 2003 and 2007 for trips by FÁS executives, spouses, board members and former board members to Florida.

Molloy accepted an invitation from the *Pat Kenny Show* on RTÉ Radio to go on air to explain himself. He said that he had been 'entitled' to first-class air travel but had 'traded down' his ticket so that his wife could travel with him. Despite an initial defence of Molloy by his fellow Offalyman Cowen, Molloy had to go, surrendering his €272,000 annual salary but consoled by a severance payment of €111,000 and a pension top-up of €330,000. The FÁS board gave him the same glowing tribute that would be paid to any departing chief executive, no matter what the circumstances.

But who was on that board? Well, it was a combination of various civil servants, including representatives from the IBEC and the ICTU. Three of the four pillars of social partnership were involved, with the community and voluntary sector being the exception. The chairman of FÁS was Impact's Peter McLoone. So where was his condemnation of Molloy's outrageous use of taxpayers' money? Was he muted by the fact that he'd flown business class to Florida with Molloy for an essential visit to NASA to see how the FÁS astronaut programme was faring?

McLoone didn't make the mistake of doing many radio interviews while the controversy raged, especially when details of $400 beauty treatments and $900 rounds of golf – all put through as *expenses* – began to emerge. He was unavailable when we tried to get him for *The Last Word*, and by the time he was available again there were more pressing issues, such as the pension levy, to discuss.

This is what he had to say about the introduction of the pension levy: 'People are angry at the unfairness of this measure, when the bankers and property speculators who caused the mess are being let off scot-free.' Leaving aside the fact that nobody was getting away 'scot-free', McLoone failed to attribute any blame to the government, which was equally culpable for the mess and which had been guilty of squandering the boom through massive public spending increases in order to keep McLoone, his comrades and the electorate happy.

If the standards of responsibility that unions often say they want applied to corporate life had been applied in this case, McLoone might have been required to offer his resignation. FÁS had a €1 billion budget, and clearly some of it was being wasted on feather-bedding key executives and the board, as a subsequent Oireachtas committee report found. However, the unions' reaction was to claim even more money for the organization – to deal with the mounting unemployment crisis – seemingly without asking how well it would be spent or what benefits its training would provide to recipients. The assumption appeared to be that FÁS had to be a 'Good Thing' because it is intended to be so, and because those who run it regard themselves as pillars of Irish society.

The parallels with the HSE are uncanny – and, as they seek more money, the unions rarely complain about waste there either.

A coarsening of the debate between unions and employers as to appropriate behaviour is likely to intensify during the downturn. Clearly, there has been enormous greed on the part of many corporate bosses who want seven-figure salaries, large shareholdings in their own enterprises and big investments in other companies too. Higher taxes for them are clearly appropriate and affordable. Unfortunately that will not fill the gap between government spending and revenues.

If some trade union bosses had the power, anyone with a salary of more than €100,000 would be considered rich and ripe for the plucking. That would include owners of small- and medium-sized businesses. Last year I conducted a live interview with Jack O'Connor in which he sneered at how many corporate types living near him could afford to drive expensive Mercedes cars while their workers were expected to make do with pay freezes or pay increases below the rate of inflation. It was an unfortunate argument to make on the day luxury car-parts manufacturer Iralco announced that its Irish operation – based in Collinstown, County Westmeath – was to go into liquidation, at the cost of 420 jobs.

Many of the Mercedes drivers about whom O'Connor was complaining own and / or run small- and medium-sized enterprises and work hard for their rewards. Their contribution to job and wealth creation should not be diminished or dismissed. If the Mercedes drivers have their wealth and income confiscated, they won't be buying replacement cars – and what will the workers in the plants that make the parts do then? And if they stop eating out, or spending leisure time in Ireland, or investing in high-quality – but more expensive – premium Irish products for their homes and businesses, what will the workers in those industries do? If people stop spending because the government takes most of their earnings in tax, where are the enterprises that will generate new jobs and a new taxation base going to come from?

There is a gap in Irish society that is not recognized often enough, and it is a generational rather than a class one. About 60 per cent of home-owners in this country have no mortgage. They have paid it off. Their children, if they had them, are no longer a financial burden. That gives them an enormous financial advantage over younger people, who may have the expense of children and car loans on top of mortgages taken in the last decade at a time when house prices were at their peak. Someone of Jack O'Connor's age earning €100,000 a year who has a small or no mortgage and whose kids have left home is indeed very well off. A man in his thirties who has bought a house in Dublin for his wife and three kids – to take a random example – who earns €100,000 is not rich. In fact, although few will stand up for someone on such a salary, he may not be living a particularly ostentatious lifestyle. If he is running his own business, rather than being an employee, he is likely to have taken risks in borrowing money. Begrudging him a nice car hardly seems fraternal, especially if he has been providing employment because of his own efforts.

Too many people got rich quick because of property investments, or suffered from the delusion that property investment made them rich, but to criticize somebody who earns from productive labour or investment, and to argue that they should be screwed for tax to support those who have not made the same effort, hardly seems like a plan to get the country out of the mire. Basing a strategy on such politics is hardly a good use of union power.

PART X

The comeback kings

44

The resurrection of the beef baron

It is possible to suffer near financial ruin, and to have power stripped away, but to recover and make a spectacular comeback. It has happened in Ireland in the last twenty years.

The first part of this story bears an uncanny resemblance to what has happened to the Irish economy in the last two years, as it is about a leading company that came close to collapse nearly twenty years ago, only to be rescued by state action. It is in the second part that encouragement can be found, because there the tale is not just of recovery but of emerging even bigger and more successful than before. This example of triumph over adversity is – unfortunately, from some people's point of view – one of the most controversial and divisive businessmen in the history of the state: Larry Goodman.

While Larry Goodman now has a relatively low profile, and may be unknown to a generation of people not involved with agriculture, he was an extraordinarily large and powerful figure two decades ago. At one stage in the late 1980s his beef-processing business accounted for up to 6 per cent of Gross National Product (GNP), the measure of all income in the country. He was the biggest beef processor in Europe and the man who controlled 40 per cent of the beef kill in Ireland.

We were still an agriculturally dependent economy then, with the pharmaceutical sector, run by foreign multinationals, our other main industry. The IFSC was only in its infancy, Intel had not yet arrived in Leixlip and become the hub for our technology sector, and there was no construction boom to provide jobs. Goodman provided jobs – albeit not particularly well-paid ones – and his companies had a policy of paying farmers cash on the day they delivered their cattle.

However, Goodman's business practices were so suspect that they resulted in the creation of the first major tribunal of investigation into modern Irish business and its relationship to government. He admitted to the Beef Tribunal that access to ministers gave him a commercial advantage over rival companies and that he had no compunction about using it. But it went far deeper than that.

The findings by Mr Justice Liam Hamilton at the conclusion of the tribunal's lengthy hearings (at which Goodman's counsel was Dermot Gleeson) were anodyne, but revelations at subsequent tribunals suggested that Goodman was very lucky that evidence about the extent of his relationship with Fianna Fáil, and Charles Haughey in particular, was not disclosed to Hamilton. Had it been, Hamilton would have been under serious pressure to come up with conclusions other than those he gave. His finding – that there was nothing to suggest that the granting of state benefits to Goodman in this period was motivated by any kind of personal or political favouritism – almost certainly would have been different had all the information been available.

For example, there was a £50,000 donation directly to the Haughey-controlled party leader's account on the day of the 1989 general election; Haughey ordered it to be kept 'anonymous'. And there was a £25,000 donation two days later, apparently for the Brian Lenihan liver transplant fund, which was also paid into the party leader's fund for use by Haughey.

There was an extraordinary relationship with backbench TD Liam Lawlor, who, as the Planning Tribunal found out over a decade later, had 'borrowed' enormous sums from Goodman to help him in a property deal and to fund a research company, which transpired to be of dubious repute. Lawlor failed to repay £250,000 of the money. Goodman complained he had been 'cheated' by Lawlor. The latter was a director of Food Industries, Goodman's ill-fated foray into the non-beef Irish agriculture sector, and, as a member of a key Oireachtas committee in 1988, controversially supplied Goodman with important information on the upcoming sale of a state asset, Irish Sugar, although Goodman did not buy it.

Two things in particular were striking about Goodman's relationship with the state: the approval of grant aid for the expansion of his beef-processing facilities and the provision of export credit insurance for his trade with countries like Iraq.

Goodman struck a deal in late 1987 with the Industrial Development Authority for the provision of generous grants – running into tens of millions of pounds – as well as cheap exchequer-subsidized loans, despite the country's financial position being almost as perilous as it is now. The money was dependent on the achievement of fairly stringent performance targets, much to Goodman's displeasure. When Goodman and the IDA made the announcement, the new Fianna Fáil agriculture minister Joe Walsh went to considerable lengths to claim it as a government job-creation initiative.

In early 1988 Goodman lobbied hard to have the performance clause dropped from the IDA deal. After another IDA refusal on 1 March, Goodman went to meet Haughey. The Beef Tribunal report confirms that at the very next cabinet meeting it was determined that the performance clause should be removed, a decision that actually went beyond the government's powers.

This wasn't the only state support Goodman was getting. He exported a great deal to Iraq, then fighting a war with Iran, which remained a smaller customer. To cover the possibility that he wouldn't be paid, he needed export credit insurance. Minister for Industry and Commerce Albert Reynolds provided it, notwithstanding the obvious dangers of not being paid for meat exported to countries at war.

However, Goodman cheated the system by exporting large amounts of non-Irish beef to Iraq, even though it had been certified in writing that all of his beef was the product of the Irish Republic. Meat bought from Irish farmers accounted for only 15 per cent of all the beef exported to Iraq; the rest was taken from the EU beef mountain and had been bought and paid for previously. When Des O'Malley, the replacement for Reynolds as minister, discovered this, he cancelled Goodman's export insurance cover. Goodman sued for damages immediately, claiming he had been grievously wronged. He sought damages of around £150 million in insurance cover, plus damages and costs, and did not drop the case until 2004.

Goodman went on a major acquisition spree before he crashed in 1990. Having established Food Industries in Ireland as a company to exploit the non-beef sector – and which he had quoted on the stock market, while keeping 68 per cent of the shares for himself – his biggest expenditure was in the UK. He bought a sizeable shareholding in Unigate, a large dairy company quoted on the stock market, and also, disastrously, a chunk of Berisford, the British Sugar company that dabbled in property investment. It may have been that these invest-ments were desperate attempts to gain control over new cash flows. At that point no one was aware of just how much money he was owed by Iraq.

While struggling financially from these bad stock market investments – on a smaller scale to those incurred by Seán Quinn nearly two decades later – Goodman suffered an even greater setback. In August 1990 Saddam Hussein, the Iraqi dictator, had his armed forces annex Kuwait. War loomed as the United States prepared to secure its oil supplies. The chances of Goodman's getting paid for his beef – the bill for which now amounted to a massive £170 million – were practically zero.

Within days the Goodman organization was on the verge of collapse, owing £510 million to thirty-three banks. The size of the debts was almost unheard of in Irish business in those days.

In a bizarre twist O'Malley introduced special new legislation with the specific purpose of saving Goodman. The Dáil was recalled in an emergency session to bring in the Examinership Act, which allowed a company to stave off receivership or liquidation by getting protection from its creditors for a limited number of days. In that time the court-appointed examiner draws up a scheme of arrangement: through this agreement creditors are paid a portion of what they are owed, usually through asset sales, the ownership of the company is restructured and, crucially, the company continues to trade.

Instead of throwing Goodman out on his ear for losing so much money, the banks allowed him to keep 40 per cent of the shares in the new company while they took the rest. He was also allowed to keep £8 million in personal assets. Their reasoning was that they needed Goodman: he had the expertise in beef processing that they didn't, and his skills in this area were in no way connected with what had gone wrong. The pain for Goodman was the loss of his extensive property portfolio, which was seized and sold.

Just four years later, with the help of a group of businessmen in County Louth, Goodman raised the money to buy out the banks for just £50 million – which meant that the banks gave up on recovering about £300 million of debts still owed. In this deal, the newly named Irish Food Processors was allowed to regain total control of Goodman's beef industry assets; and the banks were given the rights to any cash that was won in ongoing legal actions, such as the action over the revoked export credit insurance. Ten banks agreed to provide Goodman with working capital for future requirements.

IFP went on to establish itself as the biggest beef processor in Ireland and as one of the largest in Britain. Goodman had 35 per cent of the new entity and his friends who helped raise the finance to buy out the banks got 65 per cent. Within four years he bought them out.

The company now has meat plants in the Republic in Cahir, Bandon, Waterford, Rathkeale, Longford, Nenagh, Clones, Dublin and Ballybay. It also has Northern Ireland plants in Newry and Lurgan. The last accounts for the Goodman Group's Irish Food Processors were published for the year-end 31 March 2002, after which he was so confident about his financial status that he opted for unlimited liability. Those last accounts showed sales revenues of €874 million and pre-tax profits of €41.5 million. The group had €144 million in cash on its balance sheet and a net worth of €194 million. Goodman took €38 million in dividends in the last two years that IFP remained a limited company and had to file accounts in the Companies Office.

The group became way bigger in Britain than in Ireland, benefiting enormously from the thirty-month contract it won to slaughter the British beef herd in 1996 because of fears of BSE-infected meat.

Goodman now processes 22 per cent of the Irish cattle kill and has a 15 per cent cut of the UK kill. His annual turnover is estimated to be far more than €1 billion. Using his expertise in rendering, the group is building a special biofuel processing plant in Manchester capable of converting animal fat or tallow into 110 million litres of biodiesel per year. He owns 30 per cent of the used cooking oil market in Britain (used cooking oil is another source for biodiesel) and has secured an excise-free quota of 97 million litres from the Irish government under its new biodiesel scheme, even though the fuel won't be made here.

Goodman is one of Ireland's largest property investors, having repurchased all of the commercial blocks he was forced to sell in 1990 and added many more. His rent roll from the state is estimated at about €5.5 million annually. It includes the Setanta Centre, which he repurchased from Green Property in 2003 for €85 million, home to the unit of the Revenue Commissioners that audits so-called high net-worth individuals. He is believed to own more than 2,000 acres of land in the north-east, and in January 2009 applied for the rezoning of a 950-acre site near Dundalk in order to build a major hotel and golf course. He has also applied for the rezoning of the old Ravensdale meat processing plant, to provide housing on twenty-five acres.

While the current credit crunch may delay his plans, he is not under any financial pressure, such is his assumed wealth. Last year he took delivery of a new eight-seater Dauphin AS 365 N3, which has a range of nearly 800 kilometres, a top speed of nearly 280kph and a price tag of €8 million, and a new Citation X executive jet, which can travel intercontinental routes non-stop.

As a shareholder in the highly profitable Blackrock Hospital Group, which runs the Blackrock Private Hospital in Dublin, and in the Galway Clinic, he has become a major investor in Ireland. In 2006 he took a substantial stake in C&D Foods, the County Longford pet-food company that, after losing its Edgeworthstown plant in a major fire, was threatened with collapse. C&D had been started by Albert Reynolds in 1969 and run by his son Philip since 1990. In 1992, evidence O'Malley gave to the Beef Tribunal about the sums being claimed by Goodman in export credit insurance caused such a row with Reynolds that it brought about the collapse of the first Fianna Fáil–PD coalition, which Reynolds led in succession to Haughey.

This comeback would have seemed impossible in the early 1990s. In May 1991 the ITV programme *World in Action* broadcast an exposé of Goodman's business practices that had been put together painstakingly by the investigative journalist Susan O'Keeffe. The evening after its broadcast Goodman called a press conference in the Shelbourne Hotel, where he sat with his solicitor James Osborne, the man who was later to be chairman of Punchestown Racecourse and a director of Ryanair. I was the reporter on duty for the *Sunday Business Post* but at Susan's request was doubling up as her unofficial minder, because she wanted to be present when he denounced the programme and her methods. Her programme led to the setting up of the Beef Tribunal at which some of Goodman's extraordinary business practices were exposed.

In March 1996, long after the Beef Tribunal had reported, I took a phone call at my desk in the *Irish Independent* from my good friend Veronica Guerin. We had worked together at the *Sunday Business Post*, where I was her copy editor. On one occasion I spent two days rewriting an extraordinary tale she had put together about a farmer who had taken a £25 million loan from Goodman that somehow got stuck in a Cyprus bank account. Veronica and I often swapped stories, depending on how busy we were or whether we wanted to protect sources. 'I have a story for you,' was often her opening line, rather than hello, and it was again on this particular day. 'Larry Goodman wants to meet you.'

'Why would I want to meet him?' I asked. 'And anyway what are you doing relaying messages from Goodman after all the stuff you've written about him over the years?'

'He talks to me now,' she laughed.

A couple of hours later I met with Goodman in an office in Ballsbridge. He was furious with Fine Gael's agriculture minister Ivan Yates over something, but equally so about a letter that he handed to me. It was from a Fine Gael trustee called Sean Murray and had been sent to Goodman not long after the Beef Tribunal report had been published, asking for a political donation. While I could see that Goodman was using me and the paper to settle a score, it was still a legitimate story, and once I confirmed its veracity it became a front-page report in the *Irish Independent*.

Goodman enjoyed getting even with people. That's what drives wealthy and powerful people when they've lost what they had – they want to get it back. That's what's going to happen as Ireland tries to recover from its current mess. Goodman was in his mid-fifties when disaster struck him, still young enough to want to do it all again.

Some of the most unpopular figures in modern Ireland are going to come back again, as long as they get some leeway from their banks, using the experience of Goodman as an inspiration. Those who decry the type of business standards that they believe Goodman represented may wince at the thought.

45

The man they love to hate

Michael O'Leary divides public opinion like no other Irish businessman. The chief executive of the highly successful airline Ryanair is one of the few senior business figures who will comment regularly on a government's economic policies and actions. While he conducts interviews on the basis that he wants to deal only with aviation issues, he rarely manages to restrain himself from being sidetracked. Get him going and he will pass general and trenchant comment on the performance of politicians. In particular, he lacerates them if he believes they are pandering to vested union interests. He may be highly opinionated, robustly combative and at times, rude almost to the point of being obnoxious, but the way he rails against what he considers to be the dead or nervous hand of officialdom and bureaucracy appeals to many people.

He excites and divides listener opinion like almost no other radio guest when he comes on air. Unprompted text messages flood in to demand that he stand for election or be appointed directly to cabinet. His track record of achievement at Ryanair – where he has built one of Europe's biggest airlines from the most peripheral island in Europe – convinces many that he is a man who can get things done.

For every person who regards O'Leary as a corporate hero, as someone who cuts through the waffle, who is fearless in confronting vested interests and who is brave enough to make decisions, there are just as many who regard O'Leary as an ignorant buffoon – foul-mouthed, overly opinionated, intolerant, rude, aggressive, ruthless and representative of the worst excesses of capitalism. To these people, the idea that O'Leary's ruthless pursuit of profit and savage cutting of costs should be applied to public spending is anathema; the suggestion that he should be put in a position of institutional power is equally appalling.

Few politicians have promoted him as an example of how Irish business should behave, and it is not an exaggeration to say that there are numerous trade unionists who hate him and what he stands for, even if many of their members have added to Ryanair's fortunes by availing of its cheap fares.

What O'Leary said about former Taoiseach Bertie Ahern and Mary O'Rourke when she was transport minister crossed the bounds of previously acceptable discourse and appalled the establishment.

For years, O'Leary showed little or no respect towards Ahern, disparagingly called him the 'Prime Minister', mocked the government's aviation policies and accused Ahern of kowtowing to the power of his friends in the trade unions. Some of the insults were personal, in particular those that have accused Ahern of being a 'ditherer' in relation to his inaction on the building of a second terminal at Dublin Airport. When Ahern finally gave it the go-ahead, he allowed the Dublin Airport Authority to do the job instead of the private sector and to commit €1.2 billion to the project – to the predictable consternation of O'Leary. O'Leary claimed the terminal decision was a classic example of Ahern's limited ambition when it came to facilitating competition in key economic areas – and that it came too late.

While Ahern dismissed most of the attacks, some clearly irked. Once he declared angrily that he would not be 'bullied' by O'Leary. I asked Ahern during one live interview to relate to listeners his feelings about O'Leary's strident, personalized and very public criticism; he laughed it off with 'Sure, that's just Michael. You know what he's like.' But there was no masking the undercurrent to his laughter: he didn't like it.

There were many times when O'Leary's decisiveness contrasted positively with Ahern's dithering; the former's desire for confrontation could bring about results that consensus would never have achieved. Admittedly, his overstepping of the mark at times denied him what he wanted, and his impetuousness cost Ryanair serious money – for example, when he made his smart-alec purchase of 30 per cent of Aer Lingus.

O'Leary got his break working for one of Ireland's original entrepreneurs, Tony Ryan. The son of a Tipperary train-driver, Ryan was working as an executive for Aer Lingus when he had the idea of setting up an aviation finance company that bought large passenger aircraft from manufacturers and then leased, or rented, them to airlines which could not afford to buy them for themselves. Guinness Peat Aviation (GPA) was established in 1975 and in little more than a decade established itself as a world leader from its base at Shannon Airport. Ryan became one of Ireland's richest men, so wealthy that in 1988 he purchased 5 per cent of Bank of Ireland for about £30 million.

In 1993 O'Leary – as Ryan's personal assistant – was handed the task of rescuing Ryan from personal financial ruin. It all happened very suddenly. In 1992 the great Irish business success story came crashing down to earth. GPA had placed orders for more than 400 new aircraft, costing over $20 billion. It planned to strengthen its balance sheet by raising new capital on joining the stock market. Unfortunately, the company got its timing wrong. The aviation industry went into a tail-spin and the prospect of placing the new aircraft with customers dimmed. Worse, some customers could no longer afford the lease charges and sent aircraft back to GPA.

The Irish company would still have succeeded in raising new capital had it not been overly ambitious in the price it sought for the new shares. Instead, investors rejected the offer of buying them when GPA refused to lower its targets. The stock market flotation was pulled, but the company's problems were only beginning. Suddenly GPA was massively short of cash and attempted to cancel its orders for new aircraft. The company had planned to sell only $850 million worth of shares, but that would have provided the base for leverage of another $3 billion in borrowings. Without that money GPA could not pay for the delivery of the first batches of new aircraft and was totally stumped as to what to do with the rest of the planes.

In less than nine months the company was headed for liquidation, only to be rescued by the giant US multinational GE Capital, which was one of its main competitors in aviation finance. The story goes that as negotiations to rescue the ailing Irish firm dragged on, Ryan lost patience with the terms being demanded and complained bitterly that his company was being raped. GE's Jack Welch, one of America's most famous corporate bosses, was reported to have looked at him and said: 'That's what happens when you go around with no clothes on.' Many years later I spent an hour interviewing Welch and asked if it was true that he had said that. He declined to comment.

The deal gave existing investors only a small amount of money as compensation for what had once seemed a fantastic investment, even if it allowed most of the key executives to retain their well-paid jobs. Many faced ruin because of the loans they had taken out to buy shares in GPA. It was a disaster for Ryan professionally and personally, but it could have been even worse had he been forced to repay in full a $35 million loan he had taken from Merrill Lynch shortly before the intended stock market flotation, which he intended to use to buy a raft of new shares in GPA on the cheap. He had expected to sell these new shares into the flotation, at a much higher price. However, the collapse in the share price meant his shares were suddenly almost worthless. He wouldn't be collecting the $38 million success fee that would have been paid on a successful stock market flotation. And he still had a huge bank loan to repay.

Ryan had other assets, including a majority shareholding in a small loss-making competitor to Aer Lingus called Ryanair. He owned a raft of expensive mansions and estates around the world in places like Monaco, Mexico, Spain, Tipperary and Kildare. He had a major art collection. He had wealth the banks could seize but not enough to cover all his debts. He faced ruin.

Michael O'Leary persuaded the American bank to accept repayment of only a small amount of the debt owed. This gave Ryan the breathing space that he needed and O'Leary the opportunity to build Ryanair.

The airline was set up by a Ryan trust fund in the mid-1980s, although he denied controlling it for fear of alienating airline clients of GPA. For years it was a basket-case, its tickets too highly priced, the competition from the state-owned airline Aer Lingus, which had a monopoly on the best routes, too great. It accumulated losses of over £20 million in its first four years, massive money at the time. Ryan came close to selling it many times.

O'Leary took control of the operations and changed the airline's methods dramatically: he dropped prices as much as he could, cancelled flights at short notice if they weren't full enough, turned flights into shopping opportunities by having air hostesses double as saleswomen, demanded that staff have planes back on their return legs in double-quick time and did everything possible to lower his costs. He didn't allow anyone to deflect him from a course of action when it was embarked upon, most particularly the unions, who didn't know what had hit them. He boasted about becoming a low-cost operator, something that many other Irish companies in other industries later sought to emulate, and succeeded in meeting his objectives.

He was helped by the government's eventual decision to allow greater competition to Aer Lingus and by discount deals on charges at the state's main airports. Trade unionists argue that these were the essential moments in the Ryanair expansion, but, although important, they weren't critical: Ryanair succeeded because it had a managing director with obsessive drive, a willingness to confront vested interests, a better understanding of what consumers want and are prepared to pay for, an ability to tap the capital markets for finance when required and the bravery to make decisions quickly and then act upon them.

O'Leary's ability to react to a crisis was emphasized by his reaction to the 9/11 attacks upon the United States. As most panicked about the safety of air travel because of terrorism, O'Leary decided on two things. He announced a seat sale, offering tens of thousands of seats almost for free, just to ensure that his planes stayed in the air and that public confidence in flying would be restored quickly. Then he didn't wait around to see if he would be right. He went to Boeing, the world's largest aircraft manufacturer, and ordered hundreds of new aircraft for billions of euro. He got them at knock-down prices as other airlines panicked and cancelled orders. That's what private enterprise can do. Had he been wrong, he wouldn't have asked for or been given a state bailout.

When O'Leary saved Ryanair from extinction, he performed something of a national service by breaking the Aer Lingus monopoly on air travel into and out of this country, forcing it to be more commercial in its operations. And he did the public and the state enormous service by creating one of Europe's most successful airlines, despite inheriting a company that was an absolute mess both strategically and financially.

O'Leary's instinct for what passengers really want is extraordinary because it does not correspond to what appears in the business manuals. He believes that price is everything: people want reliable travel at affordable prices. Why be snobbish about something that is nothing more than an airborne bus service, to get someone from A to B, an activity that once had a cachet only because it was new? As far as O'Leary is concerned, if people don't like the service or his operating methods, they can fly with somebody else.

Tens of millions of people throughout Europe now annually enjoy the availability of cheap fares such as were never even dreamt of previously. The social benefits resulting from the opening of foreign travel to the vast majority of Irish people are incalculable. Passengers, at low prices, take weekend breaks and short holidays all across continental Europe, follow provincial rugby teams to Britain or the South of France, and go to soccer matches in England and Scotland regularly. Cheap Ryanair flights persuaded many people to buy holiday homes in Europe, although that might not be something to recommend itself now. Among the airline's many users were the price-conscious and low-income earners, who do not share their unions' concerns about O'Leary's modus operandi.

Hate is not too strong a word to describe how some think of O'Leary. In late 2006 SIPTU president Jack O'Connor appeared on RTÉ's *Questions and Answers* programme the Monday after Ryanair announced its bid to take over Aer Lingus. Not surprisingly, he was angry about what had happened and dismissive of the merits of the proposed buyers; he demanded that the government take action to block any takeover.

Asked if he could credit Ryanair with anything good, he couldn't. Not just one thing? No, he replied defiantly. No, nothing at all, he insisted. Not even cheap seats for union members, who previously couldn't afford to fly at all? What about all the Irish jobs at Ryanair? Did they cease to matter because they weren't card-carrying union members? What about the members of pension funds who had benefited from investment in Ryanair shares?

Here's one of the many ironies: the trade unions had fought against the rise of Ryanair because they didn't want competition to Aer Lingus. Now that Ryanair had grown large enough to buy Aer Lingus, the unions didn't want that because it would destroy competition.

Admittedly, O'Leary's treatment of workers has been controversial, and he refuses to deal with trade unions. Staff have to work very hard, and often at unsocial hours, but he has no problem in getting people to work for him because they are paid reasonably well if they are productive. For years the average pay at Ryanair across all staff has been higher than at Aer Lingus, even before Aer Lingus began its project of reducing costs to allow it to compete with Ryanair on price.

The no-frills policy has been taken to extremes at times, especially in the disgraceful treatment of wheelchair-bound passengers. The imposition of a levy on all passengers to cover the cost of assisting the few is scandalous but total average revenue per passenger remains 25 per cent below what Aer Lingus takes. This may explain why regular bad publicity about such things seems to do Ryanair little or no harm.

As O'Leary is not slow to boast, the average fare between Ireland and Britain before Ryanair revolutionized air travel was €270, more than a week's wages to most people at the time. It was why so many emigrants travelled by boat. Only two million or so passengers per year travelled into and out of the country. Today Ryanair's average fare is just over €40. Each year about six million people fly on Ryanair into and out of Ireland – notwithstanding the €10 per ticket travel tax introduced by the government in March 2009, despite vehement opposition from O'Leary and his cancellation and reduction of some routes in response.

For all of the people who complain about poor customer service, the inefficiency of staff, the distance of some airports from final destinations, the baggage charges and credit card levies – as well as O'Leary's sometimes objectionable and outrageous tactics in public – sixty million people a year fly with Ryanair. He provided choice.

Ryanair, rather than Aer Lingus, is effectively now the national airline. It operates far more routes from Dublin, Cork and Shannon than the former national flag carrier, now partly in the commercial sector. O'Leary seems to have done more for the Irish tourism sector than any state-funded marketing plans. He operated out of regional airports like Farranfore in Kerry, Knock in Mayo and Derry when Aer Lingus cut back on such services.

O'Leary has created Ireland's greatest business success story of the last twenty years. Yet it was jealousy and dislike of him, as much as genuine competition fears, that scuppered his chances of taking control of Aer Lingus after he opportunistically took a 30 per cent shareholding in the former state carrier, to the consternation of unions and government. The government may now wish it had taken the €500 million on offer from him in 2006, or even the €200 million he offered for his shares late in 2008, considering how much they are worth now and the government's need for cash. The ructions from the unions if the government had sold to O'Leary, of all people, would have been deafening, and no government was ever going to risk it.

In common ownership Ryanair and Aer Lingus would have been utterly dominant on the Ireland–Britain route and this would have created an opportunity for anti-competitive price fixing. However, other European carriers – as single airlines or combinations under the same grouping – have been allowed 70 per cent plus control of their domestic markets. The trade unions have no problem with protected state monopolies in other areas of business that do not match Ryanair's return on capital or ambition. They didn't seem to have confidence that a state regulator would have the strength to protect against price gouging of consumers, but the same argument could be applied to the interaction of regulators and semi-state companies. Maintaining trade union control and inflexibility at Aer Lingus may have been a motivation.

What has been created by Ryanair, from an Irish base, is extraordinary and would be celebrated in any other country and held up as an example of what needs to be done to restore the country to economic good health. At its peak in 2007 the stock market valued the company at €8.7 billion, less than Anglo Irish Bank but far more sustainable. Even though it had fallen to €4.8 billion by April 2009, it remained the second-largest company on the Irish stock market, worth more than the entire Irish banking sector combined. Ryanair's size, range of routes, availability and, most importantly, comparatively low fares have allowed it to keep market share at a time when many other airlines have been failing.

O'Leary does it all for profit, of course. He is unashamed in his desire to provide for himself financially. He had been on a profit-share arrangement at Ryanair when he took over, but this became far too expensive for the airline, so instead Ryan allowed him a 22 per cent shareholding for just £1 million. He has shares in Ryanair worth over €200 million and has sold shares worth at least that amount over the years for reinvestment elsewhere. His personal investments have been in farmland and properties in Dublin 4 and Lake Como, which will have suffered a serious loss in value in recent years. However, unlike many other Irish business leaders, he has an aversion to debt, something that is also obvious in his business management, as Ryanair consistently has cash in hand rather than borrowings.

O'Leary could easily have abandoned Ireland, especially for tax reasons; many other men of his wealth have been tempted. O'Leary hasn't done that. Paying his taxes has given him an entitlement not just to have his say but to be listened to. One year he arrived outside Leinster House with a specially printed giant personal cheque for €14 million, his contribution to the taxpayer. For all these reasons and more, including a willingness to talk honestly, without fear or favour, about how public money should be spent, he could be one of the powers in Ireland to whom we look for leadership.

It won't happen. Too many people not only dislike him but despise him. O'Leary would not be upset by that, because the lack of respect would be mutual. As he sees it, he upsets cosy arrangements, such as those enjoyed by pampered management and unions at Aer Lingus and the Dublin Airport Authority, by highlighting their waste and inefficiencies in the industrial language everyone can understand. He is not always correct in his analysis but he is right more often than he is wrong, which only makes things worse for his enemies.

Irish people either admire his entrepreneurship or resent his controversial way of conducting business. It is possible to be in the first camp while expressing misgivings about some aspects of his personal behaviour.

Whatever people think of him, if Ireland is to be successful again the country needs more people like him in positions of influence and power. There was an argument that he should have been asked to serve the national interest through involvement with something like NAMA: as a strong man, he would have been fearless in confronting banks and property developers. The likelihood is that the government won't ask for his help, not publicly at least, and probably not even in private.

PART XI

And in conclusion . . .

Update for the 2010 edition

46

To tax or not to tax

Who remembers the dismal days of the 1980s? High unemployment, high taxation, high interest rates, rampant emigration and balance of payment problems – as imports outstripped exports – dominated the economic and political agenda. The government finances were a mess. Confidence sank. We clung to sporting successes like limpets, for anything to improve our mood.

The businessman making the speech certainly remembered those days. 'Ireland wasn't exactly a great place to do business. We were conservative, flair was hardly in evidence and we lacked business confidence,' he argued. Entrepreneurs 'weren't necessarily admired or respected back in the seventies and eighties. Risk-taking was seen as something akin to back-street gambling; there was a whiff of sulphur about it. It just wasn't quite respectable.'

The businessman attributed the success of the following two decades to the 'profound cultural shift in how we did our business', the pro-business environment championed by government and Ireland's position in the EU as an attractive base for foreign investment.

'The legislative and regulatory environment reflected this spirit of adventure. The government approach was expansive ... After years of meddling government finally stood aside and allowed people to get on with it. Taxes were cut and the economy was allowed to open up. The effect was like putting a flower out in the sun. The economy blossomed.'

His speech was delivered in 2007, before Sean FitzPatrick flew too close to the sun and crashed back to earth.

Capitalist business principles had a relatively short run in Ireland, because of their abuse by men like FitzPatrick. Still, businessmen and companies continue to hold power in modern Ireland, but in smaller numbers and to a lesser extent. How much 'soft power' they will be allowed to exercise, either by being allowed to get on with things much as they like, or by influencing public policy decisions, remains to be seen. Those who retained capital amid the economic carnage, and who now have it to reinvest, would appear to be in a very powerful position, not just to profit for themselves but to do a lot of social good along the way. But will they see opportunity in a depressed, high-tax Ireland or will they send their money abroad instead?

Few businessmen are likely to stand up and complain publicly about high taxes, especially if their own annual incomes are published and remain very high relative to what everyone else is earning. Nobody wise would want to come across as David Drumm did in an interview with the *Financial Times* in 2008, in which he said that the Irish people were sensible and would 'tighten their belts' if faced with a downturn. But it would appear that discretely, behind the scenes, wealthy businessmen will continue to bend the ears of ministers and will continue to be heard, particularly if they have capital to invest.

When trade unions meet with government ministers and officials it is often in the full glare of the media spotlight (although there are many private meetings too). Meetings between the business elite – who are not the type to be represented by IBEC – and government often take place in greater privacy. In late July 2009 one such meeting took place at the British Embassy in Ballsbridge. The outgoing ambassador David Reddaway invited a group of Irish politicians, officials and businessmen to meet with Peter Levene, the chairman of Lloyds TSB, owner of Halifax Bank of Scotland, which had developed a significant presence in the Irish market in recent years through Bank of Scotland Ireland, but which was rumoured now to be considering its exit from the Irish market. (Eventually, in February 2010, it announced that it was shutting its 44 retail outlets with the loss of 750 jobs but that it would continue its commercial and corporate banking activities, keeping 850 jobs.) The group, over dinner, discussed Ireland's economic prospects and what could be done.

Among those who attended were the finance minister, Brian Lenihan, and the head of the NTMA, Michael Somers. From banking there was Anglo's chairman O'Connor and Cormac McCarthy, chief executive of Ulster Bank. There was a range of businessmen, including Dermot Desmond, Denis O'Brien, Michael O'Leary, Michael Chadwick of the Grafton Group, Johnny Ronan and former Kerry Group boss Denis Brosnan, who was helping the government on a task force for the economic future of the mid west. Richard Burrows, recently retired chairman of Bank of Ireland but soon to be appointed chairman of the giant British American Tobacco (BAT) group, was there, as was Kieran McGowan, the former chief executive of the Industrial Development Authority, who now served on a range of public company boards.

They had plenty to talk about. Earlier that day Somers had delivered a bullish assessment of Ireland's ability to continue to borrow money, somewhat at odds with his earlier comments. In a radio interview I conducted with him he had publicly reassured people that we had started from such a low base that we had plenty of capacity and that the price of borrowing was not as expensive as it had been. Lenihan was ploughing ahead with plans for NAMA, which would have implications for many of those present, and the meeting provided an opportunity to hear the final views of some of these experienced businessmen.

No formal minutes of the meeting were kept, so details of what was said and by whom are unlikely ever to emerge. It was a cordial chat over dinner, but few of those present pulled any punches as to what they thought needed to be done to save the economy. The men – and it was an all-male affair – all had ideas for Lenihan to take away with him. Their views in relation to taxation policy – no more increases – and public spending – cut, cut, cut – were put forcibly.

Many of these same men turned up at Farmleigh in the Phoenix Park, the state residence where visiting dignitaries are accommodated, for a special Global Irish Economic Forum over the weekend of 18–20 September, just over a week before the first anniversary of the government's granting of the blanket guarantee against the liabilities of the banks. The gala gathering was organized by the Minister for Foreign Affairs, Micheál Martin; the idea was to tap into the Irish diaspora to see if further investment could be attracted to Ireland. It was planned as the Irish equivalent to the famous World Economic Forum in Davos.

Among the 150-plus business leaders who had been invited were many of the wealthy Irish luminaries who feature in this book: Tony O'Reilly, Denis O'Brien and Dermot Desmond for example, although O'Reilly changed his mind about attending shortly before the event, citing other commitments; these commitments almost certainly included his ongoing battle with O'Brien for control of INM. During an impromptu press conference outside Farmleigh, O'Brien took the opportunity to castigate

O'Reilly for his failings at the beleaguered media conglomerate – his difficulties in finding the €200 million that had to be paid to bondholders – and to promote his own ambitions for the company.

Also invited were Irish business figures who had made the bulk of their fortune abroad: Peter Sutherland, the former EU commissioner who became chairman of Goldman Sachs, BP and Royal Bank of Scotland; Niall FitzGerald, the deputy chairman of Thomson Reuters; and Gerry Robinson of Moto Hospitality. High-flying Irish executives such as British Airways chief Willie Walsh and Alan Joyce of Australian airline Qantas were there as well.

It was a working weekend, with an overall forum and then a number of working groups attended by various cabinet ministers. RTÉ television cameras were allowed access to just one session – one in which Desmond took the opportunity to launch his latest initiative, an idea for a cultural university, without having to suffer public questioning of its viability.

All participants paid their own way but were rewarded with free tickets to the All-Ireland football final. The entire event was overwhelmingly male and chiefly for those aged over forty, including some who were highly indebted personally or corporately because of poor business decisions, some of which related to property. There were few young or female entrepreneurs present who might have learned from the successes or failures of the elite who did make the cut.

Notable by his absence was Michael O'Leary, who, rejecting his invitation, dismissed the entire exercise as a public relations stunt.

Some of the foreigners present to whom I spoke were also far from impressed; I found them shocked by the self-congratulatory tone of several of those present, as if these participants did not realize that they too bore responsibility for the mess Ireland was in. They bemoaned the absence of people from Continental Europe in particular and accused the organizers of an undue bias towards English language countries; the second referendum on the Lisbon Treaty, which the government considered crucial to our continued engagement with the European Union, was then less than a fortnight away.

The star of the show was an American with Irish roots, the former Intel chief executive Craig Barrett. He had been instrumental in developing the semi-conductor manufacturer's vital Kildare plant, delivering thousands of jobs directly and thousands more to suppliers, becoming one of Ireland's most important investors.

Barrett delivered a wake-up call that unfortunately had too small an audience. In a speech that reportedly lasted less than five minutes Barrett enumerated the failures of this country, saying that of the fourteen reasons why the American giant had originally invested in the country (in 1989), only one still applied: our low level of corporation tax. In particular, he lamented the shortcomings of the education system – which is no longer producing sufficiently qualified people for the skilled jobs that are being offered – and the neglect of research and development, with the result that new ideas and processes had to be imported into an Ireland that did not have the means to originate them. I met Barrett in February 2010 to conduct a lengthy interview with him for the *Last Word* and he confirmed that reports of what he had said at Farmleigh were accurate: in particular, he was very critical of our standards of maths and science teaching, saying that our students were below average. Our graduates would have to be better than average, not below, if our high wage rates were to be maintained.

After more than a decade of the biggest surge in prosperity the country has ever known, in which we reached more or less full employment, we had little or nothing to show for it.

The levying of tax is one of the real powers that a government has – it can extract as much money from our pockets as it wants – but it also has a responsibility not to destroy confidence in the economy. In 2007 the government appointed a special Commission on Taxation, made up of various interested parties, and charged it with the task of coming up with fairer ways of distributing the tax burden. It asked the commission to propose ways of making the annual intake more certain, as well as ways of 'broadening' the tax base to include a wider range of sources. The work started too late and the report arrived after it was needed: when its work started, construction and related activities made up 20 per cent of the economy but within two years that went to near zero. As one minister told me after its publication, 'we received a peacetime document during a wartime situation'. The report was shelved quickly, particularly when there was an immediate public uproar at the idea of introducing a property tax for people suffering from falling house prices and negative equity.

The Fianna Fáil–Green government had said that while taxes would have to be increased, they should not rise so dramatically as to remove the incentive to work or to create wealth. Then they raised taxes dramatically in the April 2009 'supplementary' budget. The move fitted with the usual political reluctance to cut services and public sector jobs for fear of losing votes.

Shortly before Lenihan's supplementary budget, a prominent Fianna Fáil politician delivered a speech that appeared to put him at odds with the approach Lenihan was planning. 'What is clear is that spending must be cut back deeply and taxes must be increased prudently – not to levels that will encourage those who contribute most to the exchequer to up sticks, as they did in the 1980s and flee the net, leaving us with less tax instead of more,' he said.

'We must never succumb to the failed, excessive tax-raising recipes of the past – recipes for putting our economy on a long-term diet – starved of investment, starved of well-paid jobs, starved of risk-taking and wealth creation. It was the abandonment of the socialist policies of the eighties that gave everyone in this country the opportunity to remain here on this small island and make a decent living over the past fifteen years.'

Charlie McCreevy – for it was he – pointed out that as a small open economy, 'We have huge opportunities relative to our size to sell into a vast global economy many thousand times bigger than ours. It means that we only need to capture and retain competitive advantage in a small number of areas to make a big impact on our domestic economic fortunes.'

He gave examples of what he regarded as 'wrong turns' that would destroy us: 'If we decided that we weren't going to be more flexible in our work practices or in our earnings structures. If we decided we weren't going to adapt our education system or upgrade our infrastructure. If we decided we were going back to the eighties and abandon a tax system that rewards self-starters and risk-takers and instead start driving them out with punitive taxes on capital and labour – if we were to take just one of those wrong turns, then of course our best days would be behind us.'

In his April budget speech Lenihan announced that he would seek to raise an additional €1.75 million in new taxes in 2010, with details to be announced in December 2009, and a further €1.5 billion in 2011. Between April and December Lenihan's attitude shifted. When I asked him about his budget intentions during an interview in September 2009, he made the surprising statement: 'Read my lips, no new taxes.' I asked if he would regret saying that if I repeated the tape come budget time, but he was adamant that he would live up to his new commitment, save for the introduction of the carbon tax that the Greens wanted as part of the programme for government. And, true to his word, when December came, he left taxes alone. What had changed?

Lenihan had listened to the views of tax experts, who reckoned that the increase in health and income levies during 2009 was the same as putting 9 per cent on to the top rate of tax in one fell swoop. The top marginal tax rate – when various income levies are taken into account – was at 52 per cent now, the highest it has been since 1992. Lenihan decided that it is hard to encourage people to work harder when over half of their money goes to the Revenue Commissioners. Lenihan decided the government needed to concentrate on reducing its spending, instead of raising tax rates in an attempt to increase revenues. He believed there are two dangers involved in the latter approach: one is the danger of driving investment, both local and international, out of the country in a high tax environment; the other is that by pitching rates too high the actual tax take falls instead of rises.

Although there have been many arguments that the rich do not pay their fair share, Lenihan also highlighted that 50 per cent of workers were outside the tax net and that only 11 per cent were paying at the higher rate. He believes that every earner should pay some direct tax – even if just a small amount – because they would not appreciate the services they received from the state if they did not make a contribution through tax.

While much of the media attention – through rich lists and similar efforts – may have been focused on the extraordinary loss of wealth in the millionaire classes, or on the plight of those who had lost their jobs, it seems that Lenihan was conscious of what might be called the middle classes, or the coping classes, the people who do not usually demonstrate in the streets or seek public sympathy, but who do vote. This class, for which little sympathy is expressed publicly, has also suffered a major write-down of personal assets – houses and pension funds – which has undoubtedly prompted much of the reduction in spending and government tax revenues. As far as Lenihan was concerned, the children of these people have a habit, on becoming adults, of simply leaving the country if they feel work or initiative is more likely to be punished than rewarded. Excessive taxes do not necessarily just mean lower consumption and investment; they can lead to capital flight and a brain drain as well.

The old political liking for those who might have capital to invest may also explain why Lenihan's April 2009 supplementary budget failed to assault the worldwide income of Irish citizens who chose to limit the amount of days they spend in Ireland despite holding vast assets here. Lenihan's explanation – that they paid tax on their Irish income – was a reiteration of old excuses and motivated by the fear that their remaining capital would move, particularly at a time when Ireland appeared to be a less attractive location for foreign investment. As the pressure mounted, he announced in December 2009 that a levy of €200,000 per year would apply to those who claimed non-residency. Tax experts remained unconvinced that it would be workable.

In the latter years of the economic boom, the domination of property speculation was at the expense of productive investment. The property boom was like a praying mantis, seducing us and then destroying us. It made us forget that the real drivers of the previous decade's boom were EU transfers for investment in infrastructure; a liberalization of capital movements that brought massive foreign direct investment (particularly from the employment-creating American-owned multinationals); increased private sector local investment (albeit too much in property); and the weakness of our currency – be it the pound or euro – against the dollar and sterling, as was the case until it strengthened dramatically this decade.

The speed of recovery in the US is central to that of the Irish recovery. But, just as the global credit crisis on its own was not the cause of our problems – given that we had stored up enough for ourselves – we cannot depend on an international recovery suddenly making things all right for us again.

The European Commission – and others – believes that the best way for Ireland to return to growth is to cut spending rather than to increase taxes. However, its main interest is in forcing us to reduce the size of the gap between government spending and income. It has given us the tough task of reducing that gap to 3 per cent of national income by 2013. Although it has the power to force us to achieve that, it won't insist on how this is to be done, as long as it is done. The rating agencies, however, could punish us by increasing the cost of borrowing – or by restricting our borrowing – if there is too much emphasis on tax increases. Foreign multinationals could also punish us by removing jobs or by stopping investment. These outside influences have the power to prevent us from doing too much damage to ourselves by going for the softer, but not necessarily better, option of increasing taxes.

The *Financial Times*, the newspaper that Brian Lenihan and, by implication, Charlie McCreevy attacked, suggested in an editorial early in 2009 that Ireland, unable to devalue its currency as it did successfully in 1986 and 1993 because of euro membership, had no option but to deflate. This would mean that, to accompany falling asset prices, and indeed consumer prices, wages would also have to fall in absolute terms. This has happened in parts of the private sector, where many nervous employees are accepting pay reductions for fear of losing their jobs, and to a limited degree in the public sector, where the pension levy is described by many as an effective pay cut, although it also remains a limited contribution to the provision of a guaranteed pension paid out of current government cash flow. There would be two benefits to deflation: the government would be able to reduce its public sector pay bill, as it is no longer affordable, and the wider economy would benefit from the cheaper services and products that the state would then be able to provide. The trade union movement, however, was implacably opposed to such a move.

47

Getting ready for battle

The country's leading trade unionist was in full flow. 'They came for the public servants and I did not protest because I was not a public servant. Then they came for the people on welfare and I did not protest because I was not on welfare. Then they came from the people on the minimum wage and I did not protest because I am not on the minimum wage. Then they came for the semi-states, but I did not protest because I did not work in the semi-states. Then they came for me, but there was no one left to protest.'

ICTU general secretary David Begg told the December 2009 demonstration outside the Dáil Éireann that he had adapted his words from those of the German pastor Martin Niemoller, who had written a description of Nazi activity during the 1930s. That Begg – by common consent, a decent individual – would consider a comparison between the treatment of Jews in Germany during the Holocaust, and that of anybody in Ireland by the coalition government, legitimate or fair was an astonishing indication of both how high tensions were running among the unions and of how difficult negotiating with them would be for the government. Begg has shown a weakness for hyperbole in recent times – also claiming the trade union movement is the only 'actor in the market either interested in or capable of achieving social justice' – and his economic analysis failed to find widespread support outside of the higher echelons of the trade union movement.

In advance of the budget ICTU released details of a ten-point plan for economic recovery that was long on aspirations but short on workable specifics. Most notable, however, was the claim that the state should continue to borrow heavily for longer than the government had planned. Instead of returning to a maximum borrowing requirement of 3 per cent of GNP by 2013 (the European Commission subsequently extended this to 2014), Begg suggested returning to that limit by 2017.

It was as if Begg and the unions had not recognized the damage done to the economy by reckless lending and borrowing. Begg acted as if the creditworthiness of the state had not been severely affected, as if finance would continue to be readily available, as if it didn't matter that it would be far more expensive to purchase than heretofore. Getting loans was one thing but where would the money be found to make repayments?

Like it or not, the problem of the exchequer finances will dominate the economy for the best part of the next decade (along with NAMA and the banks). What's called a 'structural deficit' – which means we have established a permanent public cost base that will exceed revenues even when the economy is growing strongly – has emerged. It could be as high as €14 billion.

Countries that concentrate on cutting spending rather than increasing taxes recover from slumps far more quickly. There is a considerable body of evidence from international experience that demonstrates this; hell, we have plenty of evidence of it in this country from the 1980s if anyone wants to remember that far back. But the unions strongly oppose the idea, as much on emotional as intellectual or economic grounds. SIPTU's Jack O'Connor argued against cutting public spending on the basis that the people who would suffer were not responsible for the bust. Maybe not, but, according to the government, as well as many independent observers, the gap between the government's income and expenditure cannot be made up solely by tax increases on the wealthy. In the high tax economy that would result from this approach, there would be a flight of capital that would damage the ability to create and maintain jobs.

Colm McCarthy's 'An Bord Snip Nua' report, published in late summer 2009, was supposed to set the agenda for this cost cutting. It enraged the unions and terrified the Fianna Fáil backbenches. It suggested €5.3 billion in spending cuts and the loss of 17,300 jobs. While the numbers seemed enormous, they none the less constituted roughly just 7 per cent of annual government spending (when capital expenditure is included) and less than 5 per cent of public sector jobs. It was far less than a commercial enterprise of the same size would have done to ensure its survival.

Of course, the public sector employs those who provide essential services, such as nurses, teachers, doctors and Gardaí, as well as the people who had to deal with the severe flooding of November 2009, for example, and the consequences of the harsh snowfalls of late December 2009 and early January 2010. Public sector workers are angry because they feel they are being victimized for the failings of others. Many argue, with good reason, that they do hard and important jobs for which they feel undervalued and unappreciated. They feel that they did not share the benefits of the boom – notwithstanding that many experienced a doubling of their wages over a decade – and that they are now being singled out for worse treatment than others are experiencing. They feel that the private sector media are deliberately attempting to vilify them, and that the government is deliberately attempting to divide and conquer.

However, this doesn't mean that waste shouldn't be eradicated. There seems to be a widespread assumption – at least among trade unionists – that all of the government's day to day spending, about €55 billion in a year, is somehow money well spent and that any reduction in that amount would lead to a noticeable and dangerous reduction in the quality of services provided. One of the criticisms made of McCarthy was that he has not given enough consideration to the damage that would be done by his cuts, that he was only interested in finding ways to save money. However, to take just one example, a report on resource allocation in the Gardaí, conducted by the American head of the Garda Siochana Inspectorate, Kathleen O'Toole, showed how 2,000 Gardaí had been added prior to the 2007 general election for political reasons and without sufficient and due consideration as to how they would be deployed effectively. Her report portrayed management structures that were backward in comparison with international norms and that almost guaranteed extravagant waste and poor delivery of services.

The trade union movement argued that it had been willing to work towards transformative structural change in the organization and delivery of public services, but that the government had walked away from this proposal during negotiations prior to the December 2009 budget, preferring instead to insist on pay cuts.

The government had sought a permanent €1.3 billion reduction in its public sector pay bill as part of an attempted €4 billion reduction in the gap between its annual spending and income. Job losses were ruled out, even in instances where there could have been lay-offs without doing damage to services, because the redundancy payments could not be afforded or agreed with the unions and there was no desire to add to the state's social welfare bill. Rather than agreeing to pay cuts, the unions suggested that public servants take an additional twelve days of unpaid leave in 2010. Estimates as to how much this would save the state ranged from €300 million to €800 million, leaving a large part of the gap still to be filled as well as raising serious questions as to just how this idea would work practically. And, just as importantly, the unions wanted full pay restored the following year, meaning the ambition of reducing the public sector pay bill permanently was not being addressed.

There was public outrage when the proposed deal with the unions was revealed. The government backed away, faced with internal political dissent and scathing media coverage. Unfortunately for the unions, the subsequent revelation that public sector reform had in fact been offered to the government came too late, and was too little to overcome the impression that had been fixed in the public's mind of a bloated public service that was unwilling to offer meaningful and deserved change without getting something in return.

The budget cuts, when they were announced, met with little disapproval outside of the public sector. A one-day stoppage by public sector workers in late November had not been a success, mainly because the media focused on the sudden extraordinary delays in traffic heading north of the border. Even though many of those who decided to take advantage of the schools being closed may have been parents of pupils, the perception developed, rightly or wrongly, that a very sizeable number were public sector workers taking the day off to spend their shopping money in the Six Counties.

The unions were left in a very difficult position. Even if, as they claimed, they had put forward what may have been excellent suggestions for long-overdue reforms of work practices in the public sector, the details were complicated; and many felt these changes should have been applied in any event, and not used to barter away pay cuts. It is difficult for many voters to believe that previous benchmarking and other pay increases were not linked to reform. Offers of change now ring hollow.

Trade union leaders are just like politicians in serving the constituency that pays them. Their responsibility is to get the best deal for their members, but that does not necessarily equate with what is best for the country. In the run-up to the budget, SIPTU's O'Connor complained bitterly about the loss of social partnership, and about what he called dangerous efforts to deflate the economy, and went so far as to call for a change of government if Brian Cowen's administration didn't do as he requested.

In his post-budget comments Begg insisted that the trade union movement was not 'formally' planning to oust the government in response to the budget. But Larry Broderick of the Irish Bank Officials' Association said that the trade union movement needed to respond to cutbacks with 'a strategic approach, focusing on local issues, non-cooperation and taking the government out of power'. Broderick warned that the country faced a 'very serious winter of discontent'. He ignored the fact that the jobs of all of his members – until that stage at least – had been protected by the provision of the bank guarantee and that many had actually had pay increases confirmed and sanctioned by the Labour Court despite the near-bankrupt status of the employers. Begg said Broderick's comments reflected the general feeling among ICTU members and the ICTU executive condemned the budget as 'a savage and brutal attack on working people and the most vulnerable – the single worst budget in the history of the state'. It unanimously adopted a motion describing the budget as a 'profoundly ideological exercise' that attacked working people, the unemployed and families. Notably Begg was a director of the Central Bank at the time of its failure to properly regulate what was happening at the banks. As a director he shares in the responsibility for the oversight of the bank, irrespective of the views he may have expressed in his professional capacity as general secretary of the ICTU. He has retained his place on the Central Bank board, keeping his seat at the heart of the establishment. So what would the government do in response? Begg was no doubt mindful of the appeal to some workers of men like Eamon Devoy of the TEEU and Brendan Ogle of Unite, both of whom represent workers in the ESB, which provides the bulk of the country's electricity to homes and businesses. Soon after the Dáil approved his budget cutbacks to public sector pay, Lenihan indicated that he would like to do the same at commercial semi-state companies, owned, but not controlled, by the state. Ogle warned of a 'ferocious response' if efforts were made to cut the pay of the workers he represented. He said he had no intention of launching protest marches; he would simply turn off the lights. Ogle was a man to be taken very seriously, given that he rose to prominence as a train driver who formed a militant break-away worker's organization and successfully orchestrated a number of train stoppages in the early part of this decade. Devoy would have been quick to get his electricians to do the same. Not surprisingly, the government moved away from a confrontation it might not have won.

This is where the power of the trade unions – which represent public sector workers and about 15 per cent of private sector workers – promises to be crucial throughout 2010. These unions have the power to disrupt if they do not get what they want and therefore make things worse. Their arguments may have some merit, but will they succeed on that basis or on the strength of their threat?

The unions, aware that many of their members did not want to engage in action that would cost them wages they could ill afford to lose, began a campaign based on a form of 'work to rule', which it said would inconvenience management and government without impacting severely on the provision of services to the public. It was a fine line to walk, and the government prepared plans to suspend state employees who did not do as instructed. Both sides moved slowly towards possible confrontation.

Had Bertie Ahern remained in power, it is likely that a deal – good or not – would have been struck. Ahern likes to be remembered as a deal-maker but a more accurate assessment of his legacy is that he did not mind the nation's money as carefully as he looked after his own.

Ahern has complained bitterly that 'some people are trying to rewrite history' and that 'people need to recognize that and not be deluded by the spin that it is only Ireland that is experiencing tougher times'. Ahern's claim that 'the state was in safe hands' while he was in charge, and that his critics won't admit that the problems were caused by external factors, came to be seen as arrogant drivel that could not be sustained by objective examination of the evidence. It ignored the fact that Ireland had had a chance to protect itself somewhat from the full consequences of the economic crash but instead followed policies that put us top of the queue of likely international bankrupts (with the exception of Greece).

Brian Cowen, as Minister for Finance, assisted him in his profligacy for four years, and then, as Taoiseach, took the approach of rueing the over-dependence on property and construction, as if someone else had been responsible for that policy. Cowen has taken enormous stick for the way he has dealt with the crisis, and in particular for his uninspiring public performances that were said to lack leadership. And even when the government has taken tough and politically unpopular decisions, the kudos have gone to his successor in finance, Brian Lenihan.

Taking its time and trying to mitigate the severity of its actions didn't save the government from being routed at the 2009 European and local elections, however. Nor did they save Bertie Ahern's brother Maurice from trailing in at fifth place in a Dublin Central by-election, despite his brother's enormous local pulling power, leading junior finance minister Martin Mansergh to comment that in future the government 'may as well be hung for a sheep as a lamb'.

Fianna Fáil's opinion poll ratings started to rise off the floor late in 2009 and at the beginning of 2010, partly as a result of their being seen to be firm with the unions. How long that would last remained to be seen, particularly as anger grew at the revelation that the country's top civil servants – 160 deputy secretaries and assistant secretaries in the various ministerial departments – and over 400 council executives, HSE bosses, senior Gardaí and army officers were going to suffer only half of the pay cuts proposed for them in the budget on the basis that they had lost their previously guaranteed bonuses.

Meanwhile, unemployment in the private sector continued to soar, businesses closed and domestic spending remained in the doldrums, developments that were mitigated only by a robust export performance from the private sector. The government looked at the experience of Greece and realized that it had to hold the line on reducing public sector costs if we were to retain the confidence of the international lenders upon which we had become totally dependent, irrespective of the unions' disapproval or whatever damage they were willing to do. And the crisis of our banking catastrophe threatened to get far worse.

48

The banks – having it all their own way

In the nod and wink culture of Irish politics, the phrase 'an Irish solution to an Irish problem' has often been used to confer praise as much as to denote disapproval. Sometimes we boast of our cleverness in coming up with a way of dealing with a problem that others wouldn't have thought of; others see that attitude as not just typical of how delusional we can be when confronting what really needs to be done but as a source of our problems in itself.

NAMA – as outlined in Chapter 39 – is most definitely an 'Irish solution to an Irish problem'. More and more details of how it would be run, and how it would value the loans transferred to it from the banks, emerged during the latter half of 2009, after the first edition of this book was completed. The arguments as to whether it was a good idea, or whether it would work to resolve the banking and property crisis or make things worse by creating a further mountain of debt for future generations to repay, continued as the timeframe for its implementation was extended and changes to its structure were required.

However, NAMA received initial approval from the European Central Bank and European Commission – although final approval was delayed and changes were demanded – and, according to e-mails released to the *Irish Times* under the Freedom of Information Act, a ringing endorsement from the International Monetary Fund. The IMF's banking recovery expert Steven Seelig wrote to the Department of Finance to say that its definition of 'long-term economic value' on bank loans was 'masterful', as it was 'both sufficiently specific and sufficiently vague to allow appropriate flexibility. I hope you can retain this language.'

The issue of 'long-term economic value', as decided by the department, was highly contentious. As expected, it confirmed that NAMA would not pay the banks the full amount at which the loans on its books were valued. However, it decided to pay the banks more than the current value of the loans, on the basis that they were undervalued during 2009 and that the property underlying the loans would recover at least some of its old value over the following ten years that NAMA was expected to be in existence.

The government announced that it was buying loans that were valued on the books of the banks at €77 billion, a figure that included €9 billion in unpaid interest that had been added on to the original borrowed sum. It said that these loans were worth just €47 billion (based on the value of the underlying assets that provided security for the repayment of the loans) but that it would buy these assets for €54 billion. It disagreed that the current market value correctly represented the true worth of the assets, or the 'long-term economic value'. Instead of taking advantage of the distressed condition of the banks to buy itself loans at less than their estimated value, the state decided to cut the banks a break by overpaying in the hope that the value of the loans would eventually recover. It was a perversion of normal investment behaviour and left the state open to major losses in the future if the loans were not repaid or if the assets supporting them were sold for less than the amount paid for them.

There was a reason for this extraordinary decision: paying the current market value of the loans would potentially bankrupt most of the banks. The losses that they would incur on the sale of the loans would more than wipe out their remaining capital. If the state wanted those banks to remain in business – which, essentially, it had committed to when it introduced the bank guarantee in September 2008 – it would have to invest tens of billions of euro in capital that would have to be borrowed. The state's own balance sheet would change materially as a result, making further borrowing for other purposes, if even possible to attain, more expensive. State officials also felt that, while the massive outflow of deposits from Anglo after nationalization arose mainly from reputational issues – who would want money there, irrespective of the government guarantee that it will be repaid? – there might be similar large outflows at any other nationalized bank. The liquidity of the banks, and therefore of the economy, as much as solvency, remained a key issue for the state, and the NAMA strategy was designed very much with that in mind.

However, the 'long-term economic value' was being calculated upon assumptions that were the subject of much criticism too.

There was some surprise in September 2009 when it emerged that John

Mulcahy had been chosen to oversee the valuation process for the loans that would be transferred to NAMA, but this turned to astonishment when he predicted a recovery in property values to near their most inflated point over the lifetime of NAMA.

As chief executive of estate agent Jones Lang LaSalle for decades, Mulcahy had been central to many of the biggest commercial property transactions and had represented many of the country's richest developers. I first met him with Mark Kavanagh, one of the main developers of the IFSC, at a dinner organized by P. J. Mara in the early 1990s, and came across him many other times in the company of some of the country's richest businessmen. Mulcahy was one of the agents involved in the sale of the Irish Glass Bottle site to the Becbay consortium, for example. He is married to Margaret Clandillon, an aviation leasing expert who once worked in GPA at the time Mara was advising it.

When Mulcahy appeared at an Oireachtas committee in September to explain his suitability to be chief valuer for NAMA, he said he had been a 'bear of property for the last four years', that he had lost speaking engagements as a result and that he was not very popular for his views. However, he did speak at one investment event that I chaired in October 2007 and I do not recall him being particularly negative about the Irish property market: indeed, he was one of many who argued with Gerry McCaughey of Century Homes, who electrified the event by warning, correctly, that the Irish housing construction market was heading for a serious slump.

Mulcahy said that, historically, property prices rebound by 88 per cent within seven years of their troughs. The statistics may well bear him out on this, but the extent of the crash in the property market in this country far exceeds anything that has ever happened before. The capacity of banks to lend over the next decade is so constrained that it makes such a recovery most unlikely, even if irrational exuberance were to take hold again. Mulcahy's own words from a 2006 conference – 'when government intervenes in the property market, or in any other market for that matter, the issue is not what good it will do but, rather, how much harm it will do before the intervention is reversed' – may come back to haunt him.

The valuers employed by NAMA had their work cut out, as they had to deal with the repercussions of previous valuations. The loans to be transferred may have had a 'book value' of €77 billion, but many of those valuations may have been wild overestimates. Often banks had relied unduly on the valuations provided by commercial property estate agents for buildings and land, and tailored their loans accordingly without making their own assessment as to whether these valuations were attainable or sustainable. Sometimes they had lent without even getting valuations done.

There was also an issue with what came to be known as 'phantom equity'. Instead of putting cash as equity into an acquisition or development project – to make up about 30 per cent of the purchase price, with the balance supplied as loans by the banks – some developers pledged separate investment properties as their deposits. But when the value of those properties plummeted – and there may have been separate legal charges on them anyway, which meant that they too were going to end up in NAMA – the value of the equity proved illusory. Borrowed money could also be 'phantom equity': it was often promised as equity and secured on personal guarantees that the borrowers were now unable to cover.

The problems multiplied when it was discovered that in many cases no proper title to the properties had been provided. The methods used to avoid stamp duties – as described earlier in the book – created other issues as to the true ownership of title, further delaying the transfer of security to NAMA. Then there was the issue of multiple lenders: if a developer had sourced money from more than one bank, especially if one was foreign, then sorting who had the claim to ownership of a piece of property that was to be transferred to NAMA because of 'duplication of security' became excruciating. It is now suspected that some borrowers behaved in ways that were reckless and bordered on fraud, while some lenders were careless and too greedy to check things out properly. Banks are also concerned that some debtors are moving to protect their assets, including family homes, from the possibility of seizure by the banks or NAMA by transferring them into their wives' or children's names.

The legislation that brought NAMA into being was passed by the Dáil in late 2009 and Brendan McDonagh was confirmed as its full-time chief executive. In early January 2010 he defended the pricing of the loans as announced by NAMA despite widespread scoffing – and evidence from values disclosed in court cases – that the present value of €47 million attributed was hopelessly optimistic. The original estimates were that Anglo would put €28 billion into NAMA, AIB €24 billion, Bank of Ireland €16 billion and INBS €8 billion, but at the time of writing nothing has been confirmed.

Even if the IMF liked the sleight of hand involved in NAMA, others of great international repute didn't. Nobel Prize-winning economics professor Joe Stiglitz, on a visit to Ireland, described NAMA as

highway robbery which we see happening all over the world, with guns pointing at the heads of political leaders and the bankers claiming the sky will fall down and the economy will be devastated unless they get this money.

Countries which allow banks to go under by following the ordinary rules of capitalism have done fine. The US has let 100 banks go this year alone, as did Sweden and Norway during their crises. In the US, it's just the big, politically powerful banks that have not been allowed to go down, for political reasons.

If you spend your money in bailing out banks without taking all the equity you will end up with a huge national debt, a liability with no assets to show for it. Now that will scare off investors in the future.

Within weeks of McDonagh's statement it became clear that the government would not be buying many of the loans because they did not have adequate security attached to them. That, added to the reduced valuation on the other loans, meant that the government would not be issuing anything like €54 billion in bonds to the banks, as had been intended. The European Commission would not allow something that was starting to look suspiciously like state aid that Ireland expected the ECB to fund. But that news was not as good as many believed it to be. It meant the banks needed more capital, cash up front and probably from the state.

Yet the government and its advisers radiated confidence. Alan Ahearne, the academic appointed as adviser to Lenihan, said that 'we will fairly soon have a banking system that is fit for purpose. Putting them [the loans] together, which happens in an asset management company, allows you to maximize the value of your assets.'

A fully functioning banking system is a major requirement for the economy. The amount of private debt outstanding is an enormous issue – at over €170 billion it's proportionately one of the highest amounts of household debt in the developed world. Of that amount about €140 billion is related to the purchase of property. But just as big an issue was the ongoing provision of finance for business. Would businesses be able to provide complementary finance for whatever capital they had? The foreign banks either pulled out of Ireland or scaled back their operations from late 2008 onwards. The power of the banks was misapplied disastrously from 2004 onwards by over-lending, but since 2008 there has been an equally damaging about-turn, leading to serious under-supply of new lending and offensive and unfair treatment of existing customers.

The problem was twofold. There was a lack of finance at the banks themselves but also a sudden aversion to risk, with customers being regarded as potential failures rather than as profitable opportunities.

As outlined earlier in this book, the banks had been borrowing on a short-term basis to fund long-term lending commitments. While the ECB maintained the Irish banks in business – using an estimated 15 per cent of its bank funding to do so, even though the Irish banking system accounted for just over 5 per cent of total euro-zone bank assets – this could not continue indefinitely. AIB and Bank of Ireland had to source replacement funding, and, despite the extension of the state guarantee to five years' duration after a quick Dáil vote in December 2009, this became increasingly expensive and difficult to achieve, in the light of a shortage of funds and plenty of other banks chasing what was available. The cost of this money eroded profits at the banks, although they tried as hard as possible to recoup it from their own customers.

The issue of personal guarantees became a major one for business people during 2009 and early 2010. The banks demanded pledges that the borrowers would surrender personal assets if their privately owned businesses were unable to make repayments. This requirement, which runs contrary to the principle of limited liability in companies and which is not invoked in other economies, was initiated by Anglo to give it added security and then copied by others. Nobody ever expected it be enforced in Irish business.

In certain cases, banks had allowed loans to 'roll over', either by demanding only the interest repayments, with capital to be repaid later when the asset was sold, or by adding the interest to the original loan, all for subsequent repayment, but by 2009 this was no longer possible and there was a procession of high-profile attempts to enforce personal guarantees.

Paddy Kelly was the first to go under, as banks sought the repayment of €110 million covered by personal guarantees. Of hotelier Hugh O'Regan's €37.5 million debts to Anglo, over €26 million was covered by personal guarantees, which of course O'Regan could not repay. Niall McFadden of Boundary Capital, a major investor in the planned redevel-opment of the Arnotts department store on Henry Street in Dublin 1, gave personal guarantees of €15 million and €14 million to Anglo and National Irish Bank respectively.

This experience made borrowers very wary when it came to negotiating new finance from the banks. The demands for security became even more onerous. Yet the banks continued to insist that they were open for business. Mark Cunningham, the new head of business banking at Bank of Ireland, told an Irish Small and Medium Enterprise (ISME) conference in November that there was no shortage of money in his bank, with the level of deposits even higher than when the SSIAs were in full flow. But that was only part of the picture, because much more money was needed from elsewhere to fund his bank's activities. Cunningham chose to highlight a shortage of good lending propositions as the reason for the slump in lending.

It also became clear that even if a scaled-back NAMA came into existence, the bonds supplied to the banks would not necessarily be presented to the ECB as security for new borrowing by the banks. They would be used simply to boost the banks' balance sheets. In one of his last public appearances before stepping down as chief executive of AIB, Eugene Sheehy bluntly told an Oireachtas committee there would be 'no sudden burst of lending' after NAMA's establishment. In early February 2010 the *Irish Times* published another e-mail from the IMF's Seelig to the Department of Finance, which it had obtained as early as April 2009. Seelig had warned that NAMA would not release significant new funds that could be used by the banks for lending. The availability of bank finance had been the government's key rationale when convincing people that NAMA's creation was absolutely necessary. Critics who said consistently that this was nonsense now had firm evidence to support their view that the government had always been aware of this fact but denied it.

One of the most significant, brave and innovative decisions made by Lenihan in 2009 was his appointment of Patrick Honohan as the new governor of the Central Bank after John Hurley's retirement. He was an outsider, with all previous appointments in the 66-year history of the bank being internal promotions or, more usually, long-service rewards for senior civil servants at the Department of Finance. Although Honohan had worked previously in the Central Bank, he had left to join the International Monetary Fund. He had been an adviser to Garret FitzGerald's 1982–7 government before beginning an acclaimed career at the World Bank.

He had taken up the position as professor of international financial economics at Trinity College Dublin a few years earlier and become very critical of domestic economic policy, writing a number of newspaper and academic articles about the loss of competitiveness, employment issues and banking. He accused the Irish banks of getting caught up in a 'mass psychology', which saw them putting 60 per cent of their assets into property. He had expressed serious doubts about the working structure of NAMA and provided ideas as to how to limit the risk to the taxpayer. Crucially, he warned against using NAMA 'as a covert way to recapitalize the banks by paying too much for their problem loans'.

Honohan also wanted an inquiry into what had gone wrong. Colm McCarthy was the first significant figure to call for an inquiry into the causes of the banking catastrophe, arguing in August 2009 that the public could not be persuaded of the merits of major cutbacks unless it was made aware of what had happened and how. He was more or less ignored. But the real impetus developed in December 2009 when Honohan called for a commission of inquiry along the lines of the US investigation into 9/11.

The timing of Honohan's intervention was significant. His call came just as the 'we must move on' brigade was becoming far more prominent and confident in public debate, playing upon the understandable desire of many people to move away from the gloom that has enveloped the country. The clichés abounded: 'we are where we are and have to accept it', we 'can't change the past much as we might like to' and 'we have to be positive moving forward'.

Cowen's initial reaction to Honohan's suggestion was not encouraging. He fell back on the old crutch of ascribing our woes to international events before holding out the possibility that maybe something along the lines Honohan suggested – using economists and social scientists as well as politicians – might be considered at some date well into the future. But the political pressure mounted over the Christmas period, especially from the Green partners in government. Eventually, the government conceded but hardly in a satisfactory way: it said that it had received strong legal advice to the effect that a full public inquiry into the banking crisis could influence court cases, and so went for a private or secret investigation instead. This horrified those who believed a public examination would not only be useful in avoiding a repetition of past mistakes, but would also expose those responsible for the mess and ensure they would be in no position to dictate the terms of attempted recovery.

The banking disaster, for the most part, did not involve illegality or recklessness but rather straightforward stupidity and mismanagement. However, there are many people who may not want to be exposed publicly: senior politicians, civil servants from the departments of the Taoiseach and Finance, Central Bank officials and financial regulator officials, just as much as those who worked in the banks.

Where criminality may have occurred, there is no established track record of vigorous prosecution in this country. If Bernie Madoff, the American investment guru who fleeced wealthy clients of billions before admitting his lies and being sent swiftly to jail for theft, had been Irish, he would probably still be awaiting prosecution; the case might not even have got to court.

After all, this is a country where a former government minister, Ray Burke, was declared corrupt by a Dáil-appointed tribunal, overseen by a High Court judge, and has had his tax evasion exposed, but he has spent no more than six months in jail. He continues to draw a pension worth over €100,000 annually from the state. When Frank Dunlop was jailed in mid-2009 it was claimed that this proved 'nobody is above the law'. Dunlop admitted corruption in a case involving minor politicians, all of whom said they would protest their innocence if ever prosecuted. He was one of the few exceptions who proved the rule and, in any case, he was more of a middleman than a player. Bigger fish than Dunlop suffered the indignity of adverse tribunal findings but paid no real price other than enduring embarrassment.

When the events that destroyed the economic well-being of the country are examined, those who clearly broke, rather than bent, the laws, or those who took advantage of poorly written laws, may have little to fear, other than a reduction in their wealth. Will those who donated to political parties, or those who possess capital that can assist in reconstruction, be left off the hook? What if state officials participated in legally dubious or selfish activities? Can this be justified by claims that it was in the national interest? If so, who defines what the 'national interest' is?

Whatever a banking inquiry may disclose, it seems that the events of the night of 29 September 2008, leading up to the decision to implement the bank guarantee, will remain hidden, as they are excluded from the terms of reference for the inquiry. The *Sunday Times* has sought the disclosure of two memoranda that documented the official record of the meetings that evening. But the Information Commissioner, Emily O'Reilly, a former journalist, decided that these were to be kept secret, despite a recommendation from Sean Garvey, a senior investigator in the Office of the Information Commissioner, that they be released because of the 'strong public interest'.

Garvey argued that, although the information was given by the banks in confidence, 'the public interest in the department being held to account for its decision to commit billions of euro to the banking sector in the context of the guarantee would outweigh any damage to confidentiality in its dealings with the sector'.

O'Reilly decided that the records should remain secret based on an exemption in the FoI Act for records used at a government meeting; in such cases, public interest does not take precedence over the department's request for secrecy. Garvey argued that the 'department has not provided any evidence that these two records were provided to government members for a government meeting', but O'Reilly accepted an objection from the Finance Department that the documents were used for the conduct of an 'incorporeal' cabinet meeting. The department had threatened O'Reilly with High Court action to prevent the release of the records. Garvey said that the documents 'appear to record the views of senior banking executives on the difficulties that faced them and the response of the Taoiseach, Minister [for Finance] and the department to the views'.

The details of what was possibly the most momentous and costly decision in the history of this state are to remain hidden. The rich, powerful and well connected, the people who really run Ireland, are to remain protected.

Postscript: Where are they now?

Liam Carroll: Although Paddy Kelly was the first of the major property developers to admit he was bust and get on with handing over his assets to his creditors, the collapse of the always controversial Liam Carroll was a more significant event.

Carroll's Zoe group tumbled in late 2009 when it failed to secure court protection from immediate repayment of debts of more than €1.3 billion. Two other major holding companies owned by Carroll, Dunloe and Orthanc, brought estimated liabilities to about €3 billion for the group.

Carroll started a fire-sale of assets in early 2009 and asked creditors to accept only 60 per cent of what they were owed. Banks were asked to accept a moratorium on repayments and to roll interest on to the original principle. He got extra finance from AIB and Bank of Ireland but ACCBank scuppered the plan. Owned by the Dutch Rabobank, it was not prepared to sell its loans to NAMA, wanting instead to get as much of its €136 million back itself and as quickly as possible.

The other banks stood by as Carroll tried to save himself by applying to the High Court for the appointment of an examiner, which would have given him more time to restructure. Carroll claimed that he would have net assets of €300 million again within three years if the banks agreed to restructure the loans. Justice Peter Kelly said this was nonsense. 'Given current market conditions and with little or no prospect for improvement in the future, on the basis of all the current economic indicators, this degree of optimism on the part of the independent accountant borders, if it does not actually trespass, upon the fanciful.'

Carroll appealed to the Supreme Court, lost, and then, incredibly, tried again to have an examiner appointed, using a plan based on different numbers. This claim was run by his executives, who claimed that Carroll had been ill during the first application and had withheld crucial information. ACC objected this time and Justice Frank Clarke rejected the application because 'it is the fact that it needs to be right on so many independent factors before it could even approach balance sheet solvency and cashflow solvency [which] leads me to the conclusion that it is significantly improbable that the financial status of the Zoe group . . . would be such as would give it a reasonable prospect of survival.' The game was up.

Carroll's hotels have been closed and the rooms are available as cheap self-catering studio apartments. INBS is seeking judgment to get €60 million from him under a personal guarantee; Carroll says he owes only €30 million. Carroll had offered personal guarantees for €34 million to allow for the drawdown of additional funds to pay Zoe's unsecured creditors. He pledged part of his pension fund as further security for loans. His shareholdings in Aer Lingus, Greencore and ICG were sold at losses amounting to hundreds of millions of euro. Work has stopped on the headquarters that he was building for Anglo in the docks: its shell stands as a fitting monument to the collapse of the boom. In April 2009, just months before his collapse, he had transferred the family home, as well as a large landbank, into his wife's name.

In January 2010 AIB started court action to recover more than €550 million in unpaid loans and interest from Zoe. Judge Peter Kelly expressed amazement that the security AIB had on the properties was so 'tenuous', 'fragile' and 'a far cry from a legal mortgage'. Kelly accused AIB of not having bothered to inspect the title to the Carroll properties and of failing to have conducted a proper investigation into its security. It took weeks to sort out in AIB's favour.

Bernard McNamara: In late 2009 Bernard McNamara's mezzanine investors in the Irish Glass Bottle deal – the group put together by Davy Stockbrokers and including the likes of Martin Naughton, Lochlann Quinn, Coolmore Stud and Barry O'Callaghan – sought the return of their money: €62.5 million from McNamara personally and €98 million from his company Donatex and went to the Commercial Court to get judgment.

After pleading with his creditors to wait, offering just €100,000 per month towards repayment, McNamara was forced to concede that he had no unencumbered assets and that he was no longer a man of significant net worth.

McNamara had been undone by the way he raised money for his Glass

Bottle adventure. He had borrowed massively from investors who were not going into NAMA and to whom he had given a personal guarantee over the loan repayments. The loans became repayable if, within thirty months of January 2007, Becbay had not applied for all necessary Section 25 certificates to get fast-track planning permission from the DDDA or had not received planning permission for development from Dublin City Council. McNamara has taken a €102 million action for damages against the DDDA, but any winnings would be distributed among his creditors.

McNamara was forced to surrender assets that his banks sold quickly. In January 2010 the *Sunday Business Post* reported that Bank of Ireland had taken control of a London development bought with help from investors assembled by Davy. In 2007 McNamara paid €65 million for 1 Park Place in Canary Wharf, but Bank of Ireland flogged it for just under €20 million, which suggests that the investment for McNamara and the Davy clients was wiped out, and that the bank may have lost over half of the loan it had advanced.

In December, McNamara told the *Sunday Independent* that banks had done massive damage to the economy and contributed to spiralling unemployment by curtailing their lending. He criticized the government's non-funding of large-scale development projects. 'I can't understand why so many projects have been stopped. These would have been major projects which would have created or sustained many jobs that could and should have gone ahead but they didn't.'

He later admitted that he was likely to lose his Ailesbury Road mansion, once valued at over €30 million, as he had pledged all of his assets to the banks to cover debts estimated at over €1.5 billion. He said his building contracting firm, Michael McNamara & Sons, from which he was resigning as a director, would not be affected. It is owned in the Isle of Man and by those whom McNamara has described as separate owners, but many wondered just how it could be regarded as outside of his assets.

DDDA: The publication of the Dublin Docklands Development Authority's 2008 annual accounts came in November 2009, on the same day that the government authorized publication of the special commission's report on the Catholic Church's cover-up of child sex abuse by its priests in Dublin. It may have been a coincidence, but it was a good day to bury the bad news that the state's loss on this particular corporate adventure was €213 million and that the involvement in the Irish Glass Bottle site was the main cause of the disaster. The site was valued now at just €60 million and that didn't take into account the likely cost of capping and monitoring methane gas emissions.

The DDDA's new chairman, Niamh Brennan – wife of former PD leader Michael McDowell but a corporate financial expert in her own right – admitted to still not understanding the commercial rationale behind the DDDA's involvement in the Glass Bottle site, but has mused aloud at the disproportionate amount of influence held by Anglo Irish Bank. Chief executive Paul Maloney left not long after her arrival.

The DDDA has swung from having an excessively pro-development, entrepreneurial culture to being almost paralysed, terrified of doing anything wrong in its planning decisions and without the money to participate in anything itself.

Derek Quinlan: When the going got tough for Derek Quinlan, he got going . . . to Switzerland.

The *Sunday Times* revealed in August 2009 that Quinlan had not just retired from his investment firm Quinlan Private – as disclosed a month earlier – but decamped to Switzerland, establishing a new home and enrolling the children of his second family in school there. In early 2010 it was disclosed that he had resigned as a director of his company in late November, leaving the remaining directors at Quinlan Private – Olan Cremin, Peter Donnelly, Thomas Dowd and Mark O'Donnell – as its four partners. One of their main jobs was to raise finance from syndicate members to restructure investments where the value of properties had fallen.

More personal assets of Quinlan's were put up for sale, including his mansion, bought for €45 million, in Cap Ferrat, where his neighbours include Chelsea football club owner Roman Abramovich and Microsoft co-founder Paul Allen. He had spent €20 million on improving the house by adding art, an internal lift, a lawn tennis court, a private beach, putting greens and an infinity pool. It was up for sale at a hopelessly optimistic €125 million.

The extent of Quinlan's debts – both personal and corporate – has never been confirmed, but it has been speculated that they were in the region of €2.5 billion, much of it with state-owned Anglo Irish Bank. It is not yet clear whether Quinlan's move to Switzerland will complicate the recovery of his debts to Irish banks. When I asked Brian Lenihan specifically about Quinlan during a radio interview in late 2009, he promised that everything possible would be done to secure repayment of debts Quinlan owes to Irish banks.

Michael Fingleton: Michael Fingleton didn't pay back his controversial €1 million bonus from Irish Nationwide Building Society as he had promised publicly. The former INBS chief executive had made the commitment in a statement in April 2009, but it turned out to be a ruse to get a media siege off the doorstep of his luxury home in Shankill, County Dublin. Late in 2009 the Department of Finance and INBS confirmed he was sticking to his original position: the bonus was legitimate and he was under no legal obligation to repay it. Fingleton also transferred ownership of his family home to wife Eileen, along with three acres of land.

Fingleton did not escape further media scrutiny. An RTÉ *Primetime Investigates* documentary in December 2009 revealed that he personally sanctioned a loan of €1.6 million for Charlie McCreevy in 2006 to assist the European Commissioner purchase a €1.5 million investment property at the K Club in Straffan, the venue of that year's Ryder Cup. Giving more than a 100 per cent loan was a breach of the society's internal guidelines, but Fingleton personally approved it. Properties at the venue have more than halved in value since. Fingleton has revealed himself to be sensitive to criticism, going so far as to demand the rewriting of a Dáil record to expunge critical comments of him by a Fine Gael TD.

Denis O'Brien: The battle for control of INM ended badly for Denis O'Brien – and only marginally better for the O'Reilly family. An extraordinary deal had to be cut with the bondholders, who were owed just €200 million, without which the company would have gone into receivership or examinership. The bondholders got 46.3 per cent of the company in exchange for €123 million of the debt. INM then launched a rights issue to raise up to €92 million, which also went to the bondholders. O'Reilly's holding was diluted to 14.5 per cent and O'Brien's to 14 per cent. Neither subsequently went into the market to buy more shares. As a result of the four months' delay in getting things sorted, INM owed, and paid, €13 million in interest and penalties to the bondholders.

The understanding between the parties collapsed, as O'Brien engaged in a series of high-profile attacks on the strategy adapted by the board. Somehow his side had missed the significance of a motion carried at the annual general meeting earlier in the year, which gave the board the authorization to issue new shares without seeking new permission from shareholders if the shares were not being issued for cash. O'Brien decided against charming the bondholders. 'If they think Denis O'Brien is going to write a cheque to the bondholders then they are smoking dope,' he said.

In late August, O'Brien told Gavin O'Reilly that he wasn't up to the job of negotiating with banks and bondholders, that O'Brien's directors on the INM board had been treated 'disgracefully' and that generally he was a failure. He followed this up with a letter alleging that the board 'still continues to operate very much under the influence and control of A. J. O'Reilly and the O'Reilly family and this is compromising the board's independence and judgement'. He said Gaffney, Connolly and Buckley – his board directors – were 'thwarted and obstructed at every turn by the existing management and board members'. O'Reilly responded by issuing his note of the phone conversation with O'Brien, in which O'Brien had said: 'I will destroy you and your father and I will go after everything.'

However, O'Brien's attempts to remove chairman Brian Hillery and independent director Baroness Margaret Jay failed, and his demand for the immediate closure of the Independent titles in London was, at €35 million, deemed too costly. He flip-flopped on the eventual sale of the South African outdoor advertising business for almost €100 million. He pitched a number of plans to banks, bondholders and management that would have given him control of the company in return for an investment of €100 million in cash, but nobody was interested. O'Brien's loss on his foray is estimated at over €400 million.

O'Brien faced into 2010 knowing that the Moriarty Tribunal was about to issue a report into his acquisition of the second mobile phone licence that would be about as far away from his liking as possible. The consequences are unknown at the time of writing. He continued to stand by his friends, bringing Sean FitzPatrick to the top table at an Amnesty International fund-raising lunch late in 2009.

He became a high-profile and regular face in the media after the earthquake in Haiti, where his company Digicel is a major employer. He travelled to the country, pledging aid and asking others to contribute, and then went to the World Economic Forum in Davos, where, alongside former US President Bill Clinton, he spoke of how he believed there were great opportunities for business investment in the impoverished island that would be profitable for everyone.

*

Michael Lowry: In early 2010 independent TD Michael Lowry launched a pre-emptive strike against the looming findings of the Moriarty Tribunal, bemoaning that he had not been given sufficient opportunity to explain his actions while Minister for Communications. Moriarty will have come to his own conclusions by the time this book goes to press.

Lowry remained unabashed about his enthusiasm for property speculation. In late October 2009 he emerged as one of the public spokesmen for an incredible new idea, a proposed €450 million development for North Tipperary put forward by Richard Quirke, a former local Garda who became rich by operating 'gaming machines' in Dublin city centre 'emporia' and who had used the cash to speculate profitably in property.

Quirke offered to buck the conventional wisdom that property development was a dead duck by building a giant casino, a 500-room luxury hotel, a golf course, an all-weather horse-racing track, a separate greyhound-racing circuit, shops and a full replica of the White House that re-creates original interiors apparently lost to renovation. There was a plan for an entertainment centre, with a retractable roof, capable of holding 15,000, as a rural alternative to the O2 in Dublin; it would have a chapel, parking for 8,000 cars and aerial access.

Quirke said he had spent €30 million on assembling the 800-acre site and lodged the planning application with North Tipperary County Council, promising 1,000 local jobs during the construction phase and 2,000 afterwards. Lowry was confident that there'd be no local objections and that work could start during 2010.

Quirke had more than a few obstacles to overcome despite Lowry's optimism. There was a massive surplus of hotel accommodation in the country; golf clubs did not have sufficient numbers of paying members to cover overheads; Horse Racing Ireland was talking of shutting courses because they could not pay their way and shopping was no longer the national pastime now that incomes had been hammered and debts were being unwound.

Quirke said he would not approach Irish banks 'even if they were interested' as he 'would not go near them'. He did not seem worried that finding foreign banks to lend money to what Lowry called 'the most sophisticated and ambitious project the country has ever seen' would be a difficult task, given this country's reputation.

A casino would be the cash cow, subsidizing other parts of the operation and providing the money to repay the loans and dividends for investors. So, while Lowry said this project wouldn't cost the state a cent in grant aid, 'floating on its own commercial merit', and indeed could provide enormous tax income from the jobs, VAT and other sources, it remained dependent on the government changing the laws that limit the size of casinos.

Lowry said the Taoiseach and ministers had been made aware of the project and he was confident of their support. Minister for Justice Dermot Ahern was conducting a review of the legislation with a view to changing it. The question arose as to whether Lowry's continued support for the government depended on the super-casino legislation going through.

Bertie Ahern had cut a deal with Lowry – on terms that remain secret – after the last election to secure his vote. The former Taoiseach had promised to help Lowry's constituency, using state money to do so. With money now running out, would sanctioning the casino provide a welcome, and apparently cheaper, alternative?

When I asked Lowry if he'd be an investor in the Quirke project, he laughed and said no. He denied being paid to be a spokesman or consultant. He may be satisfied by the currency of local kudos. It is not known if, should the replica White House be built, Quirke intends to give Lowry weekly use of the replica Oval Office to serve as his constituency office.

Jim Flavin and DCC: A January 2010 report by High Court-appointed inspector Bill Shipsey into illegal share trading by the company DCC exonerated the guilty party – businessman Jim Flavin – of an established breach of the law on the basis that he hadn't known what he was doing, hadn't meant to act illegally and had taken legal advice that gave him the go-ahead.

The complicated DCC case had been ruled upon by the Supreme Court in 2005. It found, as part of a civil case for damages, that Flavin, as chief executive of DCC and also as a director of Fyffes, had acted illegally by selling DCC's shares in Fyffes while in possession of confidential information that was highly pertinent to the inflated Fyffes share price at the time of the sale.

Shipsey found that Flavin's actions were 'inadvertent breaches of the law'. Flavin did not know the relevant law but had acted in good faith on the basis of what he had been told by highly paid advisers. He had made 'an error of appreciation and judgement' and Shipsey found that Flavin's belief that he was not in possession of price sensitive information was 'rational, if legally wrong'.

The reaction of the boss of the ODCE, Paul Appleby, was just as notable. In explaining why he would not be taking any further action in relation to the biggest insider dealing scandal ever disclosed in this country – and for which DCC had to pay nearly €40 million in damages to Fyffes – Appleby said that 'there's no way that any court would sanction a director for having followed the company's legal advice'.

Seán Quinn: Seán Quinn was seduced by property – and many of his businesses depend on construction for their profits – and by Anglo Irish, a bank that relied excessively on its property lending. There was uproar when it emerged late in 2009 that Quinn Group had paid €200 million in a dividend to Quinn's five children, at a time when it still owed massive undisclosed sums to Anglo. Quinn first said this was for the family's 'private wealth management', but it subsequently emerged that the money may have been used to cover losses incurred by another family company, Quinn Finance, during the Anglo foray.

Slowly, more information has emerged as to the extent of Quinn's errors. Quinn Group said all its losses had been disclosed and accounted for, but in January 2010 the *Sunday Times* reported the contents of an internal Anglo document completed just two weeks before the January 2009 nationalization of the bank. It said that Anglo believed Quinn had lost €2.5 billion on his ill-fated adventure in Anglo shares, a figure that would have reached nearly €3 billion had it not been for the ready-up involving the Anglo Ten. Quinn has refused to comment further on the losses suffered, saying that the Quinn Group's exposure has all been properly accounted for and declared. However, it seems certain that there were further substantial losses that Quinn suffered in a personal capacity that may never be known.

The Quinn situation raises an interesting question: what will the public attitude be now towards the likes of entrepreneurs such as Quinn, whose greedy risk-taking contributed to the ruin of Anglo and, by extension, went a significant way towards destroying the economy?

The dilemma is that no state agency or planned economic model could have done what Quinn did for this country, and in particular for the border region, for over twenty years. No state-run economy would have financed private sector competition in cement, glass or insurance, or have sanctioned the building of a giant four-star hotel in west Cavan. This country was obsessed with attracting foreign investment but often we took the domestic risking of capital for granted. Few local business people would have had the imagination or taken the chances to buck what already existed, as Quinn did.

Entrepreneurs are optimists by nature who look for new opportunities to create things and make profits. Their optimism is what drives them. It is rare for them to contemplate failure or things outside of their control going wrong. Some don't want to sell prized possessions even when enormous profits are on offer unless there is a chance to reinvest profitably without having to give up money in tax.

Clearly Quinn paid too expensively for shares that were massively exposed to a downturn in the Irish property and construction sector. He had been told many times that his efforts would never succeed and had proved his doubters wrong, at least until his Anglo experience.

So: should Quinn be punished and shunned for what he did or he should he be given a free pass of sorts, to go and create again? The state's policy decision, via the Financial Regulator, when he first got into trouble at Anglo was pragmatic: it tried to help him out of the mess. But what should be done now that he has been exposed?

Quinn seems to have learned something from the debacle, as he has adopted a new business structure that will not only spread managerial and investment responsibility beyond his family but will dilute the family shareholding and allow others the chance to invest in a planned sale of shares via the stock market. In theory, excessive entrepreneurialism should be tempered in just such a new control structure. The scale of his operations remains so large that he will probably need to continue his international diversification. There may be a risk that he will follow Goodman's example by deciding that foreign investment has the benefit of less public attention than anything done in Ireland, as well as being potentially more profitable.

Quinn remains confident, as is his nature. His company web-site boasts a recent photograph of the Fermanagh-born native and Cavan resident welcoming US President Barack Obama to his Prague Hilton Hotel, the chosen overnight venue for Obama on a visit to the Czech Republic. He has advertised extensively on television over the last year, the Quinn Group becoming sponsor of the *Late Late Show* as it sought to improve its image.

Anglo Irish Bank: In December 2009 former Anglo Irish Bank chairman Sean Fitzpatrick was confronted by a RTÉ camera crew from Primetime Investigates. *Answer a few questions, please. No, respect my privacy*, he replied, before he scurried away. It made for entertaining television and at least suggested that somebody was going after him. It emerged in the following days that, by that time at least, neither the Garda Fraud Squad nor the Office of the Director of Corporate Enforcement had interviewed him. By March Anglo moved to recover the money he had borrowed from it, starting legal proceedings to recover about €70 million of his loans that he had not repaid. The sum involved suggested that Fitzpatrick had sold some assets and made repayments of nearly €40 million, but given that much of his wealth had been tied up in now worthless Anglo bank shares – and stakes of greatly diminished value in rivals AIB and Bank of Ireland – it was difficult to envisage much of that outstanding debt being recovered. Fitzpatrick's pension also become an item for debate as it gave him an estimated weekly income of €10,000.

Anglo had already brought court proceedings against David Drumm seeking the repayment of loans of €8.3 million, although he countersued for unpaid bonuses and the distress caused by his loss of office. The bank also sought to set aside the transfer of the family home into the sole ownership of his wife, Lorraine. Land Registry records showed that No. 20 Abington, Malahide, was first registered in both names in 2003 but transferred on 13 May 2009 into the sole name of Lorraine Drumm as 'full owner' care of the Dublin offices of solicitor Noel Smyth.

Anglo claimed this property was Drumm's main asset and that the transfer, as it was a fraud on his creditors, was void; it would prevent the property's being used to reduce Drumm's liability to Anglo, even though the house had originally been part of the security for his loans. Drumm claimed the transfer had been made for 'taxation reasons'. He had tried to sell the six-bedroom, 5,200-square-foot house in 2009, putting it on the market for €2.79 million, but withdrew it from sale after dropping the price to €2.3 million didn't work.

Drumm claimed that he had sufficient assets to meet his liabilities to the bank, that the demand for immediate repayment was premature, in breach of loan agreements with him, and that he was being harassed. But the bank alleged Drumm had delayed in filing a statement of affairs; and it is believed that some of Drumm's loans had been secured on Anglo shares, which became worthless when the bank was nationalized. Drumm counter-claimed for €2.6 million over the termination of his employment and loss of bonuses.

Drumm lives in Cape Cod now but has visited Dublin on a number of occasions; in particular, he may be central to the investigation into the

€451 million lent to the so-called Anglo Ten, who bought the 10 per cent shareholding in Anglo from Seán Quinn. Of that loan, only €120 million can be recovered at best. Drumm has said that the Financial Regulator, Central Bank and Irish Stock Exchange all approved the deal with the Anglo Ten.

Further disclosures from Anglo included details of massive loans to senior executives and directors, for amounts that were massive multiples of their income. Anglo has set aside €31 million to cover any losses on loans to directors and former directors.

Meanwhile, Anglo is also looking to its future, with plans to split in two, as a 'bad bank' and as a new business lender. Anglo chairman Donal O'Connor repeatedly told an Oireachtas committee that the cost of an immediate closure of Anglo would be greater than the cost of keeping it open as a 'going concern'. But how much more capital will it require from the state and how many more cash injections will the European Commission allow?

The €3.8 billion in capital put into Anglo will have to be doubled at least and possibly trebled. NAMA is taking €28 billion of Anglo's worst loans and leaving it with €44 billion on a new, much smaller balance sheet, which will require extra capital. Anglo is being allowed to operate with less than the minimum required capital, under a derogation secured from the Financial Regulator. The plan put to the EU sought a capital injection of €5.7 billion, but bitter experience has shown that such estimates may be less than what's required.

Anglo lost €4.1 billion in the six months to 31 March 2009, the biggest corporate loss in the history of the state. Its year-end was then changed from 30 September 2009 and its accounts for the year-end 31 December have not been published yet. There is little or no transparency at the nationalized Anglo. When it is asked how it is dealing with its biggest loans, it cites client confidentiality. While this may be legally correct, the taxpayer has no way of knowing how the bank, owned by the taxpayer, is seeking recovery from its largest clients, as it does so under the cover of darkness.

AIB and Bank of Ireland: The scale of the disaster at AIB continued to mushroom. In August 2009 it announced that €4.9 billion of the loans it had given would not be repaid. However, by November it was admitting that its bad debts could be at least €1 billion higher, and that another €10.5 billion of loans were 'impaired', a near €4 billion increase on its previous estimate. AIB was due to transfer property loans of over €24 billion to NAMA. Having already received €3.5 billion in state investment, by early 2010 the bank required another €4 billion at the very least. It would have to sell its American investment – a 24 per cent stake in M&T – and its Polish banking operations, although both are highly profitable, but that would not be enough.

The European Commission also refused to allow the payment of guaranteed dividends on the preference shares, creating an additional problem for government. AIB was due to make annual repayments of €280 million in cash under the terms of the investment. If this is prevented, the state will have to take shares instead, bringing it perilously close to majority control, even before the injection of more capital. Bank of Ireland had much the same problem.

The controversy over its appointment of Richie Boucher as chief executive of that bank had led the government to insist that no similar promotion would be allowed at AIB when the time came to replace its departing chief executive, Eugene Sheehy. AIB somehow failed to find an external candidate who would do the job – even though head-hunters had an external list of four – and insisted that Colm Doherty, the head of its capital markets division and a main board director since 2003, should be promoted to the job.

Lenihan at first refused to endorse the promotion, twice trying, unsuccessfully, to persuade chairman Dan O'Connor to take the job as acting chief executive. After a lengthy stand-off the government has compromised by allowing Doherty to become managing director instead of chief executive (whatever difference that makes) and Dan O'Connor – on the main board since 2007 – to assume his role on a full-time basis. This hardly represents a regime change.

The idea was for Doherty to run the business while O'Connor dealt with the government and with the EC in Brussels. The concept of a clean slate, of getting rid of those who oversaw the mess at the bank, to be replaced by people who were not responsible, seemed to disappear. The government postured, saying that it had forced AIB to pay Doherty no more than €500,000, a fall of €133,000 on his previous package, as if this was the main issue. Doherty is well able to argue his case forcibly as well as stylishly. It is expected that he will seek aggressively to cut costs during 2010 once the bad loans are transferred to NAMA. Thousands of jobs are at risk of being axed.

Meanwhile, the two chairmen of the main banks on the night of the bank guarantee, having left their positions, managed to go on to bigger and better things. Richard Burrows, former governor of the Bank of Ireland, got a new job as chairman of British American Tobacco, one of the biggest companies on the London stock market. Dermot Gleeson was chosen to chair Travelport, a travel software company, on the occasion of its stock market flotation in London.

Brian Lenihan: Shortly after delivering his December 2009 budget, the Minister for Finance, Brian Lenihan, went for a medical check-up. It was discovered that he had pancreatic cancer. He announced this publicly in early January 2010, but, despite needing radiation and chemotherapy treatment, he pledged to continue in his job for as long as possible, having been asked to do so by Taoiseach Brian Cowen. The vast majority wished him well, mainly on a personal level, but on a political basis too. Whatever criticisms people had of NAMA and his budgetary policy, Lenihan benefited from having been outside of Ahern's cabinet during the time of dreadful decisions and from being seen to be strong, logical and fair-minded. While the polls suggested many would have liked to see the government replaced, for as long as Fianna Fáil remained in power Lenihan's presence was regarded as essential.

Lenihan put his December 2009 budget into effect via the 2010 Finance Act, in which he added various measures designed to make Ireland a more attractive place for foreign investment – including an acknowledgement of the role of Sharia Law, apparently to attract money from the Middle East. He introduced various anti-avoidance measures to limit the ways some rich people could reduce their tax bills. The infamous tax break that had been to the benefit of Ken Rohan – allowing him to claim the cost of maintaining corporately owned antique furniture in his stately home – was removed. Crucially, Lenihan also transferred responsibility for the state shareholdings in the banks to the NTMA, now under the control of John Corrigan, and away from the Department of Finance. With expectations rising that majority control of the banks was becoming inevitable, this took much of the political responsibility away from the government, but brought about criticism that the transparency of the process would be compromised.

Cowen, meanwhile, appealed to a sense of patriotism in asking people to accept a lower standard of living as part of a process of rebuilding the economy. He attended a Dublin Chamber of Commerce event in February 2010 and spoke of people standing outside the GPO in 2016 at the centenary commemoration of the Easter Rising and of displaying pride at the sacrifices that they had endured in dealing with this financial crisis. The line that 'patriotism is the last refuge of the scoundrel' came to mind.

Acknowledgements

Firstly, I owe many thanks to Patricia Deevy and Michael McLoughlin of Penguin for giving me the idea for this book, tolerating my tardiness in taking up the offer, encouraging me to stick with it as I wavered and for showing the patience to allow me to finish it. The copy editor, Donna Poppy, did a superb job in cleaning up the writing and also deserves much praise as well as thanks. I would also like to thank my literary agent, Faith O'Grady, for her encouragement and help at vital times. For research work my thanks to Jana Braddock and Ronan Lawlor.

Some of the people whom I should thank would not want me to do so publicly, having spoken to me or guided me on condition of anonymity. Others I am not naming for fear that they suffer professional consequences for doing so: while all they have told me is true and offered in good faith, they might not be thanked by some of their professional colleagues for doing so. Indeed, I would not want some people jumping to conclusions that those named in the acknowledgements might be somehow responsible for anything that has appeared in this book. Even when the assumptions may be wrong it can be difficult for suspected sources to deny it, even though they and I might know that they had nothing to do with it. These sources know who they are and I hope that the thanks I have offered in private will be sufficient.

There is not enough space to thank the many people who have helped me during my career in journalism, from *Business & Finance* magazine to the *Sunday Business Post* to the *Irish Independent* and then, in particular, to the *Sunday Tribune*. Again, to all of you, sincere thanks.

But I must acknowledge those who have helped in the latest phase of my career as a broadcaster and columnist. At Today FM, which I joined full-time at the start of 2003, I have to thank Willie O'Reilly, John McColgan and Eamon Fitzpatrick, particularly for the confidence they showed in me during difficult times. My current production team of Mary O'Hagan, Killian Murray, Patrick Haughey, Mary Carroll and Cian O'Flaherty deserve enormous thanks for facilitating my schedule, but I think they know much I appreciate their expertise, diligence and enthusiasm. Former producers – in particular, Barbara Loftus – have also helped me enormously. I would also like to thank my newspaper editors Frank Fitzgibbon at the *Sunday Times* and Tim Vaughan of the *Irish Examiner*, for showing patience over the delivery of my weekly copy, especially when I have been juggling commitments, David McRedmond, as chief executive of TV3, and Ciaran O'hEadhra of Asgard Media, with whom I work on gaelic games and soccer coverage on TV3.

Most of all, though, I have to thank my family, especially Aileen, who was left with the burden more often than she might have expected. The children rightly became fed up with hearing too often over the last year that 'Daddy has to work on his book again' and I know they were delighted when my weekends were freed from the task. So was I: the guilt lifted and I was able to enjoy their company in full again. I hope when they are older, in years to come, they will read this book, gain a little insight into the Ireland in which they grew up and decide that their daddy's effort – and use of time – was worthwhile.

Index

He just wanted a decent book to read ...

Not too much to ask, is it? It was in 1935 when Allen Lane, Managing Director of Bodley Head Publishers, stood on a platform at Exeter railway station looking for something good to read on his journey back to London. His choice was limited to popular magazines and poor-quality paperbacks – the same choice faced every day by the vast majority of readers, few of whom could afford hardbacks. Lane's disappointment and subsequent anger at the range of books generally available led him to found a company – and change the world.

'We believed in the existence in this country of a vast reading public for intelligent books at a low price, and staked everything on it'
Sir Allen Lane, 1902–1970, founder of Penguin Books

The quality paperback had arrived – and not just in bookshops. Lane was adamant that his Penguins should appear in chain stores and tobacconists, and should cost no more than a packet of cigarettes.

Reading habits (and cigarette prices) have changed since 1935, but Penguin still believes in publishing the best books for everybody to enjoy. We still believe that good design costs no more than bad design, and we still believe that quality books published passionately and responsibly make the world a better place.

So wherever you see the little bird – whether it's on a piece of prize-winning literary fiction or a celebrity autobiography, political tour de force or historical masterpiece, a serial-killer thriller, reference book, world classic or a piece of pure escapism – you can bet that it represents the very best that the genre has to offer.

Whatever you like to read – trust Penguin.